Chinese Scooters
Service and Repair Manual

by Phil Mather

Models covered

(4768 - 288 - 11AM1)

AJS Digita 50, Crazy 50, Firefox 50, Exactly 125; **Baotian** BT49QT, BT125T, Apollo 10, Apollo 12; **BTM** BT49QT, BT125T; **Branson** BS50, BS125/150; **Chituma** CTM50QT, CTM125T; **CPI** Aragon 50/125, Hussar, Formula, JR50/125, Oliver JV50/125, Popcorn JP50, VGO 125; **Daelim** Cordi 50, S-FIVE 50, E-FIVE 50, Delfino 125, Besbi 125; **Dafier** Crazy, Ghost; **Direct Bikes** DB50QT, DB125T; **FYM** FY50/100QT, FY125T; **Generic** XOR 50/125, Ideo 50, Cracker 50, Race 50, Evolution 50, ROC 50; **GIANTCO** Sprint Sport 50, Sprint City 50; **Haotian** Bubble, Cobra; **Huatian** HT50QT, HT125T; **Hyosung** SD50, SF50R, SF50B; **Jialing** JL50QT, JL125/150T; **Jincheng** JC50QT, JC125/150T; **Jinlun/CKR** JL50QT, JL125T, Retro 50/125, Cobra, Tommy, Cruiser; **JMStar** JSD50QT, JSD125T; **Jonway** Agility, Adventure; **Keeway** Hurricane 50, Flash 50, Matrix 50/125/150, F-ACT (Focus) 50/125, F-NKD, Pixel 50, Goccia 50, ARN125/150; **Kinroad** XT50QT, XT125T; **Kymco** Super 8 50/125, ZX50, YUP 50, People S 50/125/200, Agility 50/125, Agility City 50/125, Vitality 50, Dink 50, Like 50; **Lifan** LF50QT, LF125/150T; **Lingben** LB50QT, LB125T; **Lintex** HT50QT, HT125T; **Lexmoto** Molly, Flash, Tornado, Valencia, Gladiator, Dart, Firenze, Tommy, Zoom; **Longjia** JL50QT, LJ125T; **PGO** T-REX 50/125, G-MAX 50/125, PMX 50, Rodoshow 50, Ligero 50/125, Libra 50/125; **Pulse** Scout, Rhythm, Force, Phantom, Ghost, Lightspeed; **Qingqi** QM50QT, QM125T; **Sanben** SB50QT, SB125T; **Sinnis** QM50QT, QM125T; **Skygo** SG50QT, SG125T; **Sukida** SK50QT, SK125T; **Superbyke** Powerband 50/125, Powermax, M-PED, S-MAX, CQ50, CU125 and PB50-1/PB50-3; **Sym** DD50, Mio 50/100, Fiddle II 50/125, Jet BasiX 50, Jet Euro X 50/100, Jet 4R, Jet Sport X, Orbit II 50/125, Symply 50, VS125/150, City Hopper 50; **Tamoretti** Retro 50/125, Stealth 125; **TGB** 50cc 202, 101R, Hawk, 302, R50X and 125cc BK8, 204, 404, 304, Hawk; **Wangye** WY50QT, WY125T; **WK Bikes** GP50, Bellissima 50, Go 50, Mii 50, VS50/125, GP 2, Wasp 50; **Wuyang** WY50QT, WY125; **Xingyue** LLX50QT, LLX125T; **Yamati** HZM50QT; **Yiben** YB50QT, YB125T; **Yiying** YY50QT, YY125T; **Zing Bikes** LF50QT, LF125T; **Znen** ZN50QT, ZN125T; **Zongshen** LZX50QT, ZS50/100QT, ZS125/150T.

© J H Haynes & Co. Ltd. 2014

A book in the **Haynes Service and Repair Manual Series**

ABCDE
FGH

ISBN **978 0 85733 646 0**

British Library Cataloguing in Publication Data
A catalogue record for this book is available from the British Library.

Library of Congress Control Number 2013948067

Printed in India

J H Haynes & Co. Ltd.
Sparkford, Yeovil, Somerset BA22 7JJ, England

Haynes North America, Inc
859 Lawrence Drive, Newbury Park, California 91320, USA

Disclaimer

There are risks associated with automotive repairs. The ability to make repairs depends on the individual's skill, experience and proper tools. Individuals should act with due care and acknowledge and assume the risk of performing automotive repairs.

The purpose of this manual is to provide comprehensive, useful and accessible automotive repair information, to help you get the best value from your vehicle. However, this manual is not a substitute for a professional certified technician or mechanic.

This repair manual is produced by a third party and is not associated with an individual vehicle manufacturer. If there is any doubt or discrepancy between this manual and the owner's manual or the factory service manual, please refer to the factory service manual or seek assistance from a professional certified technician or mechanic.

Even though we have prepared this manual with extreme care and every attempt is made to ensure that the information in this manual is correct, neither the publisher nor the author can accept responsibility for loss, damage or injury caused by any errors in, or omissions from, the information given.

Contents

The Tip Of A (Very Big) Iceberg

by Julian Ryder

As China is the World's most populous country, it should come as no surprise that the Chinese motorcycle industry is very big indeed. Nevertheless, the sheer size of the numbers involved takes the breath away. In 2006 China's motorcycle factories produced over 20-million machines, by 2012 this had risen to 24-million a year, with 11.4 million of these machines going for export. The Chongqing province is home to the majority of the motorcycle factories and accounts for 19% of the world's total motorcycle production.

Currently the top five manufacturers in China are Lifan, Loncin, Zongshen, Jialing and Qingqi. These and many others operate joint ventures with motorcycle manufacturers from other countries, working with prestigious brands such as BMW and Honda. This has mutual benefits because whilst the customer benefits from cheaper production costs, the factories receive the benefits of working with the world's most technologically advanced firms and best styling houses.

For some time now importers of Chinese machines into western countries have engaged in rebranding in an attempt to provide more recognisable and pronounceable names. Many of the stronger brands however, are now actively promoting their identities at shows and exhibitions throughout the western world to obtain brand recognition. Model ranges which once consisted of scooters and small lightweight motorcycles have now expanded, and although there is nothing yet to seriously rival the diverse offerings from Japan and Europe, the Chinese factories are following the Korean manufacturers into the middle weight motorcycle and scooter market. That said, there is still clearly a demand for the 'generic' type of machine which is exported in large numbers to Africa, Latin America and the Middle East, and also sells well in the home market where licensing laws are strict, but China also has an eye on developing higher spec models with performance and high tech features to match those from other manufacturers.

To see how it does this, it is worth going back sixty years and contemplating the fledgling Japanese industry and what it did when faced with a similar dilemma. It went racing. In 1954, six years after the founding of the Honda Motor Company, Soichiro Honda announced his intention to race in the Isle of Man TT with a machine of his own design. It took another five years but they got there, won a team award at their first attempt and took the first of over 180 TT victories in 1961. It is worth remembering that when Mr Honda told the world he was going racing, his company were the largest manufacturer of lightweight motorcycles in the world but they were only sold on the domestic market.

Two of China's million sellers have already put a toe in the water, but only using their name. Zongshen, the eighth biggest maker on 2006 figures, ran Suzuki GSX-R1000s to win the 2002 World Endurance Championship. At the time, most journalists thought Zongshen was a tyre manufacturer, and indeed they are. It's just that they also made a million bikes a year. They also ran a 250cc team for Chinese riders, based in France and using Aprilias. When MotoGP went to China for the first time in 2005 it was noticeable that the banners celebrating Zongshen's world title singularly failed to mention the word 'Suzuki'. China's second biggest brand, Loncin, also had its name on the side of a 125 GP team that was previously badged as Malaguti and was in reality based on Honda crankcases.

The firm that looked likely to follow the Honda route and field their own machines in GP was, naturally, one of the biggest, the Grand River Group. In 2009 they developed a bike for the 125cc class, with no less a person than John Surtees fronting the effort and ex-Suzuki GP manager Garry Taylor acting as consultant. The chassis was designed by Harris Performance while ex-Aprilia engine guru Jan Witteveen designed the motor. The Grand River Group decided their Haojue brand name might not be too easy on European ears or tongues so chose the name Maxtra. Unfortunately the team were unable to use the name for legal reasons and raced under the Haojue banner in 2009. Sadly lack of performance and engine failures early in the season led to termination of the two riders' contracts and the team being disbanded.

Since then Zongshen have fielded a factory team in the TTXGP at the Isle of Man joining a small number of eRacing teams and privateers in this event which started in 2009.

Production line at the Haojue factory

Our thanks are due to Llexeter Ltd, Baotian UK and CPI Moto (UK) who supplied the scooters featured in the photographs throughout this manual. We would also like to thank NGK Spark Plugs (UK) Ltd for supplying the colour spark plug condition photos and Draper Tools for some of the workshop tools shown.

We are grateful to the UK importers who supplied literature or technical advice: Astro General Corporation Ltd, Baotain UK, CPI Moto (UK), David Silver Spares, Llexeter Ltd, Moore Large & Co Ltd, Moto GB Ltd and Sinnis International (UK) Ltd.

About this Manual

The aim of this manual is to help you get the best value from your scooter. It can do so in several ways. It can help you decide what work must be done, even if you choose to have it done by a dealer; it provides information and procedures for routine maintenance and servicing; and it offers diagnostic and repair procedures to follow when trouble occurs.

We hope you use the manual to tackle the work yourself. For many simpler jobs, doing it yourself may be quicker than arranging an appointment to get the scooter into a dealer and making the trips to leave it and pick it up. More importantly, a lot of money can be saved by avoiding the expense the shop must pass on to you to cover its labour and overhead costs. An added benefit is the sense of satisfaction and accomplishment that you feel after doing the job yourself.

References to the left or right side of the scooter assume you are sitting on the seat, facing forward.

We take great pride in the accuracy of information given in this manual, but manufacturers often make alterations and design changes during the production run of a particular machine of which they do not inform us. No liability can be accepted by the authors or publishers for loss, damage or injury caused by any errors in, or omissions from, the information given.

Identification numbers and buying spare parts

Frame and engine numbers

The frame serial number, or VIN (Vehicle Identification Number) as it is often known, is stamped into the frame, and also appears on the identification plate. The engine number is stamped into the transmission casing. Both of these numbers should be recorded and kept in a safe place so they can be furnished to law enforcement officials in the event of a theft.

The frame and engine numbers should also be kept in a handy place (such as with your driving licence) so they are always available when purchasing or ordering parts for your scooter.

Engine types can be identified by the prefix to the actual engine number; 50cc four-strokes have the prefix 139QMA or QMB, 125cc four-strokes 152QMI and 150cc four-strokes 157QMI. Two-stroke engines usually have the codes 1E40QMA or B, or 1PE40QMB.

The frame number is stamped into the frame . . .

. . . and also appears on the identification plate

The engine number is stamped into the transmission casing

Buying spare parts

When ordering replacement parts, it is essential to identify exactly the machine for which the parts are required. While in some cases it is sufficient to identify the machine by its title e.g. 'Baotian BT 50' or 'Jin Lun JL 125', any modifications made to components mean that it is usually essential to identify the scooter by its year of production, or better still by its frame or engine number prefix.

To be absolutely certain of receiving the correct part, not only is it essential to have the scooter engine or frame number prefix to hand, but it is also useful to take the old part for comparison (where possible). Note that where a modified component has superseded the original, a careful check must be made that there are no related parts which have also been modified and must be used to enable the replacement to be correctly refitted; where such a situation is found, purchase all the necessary parts and fit them, even if this means replacing apparently unworn items.

Purchase replacement parts from an authorised dealer or someone who specialises in scooter parts; they are more likely to have the parts in stock or can order them quickly from the importer. Pattern parts are available for certain components; if used, ensure these are of recognised quality brands which will perform as well as the original.

Expendable items such as lubricants, spark plugs, some electrical components, bearings, bulbs and tyres can usually be obtained at lower prices from accessory shops, motor factors or from specialists advertising in the national motorcycle press.

Professional mechanics are trained in safe working procedures. However enthusiastic you may be about getting on with the job at hand, take the time to ensure that your safety is not put at risk. A moment's lack of attention can result in an accident, as can failure to observe simple precautions.

There will always be new ways of having accidents, and the following is not a comprehensive list of all dangers; it is intended rather to make you aware of the risks and to encourage a safe approach to all work you carry out on your bike.

Asbestos

● Certain friction, insulating, sealing and other products - such as brake pads, clutch linings, gaskets, etc. - contain asbestos. Extreme care must be taken to avoid inhalation of dust from such products since it is hazardous to health. If in doubt, assume that they do contain asbestos.

Fire

● Remember at all times that petrol is highly flammable. Never smoke or have any kind of naked flame around, when working on the vehicle. But the risk does not end there - a spark caused by an electrical short-circuit, by two metal surfaces contacting each other, by careless use of tools, or even by static electricity built up in your body under certain conditions, can ignite petrol vapour, which in a confined space is highly explosive. Never use petrol as a cleaning solvent. Use an approved safety solvent.

● Always disconnect the battery earth terminal before working on any part of the fuel or electrical system, and never risk spilling fuel on to a hot engine or exhaust.

● It is recommended that a fire extinguisher of a type suitable for fuel and electrical fires is kept handy in the garage or workplace at all times. Never try to extinguish a fuel or electrical fire with water.

Fumes

● Certain fumes are highly toxic and can quickly cause unconsciousness and even death if inhaled to any extent. Petrol vapour comes into this category, as do the vapours from certain solvents such as trichloro-ethylene. Any draining or pouring of such volatile fluids should be done in a well ventilated area.

● When using cleaning fluids and solvents, read the instructions carefully. Never use materials from unmarked containers - they may give off poisonous vapours.

● Never run the engine of a motor vehicle in an enclosed space such as a garage. Exhaust fumes contain carbon monoxide which is extremely poisonous; if you need to run the engine, always do so in the open air or at least have the rear of the vehicle outside the workplace.

The battery

● Never cause a spark, or allow a naked light near the vehicle's battery. It will normally be giving off a certain amount of hydrogen gas, which is highly explosive.

● Always disconnect the battery ground (earth) terminal before working on the fuel or electrical systems (except where noted).

● If possible, loosen the filler plugs or cover when charging the battery from an external source. Do not charge at an excessive rate or the battery may burst.

● Take care when topping up, cleaning or carrying the battery. The acid electrolyte, evenwhen diluted, is very corrosive and should not be allowed to contact the eyes or skin. Always wear rubber gloves and goggles or a face shield. If you ever need to prepare electrolyte yourself, always add the acid slowly to the water; never add the water to the acid.

Electricity

● When using an electric power tool, inspection light etc., always ensure that the appliance is correctly connected to its plug and that, where necessary, it is properly grounded (earthed). Do not use such appliances in damp conditions and, again, beware of creating a spark or applying excessive heat in the vicinity of fuel or fuel vapour. Also ensure that the appliances meet national safety standards.

● A severe electric shock can result from touching certain parts of the electrical system, such as the spark plug wires (HT leads), when the engine is running or being cranked, particularly if components are damp or the insulation is defective. Where an electronic ignition system is used, the secondary (HT) voltage is much higher and could prove fatal.

Remember...

✗ **Don't** start the engine without first ascertaining that the transmission is in neutral.

✗ **Don't** suddenly remove the pressure cap from a hot cooling system - cover it with a cloth and release the pressure gradually first, or you may get scalded by escaping coolant.

✗ **Don't** attempt to drain oil until you are sure it has cooled sufficiently to avoid scalding you.

✗ **Don't** grasp any part of the engine or exhaust system without first ascertaining that it is cool enough not to burn you.

✗ **Don't** allow brake fluid or antifreeze to contact the machine's paintwork or plastic components.

✗ **Don't** siphon toxic liquids such as fuel, hydraulic fluid or antifreeze by mouth, or allow them to remain on your skin.

✗ **Don't** inhale dust - it may be injurious to health (see Asbestos heading).

✗ **Don't** allow any spilled oil or grease to remain on the floor - wipe it up right away, before someone slips on it.

✗ **Don't** use ill-fitting spanners or other tools which may slip and cause injury.

✗ **Don't** lift a heavy component which may be beyond your capability - get assistance.

✗ **Don't** rush to finish a job or take unverified short cuts.

✗ **Don't** allow children or animals in or around an unattended vehicle.

✗ **Don't** inflate a tyre above the recommended pressure. Apart from overstressing the carcass, in extreme cases the tyre may blow off forcibly.

✔ **Do** ensure that the machine is supported securely at all times. This is especially important when the machine is blocked up to aid wheel or fork removal.

✔ **Do** take care when attempting to loosen a stubborn nut or bolt. It is generally better to pull on a spanner, rather than push, so that if you slip, you fall away from the machine rather than onto it.

✔ **Do** wear eye protection when using power tools such as drill, sander, bench grinder etc.

✔ **Do** use a barrier cream on your hands prior to undertaking dirty jobs - it will protect your skin from infection as well as making the dirt easier to remove afterwards; but make sure your hands aren't left slippery. Note that long-term contact with used engine oil can be a health hazard.

✔ **Do** keep loose clothing (cuffs, ties etc. and long hair) well out of the way of moving mechanical parts.

✔ **Do** remove rings, wristwatch etc., before working on the vehicle - especially the electrical system.

✔ **Do** keep your work area tidy - it is only too easy to fall over articles left lying around.

✔ **Do** exercise caution when compressing springs for removal or installation. Ensure that the tension is applied and released in a controlled manner, using suitable tools which preclude the possibility of the spring escaping violently.

✔ **Do** ensure that any lifting tackle used has a safe working load rating adequate for the job.

✔ **Do** get someone to check periodically that all is well, when working alone on the vehicle.

✔ **Do** carry out work in a logical sequence and check that everything is correctly assembled and tightened afterwards.

✔ **Do** remember that your vehicle's safety affects that of yourself and others. If in doubt on any point, get professional advice.

● If in spite of following these precautions, you are unfortunate enough to injure yourself, seek medical attention as soon as possible.

Engine oil level check – four-stroke engine

Before you start:

✔ Make sure you have a supply of the correct oil available (see below).

✔ Support the scooter in an upright position on level ground.

✔ Start the engine and allow it to run for 2 to 3 minutes, then turn it OFF and wait a further 2 to 3 minutes before checking the oil level.

The correct oil:

● Modern engines place great demands on their oil. It is very important to use the correct oil for your engine.

● Always top-up with a good quality oil of the specified type and viscosity – check with your Owner's Handbook or dealer for details. Most specify an SAE 10W/40 engine oil to API SG and JASO MA standard. Use either engine oil packaged for scooter or motorcycle use – avoid the use of car engine oils.

● Check the oil level carefully. Make sure you know the correct level for your scooter.

● The oil level in a four-stroke engine shouldn't need frequent topping up. If it does, check for signs of oil leakage from the engine and also check for signs of oil burning (white smoke from the exhaust) which indicates a worn engine.

1 Unscrew the dipstick from the right-hand side of the engine and wipe off all the oil with clean rag or paper towel.

2 Insert the clean dipstick back into the engine but do not screw it in.

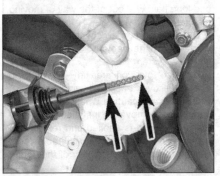

3 Remove the dipstick and check the oil level – it should be somewhere between the upper and lower level marks.

4 If the level is low, top-up with the recommended grade and type of oil, then replace the dipstick securely. Never overfill the engine with oil.

5 Using a funnel helps where it's difficult to access the filler hole with the oil container.

Engine oil level check – two-stroke engine

Before you start:

✔ Make sure you have a supply of the correct oil available.

✔ Support the scooter in an upright position whilst checking the level. Make sure it is on level ground.

The correct oil:

● A two-stroke engine burns oil during the combustion process, with the oil being held in a tank and pumped into the engine whilst it is running. Most oil tanks hold about 1 litre of two-stroke oil and it is vitally important to keep the oil tank topped-up to avoid lubrication failure. The level will fall at a gradual rate, in line with use of the scooter.

● Don't rely on the oil warning light to tell you that the oil needs topping-up. Get into the habit of checking the oil level at the same time as you fill up with fuel.

● If the engine is run without oil, even for a short time, serious engine damage and engine seizure will occur. It is advised that a bottle of two-stroke oil is carried in the scooter's storage compartment.

● Use a good quality two-stroke oil to JASO FC standard. Choose a product which is packaged for scooter or motorcycle use and is suitable for oil injection (autolube) systems.

Scooter care:

● Although the oil level in the tank will fall in line with scooter usage, if the rate of oil consumption increases, check for any sign of oil leakage between the tank and pump. Also check that the pump is adjusted correctly (see Chapter 1) to deliver the correct rate of oil to the engine, particularly if there is higher than normal blue smoke from the exhaust.

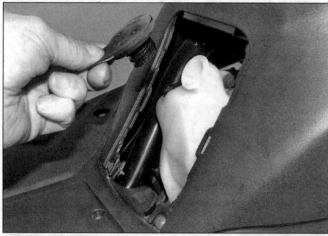

1 Remove the filler cap to check the oil level. This oil tank has an access panel in the bodywork, but other models may have the oil tank located under the seat.

2 If the level is low, top-up with the recommended grade and type of oil, then replace the filler cap securely.

Brake fluid level check

⚠️ **Warning: Brake fluid can harm your eyes and damage painted surfaces, so use extreme caution when handling and pouring it and cover surrounding surfaces with rag. Do not use fluid that has been standing open for some time, as it absorbs moisture from the air which can cause a dangerous loss of braking effectiveness.**

Before you start:

✔ Support the scooter in an upright position on level ground and turn the handlebars until the brake fluid reservoir is as level as possible.

✔ Make sure you have a supply of DOT 4 brake fluid.

✔ Access to the reservoir is restricted on a number of scooters by the upper handlebar cover. If necessary, remove the cover to check the fluid level.

✔ Wrap a rag around the reservoir to prevent any brake fluid coming into contact with painted or plastic surfaces.

Scooter care:

● The fluid level in the brake reservoir will drop at a very gradual rate as the brake pads wear down.

● If the reservoir requires repeated topping-up this is an indication of a fluid leak somewhere in the system, which should be investigated immediately.

● Check for signs of fluid leaks from the brake hose and components – if found, rectify immediately.

● Check the operation of the brake before riding the scooter; if there is evidence of air in the system (a spongy feel to the lever), it must be bled as described in Chapter 7.

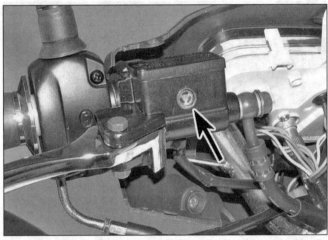

1 The brake fluid level is visible through the sightglass in the reservoir body – it must be half way up the glass, or above the LOWER line, when the reservoir is level.

2 Remove the reservoir cover screws and remove the cover, the diaphragm plate and the diaphragm.

3 Top-up with new DOT 4 hydraulic fluid. Do not overfill and take care to avoid spills (see *Warning* above).

4 Ensure that the diaphragm is correctly seated before installing the plate and cover. Tighten the cover screws securely.

Tyre checks

The correct pressures:
● The tyres must be checked when **cold**, not immediately after riding. Note that low tyre pressures may cause the tyre to slip on the rim or come off. High tyre pressures will cause abnormal tread wear and unsafe handling.
● Use an accurate pressure gauge.
● Proper air pressure will increase tyre life and provide maximum stability and ride comfort.
● Refer to your *Owner's Handbook, the Data sheets at the end of this manual, or the tyre information sticker on the scooter* for the correct tyre pressures. The pressures given in the table below are specified by tyre manufacturers for 10 inch and 12 inch tyre sizes:

Front	Rear
1.5 to 1.8 Bar (21 to 26 psi)	2.0 to 2.2 Bar (29 to 32 psi)

Tyre care:
● Check the tyres carefully for cuts, tears, embedded nails or other sharp objects and excessive wear. Operation of the scooter with excessively worn tyres is extremely hazardous, as traction and handling are directly affected.

● Check the condition of the tyre valve and ensure the dust cap is in place.

● Pick out any stones or nails which may have become embedded in the tyre tread. If left, they will eventually penetrate through the casing and cause a puncture.

● If tyre damage is apparent, or unexplained loss of pressure is experienced, seek the advice of a motorcycle and scooter tyre fitting specialist without delay.

Tyre tread depth:
● At the time of writing, for machines with an engine size greater than 50 cc, UK law requires that tread depth must be at least 1 mm over 3/4 of the tread breadth all the way around the tyre, with no bald patches. Many riders, however, consider 2 mm tread depth minimum to be a safer limit.

● For machines with an engine size not greater than 50 cc, UK law states that tread depth may be less than 1 mm if the tread pattern is clearly visible across the whole of the tread breadth all the way around the tyre.

● Many tyres now incorporate wear indicators in the tread. Identify the triangular pointer on the tyre sidewall to locate the indicator bar and replace the tyre if the tread has worn down to the bar.

1 Check the tyre pressures when the tyres are **cold** and keep them properly inflated.

2 Measure tread depth at the centre of the tyre using a tread depth gauge.

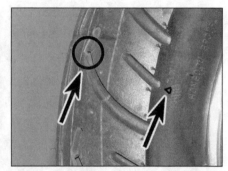
3 Tyre tread wear indicator bar and its location marking (usually an arrow, a triangle or the letters TWI) on the sidewall.

Suspension and steering checks

● Check that the front and rear suspension operates smoothly without binding.

● Check that the steering moves smoothly from lock-to-lock.

Fuel level check

● This may seem obvious, but check that you have enough fuel to complete your journey. Do not wait until the fuel gauge or warning light to tell you that the level in the tank is low before filling up.

● If you notice any fuel leaks you must rectify the cause immediately.
● Ensure you use the correct grade unleaded petrol, minimum 95 octane.

Legal and safety checks

Lighting and signalling
● Take a minute to check that the headlight, tail light, brake light, instrument lights and turn signals all work correctly.
● Check that the horn sounds when the switch is operated.

● A working speedometer graduated in mph is a statutory requirement in the UK.
Safety
● Check that the throttle twistgrip rotates smoothly and snaps shut when released, in all steering positions.

● Check that the stand return spring holds the stand securely up when retracted.

● Check that both brakes work correctly when applied and free off when released.

Chapter 1
Routine maintenance and servicing

Contents

Degrees of difficulty

Easy, suitable for novice with little experience	**Fairly easy,** suitable for beginner with some experience	**Fairly difficult,** suitable for competent DIY mechanic	**Difficult,** suitable for experienced DIY mechanic	**Very difficult,** suitable for expert DIY or professional

Specifications

Specifications are given for certain models in the *Data* section at the end of this manual. Where no data is available, refer to that contained in the *Owner's Handbook* issued with the machine when new, or to information given on decals stuck to the machine. Note that in some instances, the author has provided typical values in the text procedures.

1 Introduction

1 This Chapter is designed to help the home mechanic maintain his/her scooter for safety, economy, long life and peak performance.

2 Whenever you ride your scooter, and in some cases even when it is not in use, components wear and deteriorate. To counteract this process, every machine has a service schedule – relating either to either a period time or mileage – which stipulates when checks and adjustments should be made.

3 The majority of service items are common to all scooters, but some are specific to certain machines. Use your *Owner's Handbook*, together with the illustrations in Section 2, to identify the various components that require periodic attention.

4 Deciding where to start or plug into a service schedule depends on several factors. If the warranty period on your scooter has just expired, and if it has been maintained according to the warranty standards, you will want to pick up routine maintenance as it coincides with the next mileage or calendar interval. If you have owned the machine for some time but have never performed any maintenance on it, then you may want to start at the nearest interval and include some additional procedures to ensure that nothing important is overlooked. If you have just had a major engine overhaul, then you will want to start the maintenance routine from the beginning as with a new machine. If you have a used scooter and have no knowledge of its history or maintenance record, it would be best to combine all the checks into one large initial service, and then settle into a regular routine schedule.

5 Don't worry if you haven't got a service schedule for your particular scooter; use the information in this Chapter to identify the service items on your machine – air filter, battery, brakes etc – then create your own service schedule based on the examples we give. **Note:** *Certain maintenance information is sometimes printed on decals attached to the machine. If the information on the decals differs from that included here, use the information on the decal.*

6 Before beginning any maintenance or repair, clean your scooter thoroughly, especially around the suspension, brakes, engine and transmission covers. Cleaning will help ensure that dirt does not contaminate the working parts and will allow you to detect wear and damage that could otherwise easily go unnoticed.

7 In some cases, it will be necessary to remove body panels to gain access to service items. Follow the procedure in Chapter 8 to remove the appropriate panels.

Note 1: *The Pre-ride checks detailed at the beginning of this manual cover those items which should be inspected before riding the scooter. Always perform the pre-ride inspection at every maintenance interval (in addition to the procedures listed).*

Note 2: *The intervals listed on pages 1•4 and 1•5 are the intervals generally recommended by manufacturers but are not specific to any make or model. The Owner's Handbook for your model may have different intervals to those shown. If available, always refer to the maintenance booklet supplied with the machine for the correct intervals.*

Routine maintenance and servicing procedures

2 Typical service items

1 Use the accompanying list and the *Owner's Handbook* to identify the service items on your scooter and their locations **(see illustrations)**. The service items have been grouped under headings which identify the overall systems to which they belong. The headings also relate to the Chapters in this manual.

2 Not all the service items under each heading will require attention at the same service interval, but when you are working on a particular system it is useful to note all the parts that require attention and check them at the same time. For example, when the drive belt cover has been removed to inspect the variator and the condition of the belt, the general condition of the clutch and the kickstart mechanism can be checked. Also, if the belt has worn prematurely and is close to its service limit, a new one can be installed earlier than scheduled to prevent any damage caused by a broken belt.

Four-stroke engines
- [ ] Cooling fan
- [ ] Engine cowling
- [ ] Engine oil level
- [ ] Engine oil change
- [ ] Oil filter
- [ ] Valve clearances

Two-stroke engines
- [ ] Cooling fan
- [ ] Engine cowling
- [ ] Engine oil tank top-up
- [ ] Oil filter
- [ ] Oil pump adjustment
- [ ] Cylinder head decarbonising

Fuel and exhaust system
- [ ] Air filter
- [ ] Throttle cable
- [ ] Carburettor
- [ ] Fuel hose, filter and pump
- [ ] Idle speed
- [ ] Exhaust system mountings

Ignition system
- [ ] Spark plug

Transmission
- [ ] Drive belt
- [ ] Variator
- [ ] Kickstart mechanism
- [ ] Clutch pulley

- [ ] Gearbox oil level
- [ ] Gearbox oil change

Frame and suspension
- [ ] Front suspension
- [ ] Rear suspension
- [ ] Stand
- [ ] Steering head bearings

Brakes, wheels and tyres
- [ ] Brake cable (drum brake)
- [ ] Brake fluid (disc brake)
- [ ] Brake hose (disc brake)
- [ ] Brake levers
- [ ] Brake pads (disc brake)
- [ ] Brake shoes and cam (drum brake)
- [ ] Wheel bearings
- [ ] Tyre condition

Bodywork
- [ ] Fasteners
- [ ] Panel condition

Electrical systems
- [ ] Battery
- [ ] Headlight aim
- [ ] Brake light
- [ ] Horn

General
- [ ] Nuts and bolts

2.1a Component locations – left-hand side

1 Headlight
2 Brake levers
3 Speedometer cable
4 Battery
5 Engine oil – two-stroke engine
6 Brake light
7 Air filter
8 Rear suspension
9 Gearbox oil
10 Rear drum brake adjuster
11 Kickstarter
12 Transmission – variator, drive belt and clutch
13 Stand
14 Horn
15 Front brake
16 Wheel bearings

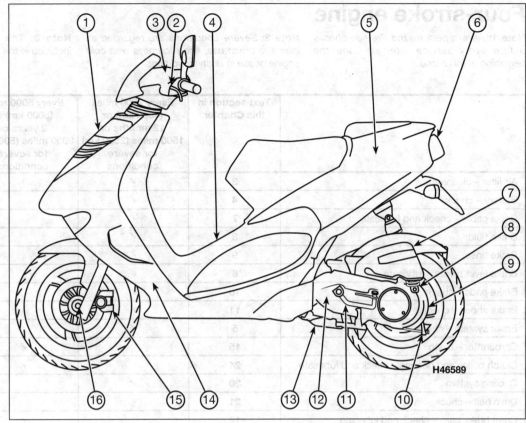

H46589

2.1b Component locations – right-hand side

1 Steering head bearings
2 Throttle cable
3 Front suspension
4 Valves – four-stroke engine
5 Spark plug
6 Carburettor – idle speed
7 Cooling fan
8 Engine oil – four-stroke engine
9 Exhaust system

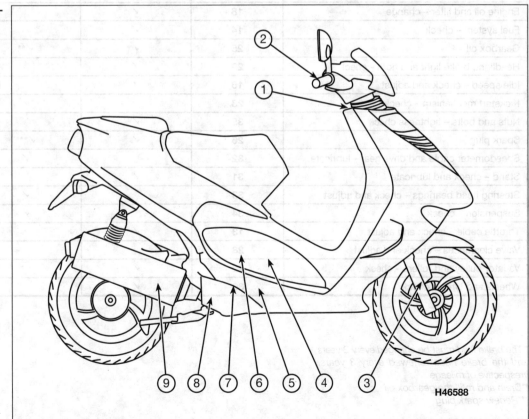

H46588

Four-stroke engine

Note 1: *Always perform the Pre-ride checks before every service interval – see the beginning of this Manual.*

Note 2: *Severe conditions are regarded as intensive urban use, short journeys with cold engine or use in dusty conditions.*

Note 3: *The 2500 mile tasks should be included in the 5000 mile service, etc.*

	Text section in this Chapter	Every 2500 miles (4000 km) or 12 months or 1500 miles (2500 km) for severe conditions	Every 5000 miles (8000 km) or 2 years or 3000 miles (5000 km) for severe conditions	Every 10,000 miles (16,000 km) or 3 years
Air filter – clean/renew	3	✓		
Battery – check	4	✓		
Brake cable – check and lubricate	7	✓		
Brake fluid	8	✓		✓*
Brake hose	9	✓		✓*
Brake lever pivots – lubricate	6	✓		
Brake pads – check	10	✓		
Brake shoes – check	11	✓		
Brake system – check	5	✓		
Carburettor – clean	15		✓	
Clutch pulley and bearing – check and lubricate	24		✓	
Cooling system	20	✓		
Drive belt – check	21	✓		
Drum brake cam – check and lubricate	12		✓	
Engine oil system – check	17	✓		
Engine oil and filter – change	18	✓		
Fuel system – check	14	✓		
Gearbox oil	25	✓	✓**	
Headlight, brake light and horn – check	29	✓		
Idle speed – check and adjust	16	✓		
Kickstart mechanism – check	23		✓	
Nuts and bolts – tightness check	35	✓		
Spark plug	26	✓	✓***	
Speedometer cable and drive gear – lubricate	32		✓	
Stand – check and lubricate	31	✓		
Steering head bearings – check and adjust	33		✓	
Suspension – check	34		✓	
Throttle cable – check and adjust	13	✓		
Valve clearances – check and adjust	28			✓
Variator pulley and rollers – check	22	✓		
Wheels and tyres – check	30	✓		

* The brake fluid must be changed every 2 years and the brake hose renewed every 3 years, irrespective of mileage
**Drain and refill the gearbox oil
***Renew spark plug

Two-stroke engine

Note 1: *Always perform the Pre-ride checks before every service interval – see the beginning of this Manual.*

Note 2: *Severe conditions are regarded as intensive urban use, short journeys with cold engine or use in dusty conditions.*

Note 3: *The 2500 mile tasks should be included in the 5000 mile service, etc.*

	Text section in this Chapter	Every 2500 miles (4000 km) or 12 months or 1500 miles (2500 km) for severe conditions	Every 5000 miles (8000 km) or 2 years or 3000 miles (5000 km) for severe conditions	Every 10,000 miles (16,000 km) or 3 years
Air filter – clean/renew	3	✓		
Battery – check	4	✓		
Brake cable – check and lubricate	7	✓		
Brake fluid	8	✓		✓*
Brake hose	9	✓		✓*
Brake lever pivots – lubricate	6	✓		
Brake pads – check	10	✓		
Brake shoes – check	11	✓		
Brake system – check	5	✓		
Carburettor – clean	15		✓	
Clutch pulley and bearing – check and lubricate	24		✓	
Cooling system	20	✓		
Cylinder head – decarbonise	27		✓	
Drive belt	21	✓	✓***	
Drum brake cam – check and lubricate	12		✓	
Engine oil system – check	17	✓		
Engine oil filter – change	18		✓	
Fuel system – check	14	✓		
Gearbox oil	25	✓	✓****	
Headlight, brake light and horn – check	29	✓		
Idle speed – check and adjust	16	✓		
Kickstart mechanism – check	23		✓	
Nuts and bolts – tightness check	35	✓		
Oil pump cable – check and adjust	19	✓		
Spark plug	26	✓	✓**	
Speedometer cable and drive gear – lubricate	32		✓	
Stand – check and lubricate	31	✓		
Steering head bearings – check and adjust	33		✓	
Suspension – check	34		✓	
Throttle cable – check and adjust	13	✓		
Variator pulley and rollers – check	22	✓		
Wheels and tyres – check	30	✓		

* The brake fluid must be changed every 2 years and the brake hose renewed every 3 years, irrespective of mileage
**Renew spark plug
***Renew the drive belt
****Drain and refill the gearbox oil

3.1a Undo the air filter cover screws (arrowed) . . .

3.1b . . . and remove the cover

3.1c Lift out the filter element, noting how it fits

3.2a Air filter housing (arrowed) located behind belly panel

3.2b Remove the cover . . .

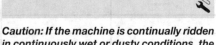

3 Air filter

Caution: If the machine is continually ridden in continuously wet or dusty conditions, the filter should be checked more frequently.

1 Remove the screws securing the air filter cover and lift it off **(see illustrations)**. Lift out the filter element – note that some filter elements are fitted in a removable panel **(see illustration)**.

2 On some machines the air filter housing is located at the front of the drivebelt cover **(see illustration)** – it may be necessary to remove some of the body panels to access the air filter housing (see Chapter 8). To facilitate access to the filter element, follow the procedure in Chapter 3 and remove the housing. Undo the screws securing the cover and lift it off, then lift out the filter element **(see illustrations)**.

3 Some manufacturers recommend that the filter element is renewed at every service interval – refer to your handbook for details. However, foam filters can usually be cleaned and reused if they are in good condition.

4 Wash the filter element in hot soapy water, then blow dry using compressed air. Do not wring the water out of the element as it may tear.

5 Soak the filter in dedicated air filter oil as recommended, or a mixture of petrol and 10% engine oil. Lay it on an absorbent surface and squeeze out the excess liquid, making sure you do not damage the filter by twisting it. Allow the filter to dry for a while.

6 If the filter is excessively dirty and cannot be cleaned properly, or is torn or damaged in any way, replace it with a new one.

7 Clean the inside of the filter housing **(see illustration)**. If the housing is fitted with a drain plug or tube, undo the plug and release any trapped fluid **(see illustration)**.

8 Check that the air intake duct is free from obstructions **(see illustration)**. If necessary, remove any body panels or the storage compartment to check that the ducting is in

3.2c . . . and lift out the filter element

3.7a Ensure the inside of the filter housing is clean

3.7b If fitted, undo the plug (arrowed) and drain the hose

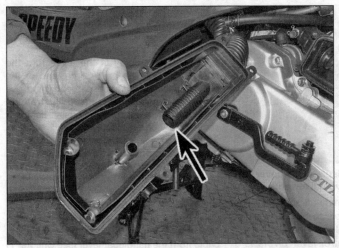

3.8 Check the air intake duct (arrowed) for obstructions

3.9 Inspect the hose union (arrowed) and clip

good condition, and renew the ducting if it is damaged or deteriorated.

9 On machines fitted with a secondary air system (SAS), check the hose union between the air intake duct and the SAS hose **(see illustration)**. Ensure that the union is not cracked or split, and that the hose clip is secure. Further details on the SAS can be found in Chapter 3.

10 Fit the filter element into the housing, then install the cover and tighten the screws securely. Don't forget to check that the intake duct hose clip is tightened securely **(see illustration)**.

4   Battery

Caution: Be extremely careful when handling or working around the battery. The electrolyte is very caustic and an explosive gas (hydrogen) is given off when the battery is charging.

1 The battery is located either underneath the seat or under the floor panel **(see illustration)**.

2 All the scooters covered in this manual are fitted with a sealed, maintenance-free battery. **Note:** *Do not attempt to open the battery as resulting damage will mean that it will be unfit for further use.*

3 All that should be done is to check that the battery terminals are clean and tight and that the casing is not damaged **(see illustration)**. Smear the terminals with petroleum jelly or battery terminal grease to prevent corrosion.

4 If fitted, ensure that the battery retaining strap is tightened securely **(see illustration)**.

5 See Chapter 9 for details of checking battery condition and battery charging.

6 If the scooter is not in regular use, disconnect the battery and give it a refresher charge every month to six weeks (see Chapter 9).

5   Brake system

1 A routine check of the brake system will ensure that any problems are discovered and remedied before the rider's safety is jeopardised.

2 Check that the brake levers are not loose or damaged, and that the lever action is smooth without excessive play. Replace any worn or damaged parts with new ones (see Chapter 7).

3 Make sure all brake fasteners are tight. Check the brake pads (disc brake) and brake shoes (drum brake) for wear (see Sections 10 and 11).

3.10 Ensure that the hose clip is secure

4 Where a disc brake is fitted, make sure the fluid level in the brake reservoir is correct (see *Pre-ride checks*). Look for leaks at the hose connections and check for cracks and abrasions in the hose and renew it if necessary (see Chapter 7). If the lever action is spongy, follow the procedure in Chapter 7 and bleed the brake.

5 Where a drum brake is fitted, check the cable for damage or stiff action, and check the cable adjustment (see Section 7).

6 Make sure the brake light operates when each brake lever is pulled in. The brake light switches are not adjustable; if they fail to operate properly, check them (see Chapter 9).

4.1 Remove the small panel underneath the floor mat to access the battery

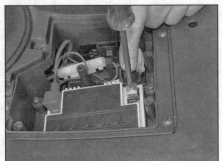

4.3 Ensure that the battery positive (+) and negative (-) terminals are tight

4.4 Ensure that the battery strap is secure

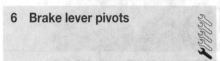

6.2a Lubricate the brake lever pivot (arrowed)

6.2b If necessary, displace the cover to access the pivot (arrowed)

6 Brake lever pivots

1 The lever pivots should be lubricated periodically to reduce wear and ensure safe and trouble-free operation.
2 In order for the lubricant to be applied where it will do the most good, the lever should be removed (see Chapter 7). However, if chain or cable lubricant is being used, it can be applied to the pivot joint gaps and will work its way into the areas where friction occurs **(see illustrations)**.
3 If motor oil or light grease is being used,

apply it sparingly as it may attract dirt (which could cause the controls to bind or wear at an accelerated rate). **Note:** *One of the best lubricants for the control lever pivots is a dry-film lubricant.*

7 Brake cable

Check and adjustment

1 Check that there is no excessive freeplay in the handlebar lever before the brake takes effect **(see illustration)**. The wheel should spin freely

when the brake is off, with approx. 10 to 20 mm freeplay measured at the ball end of the lever. However, the brake should come on before the lever is pulled back against the handlebar.
2 To reduce freeplay in the lever, turn the adjuster nut on the brake drum end of the cable clockwise; to increase freeplay, turn the adjuster nut anti-clockwise **(see illustration)**. If there is a locknut on the adjuster, tighten it securely on completion.
3 Note the wear indicator on the brake arm **(see illustration 7.2)**. If the indicator aligns with the index mark on the casing when the brake is applied, the brake shoes should be renewed (see Chapter 7).
4 If the brake is binding without the lever being pulled, first check that the lever is moving freely (see Section 6). Next, disconnect the cable from the handlebar lever (see Chapter 7) and check that the inner cable slides smoothly in the outer cable. If the action is stiff, inspect the length of the outer cable for splits and kinks, and the ends of the inner cable for frays. If any damage is found, fit a new cable (see Chapter 7).
5 If there are no signs of damage, lubricate the cable (see Steps 7 to 9). If the cable is still stiff after lubrication, replace it with a new one.
6 If the handlebar lever and brake cable are in good condition, check the operation of the brake cam (see Section 12).

7.1 Measuring brake lever freeplay

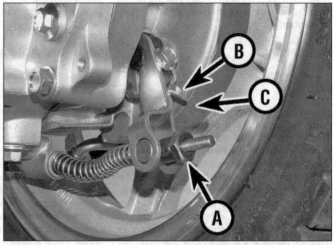

7.2 Brake adjuster nut (A), wear indicator (B) and index mark (C)

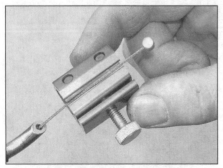

7.8a Fitting the cable lubricating adapter onto the inner cable

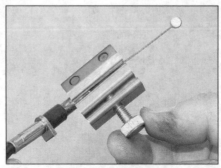

7.8b Ensure the adapter grips the inner and outer cables firmly

7.8c Connect the can of cable lubricant to the adapter

Lubrication

Special tool: *A cable lubricating adapter is necessary for this procedure.*

7 Cables should be lubricated periodically to ensure safe and trouble-free operation.

8 To lubricate a cable, follow the procedure in Chapter 7 and disconnect it at its upper end, then lubricate it with a pressure adapter and aerosol cable lubricant which is suitable for lined cables **(see illustrations)**.

9 Reconnect the cable and adjust the handlebar lever freeplay.

8   Brake fluid

1 The fluid level in the brake reservoir should be checked before riding the machine (see *Pre-ride checks*).

2 If access to the reservoir is restricted by the upper handlebar cover, check the operation of the brake. If it feels spongy, it is likely there is air in the system and the brake needs bleeding (see Chapter 7).

3 If necessary, follow the procedure in Chapter 8 and remove the handlebar cover to check the fluid level **(see illustrations)**.

4 Brake fluid will degrade over a period of time. It should be changed every two years or whenever a new master cylinder or caliper is fitted. Refer to the brake bleeding and fluid change section in Chapter 7.

> **HAYNES HINT** *Old brake fluid is invariably much darker in colour than new fluid, making it easy to see when all old fluid has been expelled from the system.*

9   Brake hose

1 Twist and flex the hose while looking for cracks, bulges and seeping fluid. Check extra carefully where the hose connects to the banjo unions as this is a common area for hose failure **(see illustration)**.

8.3a It may be necessary to remove the handlebar cover . . .

2 Inspect the banjo unions; if they are rusted, cracked or damaged, fit a new hose.

3 Inspect the banjo union connections for leaking fluid. If they leak when tightened securely, unscrew the banjo bolt and fit new sealing washers (see Chapter 7).

4 Flexible brake hoses will deteriorate with age and should be renewed every three years regardless of its apparent condition (see Chapter 7).

10   Brake pads

1 On disc brakes, the condition of the brake pads can normally be checked by looking at the underside of the caliper **(see illustration)**. On some scooters, a small plug can be removed to allow inspection of the pads **(see illustration)**.

2 If the brake pads are dirty, or if you are in any doubt as to the amount of friction material remaining on them, follow the procedure in Chapter 7 and slide the caliper off the disc to aid inspection **(see illustration)**.

3 Brake pad wear limit is either expressed in terms of the amount of friction material left on the pad backing plate (typically 1.5 mm) or by wear limit indicators which can be a groove or line around the pad periphery or a step or groove cut into the pad face.

⚠ **Warning: Brake pads often wear at different rates. If there is any doubt about the condition of either of the pads in a caliper, remove the caliper**

10.1a Check brake pad wear at the underside of the caliper

8.3b . . . to check the brake fluid level through the sightglass (arrowed)

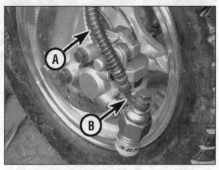

9.1 Inspect the brake hose (A) and banjo fitting (B)

and check. Brake failure will result if the friction material wears away completely.

4 Refer to Chapter 7 for details of brake pad removal, inspection and installation.

5 Inspect the surface of the disc for score marks and other damage. If the disc is badly grooved it must be machined or renewed (see Chapter 7).

11   Brake shoes

1 The brake shoes cannot be visually checked without first removing the rear wheel. However, drum brakes are normally equipped with a wear indicator **(see illustration 7.2)**.

2 As the brake shoes wear and the cable is adjusted to compensate, the indicator moves closer to the index mark on the casing. To

10.2 Displace the caliper to check the brake pads

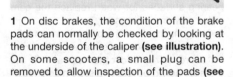

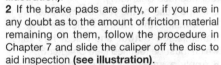

10.1b Inspection window (arrowed) for checking the brake pads

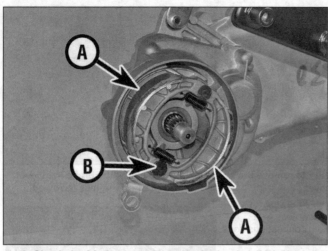

11.3 Check the friction material on the brake shoes (A). Note the brake cam (B)

12.2 Location of the brake arm clamp bolt (arrowed)

check the extent of brake wear, have an assistant apply the brake firmly; if the indicator aligns with the index mark, the brake shoes are worn to their limit and must be replaced with new ones (see Chapter 7).

3 If there is no wear indicator, follow the procedure in Chapter 7 to remove the wheel to check the amount of friction material remaining on the brake shoes **(see illustration)**.

4 Brake shoe friction material wear limit is typically 1.5 mm. Check the amount of wear at the thinnest point (at the shoe leading edge). If worn below this figure, renew the brake shoes.

5 If the brake shoes have worn unevenly, inspect the brake cam for wear (see Section 12).

12 Drum brake cam

1 Remove the wheel; on a front drum brake the brake shoes and brake cam are fitted to

the backplate, on a rear drum brake the shoes and cam are fitted to the back of the gearbox casing **(see illustration 11.3)**.

2 Follow the procedure in Chapter 7 to remove the brake shoes, then remove the brake arm clamp bolt and pull the brake cam out of the backplate or casing **(see illustration)**.

3 Clean the shaft and cam and inspect the bearing surfaces for wear; replace the cam with a new one if necessary.

4 Clean the inside of the brake drum and the casing and inspect the surface of the drum for score marks and other damage. If the drum is badly grooved it must be machined or renewed (see Chapter 7).

5 In the case of the rear drum brake, signs of oil inside the casing indicates that the transmission output shaft seal has failed which must be rectified (see Chapter 5).

6 Apply a smear of copper grease to the bearing surfaces of the cam and the shaft, and to the brake shoe pivot pin, before reassembly **(see illustration)**.

Caution: Do not apply too much grease

otherwise there is a risk of it contaminating the brake drum and shoe friction material.

13 Throttle cable

Note: *All four-stroke engines are fitted with a one-piece throttle cable. Two-stroke engines (with cable-controlled oil pumps) are fitted with three-piece cables.*

1 Ensure the throttle twistgrip rotates easily from fully closed to fully open with the handlebars turned at various angles. The twistgrip should return automatically from fully open to fully closed when released.

2 If the throttle sticks, this is probably due to a cable fault. Remove the cable (see Chapter 3) and lubricate it following the procedure in Section 7.

3 It's important that there's a small amount of freeplay in the throttle cable. This is either measured as twistgrip rotation (typically between 2 to 6 mm) **(see illustration)**, or as

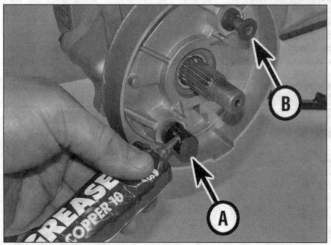

12.6 Lubricate the cam (A) and pivot pin (B) with a smear of grease

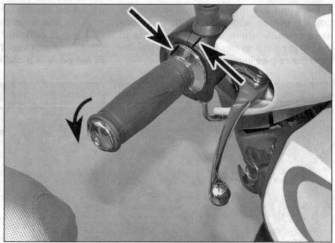

13.3 Throttle cable freeplay is measured in terms of twistgrip rotation

the amount of freeplay present at the in-line cable adjuster **(see illustration 13.7)**.

4 If there is insufficient or excessive freeplay, cable adjustment is required – follow the appropriate procedure according to the type of engine being worked on.

Four-stroke engines

5 Locate the adjuster at the carburettor end of the cable. The carburettor is accessible either through an inspection panel in the bottom of the luggage compartment **(see illustration)**, or by removing the luggage compartment itself (see Chapter 8).

6 Loosen the locknut on the adjuster, turn the adjuster until the right amount of freeplay is evident, then retighten the locknut **(see illustration)**.

7 Where an adjuster is fitted at the twistgrip end of the cable **(see illustration)** this can be used for making further adjustments. Ensure that the locknut is tightened after adjustment.

8 If cable adjustment has reached its limit, a new cable will have to be fitted (see Chapter 3).

13.5 Remove the inspection panel to access the carburettor (arrowed)

9 Once adjustment is complete, start the engine and check the idle speed. If the idle speed is too high, this could be due to incorrect adjustment of the cable. Loosen the locknut and turn the cable adjuster in – if the idle speed falls as you do, there is insufficient freeplay in the cable. Reset the adjuster. **Note:** *The idle speed should not change as the*

handlebars are turned. If it does, the throttle cable is routed incorrectly. Rectify the problem before riding the scooter (see Chapter 3).

Two-stroke engines fitted with a cable controlled oil pump

10 On these machines a three-cable system is used to actuate both the carburettor and the oil pump at the same time **(see illustration)**.

11 First ensure that there is no freeplay in the cable from the splitter to the carburettor. Remove the air filter housing (see Chapter 3) and pull back the boot on the cable adjuster on the top of the carburettor. Loosen the locknut on the adjuster, turn the adjuster to create a small amount of freeplay in the cable, then screw the adjuster out until the carburettor slide just begins to lift **(see illustration)**. Now turn the adjuster in a quarter turn. Tighten the locknut, then refit the boot and the filter housing.

12 Check the adjustment of the oil pump cable (see Section 19).

13 Now adjust the freeplay in the throttle

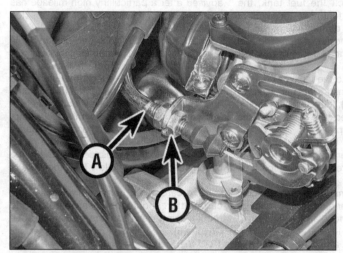

13.6 Throttle cable adjuster (A) and locknut (B), carburettor end

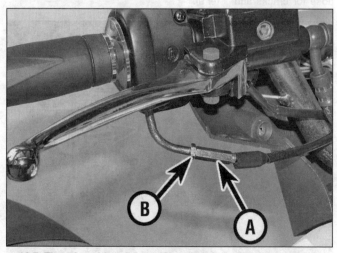

13.7 Throttle cable adjuster (A) and locknut (B), twistgrip end

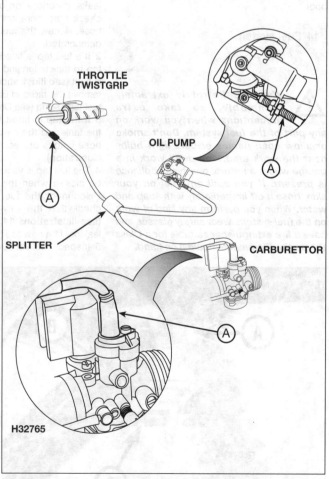

13.10 Cable arrangement for models fitted with a cable operated oil pump

Location of cable adjusters (A)

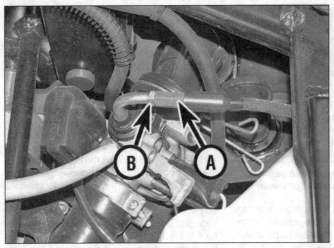

13.11 Throttle cable adjuster (A) and locknut (B), carburettor end

13.13 Throttle cable adjuster, twistgrip end. Note the boot (arrowed)

cable at the twistgrip end **(see illustration)**. Where fitted, displace the boot, then loosen the locknut on the adjuster and turn the adjuster until the right amount of freeplay is evident. Tighten the locknut and refit the boot.

14 Fuel system

⚠️ **Warning: Petrol is extremely flammable, so take extra precautions when you work on any part of the fuel system. Don't smoke or allow open flames or bare light bulbs near the work area, and don't work in a garage where a natural gas-type appliance is present. If you spill any fuel on your skin, rinse it off immediately with soap and water. When you perform any kind of work on the fuel system, wear safety glasses and have a fire extinguisher suitable for a Class B type fire (flammable liquids) on hand.**

1 Remove the body panels as necessary to access the fuel tank, tap or pump (as applicable to your scooter) and carburettor (see Chapter 8). Check the fuel tank, the tap or pump, and the fuel hose for signs of leaks, deterioration or damage; in particular check that there are no leaks from the fuel hose. Renew the fuel hose if it is cracked or deteriorated.

2 If a fuel tap is fitted to the tank, inspect the tap-to-tank union and ensure that the union nut is tight **(see illustration)**. If the union is leaking, remove the tap and check the condition of the fuel tap O-ring (see Chapter 3).

3 If the tap is fitted in the fuel line between the tank and the carburettor, ensure that the hose unions are secured by their clips **(see illustration)**.

4 The fuel tap is vacuum operated and should be closed when the engine is not running. Disconnect the fuel hose from the tap to check that the valve inside is not leaking **(see illustrations 14.2 and 3)**. If the valve is leaking, fit a new tap (see Chapter 3).

5 Inspect the vacuum hose for cracks and renew it if necessary. Ensure that the hose clip is secure.

6 Cleaning or replacement of the fuel filter is advised after a particularly high mileage has been covered or if fuel starvation is suspected (see Chapter 3).

7 Check that the fuel tank cap breather hole is clear. If the hole becomes blocked, fuel starvation will occur. Some tanks are fitted with a breather hose – check that the hose is not trapped between the tank and the frame and that the end of the hose is not blocked.

8 If your scooter is fitted with a fuel pump, ensure the fuel and vacuum hoses are securely attached to the pump and check the pump body for leaks. If you suspect that the pump is damaged or faulty, follow the procedure in Chapter 3 to test it.

9 If the carburettor gaskets are leaking, the carburettor should be disassembled and rebuilt using new gaskets and seals (see Chapter 3).

10 If the fuel gauge is believed to be faulty, check the operation of the sensor (see Chapter 9).

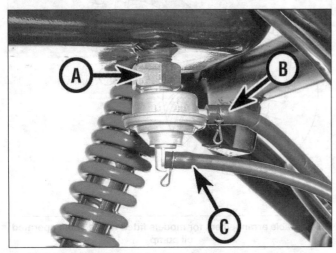

14.2 Fuel tap union (A), fuel hose (B) and vacuum hose (C)

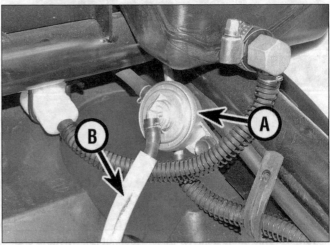

14.3 Location of the in-line fuel tap (A). Note the vacuum hose (B)

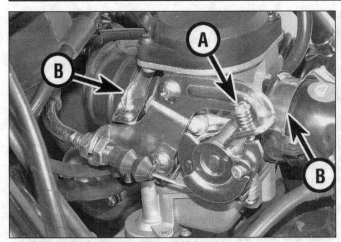

15.3 Keep the carburettor body and throttle mechanism free from dirt. Note the idle speed adjuster (A) and fixing clamps (B) – four-stroke carburettor shown

15.5a Undo the mounting screws . . .

15 Carburettor

1 Remove the air filter housing (see Chapter 3) and the storage compartment (see Chapter 8) to access the carburettor.

2 If fitted, pull back the carburettor cover, noting how it fits.

3 The exterior of the carburettor and the throttle mechanism should be kept clean and free of road dirt **(see illustration)**. Wash it carefully with hot soapy water, ensuring no water enters the carburettor body, and dry it with compressed air. Clean away any grit with a small paint brush. Oil deposits can be removed with a rag soaked in a suitable solvent. Take care to ensure the idle speed setting is not disturbed during cleaning.

4 Once the carburettor has been cleaned, don't forget to refit the protective cover. If the cover is damaged, it should be renewed (see Chapter 3).

5 A mud flap or hugger fitted in front of the rear wheel should keep road dirt off the carburettor. If the mud flap is broken or damaged, it should be renewed **(see illustrations)**. If necessary, follow the procedure in Chapter 3 to remove the exhaust system to access the mud flap.

6 Provided the air filter element is kept clean (see Section 3) the carburettor will give many thousands of miles of satisfactory service. However, dirt particles and varnish will gradually accumulate inside the body, and the carburettor should be removed and disassembled periodically to avoid the jets becoming blocked (see Chapter 3).

7 If the scooter has not been used for a long period, a sticky residue may form in the carburettor, jamming the throttle slide. Disassemble the carburettor and clean the components with a suitable solvent or carburettor cleaner (see Chapter 3). **Note:** *If the carburettor is being disassembled, read through the entire procedure and make sure that you have obtained a new gasket set first.*

16 Idle speed

1 The idle speed (engine running with the throttle twistgrip closed) should be checked and adjusted when it is obviously too high or too low. Before adjusting the idle speed, make sure the throttle cable is correctly adjusted (see Section 13) and check the spark plug gap (see Section 26). On four-stroke engines, the valve clearances must be correct to achieve a satisfactory idle speed (see Section 28).

2 The engine should be at normal operating temperature, which is usually reached after 10 to 15 minutes of stop-and-go riding. Support the scooter upright with the rear wheel clear of the ground.

> **Warning: Do not allow exhaust gases to build up in the work area; either perform the check outside or use an exhaust gas extraction system**

3 Although most manufacturers specify idle speed in engine revolutions per minute (rpm), for scooters not fitted with a tachometer it is sufficient to ensure that at idle the engine speed is steady and does not falter, and that it is not so high that the automatic transmission engages.

4 The idle speed adjuster is located on the carburettor – if necessary, refer to your *Owner's Handbook* for details **(see illustration)**. With the engine running, turn the screw clockwise to increase idle speed, and anti-clockwise to decrease it **(see illustrations 15.3 and 16.4)**.

5 Snap the throttle open and shut a few times, then recheck the idle speed. If necessary, repeat the adjustment procedure.

6 If a smooth, steady idle can't be achieved, the fuel/air mixture may be incorrect (see Chapter 3) or the carburettor may need cleaning (see Section 15). Ensure that the clamps securing the air filter housing duct to the carburettor, and the one securing the

15.5b . . . to remove the mud flap

16.4 Idle speed adjuster (arrowed) – two-stroke carburettor shown

16.6 Ensure that the intake manifold nuts (arrowed) are tight

17.8 Two-stroke engine oil pump (arrowed) located below the cylinder

17.13 Oil hose connection (arrowed) on the bottom of the oil tank

carburettor to the intake manifold, are tight. Ensure that the nuts securing the intake manifold are tight **(see illustration)**.

7 If a satisfactory idle speed still cannot be achieved, check the ignition system (see Chapter 4).

8 With the idle speed correctly adjusted, recheck the throttle cable freeplay (see Section 13).

17 Engine oil system

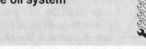

1 A routine check of the engine oil system will ensure that any problems are discovered and remedied before the engine is damaged.

2 Check the engine oil level (see *Pre-ride checks*).

Four-stroke engines

3 Ensure that the oil is changed regularly and that the oil filter is cleaned at the same time (see Section 18).

4 If you have to top-up the engine oil frequently, check around the engine unit for any oil leaks. Ensure that the cover bolts are tight and, if necessary, refer to the relevant Section in Chapter 2A or 2B and renew any damaged gaskets or seals.

5 If oil is leaking from the alternator cover on the right-hand side of the engine, it is likely that the seal on the crankshaft has failed. Remove the alternator rotor to check (see Chapter 2A or 2B). If oil is leaking from the drive belt cover, it is likely that the left-hand crankshaft

seal has failed. Remove the variator to check (see Chapter 5).

⚠ *Warning: If an oil leak can be traced to the gearbox it must be rectified immediately. The gearbox contains only a small amount of oil and any loss will soon result in serious mechanical damage and may cause the gearbox to seize.*

6 White smoke from the exhaust is caused by burning oil. A broken piston ring or worn cylinder bore will allow oil to pass the piston into the combustion chamber. Remove the cylinder to check for excessive wear or damage (see Chapter 2A or 2B).

7 There is no provision for checking the engine oil pressure. If, however, there is any doubt about the performance of the engine lubrication system, the pump should be removed for inspection (see Chapter 2A or 2B). **Note:** *Engine oil circulates to the camshaft and valve gear in the cylinder head via one of the cylinder stud holes. Lack of lubrication can be cause by a blocked oilway or fitting an incorrect cylinder head or base gasket.*

Two-stroke engines

8 Two-stroke engines are fitted with a cable operated oil pump. The pump is mounted externally on the crankcase, either in front of, behind or below the cylinder **(see illustration)**. If in doubt about the pump's location, trace the oil hose from the intake manifold back to the pump.

9 Remove any body panels or the storage compartment as necessary to access the oil

pump (see Chapter 8). Where the pump is located below the cylinder it may be necessary to remove the fan cowling or cylinder cowling to gain access (see Section 20).

10 Follow the procedure in Section 19 and check that the oil pump cable is correctly adjusted.

11 Check the operation of the oil level warning light in the instrument cluster. The light should come on temporarily when the ignition is first turned on as a check of the warning circuit, and then extinguish. If the light stays on the oil level is low and should be topped-up. If the light stays on when the tank is full, check the oil level warning circuit (see Chapter 9). If the light doesn't come on at all, check the bulb and oil level warning circuit (see Chapter 9). **Note:** *On some scooters the oil level sensor is part of the safety circuit which prevents the engine starting if there is insufficient oil in the oil tank.*

12 If a filter is fitted in the hose from the oil tank to the pump, inspect the filter **(see illustration 18.12)**. Check for sediment in the filter and replace the filter with a new one if necessary (see Section 18).

13 Check the condition of the oil inlet and outlet hoses. In particular check that there are no leaks from the hose connections to the oil tank, filter, oil pump and carburettor **(see illustration)**. Renew any hoses that are cracked or deteriorated and ensure they are properly secured by clips. **Note:** *If oil is leaking from behind the alternator cover, remove the alternator stator (see Chapter 2C) and check the oil hose connections to the pump.*

18 Engine oil and oil filter

Four-stroke engines

⚠ *Warning: Be careful when draining the oil, as the exhaust pipe, the engine, and the oil itself can cause severe burns.*

1 Oil and filter changes are the single most important maintenance procedure you can perform on a four-stroke engine. The oil not only lubricates the internal parts of the engine, but it also acts as a coolant, a cleaner, a sealant, and a protector. Because of these demands, the oil takes a terrific amount of abuse and should be replaced at the specified service interval with new oil of the recommended grade and type.

2 Before changing the oil, warm up the engine so the oil will drain easily. Stop the engine and turn the ignition OFF. Support the scooter upright and position a clean drain tray below the engine.

3 Unscrew the oil filler plug to vent the crankcase and to act as a reminder that there is no oil in the engine **(see illustration)**.

4 Unscrew the oil drain plug and allow the oil to flow into the drain tray **(see illustration)**.

18.3 Unscrew the oil filler plug

18.4 Remove the oil drain plug. Note the sealing washer (arrowed)

Discard the sealing washer or O-ring on the drain plug as a new one must be used on reassembly.

5 When the oil has completely drained, fit a new sealing washer or O-ring on the drain plug, then install the plug and tighten it securely. Avoid over-tightening, as damage to the threads will result.

6 Unscrew the oil filter assembly and allow any residual oil to flow into the drain tray **(see illustration)**. Note how the filter and spring are located in the filter cap **(see illustration)**. Discard the sealing washer or O-ring on the cap as a new one must be used on reassembly.

7 Clean the filter gauze in solvent and remove any debris caught in the mesh. Check the gauze for splits or holes and renew it if necessary.

8 Prior to installation, fit a new sealing washer or O-ring on the filter cap. Assemble the spring and filter, then install the cap and tighten it securely. Avoid over-tightening, as damage to the threads will result.

9 Refill the engine to the correct level using the recommended type of oil (see *Pre-ride checks*).

HAYNES HINT *Saving a little money on the difference between good and cheap oils won't pay off if the engine is damaged as a result.*

10 Start the engine and let it run for two or three minutes. Shut it off, wait five minutes, then check the oil level. If necessary, top-up the oil to the correct level (see *Pre-ride checks*). Check around the drain plug and filter for leaks.

11 The old oil drained from the engine cannot be re-used and should be disposed of properly. Check with your local refuse disposal company, disposal facility or environmental agency to see whether they will accept the

18.6a Unscrew the oil filter assembly (arrowed) . . .

used oil for recycling. Don't pour used oil into drains or onto the ground.

Check the old oil carefully – if it is very metallic coloured, then the engine is experiencing wear from break-in (new engine) or from insufficient lubrication. If there are flakes or chips of metal in the oil, then something is drastically wrong internally and the engine will have to be disassembled for inspection and repair.

Two-stroke engines

12 Where fitted, the oil filter in the hose between the tank and the pump should be changed at the service interval specified in the *Data* section, or sooner if there is sediment in it **(see illustration)**.

13 Remove any body panels or the storage compartment as necessary to access the oil filter. Release the clips securing the inlet and outlet hoses to the filter and slide them along the hoses away from the filter. Detach the hoses and clamp them to prevent oil loss.

14 The oil filter body is marked with an arrow indicating the direction of oil flow. Connect the hoses to the filter unions, ensuring the arrow points towards the oil pump (i.e. in the direction of oil flow), then install the hose clips.

15 Air bubbles should be bled from the filter

18.6b . . . noting the location of the filter gauze and spring

before refitting the body panels. Tilt the filter to allow the trapped air to rise through the hose into the oil tank.

---

19 Oil pump cable (two-stroke engines)

1 The oil pump is cable is connected to the throttle twistgrip via a splitter **(see illustration 13.10)**.

2 First ensure the throttle twistgrip rotates easily from fully closed to fully open with the handlebars turned at various angles (see Section 13).

3 Remove any body panels, the storage compartment or fan cowling as necessary to access the oil pump (see Section 17).

4 At the pump end, the cable is connected to the pump cam. With the cable correctly adjusted, an index mark on the cam should align with a mark on the pump body, either with the throttle closed or with the throttle fully open – if available, check with your *Owner's Handbook* for details **(see illustration)**.

5 The oil pump cable will stretch slightly in use, so only a small amount of adjustment should be necessary to re-align the marks. As a guide, there should be no discernible freeplay in the pump cable (between the pump

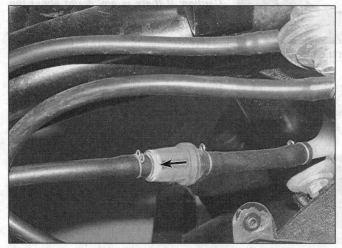

18.12 Two-stroke engine oil filter – arrow indicates direction of oil flow

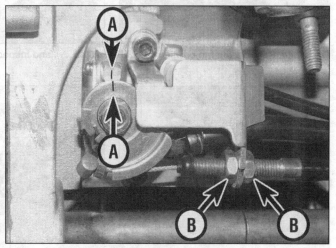

19.4 Note the alignment of the oil pump index marks (A). Note the cable adjuster locknuts (B)

19.8 Tab on cam rests against stop (arrowed) with throttle closed

and the splitter) with the throttle closed, and the pump cam should turn as the throttle is opened – at the same time as the carburettor slide lifts. If the cable is over-adjusted (too tight), too much oil will be fed into the engine causing a fouled spark plug and a smokey exhaust.

6 If the marks are not aligned, loosen the cable adjuster locknut and turn the adjuster as required until the marks align, then retighten the locknut **(see illustration 19.4)**. If the adjuster has reached its limit of adjustment, replace the cable with a new one (see Chapter 3).

7 Check that the throttle cable freeplay is correct (see Section 13).

8 On one of the machines used to illustrate this procedure, no index marks were visible on the pump cam. The recommended setting was that with the throttle closed, a tab on the cam should just rest against a stop on the

pump body **(see illustration)**. With the cam in this position, there should be no discernible freeplay in the pump cable (between the pump and the splitter). If the cable is too tight, or if there is freeplay, loosen the cable adjuster locknut and turn the adjuster as required. When the adjustment is correct, tighten the locknut.

20 Cooling system

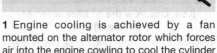

1 Engine cooling is achieved by a fan mounted on the alternator rotor which forces air into the engine cowling to cool the cylinder and cylinder head.

2 Check that the air intake in the fan cowling is not obstructed or blocked and that the sections of the engine cowling are fitted together correctly and secured with their mounting screws. **Note:** *If any sections of the engine cowling are missing, the engine will not be properly cooled.*

3 On most four-stroke scooters, a seal is fitted around the top of the cylinder head – if this is damaged or missing the cooling air will not circulate effectively.

4 Undo the mounting screws and remove the fan cowling, then inspect the fan for damage **(see illustrations)**. If any of the vanes are broken renew the fan. Check that the fan mounting bolts are tight – if the bolts are loose or if the bolt holes are worn oversize, the fan will run out of true and cause engine vibration.

5 For full details on the engine cowling removal and installation procedure, refer to the appropriate Section in Chapter 2A, 2B or 2C.

6 On some scooters, cooling air is drawn into the front of the drive belt case via ducting. Remove any body panels or the storage compartment to check that the ducting is in good condition, and renew the ducting if it is damaged or deteriorated. Check that the hose clip is secure **(see illustration)**.

7 The air is circulated by the vanes on the outside edge of the variator and exits the case via a vent on the underside – ensure that the vent is not obstructed **(see illustration)**.

21 Drive belt

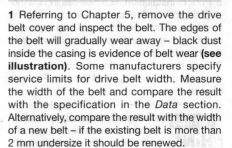

1 Referring to Chapter 5, remove the drive belt cover and inspect the belt. The edges of the belt will gradually wear away – black dust inside the casing is evidence of belt wear **(see illustration)**. Some manufacturers specify service limits for drive belt width. Measure the width of the belt and compare the result with the specification in the *Data* section. Alternatively, compare the result with the width of a new belt – if the existing belt is more than 2 mm undersize it should be renewed.

2 The drive belt must be renewed at the service interval specified in the *Data* section, or earlier dependent on belt condition (see Chapter 5).

3 In the event of premature belt wear, the cause should be investigated (see Chapter 5).

4 If the belt shows signs of fraying or cracking, or if it is contaminated with oil or grease, it should be renewed. Oil or grease inside the casing is evidence that a crankshaft, transmission shaft or clutch assembly seal has failed. Trace the source of the leak and renew the seal.

5 Clean any dust from inside the casing before installing the drive belt cover.

Caution: If there is any doubt about the condition of the drive belt, replace it with a new one. A broken belt could cause severe damage to engine or transmission components.

20.4a Remove the fan cowling . . .

20.4b . . . and inspect the fan for damage

20.6 Ensure that the hose clip (arrowed) is secure

20.7 Exit vent (arrowed) for the cooling air

21.1 Drive belt will wear along its inner and outer edges

23.1 Return spring should hold the kickstart lever in the fully-up position

23.2 Check the operation of the kickstart lever periodically

24.3 Checking for play in the clutch hub bearings

22 Variator pulley and rollers

1 Referring to Chapter 5, remove the drive pulley and the variator.
2 Disassemble the variator and check all components for wear as described. **Note:** *The self-locking variator centre nut should be replaced with a new one on reassembly.*

23 Kickstart mechanism

1 The kickstart lever should move smoothly and return to the fully-up or rest position under the tension of the return spring **(see illustration)**.
2 Although most owners will use the electric starter, it is good practice to periodically check the operation of the kickstart to ensure it is in good working order **(see illustration)**.
3 Referring to Chapter 5, remove the drive belt cover. Inspect the component parts of the kickstart mechanism for damage and wear and renew any parts as necessary. Lubricate the kickstart mechanism with high temperature grease before reassembly.

24 Clutch pulley and bearing

1 Referring to Chapter 5, remove the drive belt cover.
2 The outer half of the clutch pulley should slide outwards on the clutch hub, against the pressure of the clutch centre spring.
3 Next, grasp the pulley assembly and check for play in the pulley hub bearings **(see illustration)**.
4 To dismantle the clutch and pulley assembly in order to check the condition of the clutch and to lubricate the pulley bearing surfaces, follow the procedure in Chapter 5. **Note:** *The self-locking clutch centre nut should be replaced with a new one on reassembly.*

25 Gearbox oil

Level check

1 Where fitted, the gearbox oil level plug is located on the rear, left-hand side of the gearbox casing **(see illustration). Note:** *Not all scooters are equipped with a level plug – check with your Owner's Handbook. If required, drain and refill the gearbox to ensure that the correct level is maintained (see below).*
2 Position the scooter on its main stand. Clean the area around the level plug and then unscrew the plug from the gearbox casing. Discard the sealing washer as a new one should be used on reassembly.
3 The oil level should come up to the lower threads inside the hole, so that it is just visible on the threads **(see illustration). Note:** *The oil level should be checked with the scooter supported upright on level ground.*
4 If required, top the gearbox up with the specified gear oil. Most scooter manufacturers recommend an SAE 85W/90 gear oil, although SAE 75W/90 products are widely available. Aim to use one of those packaged for scooter use – most will come in tube form, with a small nozzle suitable for the level/filler plug hole size **(see illustration)**. Do not overfill – allow excess oil to drain out before installing the level plug.
5 Fit a new sealing washer to the level plug and tighten it securely **(see illustration)**.
6 If the oil level is very low, or oil is leaking from the gearbox, refer to Chapter 5 and

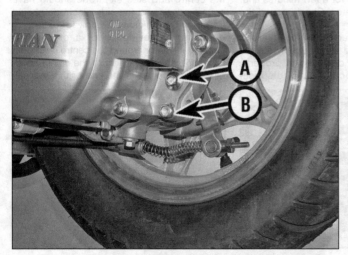

25.1 Location of the gearbox oil level plug (A) and drain plug (B)

25.3 Gearbox oil should be level with the lower threads (arrowed)

25.4 Scooter gear oil comes in handy packs to fit the filler hole size

25.5 Always fit a new sealing washer on the level plug

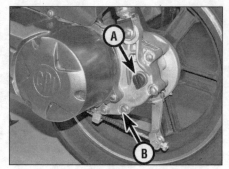

25.7 Gearbox oil filler plug (A) and drain plug (B)

25.11 Note the location of the O-ring (arrowed) on the filler plug

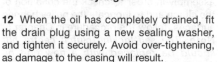
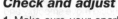

25.13 Filling the gearbox with oil using a syringe

inspect the condition of the case seals and gaskets and replace them with new ones if necessary.

> ⚠ **Warning: Do not risk under-filling or over-filling the gearbox as a transmission seizure or dangerous oil leakage may result.**

Change

7 Clean the area around the gearbox drain plug, oil level or filler plug **(see illustration)**.
8 Position a clean drain tray below the gearbox.
9 Unscrew the filler/level plug to vent the case and to act as a reminder that there is no oil in it.
10 Unscrew the oil drain plug and allow the oil to flow into the drain tray.
11 Discard the sealing washers on the plugs as new ones should be used. Check the O-ring on the filler plug and renew it if it is damaged **(see illustration)**.

12 When the oil has completely drained, fit the drain plug using a new sealing washer, and tighten it securely. Avoid over-tightening, as damage to the casing will result.
13 Refill the gearbox to the correct level using the recommended type and amount of oil. If there is a level plug, follow the procedure in Steps 3 and 4. Alternatively, the correct amount of oil can be added to the gearbox using a suitable syringe **(see illustration)**.
14 If applicable, fit a new sealing washer to the level plug and tighten it securely. Alternatively, install the filler plug.
15 Where applicable, check the oil level again after riding the scooter for a few minutes and, if necessary, add more oil. Check around the drain plug for leaks.
16 The old oil drained from the gearbox cannot be re-used, and although only a small quantity, it should be disposed of properly. Check with your local refuse disposal

company, disposal facility or environmental agency to see whether they will accept the used oil for recycling. Don't pour used oil into drains or onto the ground.

26 Spark plug

> ⚠ **Warning: Access to the spark plug is extremely restricted on some scooters. Ensure the engine and exhaust system are cool before attempting to remove the spark plug.**

Check and adjust

1 Make sure your spark plug socket is the correct size before attempting to remove the plug – a suitable plug spanner is usually supplied in the scooter's tool kit.
2 As required, remove the engine access panel or storage compartment to access the spark plug (see Chapter 8).
3 Pull off the spark plug cap, then ensure the spark plug spanner is located correctly over the plug and unscrew the plug from the cylinder head **(see illustrations)**.
4 Inspect the plug electrodes for wear. Both the centre and side electrode should have square edges and the side electrode should be of uniform thickness. Look for excessive deposits and evidence of a cracked or chipped insulator around the centre electrode. Compare your spark plug to the colour spark plug reading chart at the end of this manual.

26.3a Pull off the spark plug cap – four-stroke engine shown

26.3b Pull off the spark plug cap – two-stroke engine shown

26.3c Using the tool kit spanner to unscrew the spark plug

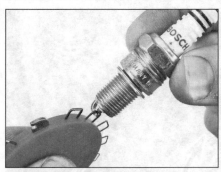

26.6a Using a wire type gauge to measure the spark plug electrode gap

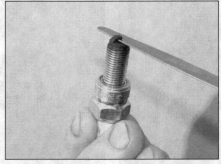

26.6b Using a feeler gauge to measure the spark plug electrode gap

26.6c Adjust the electrode gap by bending the side electrode only

Check the condition of the threads and washer, and the ceramic insulator body for cracks and other damage.

5 If the electrodes are not excessively worn, and if the deposits can be easily removed with a wire brush, the plug can be re-gapped and re-used (if no cracks or chips are visible in the insulator). If in doubt concerning the condition of the plug, replace it with a new one, as the expense is minimal.

6 Before installing the plug, make sure it is the correct type – check with your *Owner's Handbook* or the *Data* section at the end of this manual. Check the gap between the electrodes, even if a new plug is being fitted **(see illustrations)**. Compare the gap to that specified and adjust as necessary. If the gap must be adjusted, bend the side electrode only and be very careful not to chip or crack the insulator nose **(see illustration)**.

7 Make sure the washer is in place before installing the plug. Smear the plug threads with a little copper-based grease then thread it into the head by hand until it is finger-tight. Since the cylinder head is made of aluminium which is soft and easily damaged, ensure the plug threads are not crossed before tightening it securely with the spark plug spanner. Reconnect the plug cap.

 HAYNES HiNT *A stripped plug thread in the cylinder head can be repaired with a thread insert.*

27 Cylinder head (two-stroke engines)

Decarbonise

Note: *The use of modern, low ash engine oils specifically designed for use in two-stroke engines has considerably reduced the need to decarbonise the engine. However, some manufacturers still recommend decarbonising as part of the routine service schedule, and if the machine is continually ridden on short journeys which do not allow the engine to reach and maintain its normal operating temperature, the cylinder head should be decarbonised more frequently.*

1 Remove the cylinder head (see Chapter 2C).

2 Remove all accumulated carbon from inside the cylinder head using a blunt scraper **(see illustration)**. Small traces of carbon can be removed with very fine abrasive paper or a kitchen scourer

Caution: The cylinder head and piston are made of aluminium which is relatively soft. Take great care not to gouge or score the surface when scraping.

3 Press the cylinder down against the crankcase to avoid breaking the cylinder base gasket seal, then turn the engine over until the piston is at the very top of its stroke. Smear grease all around the edge of the piston to trap any particles of carbon, then clean the piston crown, taking care not to score or gouge it or the cylinder bore **(see illustration)**. Finally,

lower the piston and wipe away the grease and any remaining particles of carbon.

4 With the piston at the bottom of its stroke, check the exhaust port in the cylinder and scrape away any carbon. If the exhaust port is heavily coked, remove the exhaust system and clean the port and the exhaust pipe thoroughly (see Chapter 3). **Note:** *If the cylinder is disturbed during this procedure, fit a new cylinder base gasket (see Chapter 2C).*

5 Install the cylinder head (see Chapter 2C).

 HAYNES HiNT *Finish the piston crown and cylinder head off using a metal polish. A shiny surface is more resistant to the build-up of carbon deposits.*

28 Valve clearances (four-stroke engines)

Check and adjust

1 The engine must be completely cold for this maintenance procedure, so let the machine sit overnight before beginning. Remove any body panels necessary to gain access to the alternator and cylinder head (see Chapter 8).

2 Remove the fan cowling (see Section 20). Remove the spark plug (see Section 26).

3 Follow the procedure in Chapter 2A and remove the valve cover **(see illustration)**.

4 The valve clearances are checked with

27.2 Remove accumulated carbon (arrowed) from inside the cylinder head

27.3 Cleaning the piston crown with a soft wire brush

28.3 Remove the valve cover

28.4 Check the rocker arms (arrowed) for clearance at TDC

28.5a Timing marks or two holes (arrowed) should align with the gasket face

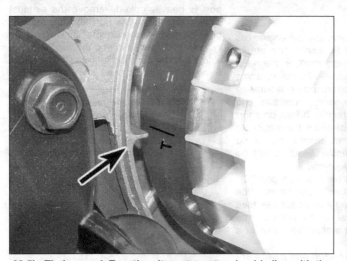

28.5b Timing mark T on the alternator rotor should align with the index mark (arrowed)

28.8 Checking the clearance on the intake (carburettor side) valve

the piston at top dead centre (TDC) on its compression stroke. At TDC the valves are closed and a small clearance can be felt at each rocker arm **(see illustration)**. Turn the engine in the normal direction of rotation until the piston is at TDC – you can do this by rotating the crankshaft via the alternator rotor.

5 To confirm that the piston is in the correct position, look for timing marks or two small

28.9 Hold the adjuster while tightening the locknut

holes on the camshaft sprocket – these should be aligned with the valve cover gasket face **(see illustration)**. Also, ensure that the timing mark 'T' on the alternator rotor is aligned with the index mark on the crankcase **(see illustration)**.

6 With the piston at TDC on its compression stroke and the timing marks aligned, the valve clearances can be checked.

7 Refer to your *Owners Handbook* or the *Data* section at the end of this manual for the correct valve clearances, noting that the clearance for the intake and exhaust valves may be different.

8 Insert a feeler gauge of the same thickness as the correct valve clearance between the rocker arm and stem of each valve **(see illustration)**. The feeler gauge should be a firm sliding fit – you should feel a slight drag when you pull the gauge out.

9 If the clearance is either too small or too large, loosen the locknut and turn the adjuster until a firm sliding fit is obtained, then tighten the locknut securely, making sure the adjuster does not turn as you do so **(see illustration)**.

Re-check the clearance.

10 Apply some engine oil to the valve assemblies, rockers and camshaft before installing the valve cover and fit a new cover gasket or O-ring. Install the remaining components in the reverse order of removal.

29 Headlight, brake light and horn

Headlight

Note: *An improperly adjusted headlight may cause problems for oncoming traffic or provide poor, unsafe illumination of the road ahead. Before adjusting the headlight aim, be sure to consult with local traffic laws and regulations – for UK models refer to MOT Test Checks in the Reference section.*

1 Before making any adjustment, check that the tyre pressures are correct. Make any adjustments to the headlight aim with the scooter on level ground, with the fuel tank half

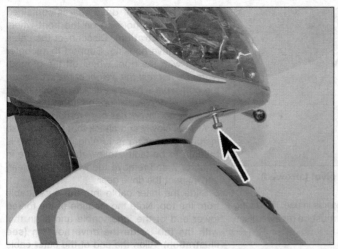

29.2a Headlight adjuster screw (arrowed) located underneath the light unit

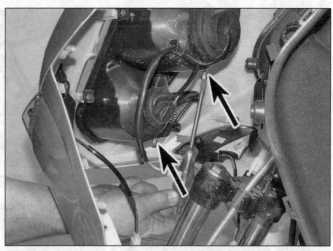

29.2b Headlight adjuster screws (arrowed) located on the back of the light units

full and with an assistant sitting on the seat. If the machine is usually ridden with a passenger on the back, have a second assistant to do this.

2 All headlight units have provision for vertical (up and down) adjustment. The headlight adjuster screw will be located either at the front of the unit, on the unit itself, or accessible through a hole or grille **(see illustrations)**. Refer to your *Owner's Handbook* for details. **Note:** *On some scooters, it may be necessary to displace the headlight panel to access the adjuster screw.*

3 Position the scooter as described in the *MOT Test Checks* in the Reference section. If necessary, start the engine, then switch the headlight main beam ON. Turn the adjuster screw to move the beam up or down as required. **Note:** *On one of the scooters used to illustrate this procedure, the adjuster screw was first loosened, then pulled back and forward in a slot to adjust the headlight.*

⚠️ **Warning: Do not allow exhaust gases to build up in the work area; either perform the check outside or use an exhaust gas extraction system**

Brake light

4 The brake light should come on when either the front or rear brake levers are pulled in. If it does not, check the operation of the brake light switch and tail/brake light bulb (see Chapter 9).

Note: *In most cases, the operation of the brake light must be checked with the engine running.*

Horn

5 If the horn fails to work, check the operation of the handlebar switch and the horn itself (see Chapter 9). **Note:** *In most cases, the operation of the horn must be checked with the engine running.*

30 Wheels and tyres

Wheels

1 Wheels are virtually maintenance free, but they should be kept clean and corrosion free and checked periodically for damage to the rims. Check cast wheels for cracks. Also check the wheel runout and alignment (see Chapter 7). Never attempt to repair damaged cast wheels; they must be replaced with new ones.

2 The front wheel bearings will wear over a period of time and result in handling problems. Support the scooter on its main stand and check for any play in the bearings by pushing and pulling the wheel against the hub **(see illustration)**. Also rotate the wheel and check that it turns smoothly.

3 If any play is detected in the hub, or if the wheel does not rotate smoothly (and this is not due to brake drag), the wheel bearings must be inspected for wear or damage (see Chapter 7).

4 Follow the same procedure to check for play in the rear wheel **(see illustration)**. There are no rear wheel bearings as such. The wheel is mounted directly onto the rear axle/gearbox output shaft which turns on bearings located inside the gearbox. If any play is detected, refer to Chapter 5 to check the gearbox. Also check that play is not due to a fault or wear in the rear suspension (see Section 34).

Tyres

5 Check the tyre condition and tread depth thoroughly – see *Pre-ride checks*.

6 Check the valve rubber for signs of damage or deterioration and have it replaced if necessary by a tyre specialist.

7 Make sure the valve stem cap is in place and tight. On some scooters, the cap doubles as a key for the valve. If a tyre loses pressure, and this is not due to damage to the tyre itself, check that the valve is tightened securely (similar caps are available in automotive accessory shops).

8 A smear of soapy water will indicate if the valve is leaking – the leak will show as bubbles in the water. If required, use the valve cap to unscrew the old valve and install a new one **(see illustration)**.

30.2 Checking the front wheel bearings

30.4 Checking for play at the rear wheel

30.8 Installing a new tyre valve with the cap/key

31.2a Main stand pivot (arrowed)

31.2b Sidestand pivot (arrowed)

31 Stand

1 Since the stand pivots are exposed to the elements, they should be cleaned and lubricated periodically to ensure safe and trouble-free operation.

2 In order for the lubricant to be applied where it will do the most good, the component should be disassembled. However, if an aerosol lubricant is being used, it can be applied to the pivot joint gaps and will usually work its way into the areas where friction occurs **(see illustrations)**. If motor oil or grease is being used, apply it sparingly as it will attract dirt (which could cause the controls to bind or wear at an accelerated rate).

3 The return spring(s) must be capable of retracting the stand fully and holding it

32.2 Disconnect the top end of the speedometer cable (arrowed)

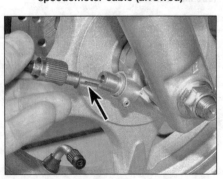

32.5a Align the forked end of the inner cable (arrowed) with the drive tab

retracted when the scooter is in use. If a spring has sagged or broken it must be renewed (see Chapter 6).

32 Speedometer cable and drive gear

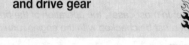

1 Remove the handlebar front cover (see Chapter 8).

2 Unscrew the knurled ring to disconnect the speedometer cable from the underside of the instrument panel **(see illustration)**. Note that the upper end of the inner cable is squared-off to locate in the speedometer drive.

3 Withdraw the inner cable from the outer cable and lubricate it with motor oil or cable lubricant. Do not lubricate the upper few inches of the cable as the lubricant may travel up into the instrument head.

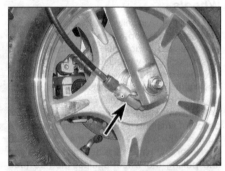

32.4 Location of the speedometer drive housing (arrowed)

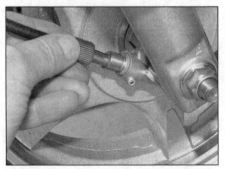

32.5b Align the outer cable with the drive housing . . .

4 The speedometer drive gear is contained within the drive housing on the front wheel hub **(see illustration)**. Disconnect the cable from the drive housing. Support the scooter upright with the front wheel off the ground. **Note:** *Do not rest the weight of the scooter on the bodywork – have an assistant push down on the rear or place a support under the frame once any bodywork has been removed.* Rotate the wheel slowly and check that the drive tab inside the housing is turning. If the drive is thought to be faulty, follow the procedure in Chapter 7 and remove the wheel, then clean and inspect the drive gear.

5 Slide the inner cable into the outer cable from the top. Note the location of the forked lower end of the inner cable and align this with the tab inside the drive housing **(see illustration)**. Align the end of the outer cable with the drive housing and tighten the knurled ring securely by hand **(see illustrations)**.

6 Insert the upper end of the inner cable into the speedometer drive, then tighten the knurled ring securely by hand **(see illustration 32.2)**.

7 Install the handlebar front cover (see Chapter 8).

33 Steering head bearings

1 The steering head bearings consist of ball bearings which run in races at the top and bottom of the steering head. The races can become dented or rough during normal use and the balls will gradually wear. In extreme cases, worn or loose steering head bearings can cause steering wobble – a condition that is potentially dangerous.

2 Support the scooter upright with the front wheel off the ground. **Note:** *Do not rest the weight of the scooter on the bodywork – have an assistant push down on the rear or place a support under the frame once any bodywork has been removed.*

3 Point the front wheel straight-ahead and slowly turn the handlebars from side-to-side. Any dents or roughness in the bearing races will be felt and the bars will not move smoothly and freely. If the bearings are damaged they must be renewed (see Chapter 6).

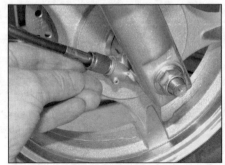

32.5c . . . and tighten the knurled ring securely

4 Next, grasp the front suspension and try to move it forwards and backwards **(see illustration)**. Any freeplay in the steering head bearings will be felt as front-to-rear movement of the steering stem. **Note:** *On trailing link front suspension, grasp the lower end of the suspension leg by the suspension arm pivot bolt for this test.* If play is felt in the bearings, follow the procedure described in Chapter 6 to adjust them.

5 Over a period of time the grease in the bearings will harden or may be washed out. Follow the procedure in Chapter 6 to disassemble the steering head and re-grease the bearings.

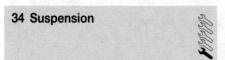

34 Suspension

1 The suspension components must be maintained in top operating condition to ensure rider safety. Loose, worn or damaged suspension parts decrease the scooter's stability and control.

Front suspension

2 While standing alongside the scooter, apply the front brake and push on the handlebars to compress the suspension several times. See if it moves up-and-down smoothly without binding. If binding is felt, the suspension should be disassembled and inspected (see Chapter 6).

3 On models with trailing link suspension, inspect the shock for fluid leaks and corrosion on the damper rod. If the shock is faulty it should be renewed (see Chapter 6). Check that the shock mounting bolts are tight.

4 On models with telescopic forks, inspect the area around the dust seal for signs of oil leaks, then carefully lever off the seal using a flat-bladed screwdriver and inspect the area behind it **(see illustration)**. If corrosion due to the ingress of water is evident, the seals must be renewed (see Chapter 6).

5 The chromed finish on the forks is prone to corrosion and pitting, so it is advisable to keep them as clean as possible and to spray them regularly with a rust inhibitor, otherwise the seals will not last long. If corrosion and pitting is evident, tackle it as early as possible to prevent it getting worse.

6 Check the tightness of all suspension nuts and bolts to ensure none have worked loose.

Rear suspension

7 Inspect the rear shock for fluid leaks and corrosion on the damper rod. If a shock is faulty it should be renewed (see Chapter 6). Check that the upper and lower shock

33.4 Checking for play in the steering head bearings

34.7 Inspect the rear shock (arrowed) for fluid leaks and corrosion

mounting bolts are tight. If necessary, follow the procedure in Chapter 3 and displace the air filter housing to inspect the full length of the shock **(see illustration)**.

8 With the aid of an assistant to support the scooter, compress the rear suspension several times. It should move up and down freely without binding. If any binding is felt, the worn or faulty component must be identified and renewed. The problem could be due to either the shock absorber or the front engine mounting/pivot assembly.

9 Support the scooter so that the rear wheel is off the ground. Grip the engine/transmission unit at the rear and attempt to rock it from side to side – there should be no discernible freeplay felt between the engine and frame. If there is movement, check the tightness of the bolts securing the front engine mounting/pivot assembly **(see illustration)**.

10 Re-check for movement. If freeplay is felt, disconnect the rear shock absorber lower mounting and displace the shock, then check again – any freeplay in the front engine mountings should be more evident. If there is freeplay, inspect the mounting bushes in the front of the crankcase and the pivot bracket for wear (see Chapter 6).

11 Reconnect the rear shock absorber, then grasp the top of the rear wheel and pull it upwards – there should be no discernible

34.4 Lever off the seals carefully and check for oil leaks and corrosion

34.9 Front engine mounting bolt (A) and pivot bracket bolt (B)

freeplay before the shock begins to compress. Any freeplay indicates a worn shock or shock mountings. The worn components must be renewed (see Chapter 6).

35 Nuts and bolts

1 Since vibration tends to loosen fasteners, all nuts, bolts, screws, etc. should be periodically checked for proper tightness.

2 Pay particular attention to the following:

Spark plug
Carburettor clamps
Gearbox oil level and drain plugs
Engine oil drain and oil filter plug
(four-stroke engines)
Stand bolts
Engine mounting bolts
Suspension bolts
Wheel nuts
Handlebar clamp bolts
Brake caliper and disc mounting bolts
(front disc brake)
Brake hose banjo bolts (front disc brake)
Exhaust system bolts/nuts

3 If a torque wrench is available, use it together with the torque specifications given in the *Data* section at the end of this manual.

Chapter 2A
50cc four-stroke engine – 139QMA/QMB

Contents

Degrees of difficulty

Easy, suitable for novice with little experience	**Fairly easy,** suitable for beginner with some experience	**Fairly difficult,** suitable for competent DIY mechanic	**Difficult,** suitable for experienced DIY mechanic	**Very difficult,** suitable for expert DIY or professional

1 General information

The 139QMA and QMB engines are derived from Honda's GY6 design engine. Differences between the QMA and QMB are minor (the QMA has a slightly higher output due to top-end improvements), but care should be taken when ordering parts to specify which type you have. The code will be part of the engine number stamped into the crankcase – see *Identification Numbers* at the beginning of this manual. Both engine types are supplied in either long crankcase 12 inch rear wheel, and short crankcase 10 inch rear wheel sizes; drive belt sizes differs between the two types.

3.5 Install the compression gauge as described

The engine is a single cylinder, overhead-camshaft four-stroke, with fan assisted air cooling (see Chapter 1). The camshaft is chain-driven off the crankshaft and operates the valves via rocker arms.

The crankshaft assembly is pressed together, incorporating the connecting rod.

The crankcase divides vertically - the left-hand crankcase is an integral part of the drive belt casing and gearbox.

2 Component access

Most components and assemblies, with the obvious exception of the crankshaft assembly and its bearings, can be worked on without having to remove the engine/transmission unit from the scooter. However, access to some components is severely restricted, and if a number of areas require attention at the same time, removal of the engine is recommended, as it is an easy task to undertake.

3 Cylinder compression test

 **Warning: Be careful when working on the hot engine – the exhaust pipe, the engine and engine components can cause severe burns.**

Special tools: *A compression gauge with an appropriate threaded adapter (see Step 5) is required for this procedure.*

1 Among other things, poor starting and engine performance may be caused by leaking valves, a leaking head gasket or worn piston, rings and/or cylinder wall. A cylinder compression check will help pinpoint these conditions.

2 Before carrying out the test, check that the valve clearances are correct (see Chapter 1).

3 Run the engine until it reaches normal operating temperature, then turn the ignition OFF. Support the scooter securely in an upright position.

4 Follow the procedure in Chapter 1, Section 26, and remove the spark plug. Fit the plug back into the cap and position the plug with the threads contacting the engine.

5 Thread the gauge adapter into the spark plug hole then install the compression gauge **(see illustration)**.

6 Open the throttle fully and crank the engine over on the kickstarter or starter motor until the gauge reading stabilises - after four or five revolutions the pressure should build up to a maximum figure and then remain stable. Make a note of the pressure reading.

7 Release the pressure on the gauge, then repeat the procedure. If the reading is different this time, repeat the procedure until you obtain several readings that are the same.

8 A reading of approximately 190 psi (13 Bars) indicates a cylinder in good condition.

4.8 Disconnect the fuel hose from the carburettor

9 If the compression builds up quickly and evenly, you can assume that the engine top end is in good mechanical condition. Worn or sticking piston rings, or a worn cylinder, will produce very little initial movement of the gauge, but compression will tend to build-up as the engine turns over. Valve seat leakage, or head gasket leakage, is indicated by low initial compression which does not build-up.

10 To confirm your findings, use a squirt-type oil can to add a small amount of engine oil into the cylinder through the spark plug hole. The oil will tend to seal the piston rings if they are leaking. Check the compression again and if it increases significantly after the addition of the oil the rings or cylinder are definitely worn. If the compression remains low, the pressure is leaking past the valves or head gasket.

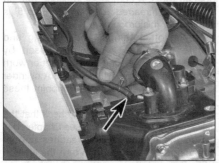

4.11 Disconnect the fuel tap vacuum hose

11 When the test is complete, follow the procedure in Chapter 1, Section 26, and install the spark plug.

Note: *High compression pressure indicates excessive carbon build-up in the combustion chamber and on the top of the piston. If this is the case, remove the cylinder head and clean the carbon deposits off. Note that excessive carbon build-up is less likely with the use of modern fuels.*

4 Engine removal and installation

Caution: The engine/transmission unit is not heavy, however removal and installation should be carried out with the aid of an assistant; personal injury or damage could occur if the engine falls or is dropped.

Removal

1 Support the scooter securely in an upright position. Work can be made easier by raising the machine to a suitable height on an hydraulic ramp or a suitable platform. Make sure it is secure and will not topple over.

2 Remove the luggage compartment and any body panels as necessary to access the engine (see Chapter 8).

3 Disconnect the battery negative terminal (see Chapter 9) and pull the spark plug cap off the plug.

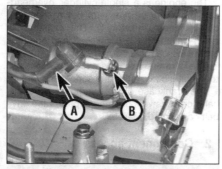

4.13 Pull back the boot (A) and disconnect the lead from the terminal (B)

4 If required, remove the exhaust system (see Chapter 3).

5 If the engine is dirty, particularly around its mountings, wash it thoroughly before starting any major dismantling work. This will make work much easier and rule out the possibility of dirt falling inside.

6 If required, drain the engine oil (see Chapter 1).

7 Remove the air filter housing and the air intake duct (see Chapter 3).

8 Disconnect the fuel hose from its union on the carburettor, being prepared to catch any residual fuel in a rag **(see illustration)**. Position a suitable container below the carburettor drain hose, then loosen the drain screw and drain any residual fuel from the float chamber. Tighten the drain screw.

9 Trace the wiring from the automatic choke unit and disconnect it at the connector. **Note:** *When disconnecting any wiring, it is advisable to mark or tag the wires as a reminder of where they connect.*

10 Either displace or remove the carburettor completely, leaving the throttle cable attached if required, or just disconnect the throttle cable (see Chapter 3). If the carburettor is displaced, ensure it is secured to a convenient part of the frame to avoid damage. Ensure that the throttle cable and automatic choke wiring is clear of the engine unit. Stuff clean rag into the intake manifold to prevent anything falling inside.

11 Disconnect the fuel tap vacuum hose from its union on the inlet manifold **(see illustration)**.

12 Where fitted, disconnect the fuel pump vacuum hose from the engine.

13 Pull back the boot, then undo the screw securing the lead to the starter motor terminal **(see illustration)**.

14 Undo the bolt securing the earth (ground) wire to the crankcase and disconnect the wire **(see illustration)**. Replace the bolt for safe-keeping.

15 Trace the wiring from the alternator and ignition pulse generator coil on the right-hand side of the engine and disconnect it at the connectors **(see illustration)**. Secure the wiring clear of the engine.

4.14 Disconnect the engine earth wire

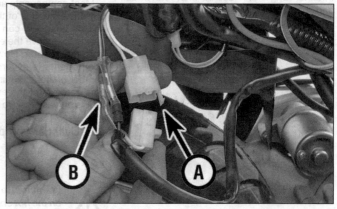

4.15 Release the clip and disconnect the alternator wiring connector (A), then disconnect the ignition wiring connectors (B)

4.18a Free the brake cable from the clip (arrowed) . . .

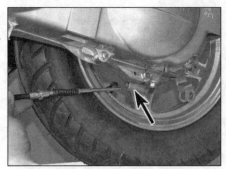

4.18b . . . and pull it through the cable stop (arrowed)

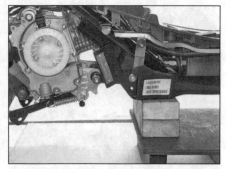

4.20 Support the weight of the machine on wooden blocks

4.23 Undo the nut on the front engine mounting bolt

4.24a Withdraw the front engine mounting bolt . . .

4.24b . . . noting the location of the spacer

16 Some scooters are fitted with a rev limiter sensor inside the drive belt cover (see Chapter 5). Trace the wiring from the casing and disconnect it at the connector. Free the wiring from any clips or ties and secure it free of the frame.

17 If required, remove the rear wheel (see Chapter 7). **Note:** *On machines where the main stand is bolted to the underside of the engine unit, the rear wheel and stand provide a convenient support for the unit once it is removed from the scooter. However, it is useful to loosen the rear wheel nut at this point before disconnecting the rear brake.*

18 Disconnect the brake cable from the brake arm (see Chapter 7). Release the cable from any clips on the underside of the drive belt casing and pull it through the cable stop **(see illustrations)**.

19 Check that all wiring, cables and hoses are clear of the engine/transmission unit.

20 With the aid of an assistant, support the weight of the machine on the rear of the frame **(see illustration)**.

21 If the rear wheel has been removed, support the gearbox on a wood block to prevent damage to the casing.

22 Remove the rear shock absorber (see Chapter 6).

23 Undo the nut on the front engine mounting bolt **(see illustration)**.

24 Have an assistant support the scooter, then carefully withdraw the engine mounting bolt **(see illustration)**. As the bolt is withdrawn, note the location of any spacers between the mounting lugs on the front of the crankcase and the pivot bracket **(see illustration)**.

25 Manoeuvre the engine unit back and out of the frame.

26 If required, remove the main stand (see Chapter 6).

Installation

27 Installation is the reverse of removal, noting the following:

● Make sure no wires, cables or hoses become trapped between the engine and the frame when installing the engine

● Tighten the front engine mounting bolt and shock absorber bolts securely. Torque settings for certain models are specified in the *Data* section at the end of this manual

● Make sure all wires, cables and hoses are correctly routed and connected, and secured by any clips or ties

● If the engine oil was drained, or if any oil has been lost during overhaul, refill or top up as described in Chapter 1 and *Pre-ride checks*.

● Check the operation of the rear brake before riding the machine (see Chapter 7)

5 Disassembly and reassembly – general information

Disassembly

1 Before disassembling the engine, the external surfaces of the unit should be thoroughly cleaned and degreased. This will prevent contamination of the engine internals, and will also make working a lot easier and cleaner. A high flash-point solvent, such as paraffin can be used, or better still, a proprietary engine degreaser such as Gunk. Use a degreasing brush or old paintbrushes to work the solvent into the various recesses of the engine casings. Take care to exclude solvent or water from the electrical components and intake and exhaust ports.

> ⚠ **Warning:** *The use of petrol (gasoline) as a cleaning agent should be avoided because of the risk of fire.*

2 When clean and dry, arrange the unit on the workbench, leaving suitable clear area for working. Gather a selection of small containers and plastic bags so that parts can be grouped together in an easily identifiable manner. Some paper and a pen should be on hand to permit notes to be made and labels attached where necessary. A supply of clean rag is also required.

3 Before commencing work, read through the appropriate section so that some idea of the necessary procedure can be gained. When removing components it should be noted that great force is seldom required, unless specified. In many cases, a component's reluctance to be removed is indicative of an incorrect approach or removal method – if in any doubt, re-check with the text.

4 When disassembling the engine, keep 'mated' parts that have been in contact with each other during engine operation together. These 'mated' parts must be reused or replaced as an assembly.

5 Complete engine disassembly should be done in the order overleaf with reference to the appropriate Sections (refer to Chapter 5 for details of transmission components):

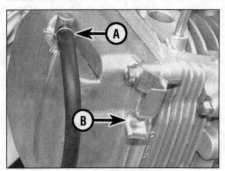

6.3 Clip (A) secures breather hose. Note location of cable guide (B)

6.4a Undo the bolts (arrowed) . . .

6.4b . . . and lift the cover off

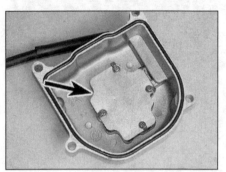

6.6 Location of the breather system baffle plate (arrowed)

- Remove the valve cover
- Remove the camshaft and rockers
- Remove the cylinder head
- Remove the cylinder
- Remove the piston
- Remove the alternator
- Remove the starter motor (see Chapter 9)
- Remove the oil pump
- Separate the crankcase halves
- Remove the crankshaft

Reassembly

6 Reassembly is accomplished by reversing the order of disassembly.

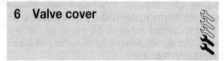

6 Valve cover

Note: *This procedure can be carried out with the engine in the scooter. If the engine has*

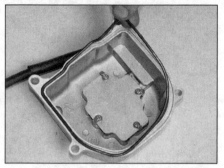

6.7 Ensure that the cover gasket is fitted into the groove

been removed, ignore the steps that do not apply.

Removal

1 Remove the body panels as necessary to access the cylinder head (see Chapter 8).
2 On some engines, it may be necessary to remove the fan cowling to access the valve cover (see Section 7). **Note:** *Some cowlings are clipped together – take care not to damage the fixing lugs when separating them.*
3 If required, loosen the clip securing the breather hose to the valve cover and detach the hose **(see illustration).**
4 Undo the bolts securing the valve cover, noting the location of any cable guides, then lift the cover off **(see illustrations).** If the cover is stuck, tap around the joint face between the cover and the cylinder head with a soft-faced mallet to free it. Do not try to lever the cover off as this may damage the sealing surfaces.

5 Remove the gasket and discard it as a new one must be used. Clean the mating surfaces of the cylinder head and the valve cover with a suitable solvent to remove any traces of old gasket or sealant.
6 Note the location of the breather system baffle plate in the valve cover **(see illustration).** If required, remove the plate and clean the inside of the cover. On installation, ensure that the screws securing the plate are tightened securely – as a precaution, clean the screw threads and apply non-permanent thread-locking compound.

Installation

7 Lay the new gasket onto the valve cover, making sure it fits correctly into the groove **(see illustration).**
8 Position the valve cover on the cylinder head, making sure the gasket stays in place. Install the cover bolts with any cable guides as noted on removal, then tighten the bolts evenly and in a criss-cross sequence. Apply the specified torque setting specified, where given (see *Data* section).
9 If removed, install the breather hose and secure it with the clip.
10 Install the remaining components in the reverse order of removal.

7 Fan cowling and engine cowling

Note: *This procedure can be carried out with the engine in the scooter. If the engine has been removed, ignore the steps that do not apply.*

1 Remove the body panels as necessary to access the engine (see Chapter 8).
2 Unclip any wiring or hoses from the fan cowling, then undo the bolts securing the fan cowling and remove it **(see illustration).** Note that on some engines, the fan cowling is clipped to the engine cowling – take care not to damage the fixing lugs when separating them.
3 Remove any spacers for the cowling bolts for safekeeping if they are loose.
4 Pull the cap off the spark plug.
5 On most engines, it is necessary to remove

7.2 Remove the fan cowling

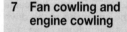

7.6a Note the location of the cowling screws (arrowed) . . .

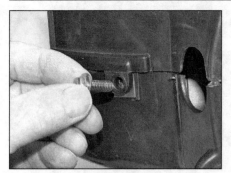

7.6b . . . then remove the screws

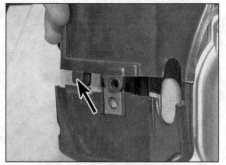

7.7a Take care when releasing any tabs (arrowed)

7.7b Note the location of the U-clips for the cowling screws

the carburettor and the exhaust system (see Chapter 3) before the upper and lower sections of the engine cowling can be removed. It may also be necessary to remove the intake manifold.

6 Note the location of the screws securing the two halves of the cowling together, then undo the screws **(see illustrations)**.

7 Ease the two halves of the cowling apart carefully – there may be press-fit tabs securing the halves together **(see illustration)**. Note the location of the U-clips where the screw fixings are located **(see illustration)**.

8 Once the upper section of the cowling is free, lift it off **(see illustration)**.

9 Check around the lower section of the cowling for additional fixings and remove them, then lift it off **(see illustrations)**.

10 On most scooters a cowling seal is fitted onto a lip around the top of the cylinder head **(see illustration)**. Check that the seal is not damaged or deteriorated and that it is a secure fit around the head. If necessary, fit a new seal.

11 Installation is the reverse of removal. Ensure that the two halves of the cowling fit together correctly – do not force them. Take care not to over-tighten the joining screws.

8 Camchain tensioner

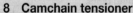

Note: *This procedure can be carried out with the engine in the scooter. If the engine has been removed, ignore the steps that do not apply.*

Removal

1 Remove the body panels as necessary to access the engine (see Chapter 8).

2 On most engines, the camchain tensioner is behind a small cover that is part of the engine cowling – undo the screws securing the cover and lift it off to access the tensioner **(see illustrations)**. If no separate cover is fitted in the cowling, remove the upper half of the cowling (see Section 7).

3 Remove the spark plug (see Chapter 1, Section 26). If not already done, remove the fan cowling (see Section 7).

7.8 Lift off the upper half of the cowling

7.9b Lift the lower section off

4 Turn the engine in the normal direction of rotation until the piston is at top dead centre (TDC) on its compression stroke. You can do this by rotating the crankshaft via the alternator rotor. The position of the piston

8.2a Cam chain tensioner cover is retained by screws (arrowed)

7.9a Note any additional fixings on the lower section of the cowling (arrowed)

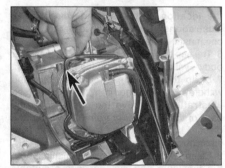

7.10 Cowling seal (arrowed) must be in good condition otherwise cooling will be impaired

can be confirmed by ensuring that the timing mark 'T' on the alternator rotor is aligned with the register mark on the crankcase **(see illustration)**.

5 Undo the tensioner cap bolt, noting

8.2b Location of the cam chain tensioner (arrowed)

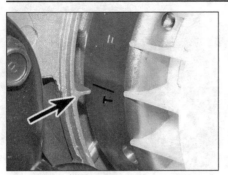

8.4 Timing mark T on the alternator rotor should align with the index mark (arrowed)

8.5a Undo the cap bolt . . .

8.5b . . . and discard the sealing washer (arrowed)

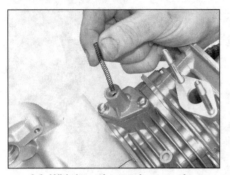

8.6 Withdraw the tensioner spring

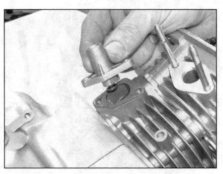

8.7a Remove the tensioner body . . .

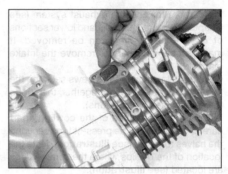

8.7b . . . and the tensioner gasket

the location of the sealing washer **(see illustrations)**. Discard the washer as a new one must be fitted.

6 The cap bolt retains a spring in the tensioner body – withdraw the spring **(see illustration)**.

7 Undo the tensioner mounting bolts and withdraw the tensioner from the cylinder **(see illustration)**. Remove the gasket from the base of the tensioner or from the cylinder and discard it as a new one must be used **(see illustration)**.

8 Clean all traces of old gasket material from the tensioner and cylinder with a suitable solvent. Take care not to scratch or gouge the soft aluminium. Be careful not to let any of the gasket material fall into the engine.

Inspection

9 Examine the tensioner components for signs of wear or damage.

10 Pull the plunger out from the tensioner body and examine the teeth on the ratchet **(see illustration)**. Now try to press the plunger back into the body – it should be locked in position.

11 Release the catch on the ratchet with a small screwdriver and ensure that the plunger moves freely in and out of the tensioner body **(see illustration)**.

12 On the 50 cc engine photographed, the spring length specification was between 45 and 50 mm. If the spring is shorter than specified, renew it. Alternatively, press the plunger into the body and temporarily install the tensioner on the back of the cylinder, then fit the spring and centre bolt. Now unscrew the centre bolt and withdraw the spring. Insert a small screwdriver into the tensioner and try to push the plunger out further against the

pressure of the tensioner blade. If the plunger moves, then the spring has lost its tension.

13 If any part of the tensioner is worn or damaged, or if the plunger is seized in the body, a new tensioner must be fitted.

Installation

14 Release the ratchet mechanism and press the tensioner plunger all the way into the tensioner body **(see illustration 8.11)**. Fit a new gasket on the tensioner body and fit a new sealing washer on the cap bolt.

15 Install the tensioner in the cylinder and tighten the mounting bolts.

16 Turn the engine in the normal direction of rotation – this removes all the slack in the front run of the chain between the crankshaft and the camshaft, and transfers it to the back run where it will be taken up by the tensioner. **Note:** *Take care when turning the engine with the tensioner spring removed to avoid the chain jumping over the teeth on the camshaft sprocket. If this happens, ensure that the timing marks on the alternator rotor and on the camshaft sprocket are correctly re-aligned with the piston at TDC before installing the tensioner spring (see Chapter 1, Section 28).*

17 Install the spring and tighten the cap bolt securely.

18 It is advisable to remove the valve cover (see Section 6) and check that the camchain is tensioned. If it is slack, the tensioner plunger did not release. Remove the tensioner and check the operation of the plunger again.

19 Install the remaining components in the reverse order of removal.

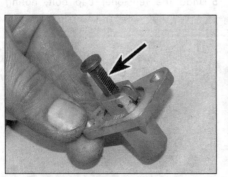

8.10 Inspect the plunger ratchet teeth (arrowed) for wear

8.11 Release the ratchet and check the operation of the plunger

9.3 Inspect the cam chain links for wear as described

9.5 The cam chain should be a firm fit on the camshaft sprocket

9.8a If fitted, remove the oil seal holder . . .

9 Camchain, blades and sprockets

Camchain

Inspection

1 The camchain runs between the drive sprocket on the crankshaft and the camshaft sprocket. To check the condition of the chain, first remove the valve cover (see Section 6).
2 Remove the spark plug (see Chapter 1, Section 26). If not already done, remove the fan cowling (see Section 7).
3 Using the alternator rotor, turn the engine slowly in the normal direction of rotation and inspect the inside edges of the chain links for wear **(see illustration)**.
4 Remove the camchain tensioner (see Section 8). Note the position of the plunger, then press a small screwdriver into the tensioner to see how much adjustment remains on the plunger. If there are only two or three clicks of movement left, the chain and/or tensioner blade are worn and must be renewed.
5 Hold the chain at the mid-way point around the camshaft sprocket and try to lift it off the sprocket **(see illustration)**. The chain should be a firm fit on the sprocket. Turn the engine carefully in the normal direction of rotation (see **Note** in Section 8, Step 16 above) and check the entire length of the chain.
6 If any of the above checks indicate that the camchain has worn, a new one must be fitted.

Removal

7 If the camchain is being removed, access will be required to the crankcase and the crankshaft. Since the camchain is on the left-hand side of the engine, refer to the procedure in Chapter 5 and remove the variator.
8 If the left-hand crankcase oil seal is fitted in a holder behind the variator, remove the holder and the seal **(see illustrations)**.
9 On some engines, the camchain can be withdrawn through an access hole on the left-hand side of the engine once it has been disengaged from the camshaft sprocket. Follow the procedure in Section 10 to displace

9.8b . . . and lever out the seal

the camshaft, then lower the chain down the tunnel in the cylinder and withdraw it from the engine **(see illustration)**.
10 If it is not possible to gain access to the camchain from the left-hand side of the engine, follow the procedure in Section 20 and separate the crankcase halves. The camchain can be removed with the crankshaft assembly.

Installation

11 Installation is the reverse of removal, noting the following:
● Before installing the chain onto the camshaft sprocket, ensure that the piston is at TDC on the compression stroke and that the timing mark 'T' on the alternator rotor is aligned with the register mark on the crankcase **(see illustration 8.4)**.
● Position the timing marks on the camshaft sprocket as noted on removal – the camshaft lobes should face down away from the rocker arms, then install the camshaft holder.

9.9 Draw the cam chain out through the access hole

● Ensure any slack in the chain is in the back run where it will be taken up by the tensioner

Camchain tensioner and guide blades

12 The camchain tensioner blade is located inside the camchain tunnel and is secured by a pivot bolt on its lower end.
13 To inspect the blade, first remove the camshaft (see Section 10). Secure the camchain to prevent it falling down into the tunnel.
14 Remove the variator (see Chapter 5).
15 Undo the pivot bolt securing the tensioner blade and lift the blade out **(see illustration)**. Note which way round the blade is fitted.
16 The guide blade can be removed when the cylinder head has been removed (see Section 11).
17 Check both blades for wear or damage and renew them if necessary **(see illustration)**.

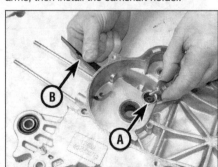

9.15 Undo the pivot bolt (A) and withdraw the tensioner blade (B)

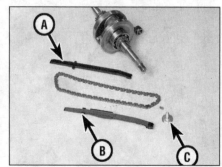

9.17 Cam chain guide blade (A), tensioner blade (B) and pivot bolt (C)

9.18a Note which way round the cam chain guide blade is fitted . . .

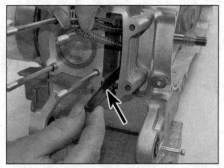

9.18b . . . and locate the lugs correctly in the top of the cam chain tunnel

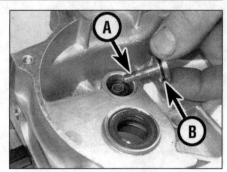

9.18c Apply locking compound to the pivot bolt threads (A). Note the O-ring (B)

Check the operation of the camchain tensioner (see Section 8).

18 Installation is the reverse of removal. Ensure that the blades are fitted the correct way round **(see illustrations)**. If an O-ring seal is fitted to the tensioner blade pivot it is good practice to fit a new one prior to installation. Apply non-permanent thread-locking compound to the threads of the pivot bolt and tighten it securely **(see illustration)**.

Camchain sprockets

19 The camshaft sprocket is integral with the camshaft. To inspect the sprocket for wear, follow the procedure in Section 10 and remove the camshaft.

20 Check for wear on the sides and tips of the sprocket teeth and for chipped or hooked teeth.

21 Similar checks should be made on the crankshaft sprocket – this is integral with the crankshaft assembly. Inspection may be possible if there is access to the sprocket on the left-hand side of the engine (see Steps 7 and 8). Otherwise the crankcase halves will have to be separated (see Section 20).

22 If the sprocket teeth are worn, the chain will also be worn. Always renew the components as an assembly – worn sprockets will soon damage a new chain.

Caution: After installing the camchain tensioner, turn the crankshaft and check that all the timing marks still align correctly. If the timing marks are not aligned exactly as described, the valve timing will be incorrect and the valves may strike the piston, causing extensive damage to the engine.

10 Camshaft and rockers

Note: *This procedure can be carried out with the engine in the scooter, although on some models access to the top of the engine is extremely restricted.*

Removal

1 Remove the valve cover (see Section 6).

2 Remove the camchain tensioner (see Section 8). Note that when the piston is at TDC on its compression stroke the valves are closed and a small clearance can be felt at each rocker arm **(see illustration)**. Look for timing marks or two small holes on the camshaft sprocket – these should be aligned with the valve cover gasket face **(see illustration)**.

3 Stuff a clean rag into the camchain tunnel to prevent anything falling into the engine.

4 The camshaft and rockers are located in a holder which is retained by long studs that also secure the cylinder head and cylinder to the crankcases. Before loosening the camshaft holder nuts, check to see if the head is also secured by any smaller bolts, and if so, loosen them first **(see illustration)**.

5 Now unscrew the camshaft holder nuts evenly and a little at a time in a criss-cross pattern, until they are all loose, then remove the nuts and any washers **(see illustrations)**.

6 Note which way round the camshaft holder is fitted. On the engine used to illustrate this

10.2a Check for a small amount of clearance in the rocker arms (arrowed)

10.2b Note the alignment between the holes in the sprocket (arrowed) and the gasket face

10.4 Always loosen the smaller cylinder head bolts (arrowed) first

10.5a Location of the camshaft holder nuts (arrowed)

10.5b Note the location of the washer under each nut

procedure, the holder was marked EX on the exhaust side **(see illustration 10.13)**.

7 Hold the camshaft in position in the cylinder head and lift off the camshaft holder **(see illustration)**. Note any dowels in the holder or head and remove them for safekeeping if they are loose **(see illustration 10.9a)**.

8 Lift the camchain off the sprocket and secure the chain to prevent it dropping into the engine **(see illustration)**.

9 Note the location of the camshaft and camshaft bearings, then lift out the camshaft **(see illustrations)**.

10 The rocker shafts are retained in the camshaft holder by the cylinder studs. Once the holder has been removed from the engine, the shafts and individual rocker arms can be disassembled. Note the position of the rocker arms and mark them so that they can be installed in their original positions, then withdraw the shafts carefully **(see illustration)**. **Note:** *If necessary, thread a suitably-sized bolt into the end of each rocker shaft to ease withdrawal.*

11 Remove the rocker arms, noting the position of any thrust washers on the shafts **(see illustration)**.

12 Assemble the rockers and any thrust washers on their shafts in the correct order so that they can be installed in their original

10.7 Lift off the camshaft holder

10.8 Lift the cam chain off the camshaft sprocket

positions. **Note:** *On engines with four-valve heads, the rockers are forked so that they bear on two valves simultaneously.*

Inspection

13 Clean all of the components with a suitable solvent and dry them **(see illustration)**.

14 Inspect the camshaft lobes for heat discoloration (blue appearance), score marks, chipped areas, flat spots and spalling. Where lobe height specifications are given in the Data Section, measure the height of each camshaft lobe with a micrometer and compare the results with the specifications

(see illustration). If damage is noted or wear is excessive, the camshaft must be renewed.

15 Check the condition of the camshaft bearings (see *Tools and Workshop Tips* in the Reference section). On some engines, the camshaft, camchain sprocket and bearings are supplied as an assembly, on others the bearings are available separately **(see illustration)**. Check with a bearing specialist or automotive engineer as to whether the bearings can be renewed.

16 Check the bearing housings in the camshaft holder and the cylinder head for score marks and spalling. Any damage is an indication that

10.9a Note the location of the camshaft and its bearings (A). Note the dowels (B)

10.9b Lift out the camshaft

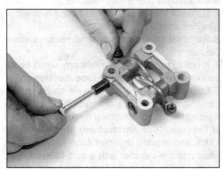

10.10 Using a suitable bolt to pull out the rocker shaft . . .

10.11 . . . then remove the rocker arm

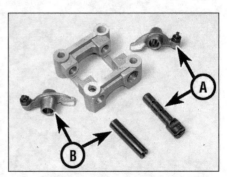

10.13 Intake rocker arm and shaft (A). Exhaust rocker arm and shaft (B)

10.14 Measuring the camshaft lobe height with a micrometer

10.15 Camshaft assembly complete with sprocket and bearings

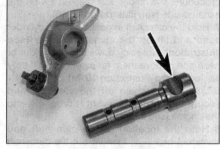

10.17 Ensure the oil passages in the rocker arms and shafts are clear. Note cut-out (arrowed) for cylinder stud

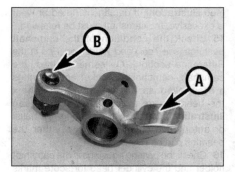

10.18 Inspect the face of the rocker arm (A) and the contact area on the adjuster screw (B)

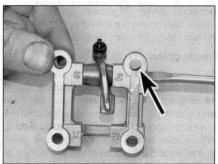

10.23 Ensure rocker shafts are clear of stud holes (arrowed)

● Position the rocker shafts so that the holes for the cylinder studs are clear **(see illustration)**.
● Ensure any dowels are correctly installed in the camshaft holder or cylinder head.
● Tighten the main cylinder head fixings before any smaller bolts.
● Tighten the cylinder head fixings a little at a time in a criss-cross sequence. Torque settings are given for certain models in the *Data* section.
● Don't forget to tighten the smaller cylinder head bolts.
● Check the valve clearances (see Chapter 1).

11 Cylinder head

Note: *On most models, this procedure can be carried out with the engine in the scooter. However, in some cases there is insufficient clearance between the cylinder head and the frame to allow the head to be removed. If so, support the rear frame, then detach the lower end of the rear shock absorber and displace the shock. Raise the rear wheel until there is enough clearance to remove the head.*
Caution: The engine must be completely cool before beginning this procedure or the cylinder head may become warped.

Removal

1 Remove the carburettor, intake manifold and exhaust system (see Chapter 3).
2 Remove the fan cowling and engine cowling (see Section 7).
3 Remove the camshaft and rockers (see Section 10).
4 If not already done, remove any small bolts securing the cylinder head **(see illustration)**.
5 Using a length of bent wire to hold the camchain, lift the cylinder head off the cylinder, feeding the camchain down through the tunnel in the head **(see illustration)**. If the head is stuck, tap around the joint face between the head and the cylinder with a soft-faced mallet to free it. Do not try to lever the head off as this may damage the sealing surfaces. **Note:** *If the cylinder is not secured to the crankcase*

the bearing has seized on the camshaft and turned inside its housing. Prior to reassembly, check that the outer race is a tight fit in its housing, otherwise use some bearing locking compound to hold it in position.
17 Blow through the oil passages in the rocker arms and shafts with compressed air, if available, to ensure that they are clear **(see illustration)**.
18 Inspect the face of the rocker arm and the contact area between the adjuster screw and the valve stem for pits and spalling **(see illustration)**.
19 Check the rocker shaft for wear. If available, use a micrometer to measure the diameter of the shaft in several places. **Note:** *Any variation in the measurements is an indication of wear on the shaft.*
20 If available, use a small hole gauge to measure the inside diameter of the rocker arm

and compare the results with the specifications in the *Data* section.
21 If any of the components are worn beyond their service limits, they should be renewed.
22 If no measuring equipment is available, assemble the rocker arm on its shaft – it should be a sliding fit with no discernible freeplay. Renew any components that are worn or damaged.

Installation

23 Installation is the reverse of removal, noting the following:
● Ensure the piston is at TDC **(see illustration 8.4)** on the compression stroke (both valves closed) before you start.
● Lubricate the shafts, bearing surfaces and bearings with clean engine oil before installation.

11.4 Remove any small cylinder head bolts

11.5 Hold the cam chain as described and lift the head off the cylinder

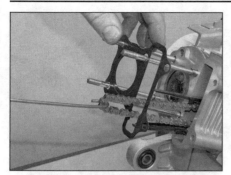

11.6a Remove the old cylinder head gasket . . .

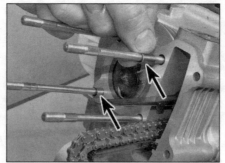

11.6b . . . noting the location of any dowels (arrowed)

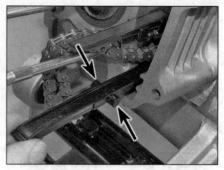

11.8 Withdraw the cam chain guide blade, noting how the lugs (arrowed) locate

(by a bolt(s)), avoid lifting it off the crankcase when the head is removed, otherwise a new cylinder base gasket will have to be fitted (see Section 13).

6 Remove the old cylinder head gasket – note any dowels in the head or cylinder and remove them for safekeeping if they are loose **(see illustrations)**.

7 Secure the camchain to prevent it dropping into the engine.

8 If required, the camchain guide blade can be removed – draw the blade out, noting how the lugs locate in the recess in the top edge of the camchain tunnel **(see illustration)**.

9 Clean all traces of old gasket material from the cylinder head and cylinder with a suitable solvent. Take care not to scratch or gouge the soft aluminium. Be careful not to let any of the gasket material fall into the crankcase, the cylinder bore or the oil passages.

10 Inspect the cylinder head gasket and the mating surfaces on the cylinder head and cylinder for signs of leaks, which could indicate that the head is warped. Refer to Section 12 and check the head mating surface for warpage.

11 After inspection, discard the old gasket as a new one must be fitted on reassembly

Installation

12 Installation is the reverse of removal, noting the following:
● Lubricate the cylinder bore with clean engine oil.
● Ensure any dowels are correctly installed in the cylinder.
● If removed, install the camchain guide blade (see Step 8).
● Install a new head gasket - never re-use the old gasket.
● Ensure the oil holes in the gasket align with the cylinder.
● Ensure the camchain is correctly located around the crankshaft sprocket.
● Install the camshaft and rockers then tighten the main cylinder head fixings evenly and a little at a time in a criss-cross pattern. Tighten the smaller cylinder head fixings. Note that torque settings are given for certain models in the *Data* section.

12 Cylinder head and valves

Note: *If a valve spring compressor is available, the home mechanic can remove the valves from the cylinder head, lap in the valves and renew the valve stem seals.*

Disassembly

1 Before you start, arrange to label and store the valves and their related components so that they can be returned to their original locations without getting mixed up **(see illustration)**. **Note:** *On some engines, only one spring is fitted to the valve.*

2 If not already done, clean all traces of old gasket material from the cylinder head with a suitable solvent. Take care not to scratch or gouge the soft aluminium.

3 Compress the valve springs on the first valve with a spring compressor, making sure it is correctly located onto each end of the valve assembly **(see illustration)**. On the underside of the head, make sure the plate on the

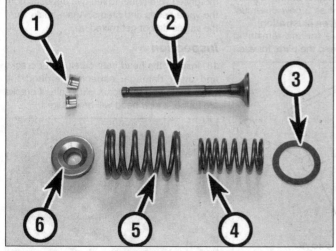

12.1 Valve components

1 Collets
2 Valve
3 Spring seat
4 Inner valve spring
5 Outer valve spring
6 Spring retainer

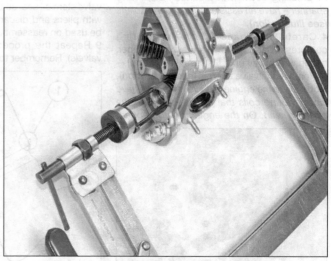

12.3a Compress the valve spring carefully . . .

12.3b . . . position a spacer (arrowed) between the spring compressor and the valve head

12.3c Remove the collets (arrowed) from the top of the valve stem

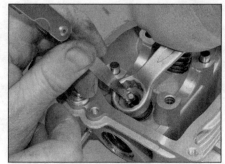

12.3d Compressing the valve springs with a ring spanner as described

12.4 Remove the spring retainer

12.5 Remove the valve springs

12.6 Lift out the spring seat

compressor only contacts the valve and not the soft aluminium of the head – if the plate is too big for the valve, use a spacer between them **(see illustration)**. Do not compress the springs any more than is absolutely necessary to release the collets, then remove the collets, using either needle-nose pliers, a magnet or a screwdriver with a dab of grease on it **(see illustration)**. **Note:** *On a small engine, if a small enough valve spring compressor is not available, the springs can be compressed by pressing down with a suitably-sized ring spanner – have an assistant remove the collets **(see illustration)**.*

4 Carefully release the valve spring compressor and remove the spring retainer, noting which way up it fits **(see illustration)**.

5 Remove the valve springs **(see illustration)**. **Note:** *On some engines the valve springs have closer wound coils that are fitted next to the cylinder head. On the engine photographed,*

the upper ends of the springs were marked with a dab of paint.

6 Lift out the spring seat **(see illustration)**, noting that on some engines, the spring seat is retained by the valve stem oil seal – remove the seat once the seal had been removed.

7 Turn the head over and withdraw the valve – if it binds in the guide (won't pull through), push it back into the head and deburr the area around the collet groove with a very fine file **(see illustrations)**.

8 Once the valve has been removed, pull the valve stem oil seal off the top of the valve guide with pliers and discard it as a new one must be used on reassembly **(see illustration)**.

9 Repeat the procedure for the remaining valve(s). Remember to keep the parts for each

valve together and in order so they can be reinstalled in the correct location.

10 Next, clean the cylinder head with solvent and dry it thoroughly. Compressed air will speed the drying process and ensure that all holes and recessed areas are clean.

11 Clean the valve springs, collets, retainers and spring seats with solvent. Work on the parts from one valve at a time so as not to mix them up.

12 Scrape off any carbon deposits that may have formed on the valve, then use a motorised wire brush to remove deposits from the valve heads and stems. Again, make sure the valves do not get mixed up.

Inspection

13 Inspect the head very carefully for cracks and other damage, especially around the valve seats and the spark plug hole. If cracks are found, a new head will be required.

12.7a Pull out the valve

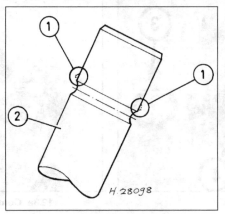

12.7b If the vale stem (2) won't pull through the guide, deburr the area (1) above the collet groove

12.8 Pull off the old valve stem oil seal

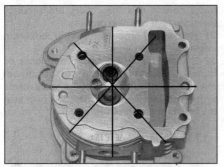

12.15 Check the cylinder head for warpage in the directions shown

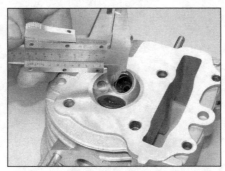

12.16 Valve seats should be the same width all the way round

12.17 Measuring the valve stem diameter with a micrometer

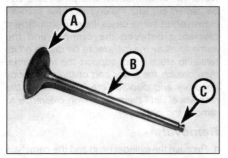

12.19 Check the valve face (A), stem (B) and collet groove (C) for signs of wear and damage

12.20a Check the valve springs for bending

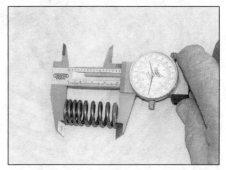

12.20b Measuring the valve spring free length

14 Inspect the threads in the spark plug hole. Damaged or worn threads can be reclaimed using a thread insert (see *Tools and Workshop Tips* in the Reference section). Most small engineering firms offer a service of this kind.

15 Using a precision straight-edge and a feeler gauge, check the head mating surface for warpage. Lay the straight-edge across the surface and measure any gap under it with feeler gauges. Check vertically, horizontally and diagonally across the head, making four checks in all **(see illustration)**. Warpage should generally be no more than 0.05 mm. If warpage is excessive, have the cylinder head machined flat or replace it with a new one. If there is any doubt about the condition of the head consult an automotive engineer.

16 Examine the valve seats in the combustion chamber. If they are deeply pitted, cracked or burned, it may be possible to have them repaired and re-cut by a specialist engineer, otherwise a new head will be required. The valve seats should be a uniform width all the way round **(see illustration)**.

17 If available, use a micrometer to measure the valve stem diameter in several places along the stem length **(see illustration)**. **Note:** *Any variation in the measurements is an indication of wear on the valve stem.*

18 If no measuring equipment is available, insert a known good valve into its guide – it should be a sliding fit with no discernible freeplay. If there is freeplay, the guide is worn. Have the guides checked by a specialist engineer. If new valve guides are available, have them installed by a specialist who will also re-cut the valve seats. Otherwise

a new cylinder head will have to be fitted. **Note:** *Carbon build-up inside the guide is an indication of wear.*

19 Inspect the valve face for cracks, pits and burned spots, and check the valve stem and the collet groove area for score marks and cracks **(see illustration)**. Rotate the valve and check for any obvious indication that it is bent. Check the end of the stem for pitting and excessive wear. If any of the above conditions are found, fit a new valve. If the stem end is pitted or worn, also check the contact area of the adjuster screw in the rocker arm.

20 Check the end of each valve spring for wear. Stand the spring upright on a flat surface and check it for bend by placing a square against it **(see illustration)**. Valve springs will take a permanent set (sag) after a long period of use. Their free length can be measured to determine if they need to be renewed – on the 50 cc model photographed, the outer spring length measures 34.1 ± 0.2 mm when new and has a service limit of 32 mm, and the inner spring length measures 30.5 ± 0.2 mm when new and has a service limit of 28.5 mm **(see illustration)**. If the spring is worn, or the bend is excessive, or the spring has sagged, it must be renewed. **Note:** *It is good practice to fit new springs when the head has been disassembled for valve servicing. Always fit new valve springs as a set.*

21 Check the spring retainers and collets for obvious wear and cracks. Any questionable parts should not be reused, as extensive damage will occur in the event of failure during engine operation.

Reassembly

22 Unless the valve seats have been re-cut, before installing the valves in the head they should be lightly lapped-in to ensure a positive seal between the valves and seats. This procedure requires fine valve lapping compound and a valve lapping tool. If a tool is not available, a piece of rubber or plastic hose can be slipped over the valve stem (after the valve has been installed in the guide) and used to turn the valve.

23 Apply a small amount of fine grinding compound to the valve face, then slip the valve into the guide **(see illustration)**. **Note:** *Make sure each valve is installed in its correct guide and be careful not to get any compound on the valve stem.*

24 Attach the tool (or hose) to the valve and rotate the tool between the palms of your hands. Use a back-and-forth motion

12.23 Apply the lapping compound sparingly, in small dabs, to the valve face only

12.24a Rotate the tool back and forth between the palms of your hands

12.24b The valve face and seat should show a uniform unbroken ring

12.27a Position the stem seal (arrowed) on the end of the valve guide . . .

12.27b . . . then press it on until it clips into place

make certain that the collets are securely locked in their retaining grooves.
31 Repeat the procedure for the remaining valve(s).
32 Support the cylinder head on blocks so the valves can't contact the workbench top, then very gently tap each of the valve stems with a soft-faced hammer. This will help seat the collets in their grooves.

13 Cylinder

Note: *On most models, this procedure can be carried out with the engine in the scooter. However, in some cases there is insufficient clearance between the cylinder and the frame to allow the cylinder to be drawn off its retaining studs. If so, support the rear frame, then detach the lower end of the rear shock absorber and displace the shock. Raise the rear wheel until there is enough clearance to remove the cylinder.*

Removal

1 Remove the cylinder head and the camchain guide blade (see Section 11).
2 Where fitted, undo the bolt(s) securing cylinder to the crankcase.
3 Hold the camchain and lift the cylinder up off the crankcase, supporting the piston as it becomes accessible to prevent it hitting the crankcase opening **(see illustrations)**. If the cylinder is stuck, tap around the joint face between the cylinder and the crankcase with a soft-faced mallet to free it. Don't attempt to free the cylinder by inserting a screwdriver between it and the crankcase – you'll damage the sealing surfaces.
4 Once the cylinder has been removed, stuff a clean rag into the crankcase opening around the piston to prevent anything falling inside.
5 Remove the cylinder base gasket, noting how it fits, then discard it as new one must be fitted on reassembly. Note any dowels in the cylinder or crankcase and remove them for safekeeping if they are loose **(see illustrations)**. Note how the camchain locates on the crankshaft sprocket and secure the chain to prevent it dropping into the crankcase **(see illustration)**.

(as though rubbing your hands together) rather than a circular motion (i.e. so that the valve rotates alternately clockwise and anti-clockwise rather than in one direction only) **(see illustration)**. Lift the valve off the seat and turn it at regular intervals to distribute the compound properly. Continue the procedure until the valve face and seat contact areas are of uniform width and unbroken around the circumference **(see illustration)**.
25 Carefully remove the valve from the guide and wipe off all traces of compound. Use solvent to clean the valve and wipe the seat area thoroughly with a solvent soaked cloth.
26 Repeat the procedure for the other valve(s).

 HAYNES HiNT *Check for proper sealing of each valve by pouring a small amount of solvent into the valve port while holding the valve shut. If the solvent leaks past the valve into the combustion chamber the valve grinding operation should be repeated.*

27 Once all the components are ready for assembly, install the valves one at a time. If the spring seat is retained by the valve stem seal, lay the seat in place in the cylinder head, then install a new seal onto the guide. Use an appropriate size deep socket to push the seal over the end of the valve guide until it is felt to clip into place **(see illustrations)**. Don't twist or cock the seal sideways, or it will not seal

properly against the valve stem. Also, don't remove it again or it will be damaged.
28 Lubricate the valve stem with clean engine oil, then install it into its guide, rotating it slowly to avoid damaging the seal. Check that the valve moves up and down freely in the guide.
29 If not already done, install the spring seat, then install the valve springs as noted on removal (see Step 5). Install the spring retainer, with its shouldered side facing down so that it fits into the top of the springs. **Note:** *On some engines, only one spring is fitted to each valve.*
30 Apply a small amount of grease to the collets to hold them in place, then compress the springs using the method employed on removal and install the collets. Compress the springs only as far as is absolutely necessary to slip the collets into place. Once installed,

13.3a Lift the cylinder off the crankcase

13.3b Support the piston to avoid it getting damaged

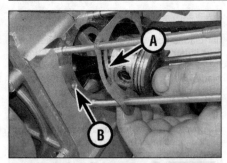

13.5a Remove the cylinder base gasket. Note the oil way in the gasket (A) aligns with the hole (B) in the crankcase

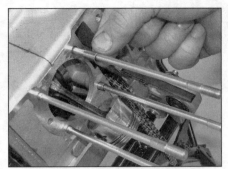

13.5b Note the location of any loose dowels (arrowed)

13.5c Note how the cam chain locates on the crankshaft sprocket (arrowed)

13.7 Inspect the cylinder bore (arrowed) for damage

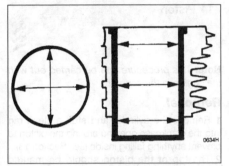

13.8a Measure the cylinder bore in the directions shown . . .

13.8b . . . using a telescoping gauge

6 Clean all traces of old gasket material from the cylinder and crankcase with a suitable solvent. Take care not to scratch or gouge the soft aluminium. Be careful not to let any of the gasket material fall into the crankcase.

Inspection

7 Check the cylinder bore carefully for scratches and score marks **(see illustration)**.
8 If available, use a telescoping gauge and micrometer to measure the inside diameter of the cylinder bore to assess the amount of wear, taper and ovality (see *Tools and Workshop Tips* in the *Reference* section). Measure near the top (but below the level of the top piston ring at top dead centre), centre and bottom (but above the level of the bottom ring with

To tighten a stud without damaging it, first lock two nuts together on the upper end of the stud. Now use a ring spanner on the upper nut to tighten the stud

the piston at bottom dead centre) of the bore both parallel to and across the crankshaft axis **(see illustrations)**.
9 Calculate any differences between the measurements to determine any taper or ovality in the bore. Where dimensions are given for bore diameter in the *Data section*, compare the results with the figure given. If the cylinder bore is worn beyond its service limits, a new one should be fitted.
10 A cylinder bore that has worn oval will reduce the efficiency of the piston rings to achieve a seal, resulting in loss of compression and increased oil consumption.
11 If no service data is available, measure an unworn part of the cylinder bore (below the level of the bottom ring with the piston at the bottom of its stroke) and compare the result to the previous measurements to determine overall wear. Alternatively, calculate the piston-to-bore clearance to determine whether the cylinder is useable (see Section 14), or check for a lip around the (unworn) top edge of the cylinder bore as a rough indication of wear.
12 If the bore is tapered, oval, or worn excessively, badly scratched, scuffed or scored, the cylinder and piston will have to be renewed as a set.
13 If there is any doubt about the condition of the cylinder, consult a specialist engineer.
14 Check that all the cylinder studs are tight in the crankcase halves. If any are loose, remove them (see *Tool Tip*) and clean their threads. Apply a suitable permanent thread locking compound, then screw them back into the crankcase securely.

Installation

15 Remove any rag from the crankcase opening. Ensure any dowels are correctly installed in the crankcase, then lay the new base gasket in place on the crankcase making sure it is the correct way round **(see illustrations 13.5b and a)**.
16 Check that the piston ring end gaps are positioned as described in Section 15.
17 If required, install a piston ring clamp onto the piston to ease its entry into the bore as the cylinder is lowered. This is not essential if the cylinder has a good lead-in enabling the piston rings to be hand-fed into the bore. If possible, have an assistant support the cylinder while this is done.
18 Lubricate the cylinder bore, piston and piston rings, and the connecting rod big- and small-ends, with the clean engine oil, then lower the cylinder down until the piston crown fits into the bore **(see illustration)**.

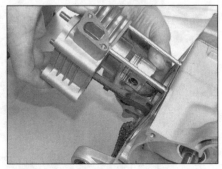

13.18 Lower the cylinder down onto the piston . . .

13.19 . . . then carefully compress each ring and feed the piston in

19 Gently push down on the cylinder, making sure the piston enters the bore squarely and does not get cocked sideways. If a piston ring clamp is not being used, carefully compress and feed each ring into the bore as the cylinder is lowered **(see illustration)**. If necessary, use a soft mallet to gently tap the cylinder down, but do not use force if it appears to be stuck as the piston and/or rings will be damaged. If a clamp is used, remove it once the piston is in the bore.

20 When the piston is correctly installed in the cylinder, support the camchain and check that the base gasket has not been displaced, then press the cylinder down onto the base gasket **(see illustration)**.

21 Where fitted, install the cylinder bolt(s) finger-tight only at this stage (see Step 2).

22 Install the camchain guide blade, then install the cylinder head (see Section 11).

23 Tighten the cylinder bolt(s).

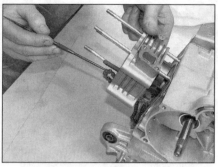

13.20 Press the cylinder down onto the base gasket

14 Piston

Note: *This procedure can be carried out with the engine in the scooter.*

Removal

1 Remove the cylinder and stuff a clean rag into the crankcase opening around the piston to prevent anything falling inside (see Section 13).

2 The top of the piston should be marked with an arrow or lettering (e.g. IN on the intake side, nearest the carburettor) to show which way round it should be fitted. If no mark is visible, scratch one lightly on the top of the piston **(see illustration)**. Note that the manufacturer's mark may not be visible until the carbon deposits have been scraped off and the piston cleaned.

3 Carefully prise out the circlip on one side of the piston using needle-nose pliers or a small flat-bladed screwdriver inserted into the notch **(see illustrations)**. Remove any burring around the circlip groove with a very fine file or penknife blade, then push the piston pin out from the other side and remove the piston from the connecting rod **(see illustration)**. Use a socket extension to push the piston pin out if required. Remove the other circlip and discard them both as new ones must be used on reassembly.

> **HAYNES HiNT**
> *To prevent the circlip from flying away or from dropping into the crankcase, pass a rod or screwdriver with a greater diameter than the gap between the circlip ends, through the piston pin. This will trap the circlip if it springs out.*
>
> *If the piston pin is a tight fit in the piston bosses, heat the piston gently with a hot air gun – this will expand the alloy piston sufficiently to release its grip on the pin.*

4 Before the inspection process can be carried out, the piston rings must be removed and the piston must be cleaned. **Note:** *If the cylinder is being renewed, piston inspection can be overlooked as a new one will be fitted.*

5 If required, the piston rings can be removed by hand; using your thumbs, ease the ends of each ring apart and carefully lift it off the piston, taking care not to expand it any more than is necessary **(see illustration)**. Do not nick or gouge the piston in the process.

14.2 Mark the top of the piston

14.3a Use the notch (arrowed) in the piston

14.3b . . . to help prise out the circlip . . .

14.3c . . . then push out the piston pin

14.5a Remove the piston rings carefully

14.5b Using a thin blade to remove the piston rings

14.9 Manufacturer's mark (arrowed) on the piston crown

Alternatively, use an old feeler gauge blade to ease the rings off the piston **(see illustration)**.
6 Note which way up each ring fits and in which groove as they must be installed in their original positions if being re-used. The upper surface of each ring should be marked at one end. Most pistons are fitted with a three-piece third (oil control) ring; there will be an upper and lower side rail and a central rail spacer (see Section 15). **Note:** *It is good practice to renew the piston rings when an engine is being overhauled. Ensure that the piston and bore are serviceable before purchasing new rings.*
7 Clean all traces of carbon from the top of the piston. A hand-held wire brush or a piece of fine emery cloth can be used once most of the deposits have been scraped away. Do not, under any circumstances, use a wire brush mounted in a drill motor; the piston material is soft and is easily damaged.
8 Use a piston ring groove cleaning tool to remove any carbon deposits from the ring grooves. If a tool is not available, a piece broken off an old ring will do the job. Be very careful to remove only the carbon deposits. Do not remove any metal and do not nick or gouge the sides of the ring grooves.
9 Once the carbon has been removed, clean the piston with a suitable solvent and dry it thoroughly. If the identification previously marked on the piston is cleaned off, be sure to re-mark it correctly **(see illustration)**.

Inspection

10 Inspect the piston for cracks around the skirt, at the pin bosses and at the ring lands **(see illustration)**. Check that the circlip grooves are not damaged. Normal piston wear appears as even, vertical wear on the thrust surfaces of the skirt and slight looseness of the top ring in its groove. If the skirt is scored or scuffed, the engine may have been suffering from overheating and/or abnormal combustion, which caused excessively high operating temperatures.
11 A hole in the top of the piston, in one extreme, or burned areas around the edge of the piston crown, indicate that pre-ignition or knocking under load have occurred. If you find evidence of any problems the cause must be corrected or the damage will occur again. Refer to Chapter 3 for carburation checks and Chapter 4 for ignition checks.

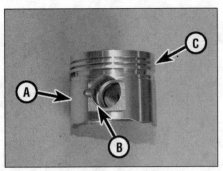

14.10 Piston skirt (A), pin boss (B) and ring lands (C)

12 Check the piston-to-bore clearance by measuring the cylinder bore (see Section 13) and the piston diameter. Measure the piston approximately 25 mm down from the bottom of the lower piston ring groove and at 90° to the piston pin axis **(see illustration)**. **Note:** *The precise point of measurement differs between manufacturers and engines, but the aim is to measure the piston in an area where it is worn.* Subtract the piston diameter from the bore diameter to obtain the clearance; piston-to-bore figures are given for certain models in the *Data* section, but note that as a general guide, this shouldn't exceed 0.10 mm.
13 If the piston-to-bore clearance is too large, check the specifications to determine whether it is the bore or piston that is worn the most. If the bore is good, install a new piston and set of rings.
14 Use a micrometer to measure the piston pin in the middle, where it runs in the

14.14 Measuring the diameter of the piston pin

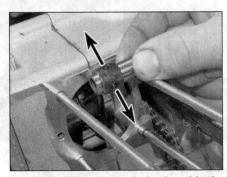

14.16 Rock the piston pin back and forth in the small-end to check for wear

14.12 Measuring the piston diameter with a micrometer

small-end bearing, and at each end where it runs in the piston **(see illustration)**. If there is any difference in the measurements the pin is worn and must be renewed.
15 If the piston pin is good, lubricate it with clean engine oil, then insert it into the piston and check for any freeplay between the two **(see illustration)**. There should be no freeplay.
16 A worn small-end will produce a metallic rattle, most audible when the engine is under load, and increasing as engine speed rises. This should not be confused with big-end bearing wear, which produces a pronounced knocking noise. Lubricate the piston pin with clean engine oil, then slide it into the small-end and check for freeplay **(see illustration)**. There should only be slightly discernible freeplay between the piston pin and the connecting rod.
17 If there is freeplay, measure the internal diameter of the connecting rod small-end **(see illustration)**. Take several

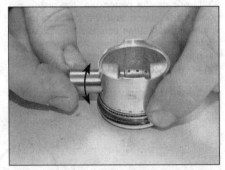

14.15 Checking for freeplay between the piston and piston pin

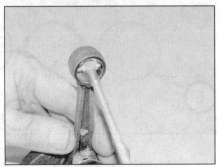

14.17 Measuring the internal diameter of the connecting rod small-end

14.18 Checking for freeplay in the big-end bearing

14.21 Ensure the circlips are seated in their grooves

measurements; if there is any difference between the measurements, the small end is worn and a new crankshaft assembly will have to be fitted (see Section 21). **Note:** *In some cases, a new connecting rod and bearings may be available, but fitting it is a specialist task which should be left to an automotive engineer. If a new rod is fitted, the big-end bearing should be renewed at the same time.*

18 With the piston removed, the general condition of the big-end bearing can be assessed. Hold the alternator to prevent the crankshaft from turning, then push-and-pull on the connecting rod, checking for any up-and-down freeplay **(see illustration)**. If freeplay is noted, refer to Section 20 to remove and inspect the crankshaft assembly.

Installation

19 Install the piston rings (see Section 15).
20 Lubricate the piston pin, the piston pin bore in the piston and the connecting-rod small-end with clean engine oil. Install a new circlip in one side of the piston, then line up the piston on the connecting rod, making sure it is the right way round (see Step 2).

21 Insert the piston pin from the other side and secure it with the other new circlip **(see illustration 14.3c)**. When installing the circlips, compress them only just enough to fit them in the piston, and make sure they are properly seated in their grooves with the open end away from the removal notch **(see illustration)**.
22 Install the cylinder (see Section 13).

15 Piston rings

1 New piston rings should be fitted whenever an engine is being overhauled **(see illustration)**. It is important that you get new rings of the correct size for your piston so ensure that any information relating to piston size and size coding is available when purchasing new parts.
2 Before fitting the new rings onto the piston, the installed ring end gaps must be checked. Insert the top ring into the bottom of the cylinder bore and square it up by pushing it in with the top of the piston. The ring should be

about 15 to 20 mm from the bottom edge of the cylinder. Measure the ring end gap using feeler gauges, slipping the gauge between the ends of the ring **(see illustration)**. Ring end gaps are given in the *Data* section for certain models. Where no specification is available, note that a gap greater than 0.7 mm should be considered too large.
3 If the gap is larger than specified it is likely the cylinder bore is worn. If the gap is too small the ring ends may come into contact with each other during engine operation, causing serious damage.
4 Repeat the procedure for the other two rings. If the piston is fitted with a three-piece third (oil control) ring, check the end gap on the upper and lower side rails only. The ends of the central rail spacer should contact each other when it is fitted on the piston.
5 Once the ring end gaps have been checked and found to be within specification, the rings can be installed on the piston. Do not expand the rings any more than is necessary to slide them into place. **Note:** *A ring installation tool can be used on the two compression rings, and on a one-piece oil control ring, if desired, but not on the side rails of a three-piece oil control ring.*
6 The oil control ring (lowest on the piston) is installed first. If a three-piece ring is used, fit the rail spacer into the groove **(see illustration)**, then install the lower side rail as follows. Place one end of the side rail into the groove between the spacer and the lower ring land. Hold it firmly in place, then slide a thin blade around the piston while pushing the rail into the groove **(see illustration)**.
7 Install the upper side rail the same way. Ensure the ends of the spacer touch but do not overlap, then check that both side rails turn smoothly in the ring groove.
8 Next install the 2nd compression ring,

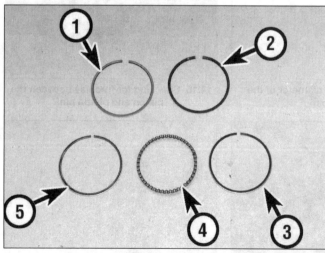

15.1 Piston ring set

1 Top (compression) ring
2 Second (compression) ring
3 Upper side rail
4 Rail spacer
5 Lower side rail

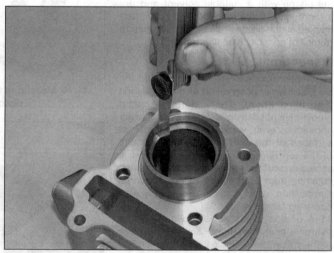

15.2 Measuring the installed piston ring end gap

15.6a Fit the oil control ring rail spacer first . . .

15.6b . . . then the lower side rail using a thin blade

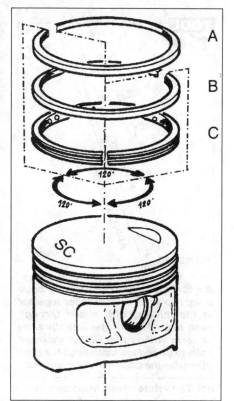

15.9b If a one-piece oil control ring is used, position the end gaps at 120° intervals

A First (top) compression ring
B Second (middle) compression ring
C Oil control ring

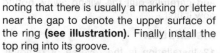

15.8 Install the compression rings using a thin blade

noting that there is usually a marking or letter near the gap to denote the upper surface of the ring **(see illustration)**. Finally install the top ring into its groove.

9 Once the rings are correctly installed, check they move freely without snagging, then stagger their end gaps as shown before fitting the piston into the cylinder **(see illustrations)**.

16 Alternator

Note: *This procedure can be carried out with the engine in the scooter. If the engine has been removed, ignore the steps that do not apply.*

Removal

1 Remove the body panels as necessary to access the alternator on the right-hand side of the engine (see Chapter 8). If required, remove the exhaust system (see Chapter 3).

2 The alternator is located behind the fan cowling. Follow the procedure in Section 7 to remove the cowling.

3 Undo the bolts securing the cooling fan to the alternator rotor and remove the fan **(see illustrations)**.

4 To remove the rotor centre nut it is necessary to stop the rotor from turning. Some manufacturers produce a service tool for this purpose which engages in the slots or holes in the rotor face – a similar home-made tool can be used or you can obtain an aftermarket version **(see illustrations and**

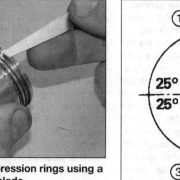

15.9a If a three-piece oil control ring is used, position the end gaps as shown – top ring (1), oil ring lower side rail (2), oil ring upper side rail (3), second ring (4)

16.3a Undo the mounting bolts . . .

16.3b . . . and remove the cooling fan

16.4a Holes (arrowed) in the face of the rotor . . .

16.4b . . . can be used to locate a holding tool

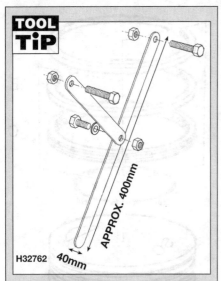

H32762 40mm APPROX. 400mm

TOOL TiP

A rotor holding tool can easily be made using two strips of steel bolted together in the middle, with a bolt through each end which locates into the slots or holes in the rotor. Do not allow the bolts to extend too far through the rotor otherwise the coils could be damaged.

Tool Tip). **Note:** *Take great care not to damage the internal coils of the alternator when locating any tools through the rotor.*

5 With the rotor securely held, loosen the centre nut **(see illustration)**.

6 Alternatively, the alternator rotor can be held with a strap wrench. If necessary, undo

16.5 Hold the rotor and undo the centre nut

the bolts securing the ignition pulse generator coil and displace it to avoid damaging it when using the strap wrench **(see illustrations)**.

7 To remove the rotor from the taper on the crankshaft it is necessary to use a puller. Engage the puller legs either in the slots in the rotor or thread them into the threaded holes in the rotor, then tighten the centre bolt exerting steady pressure to draw the rotor off the taper **(see illustrations)**. **Note:** *To avoid damaging the threaded end of the crankshaft, either leave the centre nut on the shaft with just enough clearance to allow the rotor to be dislodged, or position a soft metal spacer between the end of the shaft and the puller centre bolt.*

8 Lift the rotor off the crankshaft **(see illustration)**.

9 If it is loose, remove the Woodruff key from the shaft for safekeeping, noting how it fits **(see illustration 16.12b)**.

16.6a Displace the ignition pulse generator coil (arrowed) . . .

10 In most cases, the alternator stator coils and ignition pulse generator coil are wired together and have to be removed as an assembly. If not already done, trace the wiring back from the alternator and pulse generator and disconnect it at the connectors **(see illustration 4.15)**. Free the wiring from any clips or guides and feed it through to the alternator.

11 If not already done, undo the bolts securing the pulse generator coil, then undo the bolts securing the alternator stator and lift the assembly off **(see illustrations)**. Where fitted, draw any rubber wiring boot out of the crankcase or engine side cover and carefully pull the wiring away, noting how it fits.

Installation

12 Installation is the reverse of removal, noting the following:

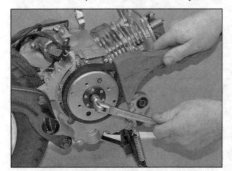

16.6b . . . before using a strap wrench to hold the rotor

16.7a Use the centre nut to protect the threads on the end of the shaft

16.7b Locate the puller as shown . . .

16.7c . . . then tighten the centre bolt

16.8 Remove the alternator rotor

16.11a Location of alternator stator mounting bolts (arrowed)

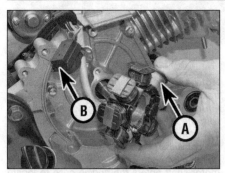

16.11b Remove the alternator stator (A) and pulse generator coil (B)

16.12a Ensure the inside of the rotor is clean. Note the slot (arrowed) for the Woodruff key

16.12b Note the location of the Woodruff key (arrowed)

● Ensure the wiring is correctly routed before installing the stator and pulse generator.
● Make sure that no metal objects have attached themselves to the magnets on the inside of the rotor.
● Clean the tapered end of the crankshaft and the corresponding mating surface on the inside of the rotor with a suitable solvent **(see illustration)**.
● Fit the Woodruff key into the crankshaft, align the slot in the centre of the rotor with the key, then install the rotor **(see illustration)**.
● Apply the torque setting for the rotor centre nut (see *Data* section) if the information is available for your model.
● Secure the wiring with any clips or ties.
● Ensure that the fan cowling is correctly installed (see Section 7).

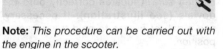

17 Right-hand crankcase cover

Note: *This procedure can be carried out with the engine in the scooter.*

Removal

1 Drain the engine oil (Chapter 1, Section 18).
2 Follow the procedure in Section 16 and remove the alternator.
3 An oil seal is fitted in the cover where the crankshaft passes through it **(see illustration)**. Check around the seal for signs of oil leakage – if the seal has been leaking a new one must be fitted once the cover has been removed.

Note: *It is good practice to renew the oil seal whenever the cover is removed.*
4 If the exhaust system support bracket is bolted to the cover, undo the bracket bolts and lift it off **(see illustrations)**.
5 Position a drain tray underneath the engine to catch any residual oil when the cover is removed, then undo the cover screws – noting their locations **(see illustrations)**.

HAYNES HINT *Make a cardboard template of the crankcase and punch a hole for each screw location. This will ensure that they are all installed correctly on reassembly – this is important as some bolts may be of different lengths.*

17.3 Location of the crankshaft oil seal (arrowed)

17.4a Undo the bolts (arrowed) . . .

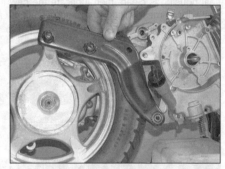

17.4b . . . and remove the exhaust system bracket

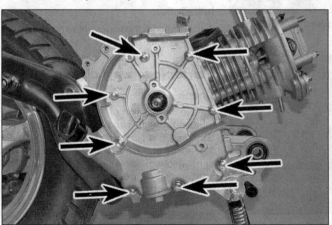

17.5a Undo the crankcase cover screws (arrowed) . . .

17.5b . . . noting their lengths and locations

17.6 Draw the crankcase cover off

17.10 Install the new cover gasket

6 Draw the cover off **(see illustration)**. If the cover is stuck, tap around the joint face between the cover and the crankcase with a soft-faced mallet to free it. Do not try to lever the cover off as this may damage the sealing surfaces.

7 Remove the gasket and discard it as a new one must be used. Note any dowels in the cover or crankcase and remove them for safekeeping if they are loose.

8 Clean the mating surfaces of the cover and the crankcase with a suitable solvent to remove any traces of old gasket or sealant. Take care not to scratch or gouge the soft aluminium.

9 To renew the cover oil seal, support the cover on the work surface and drive the seal out with a suitably-sized socket. Note which way round the seal is fitted. Ensure that the seal housing is clean, then lubricate the new seal with a smear of engine oil and press it all the way into the housing.

Installation

10 If removed, fit the dowels into the crankcase, then fit a new cover gasket, making sure it locates correctly onto the dowels **(see illustration)**. If necessary, use a dab of grease to hold the gasket in position.

11 Lubricate the inside of the oil seal with engine oil, then install the cover taking care not to damage the seal on the crankshaft threads. Make sure that the gasket stays in place.

12 Install the cover bolts, making sure they are in the correct locations, then tighten the bolts evenly and in a criss-cross sequence.

13 Install the remaining components in the reverse order of removal.

14 Fill the engine with the correct type and quantity of oil (see Chapter 1 and *Pre-ride checks*)

18 Starter pinion assembly and starter clutch

Note 1: *Two different set-ups are used to transfer the starter motor drive to the engine - a sliding pinion assembly which engages with the driven gear on the variator pulley, or a starter (one-way) clutch which is located on the crankshaft inside the right-hand crankcase cover. Note the point at which the starter motor shaft enters the engine case to locate the appropriate assembly.*
Note 2: *This procedure can be carried out with the engine in the scooter.*

Starter pinion assembly

Removal

1 Note the position of the starter motor, then remove the drive belt cover (see Chapter 5) and locate the pinion assembly adjacent to the variator pulley **(see illustration)**.

2 Withdraw the starter pinion assembly **(see illustration)**.

Inspection

3 Check the starter pinion assembly for any signs of damage or wear, particularly for chipped or broken teeth on either of the pinions **(see illustration)**. Check the corresponding teeth on the starter motor pinion and the variator driven gear.

4 Rotate the outer pinion and check that it moves smoothly up and down the shaft, and that it returns easily to its rest position **(see illustration)**.

5 The starter pinion assembly is supplied as a complete unit; if any of the component parts is worn or damaged, the unit will have to be replaced with a new one.

6 Most manufacturers recommend that the starter pinion mechanism should not be lubricated as any excess grease may contaminate the drive belt and cause it to slip. However, a smear of grease should be applied to both ends of the pinion shaft before reassembly.

Installation

7 Installation is the reverse of removal. Ensure the inner pinion engages with the starter motor shaft.

Starter (one-way) clutch

Check

8 Note the position of the starter motor, then remove the right-hand crankcase cover (see Section 17).

9 The operation of the starter clutch can be checked while it is in place. The starter driven gear should rotate freely in the *opposite* direction to crankshaft rotation (anti-clockwise), but lock when rotated clockwise **(see illustration)**. If not, the starter clutch is faulty and should be removed for inspection.

18.1 Location of the starter pinion assembly (arrowed)

18.2 Manoeuvre the pinion assembly out

18.3 Inspect the assembly for chipped or broken teeth

18.4 Check the movement of the outer pinion

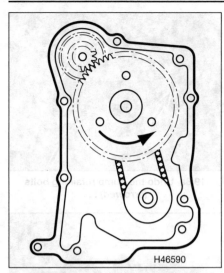

18.9 Gear should rotate freely in one direction only

Removal

10 A peg spanner is required to undo the starter clutch retaining nut **(see illustration)**. If the correct tool is not available, one can be made from a suitably-sized old socket or piece of steel tube **(see Tool Tip)**.

11 To prevent the crankshaft from turning while the retaining nut is being loosened, remove the drive belt cover and use the same method to hold the variator as when undoing the variator centre nut (see Chapter 5).

12 Undo the retaining nut. **Note:** *On some engines the retaining nut has a left-hand thread – check with your parts supplier before attempting to undo the nut. To undo a left-hand threaded nut, turn it clockwise (see Chapter 2B, Section 18).* Remove the washer, then draw the starter clutch and driven gear assembly off the crankshaft. If the assembly is a tight fit, use a puller to draw it off. **Note:** *To avoid damaging the threaded end of the crankshaft, temporarily install the alternator centre nut.*

13 If it is loose, remove the Woodruff key from the shaft for safekeeping, noting how it fits.

14 Slide the starter idler gear off its shaft and, if required, remove the shaft.

Inspection

15 Inspect both sets of teeth on the idler gear and renew it if any are chipped or worn **(see illustration)**. **Note:** *If the teeth on the larger pinion are worn or damaged, inspect the teeth on the starter motor pinion also (see Chapter 9).*

16 Check the idler shaft and bearing surfaces for signs of wear or damage, and renew it if necessary.

17 Inspect the teeth of the starter driven gear.

18 Hold the centre of the starter clutch assembly and check that the driven gear rotates freely in one direction and locks in the other direction. If it doesn't, the ring of sprags in the one-way mechanism may be jammed. Wash the assembly in suitable solvent and dry it with compressed air, if available. Lubricate

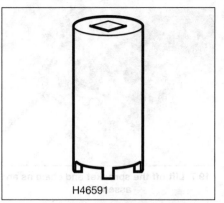

18.10 Use a peg spanner to undo the starter clutch retaining nut

the mechanism with clean engine oil and check it again. If the starter clutch still does not operate correctly, or if the driven gear teeth are worn, a new assembly will have to be fitted.

Installation

19 Installation is the reverse of removal, noting the following:
● Ensure the idler gear engages with the pinion on the starter motor shaft.
● Lubricate the starter clutch mechanism with clean engine oil.
● Fit the Woodruff key into its slot in the shaft.
● Ensure that the starter clutch assembly is pressed all the way onto the crankshaft.
● Install the washer and tighten the retaining nut securely.

19 Oil pump

Note 1: *The oil pump is located inside the engine unit and is either gear or chain-driven from the right-hand side of the crankshaft. The pump drive pinion or sprocket is integral with the crankshaft.*

Note 2: *This procedure can be carried out with the engine in the scooter.*

Removal

1 Remove the right-hand crankcase cover (see Section 17).

19.3a Using a piece of clean rag to lock the pinions together

A peg spanner can be made by cutting an old socket as shown – measure the width and depth of the slots in the retaining nut to determine the size of the castellations on the socket. Alternatively you can purchase aftermarket peg spanners, or you could make a peg spanner by cutting castellations into one end of a piece of steel tube.

18.15 Examine the idler gear teeth for wear and damage

2 If the starter one-way clutch is located inside the cover, follow the procedure in Section 18 to remove it.

3 If the oil pump is gear-driven, use a piece of clean, folded rag to lock the crankshaft and pump pinions together to prevent them turning, then undo the nut on the pump driveshaft **(see illustration)**. Remove the nut and washer, if fitted, then lift off the pump pinion, noting how it fits on the pump shaft **(see illustration)**.

4 If the pump is chain-driven, where fitted,

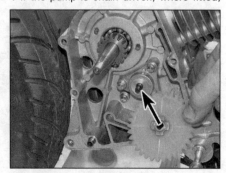

19.3b Note how the pinion locates on the pump shaft

19.4 Undo the screw securing the drive chain cover

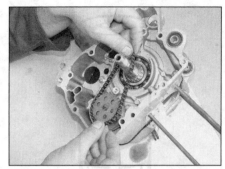

19.7 Lift off the sprocket and chain as an assembly

19.8a Undo the pump retaining bolts (arrowed) . . .

19.8b . . . and lift the pump off

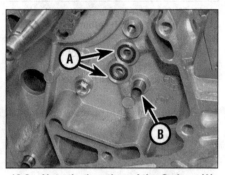

19.8c Note the location of the O-rings (A) and dowel (B)

19.9 Check that the pump rotates smoothly

remove the screw(s) securing the pump drive chain cover and remove the cover **(see illustration)**.

5 Mark the chain and sprocket so that

they can be fitted the same way round on reassembly.

6 To prevent the oil pump from turning while the sprocket nut is being loosened, remove

the drive belt cover and use the same method to hold the variator as when undoing the variator centre nut (see Chapter 5).

7 Undo the nut, then lift the sprocket and chain off the pump driveshaft and disengage the chain from the crankshaft sprocket **(see illustration)**.

8 Note how the pump is retained in the crankcase – there may be two or three retaining bolts. Undo the bolts and withdraw the pump from the engine **(see illustrations)**. Note the location of any dowels or O-rings fitted behind the pump – discard the O-rings as a new one must be fitted **(see illustration)**.

Inspection

9 Check the pump body for obvious signs of damage especially around the mounting bolt holes. Turn the pump driveshaft by hand and check that the pump rotates smoothly **(see illustration)**.

10 If required, the pump can be disassembled for cleaning and inspection.

11 Remove the screw(s) securing the cover to the pump body, then remove cover **(see illustrations)**. Note the location of any dowel between the cover and the body **(see illustration)**.

12 Note any reference marks on the pump rotors; even if the rotors are not marked, it is essential that they are reassembled the correct way round. Lift out the pump shaft and the inner and outer rotors **(see illustrations)**.

13 Clean the pump components with a suitable solvent and dry them with compressed air, if available. Inspect the pump body, rotors

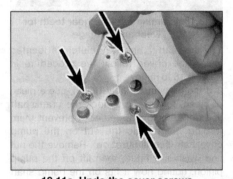

19.11a Undo the cover screws (arrowed) . . .

19.11b . . . and lift off the cover . . .

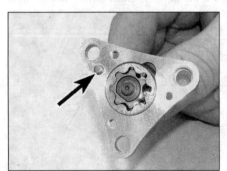

19.11c . . . noting the location of the dowel (arrowed)

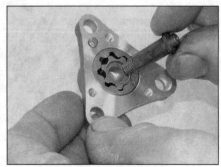

19.12a Lift out the pump shaft . . .

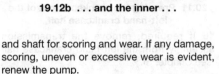

19.12b ... and the inner ...

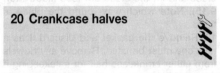

19.12c ... and outer rotors

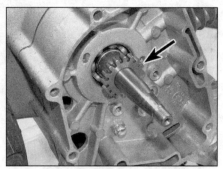

19.16 Inspect the pump pinion and the crankshaft pinion or wear or damage (arrowed)

and shaft for scoring and wear. If any damage, scoring, uneven or excessive wear is evident, renew the pump.

14 If the pump is good, reassemble all the components in the reverse order of disassembly and lubricate them with clean engine oil.

15 Fit the cover and tighten the screw(s) securely, then rotate the pump shaft by hand to check that the rotors turn smoothly and freely.

16 If the oil pump is gear-driven, inspect the pump pinion and the crankshaft pinion or wear or damage. If necessary, fit a new pump pinion. The crankshaft pinion may not be available as a separate item **(see illustration)** – if it is damaged, a new crankshaft assembly will have to be fitted (see Section 21).

17 If the pump is chain driven, inspect the pump drive chain and sprockets for wear or damage, and renew them as a set if necessary. Refer to the procedure in Section 9 for checking the sprockets. Lay the chain on a flat surface and check for play between the links – if there is any, renew the chain. Always renew the components as an assembly – worn sprockets will soon damage a new chain.

Installation

18 Installation is the reverse of removal, noting the following:

● Fit new O-rings in or behind the pump housing.

● Ensure the chain and sprocket are fitted the correct way round.

● If fitted, install the drive chain cover.

● Fill the engine with the correct type and quantity of oil (see Chapter 1 and *Pre-ride checks*)

20 Crankcase halves

Note: *To separate the crankcase halves, the engine must be removed from the scooter.*

Separation

1 Follow the procedure in Section 4 and remove the engine from the frame.

2 Before the crankcase halves can be separated the following components must be removed:

● *Cylinder head (Section 11)*
● *Cylinder (Section 13)*
● *Alternator (Section 16)*
● *Variator (Chapter 5)*
● *Camchain and tensioner blade, if accessible (Section 9)*
● *Starter motor (Chapter 9)*
● *Oil pump (Section 18)*
● *Main stand (Chapter 6)*

3 Tape some rag around the connecting rod to prevent it knocking against the cases. Although not essential, it is advisable to remove the piston to avoid damage during this procedure.

4 On some engines, the crankshaft oil seals are held in plates on the outside of the crankcases. To remove the seals, undo the bolts and remove the plates - do not try to remove the seals from the plates.

5 If the kickstart mechanism driven gear is located on the left-hand side of the crankshaft, ensure that it is removed before attempting to separate the crankcase halves (see Chapter 5).

6 Support the crankcase assembly on the work surface on its left-hand side. On most engines, once the right-hand crankcase cover has been removed, the crankcase halves are only held together by one bolt – however, always check to ensure that all the crankcase bolts have been located **(see illustration)**.

7 Loosen the remaining crankcase bolts evenly, a little at a time and in a criss-cross sequence until they are all finger-tight, then remove them **(see illustration)**. **Note:** *Ensure that all the crankcase bolts have been removed before attempting to separate the cases.*

8 Lift the right-hand crankcase half off the left-hand half **(see illustration)**. If the crankcase halves do not separate easily, first ensure all fasteners have been removed. Next, apply heat to the right-hand main bearing housing with a hot air gun and try lifting the right-hand half off again.

Caution: Do not try to separate the halves by levering against the mating surfaces as they are easily scored and will not seal correctly afterwards. Do not strike the ends of the crankshaft with a hammer as damage to the end threads or the shaft itself will result.

9 If the crankcase is an extremely tight fit on the crankshaft, a puller arrangement will be required to facilitate the procedure **(see illustration)**. If the puller is placed across the end of the crankshaft, thread the alternator

20.6 Check for any remaining crankcase bolts (arrowed)

20.7 Remove the remaining crankcase bolts

20.8 Lifting the right-hand crankcase half off

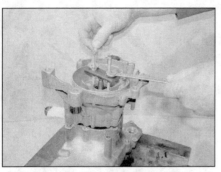

20.9 Using a puller arrangement to lift off the crankcase half

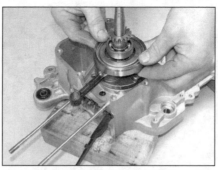

20.10 Lift the crankshaft assembly out of the left-hand crankcase half

20.11 Pressing the crankshaft out of the left-hand crankcase half

centre nut on first to protect the threads. Take care to ensure that equal pressure is applied on both sides of the puller arrangement at all times and apply heat to the bearing housing.

10 Now lift the crankshaft assembly out of the left-hand crankcase half – apply heat to the main bearing housing if required **(see illustration)**. If the camchain is still in place, ensure it is clear of the crankshaft sprocket when the crankshaft is removed. Note that the main bearings will remain in place on the crankshaft assembly (see Section 21).

11 If the crankcase is an extremely tight fit on the crankshaft, use a similar set-up to the one in Step 9, only this time press the crankshaft out of the left-hand crankcase half **(see illustration)**. Thread the variator nut onto the end of the crankshaft to protect the threads and make sure the crankshaft assembly is supported to prevent it dropping if it suddenly comes free.

12 If not already done, remove the camchain **(see illustration)**. If not already done, undo the pivot bolt securing the camchain tensioner blade and lift the blade out **(see illustration 9.15)**. Note which way round the blade is fitted.

13 Remove the gasket and discard it as a new one must be used. Remove any dowels from either crankcase half for safekeeping if they are loose.

14 Clean the mating surfaces of the crankcase halves with a suitable solvent to remove any traces of old gasket or sealant. Take care not to scratch or gouge the soft aluminium.

15 Note the position of the crankshaft oil seals and note which way round the seals are fitted. Lever the seals out carefully with a large, flat-bladed screwdriver, taking care not to damage the crankcase **(see illustration)**. Discard the seals as new ones must be fitted on reassembly.

16 If required, remove the transmission assembly from the left-hand crankcase half (see Chapter 5).

Inspection

17 Wash the cases in a suitable solvent and dry them with compressed air, if available.

18 Small cracks or holes in aluminium castings can be repaired with an epoxy resin adhesive as a temporary measure. Permanent repairs can only be effected by welding, and only a specialist in this process is in a position to advise on the economy or practical aspect of such a repair. On some engines, the crankcase halves can be renewed individually, on others the two halves are only available together as a matching set.

19 Damaged threads can be economically reclaimed by using a thread insert. Most small engineering firms offer a service of this kind. Sheared screws can usually be removed with screw extractors. Refer to *Tools and Workshop Tips* in the *Reference* section for further details.

20 Always wash the crankcases thoroughly after any repair work to ensure no dirt or metal swarf is trapped inside when the engine is rebuilt.

21 Inspect the engine mounting bushes **(see illustration)**. If they show signs of deterioration, renew them all at the same time. To remove a bush, first note its position in the casing. Heat the casing with a hot air gun, then support the casing and drive the bush out with a hammer and a suitably sized socket. Alternatively, use two suitably sized sockets to press the bush out in the jaws of a vice. Clean the bush housing with steel wool to remove any corrosion, then reheat the casing and fit the new bush. **Note:** *Always support the casing when removing or fitting bushes to avoid breaking the casing.*

22 Inspect the main bearing housings. If a bearing outer race has spun in its housing, the inside of the housing will be damaged. A bearing locking compound can be used to fix the outer race in place on reassembly if the damage is not too severe. **Note:** *If a bearing has spun in its housing, the bearing itself is likely to be damaged – see Section 21.*

23 Inspect the crankshaft assembly and bearings (see Section 21).

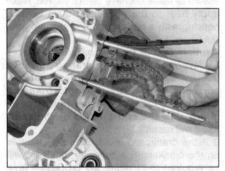

20.12 Remove the cam chain

20.15 Lever out the old seals with a flat-bladed screwdriver

20.21 Inspect the engine mounting bushes (arrowed)

20.24 Ensure the new oil seals are fitted correctly

Reassembly

24 If applicable, fit the new crankshaft oil seals into the crankcase halves and press them into place using a seal driver or socket **(see illustration)**. Ensure the seals are fitted the right way round and that they enter the cases squarely.

25 Support the left-hand crankcase half on the work surface with enough space below it to provide clearance for the end of the crankshaft when it is fully installed.

26 Lubricate the left-hand crankshaft seal and main bearing with clean engine oil and tape some rag around the connecting rod to prevent it knocking against the cases.

27 If applicable, install the camchain tensioner blade **(see illustration 9.18c)** and position the camchain in the crankcase half with clearance for the crankshaft sprocket **(see illustration)**.

28 Heat the bearing housing in the crankcase with a hot air gun. **Note:** *Avoid applying direct heat onto the crankshaft oil seal.* If required, a freeze spray can be used on the main bearing to aid installation.

29 Lower the crankshaft assembly into the crankcase half carefully to avoid damaging the seal. Ensure that the main bearing is aligned with the bearing housing and that the connecting rod is aligned with the crankcase mouth, then press the crankshaft assembly in fully so that the main bearing goes all the way into its housing. If the main bearing does not seat fully, apply more heat around the bearing housing while applying steady pressure to the crankshaft assembly.

30 If the camchain has been installed, ensure that it is correctly located around the crankshaft sprocket and secure it in position with wire or a cable-tie to avoid it becoming jammed inside the crankcase.

31 If necessary, allow the case to cool, then wipe the mating surfaces of both crankcase halves with a rag soaked in suitable solvent and fit the dowels. Install the new crankcase gasket on the mating surface of the left-hand case. If necessary, use a dab of grease to hold the gasket in position.

32 Lubricate the right-hand crankshaft seal and main bearing with clean engine oil.

33 Heat the bearing housing with a hot air gun. **Note:** *Avoid applying direct heat onto the crankshaft oil seal.* If required, use a freeze spay on the main bearing.

34 Lower the crankcase half over the crankshaft carefully to avoid damaging the seal. Ensure that the two halves of the crankcase are correctly aligned, taking special note of the position of the dowels, and that the main bearing is aligned with the bearing housing in the right-hand case **(see illustration)**.

35 Press the crankcase on fully so that the main bearing goes all the way into its housing **(see illustration)**. If the main bearing does not seat fully, apply more heat around the bearing housing while applying steady pressure to the crankcase.

36 Check that the crankcase halves are seated all the way round. If the cases are not

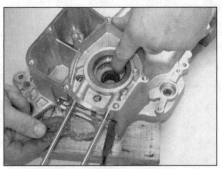

20.27 Position the cam chain in the left-hand crankcase half

20.35 . . . then press it down so that the case halves seat all the way round

correctly seated, heat the bearing housings while applying firm pressure. **Note:** *Do not attempt to pull the crankcase halves together using the crankcase bolts as the casing will crack and be ruined.*

37 Clean the threads of the crankcase bolts and install them finger-tight, then tighten them evenly a little at a time in a criss-cross sequence. **Note:** *At this stage on most engines, the crankcase halves are only retained by one bolt (see Step 6).*

38 Trim off any excess gasket across the crankcase mouth **(see illustration)**.

39 Support the connecting rod and rotate the crankshaft by hand – if there are any signs of undue stiffness, tight or rough spots, or of any other problem, the fault must be rectified before proceeding further. If the camchain has been installed, support it while rotating the crankshaft.

40 On engines where the crankshaft oil seals

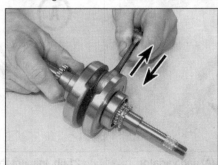

21.4 Checking for play in the big-end bearing

20.34 Lower the crankcase half into position carefully . . .

20.38 Trim off the excess gasket with a sharp blade

are fitted to the outside of the crankcases (see Step 4), lubricate the new seals with clean engine oil and install them in the cases.

41 Install the remaining components in the reverse order of removal.

21 Crankshaft assembly, big-end and main bearings

Note: *The crankshaft assembly is pressed together and is easily damaged if it is dropped.*

1 To access the crankshaft assembly, the big-end bearing and the main bearings, the crankcase must be split into two parts (see Section 20).

2 The crankshaft assembly should give many thousands of miles of service. The most likely problems to occur will be a worn small or big-end bearing due to poor lubrication. A worn big-end bearing will produce a pronounced knocking noise, most audible when the engine is under load, and increasing as engine speed rises. This should not be confused with small-end bearing wear, which produces a lighter, metallic rattle (see Section 14).

3 When the crankcase halves are separated, the main bearings will remain in place on the crankshaft assembly – they are not normally available as separate items. If the main bearings have failed, excessive rumbling and vibration will be felt when the engine is running.

4 To assess the condition of the big-end bearing, hold the crankshaft assembly firmly and push and pull on the connecting rod,

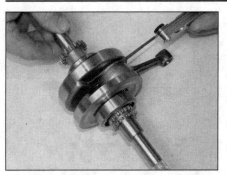

21.5 Measuring big-end side clearance as described

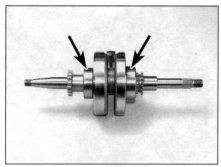

21.6 Check the condition of the main bearings (arrowed)

checking for any up-and-down freeplay between the two **(see illustration)**. If any freeplay is noted, the bearing is worn.

5 A small amount of big-end side clearance (side-to-side movement) is acceptable on the connecting rod. Some manufacturers specify a service limit for the sideplay (typically 0.2 to 0.5 mm) which can be measured with a feeler gauge **(see illustration)**.

6 Follow the procedure in *Tools and Workshop Tips* in the *Reference* section to check the condition of the main bearings **(see illustration)**.

7 If wear or damage is noted in any of the crankshaft assembly bearings, a new crankshaft assembly will have to be fitted – few manufacturers supply individual components and, due to its construction, work on the crankshaft assembly requires specialist equipment beyond the scope of this manual. **Note:** *Evidence of extreme heat, such as discoloration or blueing, indicates that lubrication failure has occurred. Be sure to check the oil pump and bearing oil ways in the crankcases before reassembling the engine.*

8 Inspect the threads on each end of the crankshaft and ensure that the retaining nuts for the alternator rotor and the variator are a good fit. Inspect the splines for the variator pulley on the left-hand end of the shaft **(see illustration)**. Inspect the taper and the slot in the right-hand end of the shaft for the alternator Woodruff key **(see illustration)**. Damage or wear that prevents the rotor from being fitted securely will require a new crankshaft assembly.

9 Inspect the oil pump and the camshaft drive sprocket teeth on the crankshaft for damage or wear **(see illustration 21.8a or b)**. On most engines, the sprockets are installed as an integral part of the crankshaft assembly – if they are worn or damaged a new assembly will have to be fitted.

22 Initial start-up after overhaul/running-in

Initial start-up after overhaul

1 Make sure the engine oil level is correct (see *Pre-ride checks*).

2 Make sure there is fuel in the tank.

3 With the ignition OFF, operate the kickstart a couple of times to check that the engine turns over easily.

4 Turn the ignition ON, start the engine and allow it to run at a slow idle until it reaches operating temperature. Do not be alarmed if there is a little smoke from the exhaust – this will be due to the oil used to lubricate the piston and bore during assembly and should subside after a while.

5 If the engine proves reluctant to start, remove the spark plug and check that it has not become wet and oily. If it has, clean it and try again. If the engine refuses to start, go through the fault finding charts at the end of this manual to identify the problem.

6 Check carefully for fuel and oil leaks and make sure the transmission and controls, especially the brakes, function properly before road testing the machine.

7 Upon completion of the road test, and after the engine has cooled down completely, recheck the valve clearances (see Chapter 1). Recheck the engine oil level (see *Pre-ride checks*).

Recommended running-in procedure

8 Treat the engine gently for the first few miles to allow any new parts to bed in.

9 If a new piston, cylinder or crankshaft assembly has been fitted, the engine will have to be run-in as when new. This means a restraining hand on the throttle until at least 300 miles (500 km) have been covered. There's no point in keeping to any set speed limit – the main idea is to gradually increase performance up to the 600 mile (1000 km) mark. Make sure that the throttle position is varied to vary engine speed, and use full throttle only for short bursts. Experience is the best guide, since it's easy to tell when an engine is running freely.

10 Pay particular attention to the *Pre-ride checks* at the beginning of this manual and investigate the cause of any oil loss immediately. Check the tightness of all relevant nuts and bolts (see Chapter 1).

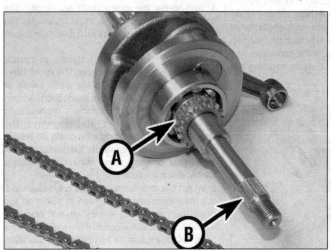

21.8a Inspect the camshaft drive sprocket (A) and variator splines (B)

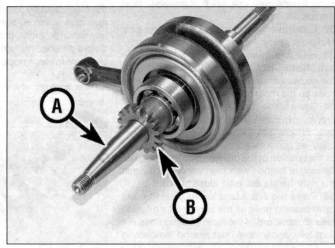

21.8b Inspect the alternator taper (A) and oil pump drive sprocket (B)

Chapter 2B
125 and 150cc four-stroke engines – 152/157QMI

Contents

Degrees of difficulty

Easy, suitable for novice with little experience	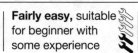	**Fairly easy,** suitable for beginner with some experience	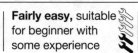	**Fairly difficult,** suitable for competent DIY mechanic	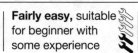	**Difficult,** suitable for experienced DIY mechanic	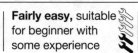	**Very difficult,** suitable for expert DIY or professional	

Specifications

Note: *These Specifications have been compiled from what limited service information is available on the 152QMI and 157QMI engines.*

Engine

Type	
152QMI	124.6 cc single cylinder, air-cooled four-stroke
157QMI	149.5 cc single cylinder, air-cooled four-stroke
Bore	
152QMI	52.4 mm
157QMI	57.4 mm
Stroke – both engines	57.8 mm
Idle speed	1500 ± 100 rpm
Oil type	SAE 10W40 API SG/CD four-stroke motorcycle oil
Oil capacity	
At oil change	900 ml
After rebuild	1100 ml
Cylinder compression pressure	213 psi (15 bars)
Piston diameter service limit	
152QMI	52.3 mm
157QMI	not available
Cylinder bore diameter service limit	
152QMI	52.5 mm
157QMI	not available

Engine (continued)

Piston-to-bore clearance service limit	0.10 mm
Piston pin outside diameter service limit	14.96 mm
Piston pin bore in piston service limit.	15.04 mm
Connecting rod small-end internal diameter service limit	15.05 mm
Piston ring-to-groove clearance service limit.	0.09 mm
Piston ring end gap service limit	
Top and second ring.	0.5 mm
Oil control ring side rail.	0.7 mm
Camshaft lobe height service limit	
Intake	25.68 mm
Exhaust.	25.45 mm
Rocker arm inside diameter service limit	10.10 mm
Rocker shaft outside diameter service limit	9.91 mm
Valve clearance	0.10 mm
Valve spring free length service limit	
Inner spring.	31.2 mm
Outer spring	34.1 mm
Valve seat width	
Standard.	1.0 mm
Service limit	1.8 mm
Valve stem diameter service limit.	4.9 mm
Valve guide inside diameter service limit.	5.3 mm
Starter driven gear hub outside diameter.	42.55 mm
Oil pump body-to-outer rotor clearance service limit	0.12 mm
Oil pump inner-to-outer rotor clearance service limit	0.12 mm
Oil pump rotor endfloat service limit	0.20 mm
Connecting rod big-end side clearance service limit.	0.55 mm

Transmission

Belt width service limit	19.0 mm
Variator rollers diameter service limit	17.4 mm
Variator body inside diameter service limit.	24.06 mm
Variator sleeve outside diameter service limit	23.94 mm
Clutch lining thickness service limit	2.0 mm
Clutch drum inside diameter service limit	125.5 mm
Spring free length service limit.	163.7 mm
Clutch inner pulley hub outside diameter	33.94 mm
Clutch outer pulley hub inside diameter.	34.06 mm
Gearbox oil type.	SAE 90W gear oil
Gearbox oil capacity	
At oil change.	180 ml
After rebuild	210 ml

Torque wrench settings

Spark plug	12 Nm
Valve cover bolts	10 Nm
Cam chain tensioner bolts	10 Nm
Cam chain tensioner blade pivot bolt	10 Nm
Cylinder head (camshaft holder) nuts.	20 Nm
Cylinder head bolts	10 Nm
Alternator nut	40 Nm
Starter clutch nut	93 Nm
Starter clutch assembly screws	12 Nm
Oil pump mounting bolts	10 Nm
Oil pump sprocket nut	10 Nm
Crankcase bolts	12 Nm
Variator centre nut	55 Nm
Clutch centre nut	55 Nm
Clutch assembly nut.	55 Nm
Gearbox cover bolts	12 Nm
Front engine mounting bolt	50 Nm
Rear shock absorber bolts.	30 Nm

1 General information

The engine is a single cylinder, overhead-camshaft four-stroke, with fan assisted air cooling (see Chapter 1, Section 20). The camshaft is chain-driven off the crankshaft and operates the valves via rocker arms.

The crankshaft assembly is pressed together, incorporating the connecting rod.

The crankcase divides vertically – the left-hand crankcase is an integral part of the drive belt casing and gearbox.

2 Component access

Most components and assemblies, with the obvious exception of the crankshaft assembly and its bearings, can be worked on without having to remove the engine/transmission unit from the scooter. However, access to some components is severely restricted, and if a number of areas require attention at the same time, removal of the engine is recommended, as it is an easy task to undertake.

3 Cylinder compression test

 Warning: Be careful when working on the hot engine – the exhaust pipe, the engine and engine components can cause severe burns.

Special tools: *A compression gauge with an appropriate threaded adapter (see Step 5) is required for this procedure.*

1 Among other things, poor starting and engine performance may be caused by leaking valves, a leaking head gasket or worn piston, rings and/or cylinder wall. A cylinder compression check will help pinpoint these conditions.

2 Before carrying out the test, check that the valve clearances are correct (see Chapter 1).

3 Run the engine until it reaches normal operating temperature, then turn the ignition OFF. With the scooter supported securely in an upright position, follow the procedure in Chapter 2A, Section 3, to install the compression gauge and take several pressure readings.

4 A reading of approximately 213 psi (15 Bars) indicates a cylinder in good condition.

5 If the compression builds up quickly and evenly, you can assume that the engine top-end is in good mechanical condition. Worn or sticking piston rings, or a worn cylinder, will produce very little initial movement of the gauge, but compression will tend to build-up as the engine turns over. Valve seat leakage, or head gasket leakage, is indicated by low initial compression which does not build-up.

6 To confirm your findings, use a squirt-type oil can to add a small amount of engine oil into the cylinder through the spark plug hole. The oil will tend to seal the piston rings if they are leaking. Check the compression again and if it increases significantly after the addition of the oil the rings or cylinder are definitely worn. If the compression remains low, the pressure is leaking past the valves or head gasket.

Note: *High compression pressure indicates excessive carbon build-up in the combustion chamber and on the top of the piston. If this is the case, remove the cylinder head and clean the carbon deposits off. Note that excessive carbon build-up is less likely with the use of modern fuels.*

4 Engine removal and installation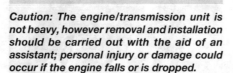

Caution: The engine/transmission unit is not heavy, however removal and installation should be carried out with the aid of an assistant; personal injury or damage could occur if the engine falls or is dropped.

Removal

1 Support the scooter securely in an upright position. Work can be made easier by raising the machine to a suitable height on an hydraulic ramp or a suitable platform. Make sure it is secure and will not topple over.

2 Remove the luggage compartment and any body panels as necessary to access the engine (see Chapter 8).

3 Disconnect the battery negative terminal (see Chapter 9) and pull the spark plug cap off the plug.

4 Remove the exhaust system (see Chapter 3).

5 If the engine is dirty, particularly around its mountings, wash it thoroughly before starting any major dismantling work. This will make work much easier and rule out the possibility of dirt falling inside.

6 If required, drain the engine oil (see Chapter 1).

7 Remove the air filter housing and the air intake duct (see Chapter 3).

8 Disconnect the fuel hose from its union on the carburettor, being prepared to catch any residual fuel in a rag **(see illustration)**. Position a suitable container below the carburettor drain hose, then loosen the drain screw and drain any residual fuel from the float chamber **(see illustration)**. Tighten the drain screw. The carburettor can remain attached to the engine, but if removing it undo the drive belt casing bolt to free the drain hose bracket.

9 Trace the wiring from the automatic choke unit and disconnect it at the connector under the right-hand floor panel **(see illustration)**. **Note:** *When disconnecting any wiring, it is advisable to mark or tag the wires as a reminder of where they connect.*

10 Either displace or remove the carburettor completely, leaving the throttle cable attached if required, or just disconnect the throttle cable (see Chapter 3). If the carburettor is displaced, ensure it is secured to a convenient part of the frame to avoid damage. Ensure that the throttle cable and automatic choke wiring is clear of the engine unit. Stuff clean rag into the intake manifold to prevent anything falling inside.

11 Disconnect the fuel tap vacuum hose

4.8a Fuel hose fits over stub on carburettor (arrowed)

4.8b Carburettor drain screw (arrowed)

4.9 Automatic choke wire connector is alongside frame rail under floor panel

4.11 Vacuum pipe fits over stub on intake manifold (arrowed)

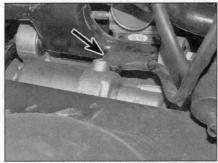

4.12 Starter motor terminal (arrowed)

4.13 Engine earth lead (arrowed)

from its union on the inlet manifold **(see illustration)**.

12 Pull back the boot, then undo the screw securing the lead to the starter motor terminal **(see illustration)**.

13 Undo the bolt securing the earth (ground) wire to the crankcase and disconnect the wire **(see illustration)**. Replace the bolt for safekeeping.

14 Trace the wiring from the alternator and ignition pulse generator coil on the right-hand side of the engine and disconnect it at the connectors **(see illustration)**. Secure the wiring clear of the engine. Pull the cap off the spark plug.

15 Remove the rear wheel if required (see Chapter 7), although the wheel and rear mudguard can remain in place. **Note:** *On machines where the main stand is bolted to the underside of the engine unit, the rear wheel*

and stand provide a convenient support for the unit once it is removed from the scooter. However, it is useful to loosen the rear wheel nut at this point before disconnecting the rear brake.

16 Disconnect the brake cable from the brake arm (see Chapter 7) **(see illustration)**. Release the cable from any clips along the edge of the drive belt casing and pull it through the cable stop **(see illustration)**.

17 Check that all wiring, cables and hoses are clear of the engine/transmission unit.

18 With the aid of an assistant, support the weight of the machine on the rear underside of the frame. If the rear wheel has been removed, support the gearbox on a wood block to prevent damage to the casing.

19 Remove the rear shock absorber (see Chapter 6).

20 Undo the nut on the front upper engine

mounting bolt that passes through the engine pivot bracket **(see illustration)**. Have an assistant support the scooter, then carefully withdraw the engine mounting bolt **(see illustration)**. As the bolt is withdrawn, note the location of any spacers between the mounting lugs on the crankcase and the pivot bracket.

21 Manoeuvre the engine unit (complete with rear wheel) back and out of the frame. Check the condition of the rubber mountings set in the upper mounting point **(see illustration)**.

Installation

22 Installation is the reverse of removal, noting the following:

● Make sure no wires, cables or hoses become trapped between the engine and the frame when installing the engine

● Tighten the front engine mounting bolt and shock absorber bolts to the torque settings

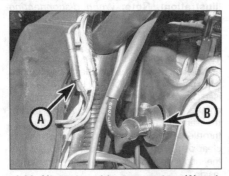

4.14 Alternator wiring connectors (A) and spark plug cap (B)

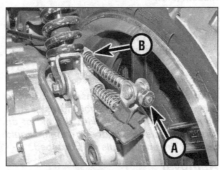

4.16a Rear brake cable adjuster nut (A) and its stop (B)

4.16b Free brake cable from clamps on top of drive belt casing

4.20a Engine mounting bolt nut . . .

4.20b . . . and mounting bolt head

4.21 Engine mounting point bushes

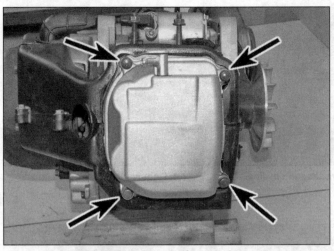
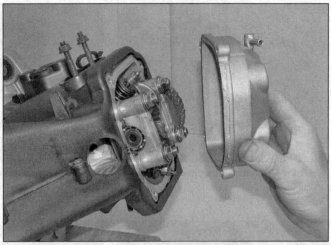

6.3a Undo the bolts (arrowed) . . .   **6.3b . . . and remove the valve cover**

in the Specifications at the beginning of this chapter.

- Make sure all wires, cables and hoses are correctly routed and connected, and secured by any clips or ties.
- If the engine oil was drained, or if any oil has been lost during overhaul, refill or top up as described in Chapter 1 and *Pre-ride checks.*
- Check the operation of the rear brake before riding the machine (see Chapter 7).

5 Disassembly and reassembly – general information

Disassembly

1 Before disassembling the engine, the external surfaces of the unit should be thoroughly cleaned and degreased. This will prevent contamination of the engine internals, and will also make working a lot easier and cleaner. A high flash-point solvent, such as paraffin can be used, or better still, a proprietary engine degreaser such as Gunk. Use a degreasing brush or old paintbrushes to work the solvent into the various recesses of the engine casings. Take care to exclude solvent or water from the electrical components and intake and exhaust ports.

 Warning: The use of petrol (gasoline) as a cleaning agent should be avoided because of the risk of fire.

2 When clean and dry, arrange the unit on the workbench, leaving suitable clear area for working. Gather a selection of small containers and plastic bags so that parts can be grouped together in an easily identifiable manner. Some paper and a pen should be on hand to permit notes to be made and labels attached where necessary. A supply of clean rag is also required.

3 Before commencing work, read through the appropriate section so that some idea of the

necessary procedure can be gained. When removing components it should be noted that great force is seldom required, unless specified. In many cases, a component's reluctance to be removed is indicative of an incorrect approach or removal method – if in any doubt, re-check with the text.

4 When disassembling the engine, keep 'mated' parts that have been in contact with each other during engine operation together. These 'mated' parts must be reused or replaced as an assembly.

5 Complete engine disassembly should be done in the following general order with reference to the appropriate Sections (refer to Chapter 5 for details of transmission components):

- Remove the valve cover
- Remove the camshaft and rockers
- Remove the cylinder head
- Remove the cylinder
- Remove the piston
- Remove the starter motor (see Chapter 9)
- Remove the alternator
- Remove the starter clutch (see Chapter 9)
- Remove the oil pump
- Separate the crankcase halves
- Remove the crankshaft

Reassembly

6 Reassembly is accomplished by reversing the order of disassembly.

6 Valve cover

Note: *This procedure can be carried out with the engine in the scooter. If the engine has been removed, ignore the steps that do not apply.*

Removal

1 Remove the body panels as necessary to access the cylinder head (see Chapter 8).

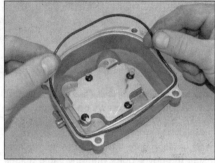

6.4 Rocker cover gasket sits in cover groove

2 If required, loosen the clip securing the breather hose to the valve cover and detach the hose.

3 Undo the bolts securing the valve cover, noting the location of any cable guides, then lift the cover off **(see illustrations)**. If the cover is stuck, tap around the joint face between the cover and the cylinder head with a soft-faced mallet to free it. Do not try to lever the cover off as this may damage the sealing surfaces.

4 Remove the gasket and discard it as a new one must be used **(see illustration)**. Clean the mating surfaces of the cylinder head and the valve cover with a suitable solvent to remove any traces of old gasket or sealant.

5 Note the location of the breather system baffle plate in the valve cover. If required, remove the plate and clean the inside of the cover. Bend back the tabs securing the plate screws carefully to avoid damaging them. On installation, ensure that the screws securing the plate are tightened securely – as a precaution, clean the screw threads and apply non-permanent thread-locking compound.

Installation

6 Lay the new gasket onto the valve cover, making sure it fits correctly into the groove **(see illustration 6.4)**.

7 Position the valve cover on the cylinder

7.2a Undo the bolts (arrowed) . . .

7.2b . . . and remove the fan cowling

7.4 Remove the spark plug cap

7.6a Undo the screws on the right . . .

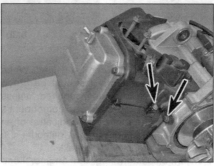

7.6b . . . and left-hand sides

7.7 Ease the cowling apart carefully

head, making sure the gasket stays in place. Install the cover bolts with any cable guides as noted on removal, then tighten the bolts evenly and in a criss-cross sequence to the torque setting in the Specifications at the beginning of this chapter.

8 If removed, install the breather hose and secure it with the clip.

9 Install the remaining components in the reverse order of removal.

7 Fan cowling and engine cowling

Note: *This procedure can be carried out with the engine in the scooter. If the engine has been removed, ignore the steps that do not apply.*

1 Remove the body panels as necessary to access the engine (see Chapter 8).

2 Unclip any wiring or hoses from the fan cowling, then undo the bolts securing the fan cowling and remove it **(see illustrations)**.

3 Remove any spacers for the cowling bolts for safekeeping if they are loose.

4 Pull the cap off the spark plug **(see illustration)**.

5 On most engines, it is necessary to remove the carburettor and the exhaust system (see Chapter 3) before the upper and lower sections of the engine cowling can be removed. It may also be necessary to remove the intake manifold.

6 Note the location of the screws securing the two halves of the cowling together, then undo the screws **(see illustrations)**.

7 Ease the two halves of the cowling apart carefully to avoid straining the tabs securing the halves together **(see illustration)**, then lift the cowling off.

8 On most scooters a cowling seal is fitted onto a lip around the top of the cylinder head **(see illustration 10.1)**. Check that the seal is not damaged or deteriorated and that it is a secure fit around the head. If necessary, fit a new seal.

9 Installation is the reverse of removal. Ensure that the two halves of the cowling fit together correctly – do not force them. Take care not to over-tighten the joining screws.

8 Camchain tensioner

Note: *This procedure can be carried out with the engine in the scooter. If the engine has been removed, ignore the steps that do not apply.*

Removal

1 Remove the body panels as necessary to access the engine (see Chapter 8).

2 On some engines, the camchain tensioner is behind a small cover that is part of the engine cowling – undo the screws securing the cover

and lift it off to access the tensioner. If no separate cover is fitted, remove the upper half of the cowling (see Section 7).

3 Remove the spark plug (see Chapter 1). If not already done, remove the fan cowling (see Section 7).

4 Turn the engine in the normal direction of rotation until the piston is at top dead centre (TDC) on its compression stroke. You can do this by rotating the crankshaft via the alternator rotor. The position of the piston can be confirmed by ensuring that the timing mark 'T' on the alternator rotor is aligned with the register mark on the crankcase **(see illustration)**.

5 Undo the tensioner cap screw, noting the location of the sealing O-ring **(see**

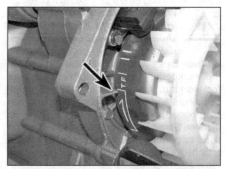

8.4 Scribed line next to T mark should align with register mark (arrowed)

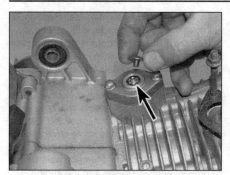

8.5 Note location of O-ring

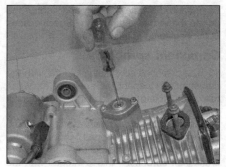

8.6 Turn tensioner screw clockwise

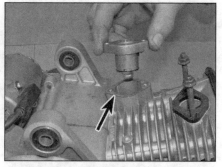

8.7 Remove the tensioner and gasket (arrowed)

illustration). Discard the O-ring as a new one must be fitted.

6 Using a small flat-bladed screwdriver, turn the tensioner screw clockwise until it goes tight – this will retract the tensioner plunger into the tensioner body (see illustration).

7 Undo the tensioner mounting bolts and withdraw the tensioner from the cylinder (see illustration). Remove the gasket from the base of the tensioner or from the cylinder and discard it as a new one must be used.

8 Clean all traces of old gasket material from the tensioner and cylinder with a suitable solvent. Take care not to scratch or gouge the soft aluminium. Be careful not to let any of the gasket material fall into the engine.

Inspection

9 Examine the tensioner components for signs of wear or damage.

10 Turn the tensioner screw anti-clockwise to release the plunger (see illustration). Now try to press the plunger back into the body – it should be locked in position.

11 By turning the screwdriver, ensure that the plunger moves freely in and out of the tensioner body. Examine the foot of the plunger for wear (see illustration).

12 If any part of the tensioner is worn or damaged, or if the plunger is seized in the body, a new tensioner must be fitted.

Installation

13 Turn the tensioner screw clockwise to retract the plunger. Fit a new gasket on the tensioner body, install the tensioner in the cylinder and tighten the mounting bolts to the torque setting in the Specifications at the beginning of this chapter.

14 Turn the engine in the normal direction of rotation – this removes all the slack in the front run of the chain between the crankshaft and the camshaft, and transfers it to the back run where it will be taken up by the tensioner.

Note: *Take care when turning the engine with the tensioner spring removed to avoid the chain jumping over the teeth on the camshaft sprocket. If this happens, ensure that the timing marks on the alternator rotor and on the camshaft sprocket are correctly re-aligned with the piston at TDC before releasing the tensioner plunger (see Chapter 1, Section 28).*

15 Turn the tensioner screw anti-clockwise to release the plunger.

16 Fit a new sealing O-ring under the cap screw, then install the screw and tighten it securely (see illustration 8.5).

17 It is advisable to remove the valve cover (see Section 6) and check that the camchain is tensioned. If it is slack, the tensioner plunger did not release. Remove the tensioner and check the operation of the plunger again.

18 Install the remaining components in the reverse order of removal.

9 Camchain, blades and sprockets

Camchain

Inspection

1 The camchain runs between the drive sprocket on the crankshaft and the camshaft sprocket. To check the condition of the chain, first remove the valve cover (see Section 6).

2 Remove the spark plug (see Chapter 1). If not already done, remove the fan cowling (see Section 7).

3 Referring to Chapter 2A, Section 9, turn the engine slowly in the normal direction of rotation and inspect the inside edges of the chain links for wear. Next, hold the chain at the mid-way point around the camshaft sprocket and try to lift it off the sprocket. The chain should be a firm fit on the sprocket. Turn

the engine in the normal direction of rotation and check the entire length of the chain.

4 If any of the above checks indicate that the camchain has worn, a new one must be fitted.

Removal

5 The camchain cannot be removed until the crankcase halves have been separated and the crankshaft has been removed (see Section 20).

Installation

6 Installation is the reverse of removal, noting the following:

● Ensure the chain is correctly installed on the crankshaft sprocket before assembling the crankcase halves. Secure the chain to one of the cylinder studs to prevent it being displaced during engine assembly.

● Pay particular attention to the alignment of the TDC timing mark 'T' on the alternator rotor and the timing marks on the camshaft sprocket before installing the chain onto the sprocket.

● Ensure any slack in the chain is in the back run where it will be taken up by the tensioner.

Camchain guide and tensioner blades

Removal

7 The guide blade can be removed after the cylinder head has been removed (see Section 11).

8.10 Check action of the tensioner plunger

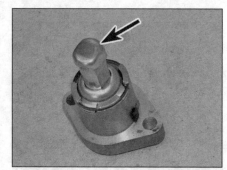

8.11 Examine plunger foot for wear

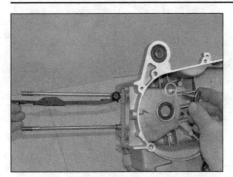

9.10 Removing the camchain tensioner blade

8 The tensioner blade is secured by a pivot bolt on its lower end. To remove the blade, first remove the camshaft (see Section 10). Secure the camchain to prevent it falling down into the tunnel in the side of the cylinder.

9 Remove the variator (see Chapter 5).

10 Undo the pivot bolt and lift the blade out **(see illustration)**. Note which way round the blade is fitted. Note the location of the sealing O-ring on the pivot bolt and discard it as a new one must be fitted.

11 Check both blades for wear or damage and renew them if necessary. Check the operation of the camchain tensioner (see Section 8).

Installation

12 Installation is the reverse of removal. Ensure that the blades are fitted the correct way round **(see illustrations 9.10 and 11.8)**. Clean the threads of the tensioner blade pivot bolt and apply non-permanent thread-locking compound. Fit a new O-ring and tighten the bolt to the torque setting in the Specifications at the beginning of this chapter.

Camchain sprockets

13 The camshaft sprocket is integral with the camshaft. To inspect the sprocket for wear, follow the procedure in Section 10 and remove the camshaft.

14 Check for wear on the sides and tips of the sprocket teeth and for chipped or hooked teeth.

15 Similar checks should be made on the crankshaft sprocket – this is integral with the crankshaft assembly (see Section 21).

16 If the sprocket teeth are worn, the chain will also be worn. Always renew the components as an assembly – worn sprockets will soon damage a new chain.

Caution: After installing the camchain tensioner, turn the crankshaft and check that all the timing marks still align correctly. If the timing marks are not aligned exactly as described, the valve timing will be incorrect and the valves may strike the piston, causing extensive damage to the engine.

10 Camshaft and rockers

Note: *This procedure can be carried out with the engine in the scooter, although on some models access to the top of the engine is extremely restricted.*

Removal

1 Remove the valve cover (see Section 6) and the fan and engine cowlings (see Section 7). Remove the cowling seal **(see illustration)**.

2 Remove the camchain tensioner (see Section 8). Note that when the piston is at TDC **(see illustration 8.4)** on its compression stroke the valves are closed and a small clearance can be felt at each rocker arm **(see illustration)**. Look for timing marks or two small holes on the camshaft sprocket – these should be aligned with the valve cover gasket face **(see illustration)**.

3 Stuff a clean rag into the camchain tunnel to prevent anything falling into the engine.

4 The camshaft and rockers are located in a holder which is retained by long studs that also secure the cylinder head and cylinder to the crankcases. Before loosening the camshaft holder nuts, check to see if the head is also secured by any smaller bolts, and if so, loosen them first **(see illustration 11.4a)**.

5 Now unscrew the camshaft holder nuts evenly and a little at a time in a criss-cross pattern, until they are all loose, then remove the nuts and washers **(see illustration)**.

6 Note which way round the camshaft holder is fitted. On the engine used to illustrate this procedure, the holder was marked EX on the exhaust side **(see illustration 10.2a)**.

7 Hold the camshaft in position in the cylinder head and lift off the camshaft holder **(see illustration)**. Note any dowels in the holder or head and remove them for safekeeping if they are loose **(see illustration 11.4b)**.

8 Lift the camchain off the sprocket and secure the chain to prevent it dropping into the engine **(see illustration)**.

10.1 Remove the cowling seal

10.2a Check for a small clearance in both rocker arms

10.2b Note alignment of the timing marks

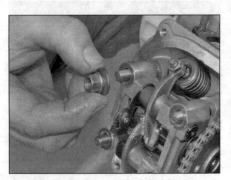

10.5 Undo the camshaft holder nuts

10.7 Lift off the camshaft holder

10.8 Lift off the camchain and secure it

10.9 Lift out the camshaft and bearings

10.10a Mark the rocker arms (arrowed) to aid reassembly

10.10b Pull out the rocker arm . . .

10.10c . . . noting cut-out for cylinder stud

10.11a Location of the decompressor cam mechanism

10.11b Decompressor stopper arm plate (arrowed)

9 Note the location of the camshaft and camshaft bearings, then lift out the camshaft **(see illustration)**.

10 The rocker shafts are retained in the camshaft holder by the cylinder studs. Once the holder has been removed from the engine, the shafts and individual rocker arms can be disassembled. Note the position of the rocker arms and mark them so that they can be installed in their original positions **(see illustration)**. Working on one shaft at a time, thread a suitably-sized bolt into the end of the shaft and withdraw it carefully, removing the rocker arm when it becomes free **(see illustrations)**. Note the position of any thrust washers on the shafts.

11 The engine used to illustrate this procedure was fitted with a reverse decompressor cam.

A one-way bearing inside the cam allows it to free-wheel when the engine is turning in the normal direction of rotation. However, if the engine kicks-back when being started and turns in the opposite direction to normal, the bearing locks and raises the lobe of the decompressor cam which opens the exhaust valve, stopping the engine. The main components of the decompressor cam mechanism are located on the right-hand end of the camshaft **(see illustration)**. A plate with a spring loaded stopper arm is located on the right-hand side of the camshaft holder **(see illustration)**. Note which way round the plate is fitted.

12 Keep the components in order so that they can be reinstalled in their correct locations **(see illustration)**.

Inspection

13 Clean all of the components with a suitable solvent and dry them.

14 Inspect the camshaft lobes for heat discoloration (blue appearance), score marks, chipped areas, flat spots and spalling **(see illustration)**. Measure the height of each camshaft lobe with a micrometer and compare the results with the Specifications at the beginning of this chapter **(see illustration)**. If damage is noted or wear is excessive, the camshaft must be renewed.

15 Check the condition of the camshaft bearings (see *Tools and Workshop Tips* in the Reference section). The camshaft, camchain sprocket and bearings are supplied as an assembly, so if any component is worn a new assembly will have to be fitted.

10.12 Components of the camshaft holder assembly

10.14a Inspect the camshaft lobes and corresponding face of the rocker arm (arrowed)

10.14b Measuring the camshaft lobe height

16 Check the bearing housings in the camshaft holder and the cylinder head for score marks and spalling. Any damage is an indication that the bearing has seized on the camshaft and turned inside its housing. Prior to reassembly, check that the outer race is a tight fit in its housing, otherwise use some bearing locking compound to hold it in position.

17 Check the operation of the decompressor cam on the camshaft and the stopper arm (see Step 11). If any of the components are worn or do not move smoothly replace them with new ones.

18 Blow through the oil passages in the rocker arms and shafts with compressed air, if available, to ensure that they are clear.

19 Inspect the face of the rocker arm **(see illustration 10.14a)** and the contact area between the adjuster screw and the valve stem for pits and spalling.

20 Check the rocker shaft for wear. If available, use a micrometer to measure the diameter of the shaft in several places and compare the results with the Specifications at the beginning of this chapter. **Note:** *Any variation in the measurements is an indication of wear on the shaft.*

21 If available, use a small hole gauge to measure the inside diameter of the rocker arm and compare the results with the specifications.

22 If any of the components are worn beyond their service limits, they should be renewed.

23 If no measuring equipment is available, assemble the rocker arm on its shaft – it should be a sliding fit with no discernible freeplay. Renew any components that are worn or damaged.

Installation

24 Installation is the reverse of removal, noting the following:
- Ensure the piston is at TDC **(see illustration 8.4)** on the compression stroke (both valves closed) before you start.
- Lubricate the shafts, bearing surfaces and bearings with clean engine oil before installation.
- Ensure the stopper arm plate for the decompressor cam is correctly installed **(see illustration 10.11b)**.
- Position the rocker shafts so that the holes for the cylinder studs are clear **(see illustration 10.10c and b)**.
- Ensure any dowels are correctly installed in the camshaft holder or cylinder head.
- Tighten the camshaft holder nuts a little at a time in a criss-cross sequence to the torque setting in the Specifications at the beginning of this chapter, not forgetting the smaller cylinder head bolts.
- Check the valve clearances (see Chapter 1).

11 Cylinder head

Note: *On most models, this procedure can be carried out with the engine in the scooter. However, in some cases there is insufficient clearance between the cylinder head and the* frame to allow the head to be removed. If so, support the rear frame, then detach the lower end of the rear shock absorber and displace the shock. Raise the rear wheel until there is enough clearance to remove the head.

Removal

1 Remove the carburettor, intake manifold and exhaust system (see Chapter 3).

2 Remove the fan cowling and engine cowling (see Section 7).

3 Remove the camshaft and rockers (see Section 10).

4 If not already done, remove any small bolts securing the cylinder head **(see illustration)**. Remove the camshaft holder dowels **(see illustration)**.

5 Using a length of bent wire to hold the camchain, lift the cylinder head off the cylinder, feeding the camchain down through the tunnel in the head **(see illustration)**. If the head is stuck, tap around the joint face between the head and the cylinder with a soft-faced mallet to free it. Do not try to lever the head off as this may damage the sealing surfaces. **Note:** *If the cylinder is not secured to the crankcase by additional bolts, avoid lifting it off the crankcase when the head is removed, otherwise a new cylinder base gasket will have to be fitted (see Section 13).*

6 Remove the old cylinder head gasket **(see illustration)**. Note any dowels in the head or cylinder and remove them for safekeeping if they are loose.

7 Secure the camchain to prevent it dropping into the engine.

8 If required, the camchain guide blade can be removed – draw the blade out, noting how the lugs locate in the recess in the top edge of the camchain tunnel **(see illustration)**.

9 Clean all traces of old gasket material from the cylinder head and cylinder with a suitable solvent. Take care not to scratch or gouge the soft aluminium. Be careful not to let any of the gasket material fall into the crankcase, the cylinder bore or the oil passages.

10 Inspect the cylinder head gasket and the mating surfaces on the cylinder head and cylinder for signs of leaks, which could indicate that the head is warped. Refer to Section 12 and check the head mating surface for warpage.

11.4a Small bolts (arrowed) secure the cylinder head

11.4b Remove the camshaft holder dowels

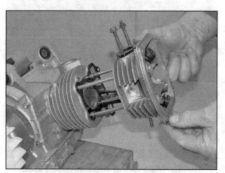

11.5 Lift off the cylinder head . . .

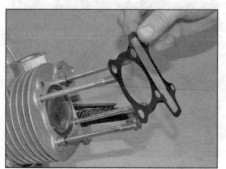

11.6 . . . and remove the head gasket

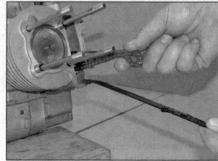

11.8 Draw out the camchain guide blade

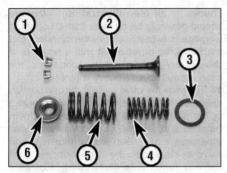

12.1 Valve components

1 *Collets*   4 *Inner valve spring*
2 *Valve*   5 *Outer valve spring*
3 *Spring seat*   6 *Spring retainer*

11 After inspection, discard the old gasket as a new one must be fitted on reassembly

Installation

12 Installation is the reverse of removal, noting the following:

● Lubricate the cylinder bore with clean engine oil.
● Ensure any dowels are correctly installed in the cylinder.
● If removed, install the camchain guide blade (see Step 8).
● Install a new head gasket – never re-use the old gasket.
● Ensure the oil holes in the gasket align with the cylinder.
● Ensure the camchain is correctly located around the crankshaft sprocket.
● Tighten the camshaft holder nuts evenly and a little at a time in a criss-cross sequence to the torque setting in the Specifications at the beginning of this chapter, not forgetting the smaller cylinder head bolts.
● Check the valve clearances (see Chapter 1).

12 Cylinder head and valves

Note: *If a valve spring compressor is available,*

12.3a Ensure the valve spring compressor is correctly located on the valve head . . .

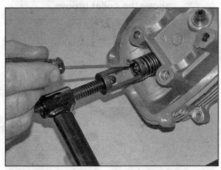

12.3c Remove the collets from the top end of the valve

the home mechanic can remove the valves from the cylinder head, lap the valves and renew the valve stem seals.

Disassembly

1 Before you start, arrange to label and store the valves and their related components so that they can be returned to their original locations without getting mixed up **(see illustration)**.
2 If not already done, clean all traces of old gasket material from the cylinder head with a suitable solvent. Take care not to scratch or gouge the soft aluminium.
3 Compress the valve springs on the first valve with a spring compressor, making sure it is correctly located onto each end of the valve assembly **(see illustrations)**. Do not compress

12.3b . . . and on the spring retainer

12.4 Remove the spring retainer

the springs any more than is absolutely necessary to release the collets, then remove the collets, using either needle-nose pliers, a magnet or a screwdriver with a dab of grease on it **(see illustration)**.
4 Carefully release the valve spring compressor and remove the spring retainer, noting which way up it fits **(see illustration)**.
5 Remove the valve springs **(see illustrations)**. **Note:** *On the engine photographed, the closer wound coils of the springs were fitted next to the cylinder head.*
6 Lift out the spring seat **(see illustration)**. **Note:** *If the spring seat is retained by the valve stem oil seal remove the seat once the seal had been removed.*
7 Turn the head over and withdraw the valve – if it binds in the guide (won't pull through), push it back into the head and deburr the area

12.5a Remove the outer . . .

12.5b . . . and inner valve springs

12.6 Remove the spring seat. Note the valve stem oil seals (arrowed)

12.7a Pull out the valve

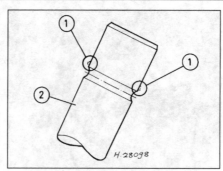

12.7b If the valve stem (2) won't pull through the guide, deburr the area (1) above the collet groove

12.15 Checking the cylinder head for warpage

12.16 Valve seats should be the same width all the way round

around the collet groove with a very fine file **(see illustrations)**.

8 Once the valve has been removed, pull the valve stem oil seal off the top of the valve guide with pliers and discard it as a new one must be used on reassembly.

9 Repeat the procedure for the remaining valve. Remember to keep the parts for each valve together and in order so they can be reinstalled in the correct location.

10 Next, clean the cylinder head with solvent and dry it thoroughly. Compressed air will speed the drying process and ensure that all holes and recessed areas are clean.

11 Clean the valve springs, collets, retainers and spring seats with solvent. Work on the parts from one valve at a time so as not to mix them up.

12 Scrape off any carbon deposits that may have formed on the valve, then use a motorised wire brush to remove deposits from the valve heads and stems. Again, make sure the valves do not get mixed up.

Inspection

13 Inspect the head very carefully for cracks and other damage, especially around the valve seats and the spark plug hole. If cracks are found, a new head will be required.

14 Inspect the threads in the spark plug hole. Damaged or worn threads can be reclaimed using a thread insert (see *Tools and Workshop Tips* in the Reference section). Most small engineering firms offer a service of this kind.

15 Using a precision straight-edge and a feeler gauge, check the head mating surface for warpage. Lay the straight-edge across the surface and measure any gap under it with feeler gauges. Check vertically, horizontally and diagonally across the head, making four

checks in all **(see illustration)**. Warpage should generally be no more than 0.05 mm. If warpage is excessive, have the cylinder head machined flat or replace it with a new one. If there is any doubt about the condition of the head consult an automotive engineer.

16 Examine the valve seats in the combustion chamber. If they are deeply pitted, cracked or burned, it may be possible to have them repaired and re-cut by a specialist engineer, otherwise a new head will be required. The valve seats should be a uniform width all the way round **(see illustration)**. Compare the measured valve seat width with the specification given in the Specifications at the beginning of this chapter.

17 If available, use a micrometer to measure the valve stem diameter in several places along the stem length **(see illustration)**. Compare the results with the figure given in the Specifications at the beginning of this chapter. Using a small hole gauge (see *Tools and Workshoip Tips* in the *Reference* section) measure the internal diameter of the valve guides. If any components are worn beyond the specified service limits they should be renewed.

18 If no measuring equipment is available, insert a known good valve into its guide – it should be a sliding fit with no discernible freeplay. If there is freeplay, the guide is worn. Have the guides checked by a specialist engineer. If new valve guides are available, have them installed by a specialist who will also re-cut the valve seats. Otherwise a new cylinder head will have to be fitted. **Note:** *Carbon build-up inside the guide is an indication of wear.*

19 Inspect the valve face for cracks, pits and burned spots, and check the valve stem and the collet groove area for score marks and cracks **(see illustration)**. Rotate the valve and check for any obvious indication that it is bent. Check the end of the stem for pitting and excessive wear. If any of the above conditions are found, fit a new valve. If the stem end is pitted or worn, also check the contact area of the adjuster screw in the rocker arm.

20 Check the end of each valve spring for wear. Stand the spring upright on a flat surface and check it for bend by placing a square against it **(see illustration)**. Valve springs will

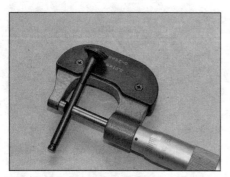

12.17 Measuring the valve stem diameter with a micrometer

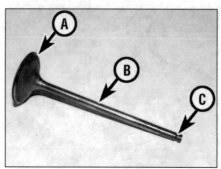

12.19 Check the valve face (A), stem (B) and collet groove (C) for signs of wear or damage

12.20a Check the valve springs for bending

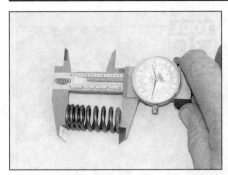

12.20b Measuring the valve spring free length

12.23 Press the stem seal down until it clips into place

Removal

1 Remove the cylinder head and the camchain guide blade (see Section 11).

2 Hold the camchain and lift the cylinder up off the crankcase, supporting the piston as it becomes accessible to prevent it hitting the crankcase opening **(see illustrations)**. If the cylinder is stuck, tap around the joint face between the cylinder and the crankcase with a soft-faced mallet to free it. Don't attempt to free the cylinder by inserting a screwdriver between it and the crankcase – you'll damage the sealing surfaces.

3 Once the cylinder has been removed, stuff a clean rag into the crankcase opening around the piston to prevent anything falling inside.

4 Remove the cylinder base gasket, noting how it fits, then discard it as new one must be fitted on reassembly **(see illustration)**.

5 Note any dowels in the cylinder or crankcase and remove them for safekeeping if they are loose. Note how the camchain locates on the crankshaft sprocket and secure the chain to prevent it dropping into the crankcase **(see illustration 13.20)**.

6 Clean all traces of old gasket material from the cylinder and crankcase with a suitable solvent. Take care not to scratch or gouge the soft aluminium. Be careful not to let any of the gasket material fall into the crankcase.

Inspection

7 Check the cylinder bore carefully for scratches and score marks **(see illustration)**.

8 If available, use a telescoping gauge and micrometer to measure the inside diameter of

take a permanent set (sag) after a long period of use. Measure the free length of each spring **(see illustration)** and compare the results with the specification. If any spring is worn, or the bend is excessive, or the spring has sagged, it must be renewed. **Note:** *It is good practice to fit new springs when the head has been disassembled for valve servicing. Always fit new valve springs as a set.*

21 Check the spring retainers and collets for obvious wear and cracks. Any questionable parts should not be reused, as extensive damage will occur in the event of failure during engine operation.

Reassembly

22 Unless the valve seats have been re-cut, before installing the valves in the head they should be lapped-in lightly to ensure a positive seal between the valves and seats. Follow the procedure described in Chapter 2A, Section 12.

23 Once all the components are ready for assembly, install the valves one at a time. If the spring seat is retained by the valve stem seal, lay the seat in place in the cylinder head, then install a new seal onto the guide. Use an appropriate size deep socket to push the seal over the end of the valve guide until it is felt to clip into place **(see illustration)**. Don't twist or cock the seal sideways, or it will not seal properly against the valve stem. Also, don't remove it again or it will be damaged.

24 Lubricate the valve stem with clean engine oil, then install it into its guide, rotating it slowly to avoid damaging the seal. Check that the valve moves up and down freely in the guide.

25 If not already done, install the spring seat, then install the valve springs as noted on removal (see Step 5). Install the spring retainer, with its shouldered side facing down so that it fits into the top of the springs.

26 Apply a small amount of grease to the collets to hold them in place, then compress the springs and install the collets **(see illustrations 12.3a, b and c)**. Compress the springs only as far as is absolutely necessary to slip the collets into place. Once installed, make certain that the collets are securely locked in their retaining grooves.

27 Repeat the procedure for the remaining valve.

28 Support the cylinder head on blocks so the valves can't contact the workbench top, then very gently tap each of the valve stems with a soft-faced hammer. This will help seat the collets in their grooves.

13 Cylinder

Note: *On most models, this procedure can be carried out with the engine in the scooter. However, in some cases there is insufficient clearance between the cylinder and the frame to allow the cylinder to be drawn off its retaining studs. If so, support the rear frame, then detach the lower end of the rear shock absorber and displace the shock. Raise the rear wheel until there is enough clearance to remove the cylinder.*

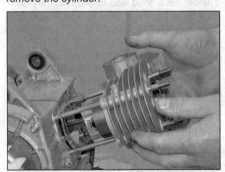

13.2a Lift the cylinder . . .

13.2b . . . and support the piston

13.4 Discard the old cylinder base gasket

13.7 Inspect the cylinder bore for scratches and score marks

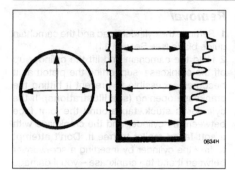

13.8a Measure the cylinder bore in the directions shown . . .

13.8b . . . using a telescoping gauge

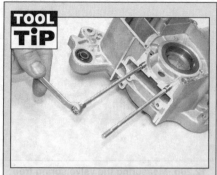

To tighten a stud without damaging it, first lock two nuts together on the upper end of the stud. Now use a ring spanner on the upper nut to tighten the stud.

the cylinder bore to assess the amount of wear, taper and ovality (see *Tools and Workshop Tips* in the *Reference* section). Measure near the top (but below the level of the top piston ring at top dead centre), centre and bottom (but above the level of the bottom ring with the piston at bottom dead centre) of the bore both parallel to and across the crankshaft axis **(see illustrations)**.

9 Calculate any differences between the measurements to determine any taper or ovality in the bore. Where dimensions are given for bore diameter in the Specifications at the beginning of this chapter, compare the results with the figure given. If the cylinder bore is worn beyond its service limit, a new one should be fitted.

10 A cylinder bore that has worn oval will reduce the efficiency of the piston rings to achieve a seal, resulting in loss of compression and increased oil consumption.

11 If no service data is available, measure an unworn part of the cylinder bore (below the level of the bottom ring with the piston at the bottom of its stroke) and compare the result to the previous measurements to determine overall wear. Alternatively, calculate the piston-to-bore clearance to determine whether the cylinder is useable (see Section 14), or check for a lip around the (unworn) top edge of the cylinder bore as a rough indication of wear.

12 If the bore is tapered, oval, or worn excessively, badly scratched, scuffed or scored, the cylinder and piston will have to be renewed as a set.

13 If there is any doubt about the condition of the cylinder, consult a specialist engineer.

14 Check that all the cylinder studs are tight in the crankcase halves. If any are loose, remove them (see **Tool Tip**) and clean their threads. Apply a suitable permanent thread locking compound, then screw them back into the crankcase securely.

Installation

15 Remove any rag from the crankcase opening. Ensure any dowels are correctly installed in the crankcase, then lay the new base gasket in place on the crankcase making sure it is the correct way round.

16 Check that the piston ring end gaps are positioned as described in Section 15.

17 If required, install a piston ring clamp onto the piston to ease its entry into the bore as the cylinder is lowered. This is not essential if the cylinder has a good lead-in enabling the piston rings to be hand-fed into the bore. If possible, have an assistant support the cylinder while this is done.

18 Lubricate the cylinder bore, piston and piston rings, and the connecting rod big- and small-ends, with the clean engine oil, then lower the cylinder down until the piston crown fits into the bore **(see illustration 13.2b)**.

19 Gently push down on the cylinder, making sure the piston enters the bore squarely and does not get cocked sideways. If a piston ring clamp is not being used, carefully compress and feed each ring into the bore as the cylinder is lowered **(see illustration)**. If necessary, use a soft mallet to gently tap the cylinder down,

but do not use force if it appears to be stuck as the piston and/or rings will be damaged. If a clamp is used, remove it once the piston is in the bore.

20 Once the piston is correctly installed in the cylinder, press the cylinder down onto the base gasket. Check that the camchain is still located around the crankshaft sprocket **(see illustration)**.

21 Install the camchain guide blade, then install the cylinder head (see Section 11).

14 Piston

Note: *This procedure can be carried out with the engine in the scooter.*

Removal

1 Remove the cylinder and stuff a clean rag into the crankcase opening around the piston to prevent anything falling inside (see Section 13).

2 The top of the piston should be marked with an arrow or lettering (e.g. IN on the intake side, nearest the carburettor) to show which way round it should be fitted **(see illustration)**. If no mark is visible, scratch one lightly on the top of the piston. Note that the manufacturer's mark may not be visible until the carbon

13.19 Feed each ring into the bore carefully as the cylinder is lowered

13.20 Check position of the camchain around the crankshaft sprocket (arrowed)

14.2 Note IN lettering (arrowed) on piston crown

deposits have been scraped off and the piston cleaned.

3 Carefully prise out the circlip on one side of the piston using needle-nose pliers or a small flat-bladed screwdriver inserted into the notch **(see illustration)**. Remove any burring around the circlip groove with a very fine file or penknife blade, then push the piston pin out from the other side and remove the piston from the connecting rod **(see illustration)**. Use a socket extension to push the piston pin out if required. Remove the other circlip and discard them both as new ones must be used on reassembly.

> **HAYNES HiNT**
> *To prevent the circlip from flying away or from dropping into the crankcase, pass a rod or screwdriver with a greater diameter than the gap between the circlip ends, through the piston pin. This will trap the circlip if it springs out.*

> **HAYNES HiNT**
> *If the piston pin is a tight fit in the piston bosses, heat the piston gently with a hot air gun – this will expand the alloy piston sufficiently to release its grip on the pin.*

4 Before the inspection process can be carried out, the piston rings must be removed and the piston must be cleaned. **Note:** *If the cylinder is being renewed, piston inspection can be overlooked as a new one will be fitted.*

5 If required, the piston rings can be removed by hand; using your thumbs, ease the ends of each ring apart and carefully lift it off the piston, taking care not to expand it any more than is necessary **(see illustration)**. Do not nick or gouge the piston in the process. Alternatively, use an old feeler gauge blade to ease the rings off the piston **(see illustration)**.

6 Note which way up each ring fits and in which groove as they must be installed in their original positions if being re-used. The upper surface of each ring should be marked at one end. **Note:** *On the engine photographed, the top ring was marked ATG and the second ring was marked A.* Most pistons are fitted with a three-piece third (oil control) ring; there will be an upper and lower side rail and a central rail spacer (see Section 15). **Note:** *It is good practice to renew the piston rings when an engine is being overhauled. Ensure that the piston and bore are serviceable before purchasing new rings.*

7 Clean all traces of carbon from the top of the piston. A hand-held wire brush or a piece of fine emery cloth can be used once most of the deposits have been scraped away. Do not, under any circumstances, use a wire brush mounted in a drill motor; the piston material is soft and is easily damaged.

8 Use a piston ring groove cleaning tool to remove any carbon deposits from the ring grooves. If a tool is not available, a piece broken off an old ring will do the job. Be very careful to remove only the carbon deposits. Do not remove any metal and do not nick or gouge the sides of the ring grooves.

9 Once the carbon has been removed, clean the piston with a suitable solvent and dry it thoroughly. If the identification previously marked on the piston is cleaned off, be sure to re-mark it correctly.

Inspection

10 Inspect the piston for cracks around the skirt, at the pin bosses and at the ring lands **(see illustration)**. Check that the circlip grooves are not damaged. Normal piston wear appears as even, vertical wear on the thrust surfaces of the skirt and slight looseness of the top ring in its groove. If the skirt is scored or scuffed, the engine may have been suffering from overheating and/or abnormal combustion, which caused excessively high operating temperatures.

11 A hole in the top of the piston, in one extreme, or burned areas around the edge of the piston crown, indicate that pre-ignition or knocking under load have occurred. If you find evidence of any problems the cause must be corrected or the damage will occur again. Refer to Chapter 3 for carburation checks and Chapter 4 for ignition checks.

12 Check the piston-to-bore clearance by measuring the cylinder bore (see Section 13) and the piston diameter. Measure the piston approximately 9 mm up from the bottom edge of the skirt and at 90° to the piston pin axis **(see illustration)**. **Note:** *The precise point of measurement differs between manufacturers and engines, but the aim is to measure the piston in an area where it is worn.* Subtract the piston diameter from the bore diameter to

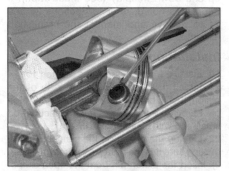

14.3a Removing the circlip with a small screwdriver

14.3b Push out the piston pin to free the piston

14.5a Remove the piston rings carefully

14.5b Using a thin blade to remove the piston rings

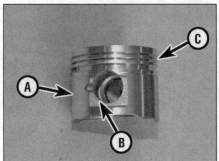

14.10 Piston skirt (A), pin boss (B) and ring lands (C)

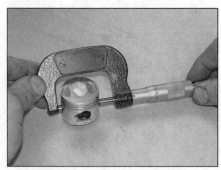

14.12 Measuring the piston diameter with a micrometer

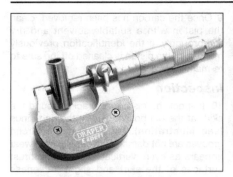

14.14 Measuring the diameter of the piston pin

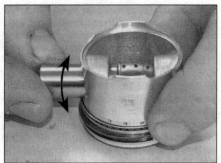

14.15 Checking for freeplay between the piston and the piston pin

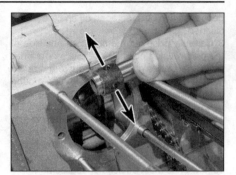

14.16 Checking for freeplay between the small-end and the piston pin

obtain the clearance; piston-to-bore figures are given in the Specifications at the beginning of this chapter.

13 If the piston-to-bore clearance is too large, check the specifications to determine whether it is the bore or piston that is worn the most. If the bore is good, install a new piston and set of rings.

14 Use a micrometer to measure the piston pin in the middle, where it runs in the small-end bearing, and at each end where it runs in the piston **(see illustration)**. Compare the result with the figure in the Specifications at the beginning of this chapter.. If there is any difference in the measurements the pin is worn and must be renewed.

15 If the piston pin is good, lubricate it with clean engine oil, then insert it into the piston and check for any freeplay between the two **(see illustration)**. There should be no freeplay.

16 A worn small-end will produce a metallic rattle, most audible when the engine is under load, and increasing as engine speed rises. This should not be confused with big-end bearing wear, which produces a pronounced knocking noise. Lubricate the piston pin with clean engine oil, then slide it into the small-end and check for freeplay **(see illustration)**. There should only be slightly discernible freeplay between the piston pin and the connecting rod.

17 If there is freeplay, measure the internal diameter of the connecting rod small-end **(see illustration)**. Take several measurements and compare the result with the figure in the Specifications at the beginning of this chapter. If the small-end is worn beyond the service limit a new crankshaft assembly will have to be fitted (see Section 21). **Note:** *In some cases, a new connecting rod and bearings may be available, but fitting it is a specialist task which*

should be left to an automotive engineer. If a new rod is fitted, the big-end bearing should be renewed at the same time.

18 Measure the piston ring-to-groove clearance by fitting each ring in its groove and slipping a feeler gauge in beside it **(see illustration)**. Make sure you have the correct ring for the groove (see Step 6). Check the clearance at three or four locations around the groove. If the clearance is greater than specified, renew both the piston and rings as a set. If new rings are being used, measure the clearance using the new rings. If the clearance is greater than that specified, the piston is worn and must be renewed.

19 With the piston removed, the general condition of the big-end bearing can be assessed. Hold the alternator to prevent the crankshaft from turning, then push-and-pull on the connecting rod, checking for any up-and-down freeplay **(see illustration)**. If freeplay is noted, refer to Sections 20 and 21 to remove and inspect the crankshaft assembly.

Installation

20 Install the piston rings (see Section 15).

21 Install a new circlip in one side of the piston, then lubricate the piston pin, the piston pin bore in the piston and the connecting-rod small-end with clean engine oil.

22 Line up the piston on the connecting rod, making sure it is the right way round (see Step 2). Insert the piston pin from the open side of the piston and secure it with the other new circlip. When installing the circlips, compress them only just enough to fit them in the piston, and make sure they are properly seated in their grooves with the open end away from the removal notch **(see illustration)**.

23 Install the cylinder (see Section 13).

15 Piston rings

1 New piston rings should be fitted whenever an engine is being overhauled **(see illustration)**. It is important that you get new rings of the correct size for your piston so ensure that any information relating to

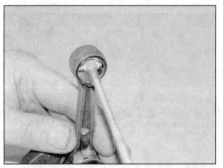

14.17 Measuring the internal diameter of the connecting rod small-end

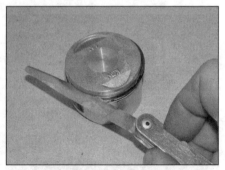

14.18 Measuring piston ring-to-groove clearance

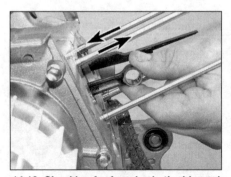

14.19 Checking for freeplay in the big-end bearing

14.22 Location of the circlip removal notch

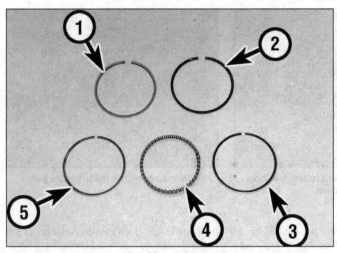

15.1 Piston ring set

1 *Top (compression) ring*
2 *Second (compression) ring*
3 *Upper side rail*
4 *Rail spacer*
5 *Lower side rail*

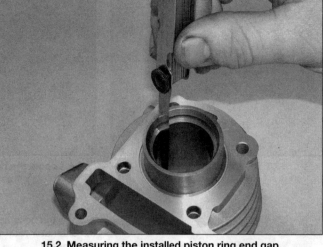

15.2 Measuring the installed piston ring end gap

piston size and size coding is available when purchasing new parts.

2 Before fitting the new rings onto the piston, the installed ring end gaps must be checked. Insert the top ring into the bottom of the cylinder bore and square it up by pushing it in with the top of the piston. The ring should be about 15 to 20 mm from the bottom edge of the cylinder. Measure the ring end gap using feeler gauges, slipping the gauge between the ends of the ring **(see illustration)**. Ring end gaps are given in the Specifications at the beginning of this chapter.

3 If the gap is larger than specified it is likely the cylinder bore is worn. If the gap is too small the ring ends may come into contact with each other during engine operation, causing serious damage.

4 Repeat the procedure for the other two rings. If the piston is fitted with a three-piece third (oil control) ring, check the end gap on the upper and lower side rails only. The ends of the central rail spacer should contact each other when it is fitted on the piston.

5 Once the ring end gaps have been checked and found to be within specification, the rings can be installed on the piston. Do not expand the rings any more than is necessary to slide them into place. **Note:** *A ring installation tool can be used on the two compression rings, and on a one-piece oil control ring, if desired, but not on the side rails of a three-piece oil control ring.*

6 The oil control ring (lowest on the piston) is installed first. If a three-piece ring is used, fit the rail spacer into the groove **(see illustration)**, then install the lower side rail as follows. Place one end of the side rail into the groove between the spacer and the lower ring land. Hold it firmly in place, then slide a thin blade around the piston while pushing the rail into the groove **(see illustration)**.

7 Install the upper side rail the same way.

15.6a Fit the oil control ring spacer first . . .

15.6b . . . then the lower side rail using a thin blade

Ensure the ends of the spacer touch but do not overlap, then check that both side rails turn smoothly in the ring groove.

8 Next install the second compression ring, noting that there is usually a marking or letter near the gap to denote the upper surface of the ring **(see illustration)**. Finally install the top ring into its groove.

9 Once the rings are correctly installed, check they move freely without snagging, then stagger their end gaps as shown before fitting the piston into the cylinder **(see illustration)**.

15.8 Install the compression rings using a thin blade

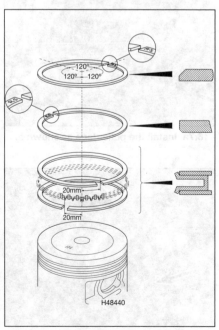

15.9 Position the piston ring end gaps as shown

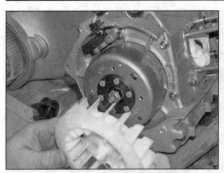

16.3 Remove the cooling fan

16.4 Locate the holding tool in the holes as shown

16.5 Loosen the rotor centre nut

16 Alternator

Note: *This procedure can be carried out with the engine in the scooter. If the engine has been removed, ignore the steps that do not apply.*

Removal

1 Remove the body panels as necessary to access the alternator on the right-hand side of the engine (see Chapter 8). If required, remove the exhaust system (see Chapter 3).

2 The alternator is located behind the fan cowling. Follow the procedure in Section 7 to remove the cowling.

3 Undo the bolts securing the cooling fan to the alternator rotor and remove the fan **(see illustration)**.

4 To remove the rotor centre nut it is necessary to stop the rotor from turning. Some manufacturers produce a service tool for this purpose which engages in the holes in the rotor face – a similar home-made tool can be used (see *Tool Tip*, Chapter 2A, Section16) **(see illustration)** or you can obtain an aftermarket version. **Note:** *Take great care not to damage the internal coils of the alternator when locating any tools through the rotor.*

5 With the rotor securely held, loosen the centre nut **(see illustration)**.

6 Alternatively, the alternator rotor can be held with a strap wrench. If necessary, undo

the bolts securing the ignition pulse generator coil and displace it to avoid damaging it when using the strap wrench.

7 To remove the rotor from the taper on the crankshaft it is necessary to use a puller. Engage the puller legs either in the slots in the rotor or thread them into the threaded holes in the rotor, then tighten the centre bolt exerting steady pressure to draw the rotor off the taper **(see illustrations)**. **Note:** *To avoid damaging the threaded end of the crankshaft, either leave the centre nut on the shaft with just enough clearance to allow the rotor to be dislodged, or position a soft metal spacer between the end of the shaft and the puller centre bolt.*

8 Remove the centre nut, washer and alternator rotor **(see illustration)**.

9 If it is loose, remove the Woodruff key from the shaft for safekeeping, noting how it fits **(see illustration)**.

10 The alternator stator coils and ignition pulse generator coil are wired together and have to be removed as an assembly. If not already done, trace the wiring back from the alternator and pulse generator and disconnect it at the connectors. Free the wiring from any clips or guides and feed it through to the alternator.

11 Undo the two long crankcase bolts securing the alternator wiring guide and remove the guide **(see illustration)**. Undo the bolts securing the pulse generator coil, then undo the bolts securing the alternator stator

16.7a Install the puller legs as shown . . .

16.7b . . . then install the puller and centre bolt

16.8 Note location of washer (arrowed) behind centre nut

16.9 Note location of Woodruff key

16.11a Long bolts secure wiring guide

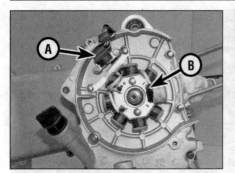

16.11b Pulse generator coil (A) and alternator stator (B)

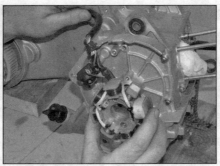

16.11c Lift the alternator assembly off

17.5 Undo the cover screws

and lift the assembly off **(see illustrations)**. Note how the wiring seal fits in the cut-out in the top of the engine casing.

Installation

12 Installation is the reverse of removal, noting the following:

- Ensure the wiring is correctly routed before installing the stator and pulse generator.
- Make sure that no metal objects have attached themselves to the magnets on the inside of the rotor.
- Clean the tapered end of the crankshaft and the corresponding mating surface on the inside of the rotor with a suitable solvent.
- Fit the Woodruff key into the crankshaft, align the slot in the centre of the rotor with the key, then install the rotor.
- Tighten the alternator centre nut to the torque setting specified in the Specifications at the beginning of this chapter.
- Secure the wiring with any clips or ties.
- Ensure that the fan cowling is correctly installed (see Section 7).

17 Right-hand crankcase cover

Note: *This procedure can be carried out with the engine in the scooter.*

Removal

1 Drain the engine oil (see Chapter 1, Section 18).
2 Follow the procedure in Section 16 and remove the alternator.
3 An oil seal is fitted in the cover where the crankshaft passes through it **(see illustration 17.6c)**. Check around the seal for signs of oil leakage – if the seal has been leaking a new one must be fitted once the cover has been removed. **Note:** *It is good practice to renew the oil seal whenever the cover is removed.*
4 If the exhaust system support bracket is bolted to the cover, undo the bracket bolts and lift it off.
5 Position a drain tray underneath the engine to catch any residual oil when the cover is removed, then undo the cover screws – noting their locations **(see illustrations)**.

6 Draw the cover off. If it is stuck, tap around the joint face and the pry-points between the cover and the crankcase with a soft-faced mallet to free it **(see illustrations)**. Do not try to lever the cover off as this may damage the sealing surfaces. Note the location of the right-hand crankshaft oil seal **(see illustration)**.
7 Remove the gasket and discard it as a new one must be used. Note any dowels in the cover or crankcase and remove them for safekeeping if they are loose.
8 Clean the mating surfaces of the cover and the crankcase with a suitable solvent to remove any traces of old gasket or sealant. Take care not to scratch or gouge the soft aluminium.
9 To renew the oil seal, support the cover on the work surface and drive the seal out from the alternator side with a suitably-sized socket **(see illustration)**. Note which way

Make a cardboard template of the crankcase and punch a hole for each screw location. This will ensure that they are all installed correctly on reassembly – this is important as some bolts may be of different lengths.

17.6a Tap around the joint face . . .

17.6b . . . to loosen the cover

17.6c Location of the right-hand crankshaft oil seal

17.9a Drive out the oil seal with a suitable socket

17.9b Installed position of the crankshaft oil seal

17.10 Fit the gasket over the dowels (arrowed)

round the seal is fitted. Ensure that the seal housing is clean, then lubricate the new seal with a smear of engine oil and press it all the way into the housing **(see illustration)**.

Installation

10 If removed, fit the dowels, then fit a new cover gasket, making sure it locates correctly onto the dowels **(see illustration)**. If necessary, use a dab of grease to hold the gasket in position.

11 Lubricate the inside of the oil seal with engine oil, then install the cover taking care not to damage the seal on the crankshaft

18.2 Check the rotation of the starter driven gear (arrowed)

18.3 Remove the starter idler gear

threads. Make sure that the gasket stays in place.

12 Install the cover bolts, making sure they are in the correct locations, then tighten the bolts evenly and in a criss-cross sequence.

13 Install the remaining components in the reverse order of removal.

14 Fill the engine with the correct type and quantity of oil (see Chapter 1 and *Pre-ride checks*)

18 Starter idler gear and starter clutch

Note: *This procedure can be carried out with the engine in the scooter.*

Check

1 Remove the alternator (see Section 16) and the right-hand crankcase cover (see Section 17).

2 The operation of the starter clutch can be checked while it is in place. The starter driven gear should rotate freely in the *opposite* direction to crankshaft rotation (anticlockwise), but lock when rotated clockwise **(see illustration)**. If not, the starter clutch is faulty and should be removed for inspection.

18.4 Use a peg spanner to undo the starter clutch nut

Removal

3 Pull out the idler gear shaft and lift out the idler gear **(see illustration)**. Note how the smaller pinion engages with the starter driven gear and the larger pinion engages with the teeth on the starter motor shaft.

4 A peg spanner is required to undo the starter clutch retaining nut **(see illustration)**. If the correct tool is not available, one can be made from a suitable length of steel tube **(see *Tool Tip*)**.

5 The crankshaft must be prevented from turning while the retaining nut is being loosened. If the cylinder has been removed, temporarily fit the piston pin into the connecting rod small-end, then pass a rod through the centre of the pin and rest the ends of the rod on wooden blocks placed across

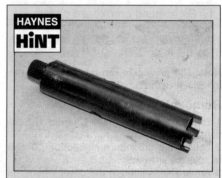

HAYNES HiNT

A peg spanner can be made by cutting castellations into one end of a length of thick-walled steel tube – measure the width and depth of the slots in the retaining nut to determine the size of the castellations. The tube should be 75 mm long to fit over the crankshaft and 31 mm diameter. Weld a heavy washer and large nut onto the opposite end of the tube so that the retaining nut can be tightened to the correct torque on installation.

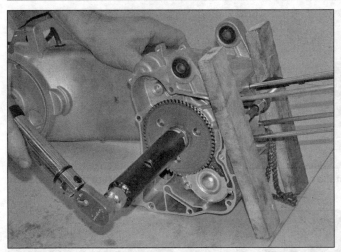

18.5a Holding the crankshaft with a rod passed through the small-end

18.5b Hold the variator to prevent the crankshaft turning

the top of the crankcase **(see illustration)**. Alternatively, remove the drive belt cover and hold the variator with a tool located in the holes provided in the pulley **(see illustration)**. Ensure the tool is fully located on the variator before commencing the procedure. Do not try to hold the crankshaft with a spanner on the variator centre nut – the starter clutch nut is extremely tight and has a left-hand thread, attempting to loosen it will simply tighten the variator nut.

6 To undo the starter clutch retaining nut turn it clockwise **(see illustration)**.

7 Remove the nut and washer, then draw the driven gear and starter clutch assembly off the crankshaft **(see illustrations)**.

8 If it is loose, remove the Woodruff key from the shaft for safekeeping, noting how it fits **(see illustration)**.

Inspection

9 Inspect both sets of teeth on the idler gear and renew it if any are chipped or worn **(see illustration)**. **Note:** *If the teeth on the*

18.6 Turn the nut clockwise to undo

18.7a Remove the nut and washer . . .

18.7b . . . and the driven gear and starter clutch assembly

18.8 Location of the starter clutch Woodruff key

18.9 Inspect the idler gear and shaft for wear

18.11a Separate the driven gear from the starter clutch . . .

18.11b . . . and lift out the needle bearing

18.12 Measure the OD of the starter gear hub

18.13a Lift out the clutch centre

18.13b Hold back the plungers to remove the sprags . . .

18.13c . . . then remove the plungers and springs

*larger pinion are worn or damaged, inspect the teeth on the starter motor shaft also (see Chapter 9).*Check the idler shaft and bearing surfaces for signs of wear or damage, and renew it if necessary.

10 Hold the centre of the starter clutch assembly and check that the driven gear rotates freely in one direction and locks in the other direction. If it doesn't, the ring of sprags in the one-way mechanism may be jammed. Wash the assembly in suitable solvent and dry it with compressed air, if available. Lubricate the mechanism with clean engine oil and check it again. If the starter clutch still does not operate correctly, it can be disassembled and the components inspected (see Step 13) – check first to see if individual items are available.

11 Inspect the teeth of the starter driven gear for wear and damage. Lift the gear out from the starter clutch and remove the needle bearing **(see illustrations)**. Inspect the bearing and

the bearing races in the starter clutch and the starter gear for wear and pitting and renew the assembly if necessary.

12 Inspect the outside surface of the driven gear hub for wear. Measure the outside diameter of the hub and compare the result with the figure in the Specifications at the beginning of this chapter **(see illustration)**. If wear is uneven or beyond the service limit a new starter clutch assembly should be fitted.

13 If required, undo the starter clutch assembly screws, then turn the assembly over and lift out the centre **(see illustration)**. Hold the spring-loaded plungers in place and lift out the clutch sprags, then remove the plungers and springs, noting how they fit **(see illustration)**. Inspect the components carefully for wear and damage, then if everything is good, reassemble the clutch. Clean the threads of the assembly screws and apply a suitable non-permanent thread-locking compound, then tighten the screws to the

specified torque setting in the Specifications at the beginning of this chapter..

Installation

14 Installation is the reverse of removal, noting the following:

- Lubricate the starter clutch mechanism with clean engine oil.
- Fit the Woodruff key into its slot in the shaft.
- Ensure that the starter clutch assembly is pressed all the way onto the crankshaft.
- Install the washer and tighten the retaining nut to the torque setting in the Specifications at the beginning of this chapter. Use the same method to hold the crankshaft as on disassembly and turn the nut anti-clockwise.
- Ensure the idler gear engages with the pinion on the starter motor shaft. Lubricate the idler gear shaft.

19 Oil pump

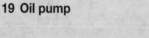

Note: *This procedure can be carried out with the engine in the scooter.*

Removal

1 Remove the alternator (see Section 16) and the right-hand crankcase cover (see Section 17).

2 Remove the starter clutch (see Section 18).

3 Undo the bolts securing the pump driven sprocket cover and remove the cover **(see illustrations)**.

19.3a Undo the bolts (arrowed) . . .

19.3b . . . and remove the sprocket cover

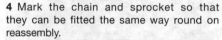

19.6 Remove the pump driven sprocket and chain

19.7a Undo the mounting bolts . . .

19.7b . . . and lift out the oil pump

4 Mark the chain and sprocket so that they can be fitted the same way round on reassembly.

5 To prevent the oil pump from turning while the sprocket nut is being loosened, use the same method to hold the crankshaft as when undoing the starter clutch retaining nut (see Section 18).

6 Undo the nut, then lift the driven sprocket and chain off the pump driveshaft and disengage the chain from the crankshaft sprocket **(see illustration)**. Note how the hole in the centre of the driven sprocket aligns with the flat on the driveshaft.

7 Note how the pump is located in the crankcase with the arrow on the outside face of the pump body pointing UP. Undo the bolts and withdraw the pump from the engine **(see illustrations)**.

Inspection

8 Check the pump body for obvious signs of damage especially around the mounting bolt holes. Turn the pump driveshaft by hand and check that the pump rotates smoothly.

9 If required, the pump can be disassembled for cleaning and inspection.

10 Pull out the pump shaft, then undo the screw securing the cover to the pump body and remove cover **(see illustrations)**. Note the location of the dowel between the cover and the body.

11 Note any reference marks on the pump rotors; even if the rotors are not marked, it is essential that they are reassembled the correct way round. Lift out the inner and outer rotors, clean the components with a suitable solvent and dry them with compressed air, if available. Inspect the pump body, rotors and shaft for scoring and wear. If any damage, scoring, uneven or excessive wear is evident, renew the pump.

12 If the pump appears to be in good condition, reassemble the inner and outer rotors. Using feeler gauges, measure the clearance between the pump body and the outer rotor, and the inner rotor and outer rotor **(see illustrations)**. Compare the results with the figures in the Specifications at the beginning of this chapter. Lay a straight-edge across the pump body and measure the

rotor endfloat **(see illustration)**. If any of the measurements are beyond the specified service limits a new pump must be fitted.

13 Fit the cover and tighten the screw lightly, then install the pump shaft to align the components. Tighten the cover screw fully.

19.10a Pull out the shaft . . .

19.10c . . . and lift off the cover. Note dowel (arrowed)

19.12b . . . and the inner and outer rotors

Lubricate the pump with clean engine oil and check that the shaft and rotors turn smoothly and freely.

14 Inspect the pump drive chain and sprockets for wear or damage, and renew them as a set if necessary. Check for wear on

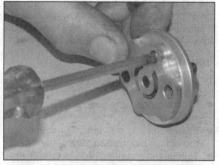

19.10b . . . then undo the cover screw . . .

19.12a Measure the clearance between the pump body and outer rotor . . .

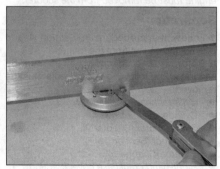

19.12c Measuring the pump rotor endfloat

20.5 Unscrew the remaining crankcase bolts

20.6 Ease off the right-hand crankcase half

the sides and tips of the sprocket teeth and for chipped or hooked teeth. Lay the chain on a flat surface and check for play between the links – if there is any, renew the chain.

Installation

15 Installation is the reverse of removal, noting the following:
- Fill the pump with clean engine oil before installation.
- Ensure the pump is fitted the correct way round **(see illustration 19.7b)**.
- Tighten the mounting bolts to the specified torque in the Specifications at the beginning of this chapter..
- Ensure the chain and sprocket are fitted the correct way round.
- Tighten the pump sprocket nut to the specified torque in the Specifications at the beginning of this chapter..
- Fill the engine with the correct type and quantity of oil (see Chapter 1 and *Pre-ride checks*)

20 Crankcase halves

Note: *To separate the crankcase halves, the engine must be removed from the scooter.*

Separation

1 Follow the procedure in Section 4 and remove the engine from the frame.
2 Before the crankcase halves can be separated the following components must be removed:
- *Cylinder head (Section 11)*
- *Cylinder (Section 13)*
- *Starter motor (Chapter 9)*
- *Alternator (Section 16)*
- *Variator (Chapter 5)*
- *Right-hand crankcase cover (Section 17)*
- *Starter clutch (Chapter 18)*
- *Oil pump (Section 19)*

3 Tape some rag around the connecting rod to prevent it knocking against the cases. Although not essential, it is advisable to remove the piston to avoid damage during this procedure.
4 The kickstart mechanism driven gear is located on the left-hand side of the crankshaft – ensure that it is removed before attempting to separate the crankcase halves (see Chapter 5).
5 The long bolts securing the alternator wiring guide and the right-hand crankcase cover also hold the crankcase halves together. Identify the remaining crankcase bolts and unscrew them, noting where they fit **(see illustration)**.
Note: *Ensure that all the crankcase bolts have been removed before attempting to separate the cases.*
6 Ease the right-hand crankcase half off the left-hand half being prepared to catch any residual oil **(see illustration)**. If the crankcase halves do not separate easily, first ensure all fasteners have been removed. Next, apply heat to the right-hand main bearing housing with a hot air gun and try lifting the right-hand half off again.
Caution: Do not try to separate the halves by levering against the mating surfaces as they are easily scored and will not seal correctly afterwards. Do not strike the ends of the crankshaft with a hammer as

damage to the end threads or the shaft itself will result.
7 If the crankcase is an extremely tight fit on the crankshaft, follow the procedure in Chapter 2A, Section 20, and use a puller arrangement to separate the crankcase halves.
8 Ensure the camchain is clear of the sprocket on the left-hand side of the crankshaft and pull the crankshaft assembly out of the left-hand crankcase half **(see illustrations)**. Apply heat to the main bearing housing if required.
9 If the crankshaft is an extremely tight fit in the crankcase, follow the procedure in Chapter 2A, Section 20, to press the crankshaft out.
10 Note that the main bearings will remain in place on the crankshaft assembly (see Section 21).
11 Remove the camchain. Undo the pivot bolt securing the camchain tensioner blade and lift the blade out **(see illustration 9.10)**. Note which way round the blade is fitted.
12 Remove the gasket and discard it as a new one must be used. Remove any dowels from either crankcase half for safekeeping if they are loose.
13 Clean the mating surfaces of the crankcase halves with a suitable solvent to remove any traces of old gasket or sealant. Take care not to scratch or gouge the soft aluminium.

20.8a Remove the crankshaft assembly . . .

20.8b . . . and disengage the camchain (arrowed) from the crankshaft

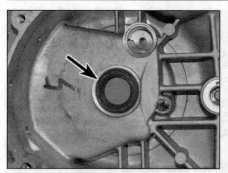

20.14 Installed position of the left-hand crankshaft oil seal

20.16 Clean the oil pump housing and oil passages carefully

20.20a Front left-hand engine mounting bush

14 Note the position of the left-hand crankshaft oil seal and note which way round the seal is fitted **(see illustration)**. Lever the seal out carefully with a large, flat-bladed screwdriver, taking care not to damage the crankcase (see *Tools and Workshop Tips* in the *Reference* section). Discard the seal as a new one must be fitted on reassembly. **Note:** *The right-hand crankshaft oil seal is fitted in the right-hand crankcase cover (see Section 17).*

15 If required, remove the transmission assembly from the left-hand crankcase half (see Chapter 5).

Inspection

16 Wash the cases in a suitable solvent and dry them with compressed air, if available. Pay particular attention to ensuring that the internal oil passages and the oil pump housing are clear **(see illustration)**.

17 Small cracks or holes in aluminium castings can be repaired with an epoxy resin adhesive as a temporary measure. Permanent repairs can be effected by specialist welding, or using one of the low temperature home welding kits such as Lumiweld. On some engines, the crankcase halves can be renewed individually, on others the two halves are only available together as a matching set.

18 Damaged threads can be economically reclaimed by using a thread insert. Most small engineering firms offer a service of this kind. Sheared screws can usually be removed with screw extractors. Refer to *Tools and*

Workshop Tips in the *Reference* section for further details.

19 Always wash the crankcases thoroughly after any repair work to ensure no dirt or metal swarf is trapped inside when the engine is rebuilt.

20 Inspect the front and rear engine mounting bushes **(see illustrations)**. If they show signs of deterioration, renew both bushes at the same time. To remove a bush, first note its position in the casing. Heat the casing with a hot air gun, then support the casing and drive the bush out with a hammer and a suitably sized socket. Alternatively, use two suitably sized sockets to press the bush out in the jaws of a vice. Clean the bush housing with steel wool to remove any corrosion, then reheat the casing and fit the new bush. **Note:** *Always support the casing when removing or fitting bushes to avoid breaking the casing.*

21 Inspect the main bearing housings **(see illustration)**. If a bearing outer race has spun in its housing, the inside of the housing will be damaged. A bearing locking compound can be used to fix the outer race in place on reassembly if the damage is not too severe. **Note:** *If a bearing has spun in its housing, the bearing itself is likely to be damaged – see Section 21.*

22 Inspect the crankshaft assembly and bearings (see Section 21).

Joining

23 Follow the procedure in Section 17 to fit a new crankshaft oil seal into the left-hand

crankcase half and the right-hand crankcase cover using a seal driver or socket . Ensure the seals are fitted the right way round and that they enter the cases squarely.

24 Lubricate the left-hand crankshaft seal and main bearing with clean engine oil and tape some rag around the connecting rod to prevent it knocking against the cases.

25 Support the left-hand crankcase half securely in an upright position on the work surface. If required, have an assistant support the crankcase.

26 Heat the bearing housing in the crankcase with a hot air gun. **Note:** *Avoid applying direct heat onto the crankshaft oil seal.* If required, a freeze spray can be used on the main bearing to aid installation.

27 Support the camchain in the camchain tunnel and insert the left-hand end of the crankshaft through the chain and the oil seal **(see illustration)**. Take care to avoid damaging the seal.

28 Ensure that the main bearing is aligned with the bearing housing and that the connecting rod is aligned with the crankcase mouth, then press the crankshaft assembly in fully so that the main bearing goes all the way into its housing. If the bearing does not seat fully, apply more heat around the bearing housing while applying steady pressure to the crankshaft assembly.

29 Check that the camchain is correctly located around the crankshaft sprocket and secure it in position with wire or a cable-tie to avoid it becoming jammed inside the

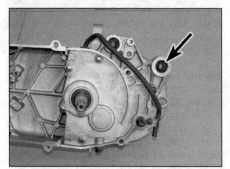

20.20b Rear left-hand engine mounting bush

20.21 Right-hand main bearing housing. Note oil passage (arrowed)

20.27 Installing the crankshaft in the left-hand casing

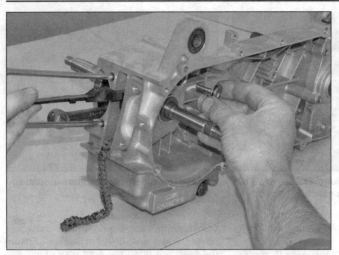

20.29 Installing the camchain tensioner blade

20.30 Fit the new gasket over the dowels (arrowed)

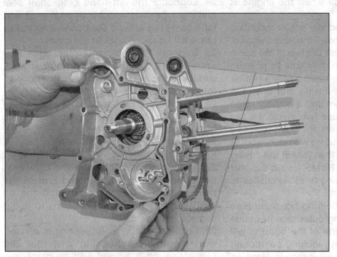

20.33 Align the crankcase halves carefully

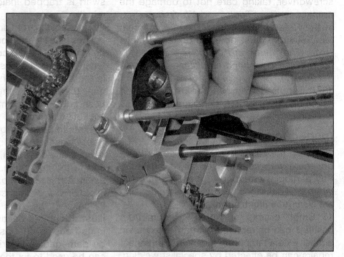

20.37 Trim off the excess crankcase gasket

crankcase. Install the camchain tensioner blade (see Section 9) **(see illustration)**.

30 If necessary, allow the case to cool, then wipe the mating surfaces of both crankcase halves with a rag soaked in suitable solvent. Fit the dowels and install the new crankcase gasket on the mating surface of the left-hand case **(see illustration)**. If necessary, use a dab of grease to hold the gasket in position. If the gasket bridges the crankcase mouth leave this section in position for support until after the crankcase halves have been bolted together.

31 Lubricate the right-hand crankshaft main bearing with clean engine oil.

32 Heat the bearing housing with a hot air gun. If required, use a freeze spay on the main bearing.

33 Fit the crankcase half over the crankshaft. Ensure that the two halves of the crankcase are correctly aligned, taking special note of the position of the dowels, and that the main bearing is aligned with the bearing housing in the right-hand case **(see illustration)**.

34 Press the crankcase on fully so that the main bearing goes all the way into its housing. If the main bearing does not seat fully, apply more heat to the bearing housing while apply steady pressure to the crankcase.

35 Check that the crankcase halves are seated all the way round. If the cases are not correctly seated, heat the bearing housings while applying firm pressure. **Note:** *Do not attempt to pull the crankcase halves together using the crankcase bolts as the casing will crack and be ruined.*

36 Clean the threads of the crankcase bolts and install them finger-tight, then tighten them evenly to the torque setting in the Specifications at the beginning of this chapter.

37 Trim off any excess gasket across the crankcase mouth **(see illustration)**.

38 Support the connecting rod and rotate the crankshaft by hand – if there are any signs of undue stiffness, tight or rough spots, or of any other problem, the fault must be rectified before proceeding further. Don't forget to

support the camchain while rotating the crankshaft.

39 Install the remaining components in the reverse order of removal.

21 Crankshaft assembly, big-end and main bearings

Note: *The crankshaft assembly is pressed together and is easily damaged if it is dropped.*

1 To access the crankshaft assembly, the big-end bearing and the main bearings, the crankcase must be split into two parts (see Section 20).

2 The crankshaft assembly should give many thousands of miles of service. The most likely problems to occur will be a worn small or big-end bearing due to poor lubrication. A worn big-end bearing will produce a pronounced knocking noise, most audible when the engine is under load, and

21.4 Checking for play in the big-end bearing

21.5 Measuring big-end side clearance

21.6 Check the main bearings on both sides of the crankshaft

21.9 Inspect the crankshaft sprockets for wear

increasing as engine speed rises. This should not be confused with small-end bearing wear, which produces a lighter, metallic rattle (see Section 14).

3 When the crankcase halves are separated, the main bearings will remain in place on the crankshaft assembly – they are not normally available as separate items. If the main bearings have failed, excessive rumbling and vibration will be felt when the engine is running.

4 To assess the condition of the big-end bearing, hold the crankshaft assembly firmly and push and pull on the connecting rod, checking for any up-and-down freeplay between the two **(see illustration)**. If any freeplay is noted, the bearing is worn.

5 A small amount of big-end side clearance (side-to-side movement) is acceptable on the connecting rod. Some manufacturers specify a service limit for the sideplay (typically 0.10 to 0.35 mm) which can be measured with a feeler gauge **(see illustration)**.

6 Follow the procedure in *Tools and*

Workshop Tips in the *Reference* section to check the condition of the main bearings **(see illustration)**.

7 If wear or damage is noted in any of the crankshaft assembly bearings, a new crankshaft assembly will have to be fitted. **Note:** *Evidence of extreme heat, such as discoloration or blueing, indicates that lubrication failure has occurred. Be sure to check the oil pump and bearing oilways in the crankcases before reassembling the engine.*

8 Inspect the threads on each end of the crankshaft and ensure that the retaining nuts for the alternator rotor and the variator are a good fit. Inspect the splines for the variator pulley on the left-hand end of the shaft **(see illustration 21.6)**. Inspect the taper and the slot in the right-hand end of the shaft for the alternator Woodruff key. Damage or wear that prevents the rotor from being fitted securely will require a new crankshaft assembly.

9 Inspect the oil pump and the camshaft drive sprocket teeth on the crankshaft for damage or wear **(see illustration)**. The sprockets are

installed as an integral part of the crankshaft assembly – if they are worn or damaged a new assembly will have to be fitted.

22 Initial start-up after overhaul/running-in

Initial start-up after overhaul

1 Make sure the engine oil level is correct (see *Pre-ride checks*).

2 Make sure there is fuel in the tank.

3 With the ignition OFF, operate the kickstart a couple of times to check that the engine turns over easily.

4 Turn the ignition ON, start the engine and allow it to run at a slow idle until it reaches operating temperature. Do not be alarmed if there is a little smoke from the exhaust – this will be due to the oil used to lubricate the piston and bore during assembly and should subside after a while.

5 If the engine proves reluctant to start, remove the spark plug and check that it has not become wet and oily. If it has, clean it and try again. If the engine refuses to start, go through the fault finding charts at the end of this manual to identify the problem.

6 Check carefully for fuel and oil leaks and make sure the transmission and controls, especially the brakes, function properly before road testing the machine.

7 Upon completion of the road test, and after the engine has cooled down completely, recheck the valve clearances (see Chapter 1). Recheck the engine oil level (see *Pre-ride checks*).

Recommended running-in procedure

8 Treat the engine gently for the first few miles to allow any new parts to bed in.

9 If a new piston, cylinder or crankshaft assembly has been fitted, the engine will have to be run-in as when new. This means a restraining hand on the throttle until at least 300 miles (500 km) have been covered. There's no point in keeping to any set speed limit – the main idea is to gradually increase performance up to the 600 mile (1000 km) mark. Make sure that the throttle position is varied to vary engine speed, and use full throttle only for short bursts. Experience is the best guide, since it's easy to tell when an engine is running freely.

10 Pay particular attention to the *Pre-ride checks* at the beginning of this manual and investigate the cause of any oil loss immediately. Check the tightness of all relevant nuts and bolts (see Chapter 1).

Chapter 2C
Two-stroke engines

Contents

Degrees of difficulty

Easy, suitable for novice with little experience	**Fairly easy,** suitable for beginner with some experience	**Fairly difficult,** suitable for competent DIY mechanic	**Difficult,** suitable for experienced DIY mechanic	**Very difficult,** suitable for expert DIY or professional

1 General information

Two-stroke engine codes 1E40QMA or B, and 1PE40QMB are likely to be found as part of the engine number. There are bottom-end differences between these engine types, such as piston pins (10mm or 12mm dia.), crankshafts, generator stators and oil pumps.

The engine is a single cylinder two-stroke with fan assisted air cooling (see Chapter 1). The crankshaft assembly is pressed together, incorporating the connecting rod. The piston runs on a needle roller bearing fitted in the small-end of the connecting rod. The crankshaft runs in caged ball main bearings.

The crankcase divides vertically – the left-hand crankcase is an integral part of the drive belt casing and gearbox.

2 Component access

Most components and assemblies, with the obvious exception of the crankshaft assembly and its bearings, can be worked on without having to remove the engine/transmission unit from the scooter. However, access to some components is severely restricted, and if a number of areas require attention at the same time, removal of the

engine is recommended, as it is an easy task to undertake.

3 Engine – removal and installation

Caution: The engine/transmission unit is not heavy, however removal and installation should be carried out with the aid of an assistant; personal injury or damage could occur if the engine falls or is dropped.

Removal

1 Support the scooter securely in an upright position. Work can be made easier by raising it to a suitable height on an hydraulic ramp or

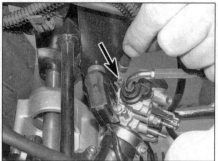

3.7 Disconnect the fuel hose (arrowed) from the carburettor

3.8 Detach the fuel tap vacuum hose (arrowed)

5 If the engine is dirty, particularly around its mountings, wash it thoroughly before starting any major dismantling work. This will make work much easier and rule out the possibility of dirt falling inside.

6 Remove the air filter housing and the air intake duct (see Chapter 3).

7 Disconnect the fuel hose from its union on the carburettor, being prepared to catch any residual fuel in a rag **(see illustration)**. Position a suitable container below the carburettor drain hose, then loosen the drain screw and drain any residual fuel from the float chamber. Tighten the drain screw.

8 Disconnect the fuel tap vacuum hose from its union on the carburettor **(see illustration)**.

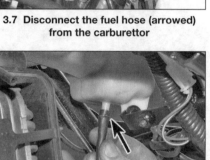

3.9a Release the clip (arrowed) and pull off the oil hose . . .

3.9b . . . then plug the tank union and hose (arrowed) to prevent oil loss

9 Release the clip securing the oil hose to the union on the oil tank and detach the hose – plug the tank union and the open end of the hose to prevent oil loss **(see illustrations)**.

10 Release the clip securing the oil hose to the union on the carburettor and pull the hose off, being prepared to catch any residual oil in a rag **(see illustration)**.

11 Detach the oil pump control cable from the pump pulley and detach the cable from its bracket (see Section 11).

12 Trace the wiring from the automatic choke unit and disconnect it at the connector. **Note:** *When disconnecting any wiring, it is advisable to mark or tag the wires as a reminder of where they connect.* Where fitted, disconnect the carburettor heater wiring.

a suitable platform. Make sure it is secure and will not topple over.

2 Remove the luggage compartment and any body panels as necessary to access the engine (see Chapter 8).

3 Disconnect the battery negative terminal (see Chapter 9) and pull the spark plug cap off the plug.

4 If required, remove the exhaust system (see Chapter 3).

13 Either displace or remove the carburettor completely, leaving the throttle cable attached if required, or just disconnect the throttle cable (see Chapter 3). If the carburettor is displaced, ensure it is secured to a convenient part of the frame to avoid damage. Ensure that the throttle cable and all wiring is clear of the engine unit. Stuff clean rag into the intake manifold to prevent anything falling inside.

14 Disconnect the starter motor terminal lead – either pull back the boot, then undo the screw securing the lead to the starter motor terminal, or trace the lead from the starter motor and disconnect it at the connector or starter solenoid **(see illustrations)**.

3.10 Disconnect the oil hose from the union (arrowed) on the carburettor

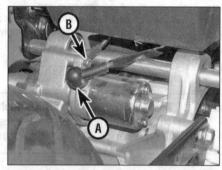

3.14a Starter motor terminal (A) and earth wire terminal (B)

15 Undo the bolt securing the earth (ground) wire to the crankcase and disconnect the wire **(see illustration 3.14a)**. Replace the bolt for safekeeping.

16 Trace the wiring from the alternator/ ignition pulse generator coil on the right-hand side of the engine and disconnect it at the connectors **(see illustration)**. Free the wiring from any clips or ties and secure it free of the frame.

17 If required, remove the rear wheel (see Chapter 7). **Note:** *On machines where the main stand is bolted to the underside of the engine unit, the rear wheel and stand provide a convenient support for the unit once it is removed from the scooter. However, it is useful to loosen the rear wheel nut at this point before disconnecting the rear brake.*

3.14b Starter motor lead terminal (arrowed) on the starter relay

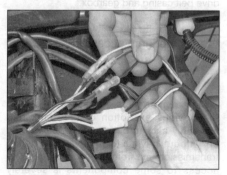

3.16 Disconnect the alternator and ignition pulse generator coil wiring

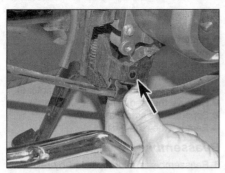

3.18 Detach the brake cable and any clips (arrowed) from the casing

3.20a Remove the shock mounting lower bolt . . .

3.20b . . . and displace the shock. Note the location of the stands (arrowed)

18 Disconnect the brake cable from the brake arm (see Chapter 7). Undo any screws securing the cable to the underside of the drive belt casing and detach the cable **(see illustration)**.

19 Check that all wiring, cables and hoses are clear of the engine/transmission unit.

20 With the aid of an assistant, support the weight of the machine on the rear of the frame, then remove the bolt securing the rear shock absorber to the gearbox casing **(see illustrations)**. If the rear wheel has been removed support the gearbox on a wood block to prevent damage to the casing. Either displace the shock or undo the nut securing the upper end of the shock to the frame and remove the shock.

21 Undo the nut on the front engine mounting bolt **(see illustration)**.

22 Have an assistant support the scooter, then carefully withdraw the front engine

3.21 Undo the nut (arrowed) . . .

mounting bolt, noting the location of any spacers between the mounting lugs on the front of the crankcase and the pivot bracket **(see illustration)**. **Note:** *On the machine used to illustrate this procedure a one-piece spacer was retained by circlips inside bearings*

3.22a . . . then withdraw the front engine mounting bolt

located in the crankcase mounting lugs **(see illustrations)**.

23 Manoeuvre the engine unit back and out of the frame **(see illustration)**.

24 If required, remove the main stand (see Chapter 6).

3.22b Engine mounting sleeve runs in bearings (arrowed)

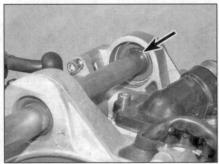

3.22c The sleeve is retained by circlips (arrowed)

3.22d Draw the sleeve out

3.22e Inspect the sleeve for wear

3.22f Check that the bearings (arrowed) are free to turn

3.23 Manoeuvre the engine unit out of the frame

Installation

25 Installation is the reverse of removal, noting the following:

● Make sure no wires, cables or hoses become trapped between the engine and the frame when installing the engine.

● Tighten the front engine mounting bolt and shock absorber bolt securely. Use the recommended torque settings specified in the *Data* section at the end of this manual if given for your model.

● Make sure all wires, cables and hoses are correctly routed and connected, and secured by any clips or ties.

● Bleed the oil pump (see Section 11) and check the adjustment of the oil pump cable (see Chapter 1).

● Check the operation of the rear brake before riding the machine (see Chapter 1).

4 Disassembly and reassembly – general information

Disassembly

1 Before disassembling the engine, the external surfaces of the unit should be thoroughly cleaned and degreased. This will prevent contamination of the engine internals, and will also make working a lot easier and cleaner. A high flash-point solvent, such as paraffin can be used, or better still, a proprietary engine degreaser such as Gunk. Use an old paintbrush to work the solvent into the various recesses of the engine casings. Take care to exclude solvent or water from the electrical components and intake and exhaust ports.

 Warning: The use of petrol (gasoline) as a cleaning agent should be avoided because of the risk of fire.

2 When clean and dry, arrange the unit on the workbench, leaving a suitable clear area for working. Gather a selection of small containers and plastic bags so that parts can be grouped together in an easily identifiable manner. Some paper and a pen should be on hand to permit notes to be made and labels attached where necessary. A supply of clean rag is also required.

3 Before commencing work, read through the appropriate section so that some idea of the necessary procedure can be gained. When removing components it should be noted that great force is seldom required, unless specified. In many cases, a component's reluctance to be removed is indicative of an incorrect approach or removal method – if in any doubt, re-check with the text.

4 When disassembling the engine, keep 'mated' parts that have been in contact with each other during engine operation together. These 'mated' parts must be reused or renewed as an assembly.

5 Complete engine disassembly should be done in the following general order with reference to the appropriate Sections (refer to Chapter 5 for details of transmission components disassembly):

● Remove the cylinder head
● Remove the cylinder
● Remove the piston
● Remove the alternator
● Remove the oil pump
● Remove the variator (see Chapter 5)
● Remove the starter motor (see Chapter 9)
● Remove the reed valve (see Chapter 3)
● Separate the crankcase halves
● Remove the crankshaft

Reassembly

6 Reassembly is accomplished by reversing the order of disassembly.

5 Cylinder head

Note: *This procedure can be carried out with the engine in the scooter. If the engine has been removed, ignore the steps that do not apply.*

Caution: The engine must be completely cool before beginning this procedure or the cylinder head may become warped.

Removal

1 Remove the luggage compartment and any body panels as necessary to access the cylinder head (see Chapter 8).

2 Pull the spark plug cap off the spark plug **(see illustration)**.

3 It will be necessary to remove the engine cowling, or part of the cowling, to access the cylinder head. On some engines, the cooling fan cowling forms part of the engine cowling. Check around the cowling and disconnect any wires or hoses clipped to it, then undo the bolts securing the cowling and remove it, noting how it fits **(see illustrations). Note:** *Some cowlings are clipped together – take care not to damage the fixing lugs when separating them.* Remove any spacers for the cowling bolts for safekeeping if they are loose.

4 Remove the spark plug, then unscrew the cylinder head nuts evenly and a little at a time in a criss-cross sequence until they are all loose and remove them together with any washers **(see illustration). Note:** *Some cylinder heads are secured by long bolts which*

5.2 Pull off the spark plug cap

5.3a Remove the fan cowling . . .

5.3b . . . then unclip any wires or hoses (arrowed) . . .

5.3c . . . before lifting off the engine cowling

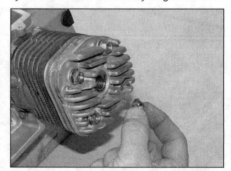

5.4 Undo the cylinder head nuts evenly

5.5 Lift off the cylinder head

5.6 Remove the cylinder head gasket

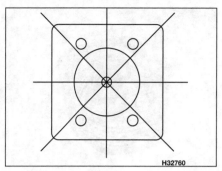

5.11 Check the cylinder head for warpage with a straight-edge

pass down through the cylinder and screw into the crankcase, others are secures by nuts on long studs. In both cases, once the cylinder head is loose care must be taken not to break the cylinder base gasket seal otherwise a new base gasket will have to be fitted before replacing the head (see Section 6).

5 Lift the head off the cylinder **(see illustration)**. If the head is stuck, tap around the joint face between the head and cylinder with a soft-faced mallet to free it. Do not attempt to free the head by inserting a screwdriver between the head and cylinder – you'll damage the sealing surfaces.

6 Remove the cylinder head gasket and discard it as a new one must be used on reassembly **(see illustration)**.

Inspection

7 Refer to Chapter 1, Section 27, and decarbonise the cylinder head.

8 Inspect the head very carefully for cracks and other damage. If cracks are found, a new head will be required.

9 Inspect the threads in the spark plug hole. Damaged or worn threads can be reclaimed using a thread insert (see *Tools and Workshop Tips* in the *Reference* section). Most small engineering firms offer a service of this kind.

10 Check the mating surfaces on the cylinder head and cylinder for signs of leaks, which could indicate that the head is warped.

11 Using a precision straight-edge and a feeler gauge, check the head mating surface

for warpage. **Note:** *Clean all traces of old gasket material from the cylinder head and cylinder with a suitable solvent. Take care not to scratch or gouge the soft aluminium.* Lay the straight-edge across the surface and measure any gap under it with feeler gauges. Check vertically, horizontally and diagonally across the head, making four checks in all **(see illustration)**. Warpage should generally be no more than 0.05 mm. If warpage is excessive, have the cylinder head machined flat or replace it with a new one. If there is any doubt about the condition of the head consult an automotive engineer.

Installation

12 Installation is the reverse of removal, noting the following:

● Ensure both cylinder head and cylinder mating surfaces are clean.

● Lubricate the cylinder bore with the specified type of two-stroke oil.

● Install the new head gasket. **Note:** *The gasket may be marked to identify which side should face up when it is in place, or there may be a raised section around the inner edge of the gasket. If so, fit the gasket with the raised section uppermost.*

● Tighten the cylinder head fixings evenly and a little at a time in a criss-cross pattern. Torque settings are given in the Data section for certain models.

● Ensure the engine cowling is correctly secured.

6 Cylinder

Note: *This procedure can be carried out with the engine in the scooter.*

Removal

1 Remove the exhaust system (see Chapter 3) and the cylinder head (see Section 5).

2 Lift the cylinder up off the crankcase, supporting the piston as it becomes accessible to prevent it hitting the crankcase opening **(see illustration)**. If the cylinder is stuck, tap around the joint face between the cylinder and the crankcase with a soft-faced mallet to free it. Don't attempt to free the cylinder by inserting a screwdriver between it and the crankcase – you'll damage the sealing surfaces. When the cylinder is removed, stuff a clean rag into the crankcase opening around the piston to prevent anything falling inside.

3 Remove the cylinder base gasket and discard it as a new one must be fitted on reassembly **(see illustration)**.

4 Scrape off any carbon deposits that may have formed in the exhaust port, then wash the cylinder with a suitable solvent and dry it thoroughly **(see illustration)**. Compressed air will speed the drying process and ensure that all holes and recesses are clean.

6.2 Support the piston as the cylinder is lifted off

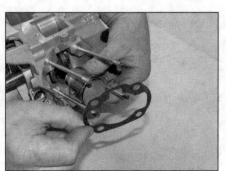

6.3 Remove the cylinder base gasket

6.4 Scrape carbon deposits out of the exhaust port (arrowed)

6.5 Inspect the bore (arrowed) for damage

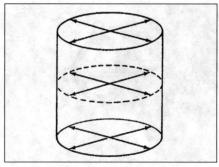

6.6 Measure the cylinder bore in the directions shown

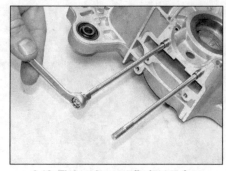

6.12 Tightening a cylinder stud as described

Inspection

5 Inspect the cylinder bore carefully for scratches and score marks **(see illustration)**.

6 If available, use a telescoping gauge and micrometer to measure the diameter of the cylinder bore to assess the amount of wear, taper and ovality (see *Tools and Workshop Tips* in the *Reference* section). Measure near the top (but below the level of the top piston ring at TDC), centre and bottom (but above the level of the bottom ring at BDC) of the bore both parallel to and across the crankshaft axis **(see illustration)**.

7 Calculate any differences between the measurements to determine any taper or ovality in the bore. Compare the results with the specifications in the *Data* section if given for your model. If the cylinder bore is worn beyond its service limits, a new one should be fitted.

8 A cylinder bore that has worn oval will reduce the efficiency of the piston rings to achieve a seal, resulting in loss of compression.

9 If no specifications are provided for your model, measure an unworn part of the cylinder bore (below the level of the bottom ring with the piston at the bottom of its stroke) and compare the result to the previous measurements to determine overall wear. Alternatively, calculate the piston-to-bore clearance to determine whether the cylinder is useable (see Section 7).

10 If the bore is tapered, oval, or worn excessively, or badly scratched, scuffed or scored, the cylinder and piston will have to be renewed as a set.

11 If there is any doubt about the serviceability of the cylinder, consult a specialist engineer.

12 Check that all the cylinder studs are tight in the crankcase halves. If any are loose, remove them and clean their threads. Apply a suitable permanent thread locking compound, then screw them back into the crankcase securely.

Note: *To tighten a stud without damaging it, first lock two nuts together on the upper end of the stud. Now use a ring spanner on the upper nut to tighten the stud* **(see illustration)**.

Installation

13 Check that the mating surfaces of the cylinder and crankcase are clean, then remove any rag from the crankcase opening. Lay the new base gasket in place on the crankcase making sure it is the correct way round **(see illustration 6.3)**.

14 Check that the piston rings are correctly positioned so that the ring locating pins in the piston grooves are between the ring ends **(see illustration)**.

15 Lubricate the cylinder bore, piston and piston rings, and the connecting rod big- and small-ends, with two-stroke oil, then locate the cylinder over the top of the piston **(see illustration)**.

16 Ensure the piston enters the bore squarely and does not get cocked sideways. Carefully compress and feed each ring into the bore as the cylinder is lowered, taking care that the rings do not rotate out of position **(see illustration)**. Do not use force if the cylinder appears to be stuck as the piston and/or rings will be damaged.

17 When the piston is correctly installed in the cylinder, check that the base gasket has not been displaced, then press the cylinder down onto the gasket **(see illustration)**.

18 Install the remaining components in the reverse order of removal.

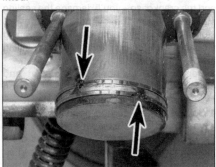

6.14 Ring locating pins (arrowed) must be between the ring ends

6.15 Position the cylinder over the top of the piston . . .

6.16 . . . then carefully feed the piston into the cylinder

6.17 Check that the cylinder contacts the base gasket (arrowed) all the way around

7 Piston

Note: *This procedure can be carried out with the engine in the scooter.*

Removal

1 Remove the cylinder and stuff a clean rag into the crankcase opening around the piston to prevent anything falling inside (see Section 6).

2 The piston top should be marked with an arrow which points towards the exhaust. If the piston was cleaned prior to disassembly,

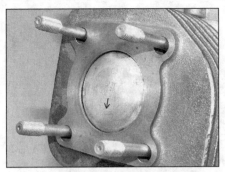

7.2 Arrow on piston top should point towards the exhaust

7.3a Remove the circlip . . .

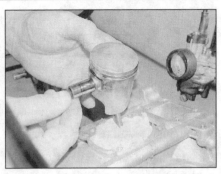

7.3b . . . then push out the piston pin

ensure that the arrow is visible or mark the piston accordingly so that it can be installed the correct way round **(see illustration)**.

3 Carefully prise the circlip out from one side of the piston using needle-nose pliers or a small flat-bladed screwdriver inserted into the notch **(see illustration)**. Check for burring around the circlip groove and remove any with a very fine file or penknife blade, then push the piston pin out from the other side and remove the piston from the connecting rod **(see illustration)**. Use a socket extension to push the piston pin out if required. Remove the other circlip and discard them both as new ones must be used on reassembly.

> *To prevent the circlip from flying away or from dropping into the crankcase, pass a rod or screwdriver with a greater diameter than the gap between the circlip ends, through the piston pin. This will trap the circlip if it springs out.*
>
> *If the piston pin is a tight fit in the piston bosses, heat the piston gently with a hot air gun – this will expand the alloy piston sufficiently to release its grip on the pin.*

4 The connecting rod small-end bearing is a loose fit in the rod; remove it for safekeeping, noting which way round it fits **(see illustration)**.

5 Before the inspection process can be carried out, the piston rings must be removed and the

piston must be cleaned. **Note:** *If the cylinder is being renewed, piston inspection can be overlooked as a new one will be fitted. The piston rings can be removed by hand – using your thumbs, ease the ends of each ring apart and carefully lift it off the piston, taking care not to expand it any more than is necessary. Alternatively, slide thin strips of plastic down between the rings and the piston, then ease the rings off* **(see illustration)**. *Do not nick or gouge the piston in the process.*

6 Note which way up each ring fits and in which groove as they must be installed in their original positions if being re-used. The upper surface of each ring should be marked at one end. Some pistons have an expander fitted behind the second ring **(see illustration)**. **Note:** *It is good practice to renew the piston rings when an engine is being overhauled. Ensure that the piston and bore are serviceable before purchasing new rings.*

7 Clean all traces of carbon from the top of the piston. A hand-held wire brush or a piece of fine emery cloth can be used once most of the deposits have been scraped away. Do not, under any circumstances, use a wire brush

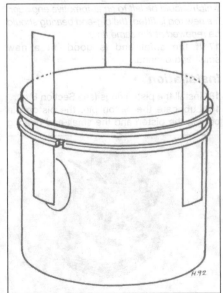

7.5 Remove the piston rings carefully without expanding them too far

mounted in a drill motor; the piston material is soft and is easily damaged.

8 Use a piston ring groove cleaning tool to remove any carbon deposits from the ring grooves. If a tool is not available, a piece broken off an old ring will do the job. Be very careful to remove only the carbon deposits. Do not remove any metal and do not nick or gouge the sides of the ring grooves.

9 Once the carbon has been removed, clean the piston with a suitable solvent and dry it thoroughly. If the identification previously marked on the piston is cleaned off, be sure to re-mark it correctly.

Inspection

10 Inspect the piston for cracks around the skirt, at the pin bosses and at the ring lands. Check that the circlip grooves are not damaged. Normal piston wear appears as even, vertical wear on the thrust surfaces of the piston and slight looseness of the top ring in its groove. If the skirt is scored or scuffed, the engine may have been suffering from overheating and/or abnormal combustion, resulting in excessively high operating temperatures.

11 A hole in the top of the piston, in one extreme, or burned areas around the edge of the piston crown, indicate that pre-ignition or knocking under load have occurred. If you find evidence of any problems the cause must be corrected or the damage will occur again. Refer to Chapter 3 for carburation checks and Chapter 4 for ignition checks.

12 Check the piston-to-bore clearance by

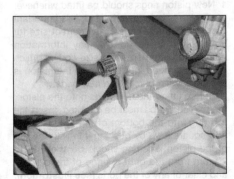

7.4 Remove the small-end bearing

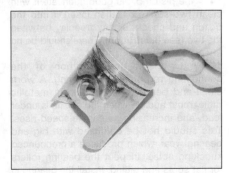

7.6 Expander fitted behind the second ring

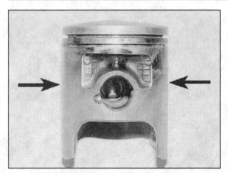

7.12 Measure the piston at 90° to the piston pin axis

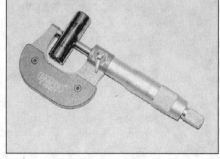

7.13 Measuring the piston pin where it runs in the small-end bearing

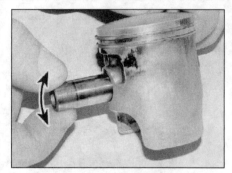

7.14 Check for freeplay between the piston and the piston pin

7.15 Rock the piston pin back and forth to check for freeplay

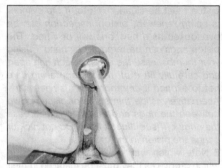

7.16 Measuring the internal diameter of the connecting rod small-end

7.20 Position the open end of the circlip away from the removal notch (arrowed)

measuring the cylinder bore (see Section 6) and the piston diameter. Measure the piston approximately 25 mm down from the bottom of the lower piston ring groove and at 90° to the piston pin axis **(see illustration)**. **Note:** *The precise point of measurement differs between manufacturers and engines, but the aim is to measure the piston in an area where it is worn.* Subtract the piston diameter from the bore diameter to obtain the clearance. If it is greater than the specified service limit (generally 0.1 mm), check whether it is the bore or piston that is worn the most. If the bore is good, install a new piston and rings.

13 Use a micrometer to measure the piston pin in the middle, where it runs in the small-end bearing, and at each end where it runs in the piston **(see illustration)**. If there is any difference in the measurements the pin is worn and must be renewed.

14 If the piston pin is good, lubricate it with clean two-stroke oil, then insert it into the piston and check for any freeplay between the two **(see illustration)**. There should be no freeplay.

15 Next, check the condition of the connecting rod small-end bearing. A worn small-end bearing will produce a metallic rattle, most audible when the engine is under load, and increasing as engine speed rises. This should not be confused with big-end bearing wear, which produces a pronounced knocking noise. Inspect the bearing rollers for flat spots and pitting. Install the bearing in the connecting rod, then slide the piston pin into the bearing and check for freeplay **(see**

illustration). There should only be slightly discernible freeplay between the piston pin, the bearing and the connecting rod.

16 If there is freeplay, measure the internal diameter of the connecting rod small-end **(see illustration)**. Take several measurements; if there is any difference between the measurements the small end is worn and either a new connecting rod or crankshaft assembly will have to be fitted (see Section 13). **Note:** *If a new rod is available, fitting it is a specialist task which should be left to an automotive engineer. If a new rod is fitted, the big-end bearing should be renewed at the same time.*

17 If the small-end is good, fit a new small-end bearing.

Installation

18 Install the piston rings (see Section 8).

19 Lubricate the piston pin, the piston pin bore in the piston and the small-end bearing

8.2a Insert the piston rings into the bottom of the bore for checking

with the specified two-stroke oil and install the bearing in the connecting rod.

20 Install a new circlip in one side of the piston, line up the piston on the connecting rod, making sure the arrow on the piston top faces towards the exhaust, and insert the piston pin from the other side. Secure the pin with the other new circlip. When installing the circlips, compress them only just enough to fit them in the piston, and make sure they are properly seated in their grooves with the open end away from the removal notch **(see illustration)**.

21 Install the cylinder (see Section 6).

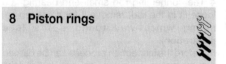

8 Piston rings

1 New piston rings should be fitted whenever an engine is being overhauled. It is important that you get new rings of the correct size for your piston so ensure that any information relating to piston size and size coding which may be stamped into the top of the piston is available when purchasing new parts.

2 Before fitting the new rings onto the piston, the ring end gaps must be checked. Insert the top ring into the bottom of the cylinder bore and square it up by pushing it in with the top of the piston. The ring should be about 15 to 20 mm from the bottom edge of the cylinder and clear of any of the ports **(see illustration)**. Measure the ring end gap using feeler gauges, slipping the gauge between the ends of the

8.2b Measuring installed ring end gap

8.5 Piston ring ends must fit each side of the locating pin (arrowed)

8.7 Using a thin blade to install the piston ring

ring **(see illustration)**. Ring end gaps are given in the *Data* section for certain models. Where no specification is available, note that a gap greater than 0.7 mm should be considered too large.

3 If the gap is larger or smaller than specified, check to make sure that you have the correct rings before proceeding. If the gap is larger than specified it is likely the cylinder bore is worn. If the gap is too small the ring ends may come into contact with each other during engine operation, causing serious damage.

4 Repeat the procedure for the other ring.

5 Once the ring end gaps have been checked, the rings can be installed on the piston. First identify the ring locating pin in each piston ring groove – the ring must be positioned so that the pin is in between the ends of the ring **(see illustration)**. Note that the ends of the ring are shaped to fit around the locating pin.

6 If the piston has an expander fitted behind

the lower ring, fit that first, ensuring that the ends of the expander do not overlap the ring locating pin **(see illustration 7.6)**.

7 The upper surface of each ring should be marked at one end; make sure you fit the rings the right way up. Install the lower ring first, taking care not to expand the ring any more than is necessary to slide it into place **(see illustration)**. Ensure that the locating pin is between the ends of the ring **(see illustration 8.5)**.

8 Install the top ring. Always ensure that the ring end gaps are positioned each side of the locating pins before fitting the piston into the cylinder.

9 Alternator

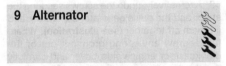

Note: *This procedure can be carried out with*

the engine in the scooter. If the engine has been removed, ignore the steps that do not apply.

Removal

1 Remove the body panels as necessary to access the alternator on the right-hand side of the engine (see Chapter 8). If required, remove the exhaust system (see Chapter 3).

2 The alternator is located behind the fan cowling. Follow the procedure in Section 5 to remove the cowling.

3 Undo the bolts securing the cooling fan to the alternator rotor and remove the fan **(see illustrations)**.

4 To remove the rotor centre nut it is necessary to stop the rotor from turning. Some manufacturers produce a service tool for this purpose which engages in the slots or holes in the rotor face – a similar home-made tool can be used (see *Tool Tip*, Chapter 2A, Section 16). **Note:** *Take great care not to damage the internal coils of the alternator when locating any tools through the rotor.*

5 Alternatively, use a proprietary holding tool or hold the rotor with a strap wrench **(see illustrations)**. If necessary, undo the bolts securing the ignition pulse generator coil and displace it to avoid damaging it when using the strap wrench (see Steps 12 and 13.

6 With the rotor securely held, unscrew the centre nut.

7 To remove the rotor from the taper on the crankshaft it is necessary to use a puller – either a manufacturer's service tool or a commercially available puller **(see illustrations)**.

8 To use the service tool, first screw the

9.3a Undo the bolts securing the cooling fan . . .

9.3b . . . and lift the fan off

9.5a Hold the rotor and undo the centre nut

9.5b Using a strap wrench to hold the rotor

9.7a Typical service tool for removing the rotor

9.7b Set-up using a two-legged puller

9.8a Tighten the centre bolt . . .

9.8b . . . to draw the rotor off the crankshaft

body of the tool all the way into the threads provided in the rotor. Hold the tool steady with a spanner on its flats and tighten the centre bolt, exerting steady pressure to draw the rotor off the taper **(see illustrations)**.

9 To use the puller, engage the puller legs either in the slots in the rotor or thread them into the threaded holes in the rotor, then tighten the centre bolt exerting steady pressure to draw the rotor off the taper. **Note:** *To avoid damaging the threaded end of the crankshaft, either leave the centre nut on the shaft with just enough clearance to allow the rotor to be dislodged, or position a soft metal spacer between the end of the shaft and the puller centre bolt.*

10 Note the location of the Woodruff key on the crankshaft and remove it for safekeeping if it is loose **(see illustration)**.

11 In most cases, the alternator stator

coils and ignition pulse generator coil are wired together and have to be removed as an assembly. If not already done, trace the wiring back from the alternator and pulse generator and disconnect it at the connectors **(see illustration 3.16)**. Free the wiring from any clips or guides and feed it through to the alternator.

12 On some scooters, the pulse generator coil is mounted onto the alternator stator backplate. Undo the backplate mounting bolts, then ease the wiring grommet and wiring through the casing and lift the assembly off **(see illustrations)**.

13 Alternatively, undo the screws securing the stator and the pulse generator separately, and lift them off together **(see illustration)**. Where fitted, draw any wiring grommet out of the crankcase or engine side cover and carefully pull the wiring away, noting how it fits.

Installation

14 Installation is the reverse of removal, noting the following:
● Ensure the wiring is correctly routed before installing the stator and pulse generator **(see illustrations)**.
● Make sure that no metal objects have attached themselves to the magnets on the inside of the rotor.
● Clean the tapered end of the crankshaft and the corresponding mating surface on the inside of the rotor with a suitable solvent.
● Fit the Woodruff key into the crankshaft, align the slot in the centre of the rotor with the key, then install the rotor.
● Tighten the rotor centre nut securely. Apply the torque setting specified in the Data section if given for your model.
● Secure the wiring with any clips or ties.

9.10 Note the location of the Woodruff key

9.12a Undo the mounting bolts . . .

9.12b . . . and ease the assembly off

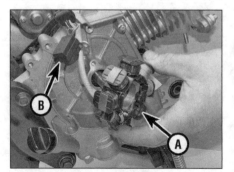

9.13 Remove the alternator stator (A) and pulse generator coil (B)

9.14a Note the location of the wiring grommet (arrowed) on the outside . . .

9.14b . . . and the inside of the casing

10.1 Starter pinion assembly is driven by the starter motor shaft (arrowed)

10 Starter pinion assembly and starter clutch

Note 1: *Two different set-ups are used to transfer the starter motor drive to the engine – a sliding pinion assembly or a starter (one-way) clutch. The sliding pinion assembly engages with the driven gear on the variator pulley, or a driven gear on the crankshaft behind the variator. The starter clutch is located on the crankshaft behind the variator. Note the point at which the starter motor shaft enters the engine case to locate the appropriate assembly.*
Note 2: *This procedure can be carried out with the engine in the scooter.*

Starter pinion assembly

Removal

1 Remove the drive belt cover (see Chapter 5)

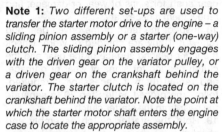

10.9 Starter motor (A), idler gear (B) and driven gear (C)

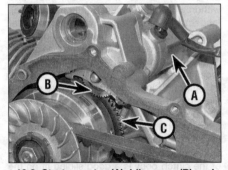

10.12 Remove the idler gear support

10.3 Remove the pinion assembly, noting how it fits

and locate the pinion assembly adjacent to the variator pulley **(see illustration)**.
2 Where necessary, undo the bolts securing the starter pinion outer support and remove the support.
3 Withdraw the starter pinion assembly **(see illustration)**.

Inspection

4 Check the starter pinion assembly for any signs of damage or wear, particularly for chipped or broken teeth on either of the pinions **(see illustration)**. Check the corresponding teeth on the starter motor pinion and the variator driven gear.
5 Rotate the outer pinion and check that it moves smoothly up and down the shaft, and that it returns easily to its rest position.
6 The starter pinion assembly is supplied as a complete unit; if any of the component parts is worn or damaged, the unit will have to be replaced with a new one.

10.10 Starter driven gear should rotate freely in the opposite direction to crankshaft

10.13a Remove the thrust washer . . .

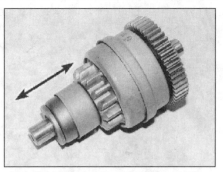

10.4 Check the pinion teeth. Outer pinion should move smoothly on shaft

7 Most manufacturers recommend that the starter pinion mechanism should not be lubricated as any excess grease may contaminate the drive belt and cause it to slip. However, a smear of grease should be applied to both ends of the pinion shaft before reassembly.

Installation

8 Installation is the reverse of removal. Ensure the inner pinion engages with the starter motor pinion **(see illustration 10.1)**.

Starter (one-way) clutch

Removal

9 Remove the drive belt cover (see Chapter 5) and locate the idler gear and starter driven gear behind the variator pulley **(see illustration)**.
10 The operation of the starter clutch can be checked while it is in place. Check that the starter driven gear is able to rotate freely in the opposite direction to crankshaft rotation, but locks when rotated in the other direction **(see illustration)**. If not, the starter clutch is faulty and should be removed for inspection.
11 Remove the variator (see Chapter 5).
12 Undo the bolts securing the idler gear outer support and remove the support **(see illustration)**.
13 Where fitted, remove the thrust washer, then draw off the idler gear **(see illustrations)**. Note if a second thrust washer is located behind the idler gear.
14 The starter clutch is a two-part assembly – grip the assembly so that the driven gear at the back is held into the body of the clutch as you draw it off the crankshaft, otherwise the

10.13b . . . and the idler gear. Note the remaining thrust washer (arrowed)

10.14 Draw off the starter clutch assembly

10.15 Remove the starter clutch bearing

10.16a Remove the large washer . . .

10.16b . . . and the crankshaft spacer

10.17 Examine the idler gear teeth. Note the location of the bearing (arrowed)

clutch sprags may become displaced inside the assembly **(see illustration)**.
15 Note the location of the clutch bearing and lift it off **(see illustration)**.
16 Where fitted, note the location of the large

washer and crankshaft spacer and remove them if required **(see illustrations)**.

Inspection

17 Inspect the teeth on the idler gear and

renew it if any are chipped or worn **(see illustration)**. Check the corresponding teeth on the starter motor pinion. Check the bearing inside the idler gear and the surface of the gear shaft for signs of wear or damage, and renew them if necessary.
18 Inspect the teeth of the driven gear and renew it if any are chipped or worn. Check the inner bearing surface of the gear and the clutch bearing for signs of wear or damage, and renew them if necessary. It required, follow the procedure in Step 20 to separate the gear from the starter clutch.
19 Hold the starter clutch assembly and check that the driven gear rotates freely in one direction and locks in the other direction. If it doesn't, the starter clutch is faulty and should be renewed. If individual components are available, check the condition of the one-way mechanism as follows.
20 Slowly rotate the driven gear and withdraw it from the clutch **(see illustration)**. Inspect the hub of the driven gear for wear and scoring and check that the spring-loaded sprags of the clutch one-way mechanism are retained by the plungers and are free to rotate **(see illustration)**
21 Although individual components are not available, the sprag and spring mechanisms can be eased out of the clutch housing for cleaning and inspection **(see illustration)**. If any of the components are damaged, fit a new starter clutch. Ensure that the toothed centre of the clutch body is a good sliding fit on the crankshaft splines **(see illustrations)**– if the teeth are worn, fit a new starter clutch.

10.20a Separate the driven gear from the starter clutch

10.20b Inspect the driven gear hub (A) and starter clutch sprags (B)

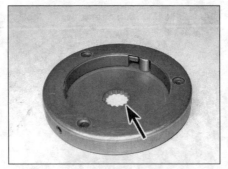

10.21a Sprag, plunger and spring of the starter clutch mechanism

10.21b Centre (arrowed) of the clutch body . . .

10.21c . . . should be a sliding fit on the crankshaft splines (arrowed)

Installation

22 Installation is the reverse of removal, noting the following:

● Lubricate the clutch bearing and the idler gear bearing with a smear of grease.
● Rotate the driven gear to install it in the starter clutch.
● Ensure the idler gear engages with the starter motor pinion.
● Tighten the idler gear support bolts securely.
● Install the variator (see Chapter 5).

11 Oil pump

Note 1: *Generally the oil pump is located on the outside of the crankcase, either in front of, behind or below the cylinder. Pumps are driven via a shaft and worm gear on the crankshaft, or by gear directly off the crankshaft. The rate of oil delivery is cable-controlled from the throttle twistgrip via a cable splitter – see Chapter 1.*
Note 2: *This procedure can be carried out with the engine in the scooter. If the engine has been removed, ignore the steps that do not apply.*

Shaft driven pump

Removal

1 Remove the body panels as necessary to access the oil pump (see Chapter 8). If required, remove the exhaust system (see Chapter 3).
2 Detach the inner cable end from the pump pulley – if necessary, loosen the cable adjuster to allow the cable end to be disengaged. If applicable, unscrew the bolts securing the cable bracket and remove the bracket with the cable attached **(see illustration)**.
3 Release the clip securing the oil inlet hose from the oil tank to the union on the pump and detach the hose **(see illustration)**. Clamp the hose and secure it in an upright position to minimise oil loss. Release the clip securing the oil outlet hose to the union on the pump and detach the hose. Wrap clean plastic bags around the hose ends to prevent dirt entering the system. **Note:** *On some engines, the*

11.2 Remove the oil pump cable and bracket

inlet and outlet hoses are protected from the exhaust pipe by a heat-proof sheath. Remove the sheath if necessary but don't forget to refit it on reassembly.
4 If not already done, unscrew the pump mounting bolts.
5 Withdraw the pump from the crankcase, noting how the drive tab on the pump locates in the slot in the pump drive shaft **(see illustration)**. Remove the wave washer **(see illustration)**.
6 The drive shaft cannot be removed unless the crankcase halves are separated. Turn the crankshaft to ensure that the pump drive shaft is rotating. If the drive shaft is thought to be faulty, follow the procedure in Section 12 and separate the crankcase halves. Stuff a clean rag into the crankcase opening to prevent dirt falling inside.
7 Where fitted, remove the O-ring from the pump body and discard it as a new one must be fitted on reassembly **(see illustration)**.
8 Ensure no dirt enters the pump body and clean it using a suitable solvent, then dry the pump thoroughly.

Inspection

9 Check the pump body for obvious signs of damage especially around the mounting bolt holes. Turn the drive tab by hand and check that the pump rotates smoothly. Check that the cable pulley turns freely and returns to rest under pressure of the return spring.
10 No individual internal components are available for the pump. If it is damaged, or, if after bleeding the operation of the pump is suspect, replace it with a new one.

11.3 Detach the oil hoses (arrowed) from the pump unions

Installation

11 Installation is the reverse of removal, noting the following:
● If applicable, fit a new O-ring on the pump body and lubricate it with a smear of grease.
● Install the wave washer, then install the pump.
● Ensure the tab on the back of the pump engages with the slot in the drive shaft.
● Ensure the hoses are secured to the pump unions with clips.
● Bleed the pump (see Steps 23 to 25)
● Check the adjustment of the cable (see Chapter 1)
Caution: Accurate cable adjustment is important to ensure that the oil pump delivers the correct amount of oil to the engine and is correctly synchronised with the throttle.

Gear driven pump

Removal

12 Remove the body panels as necessary to access the oil pump (see Chapter 8). If required, remove the fan cowling (see Section 5).
13 Detach the inner cable end from the pump pulley – if necessary, loosen the cable adjuster to allow the cable end to be disengaged **(see illustration)**.
14 On the engine photographed it was necessary to remove the alternator rotor and stator backplate to access the oil outlet hose and the pump drive pinion (see Section 9).
15 Where fitted, remove the alternator backplate gasket to access the oil pump components **(see illustrations)**.

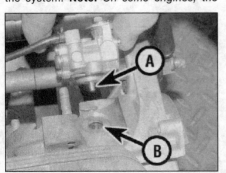

11.5a Note how drive tab (A) locates in the slot (B)

11.5b Remove the wave washer

11.7 Note the location of the pump body O-ring

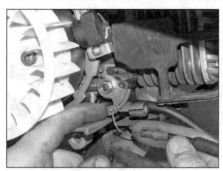

11.13 Detach the cable from the pump pulley

11.15a Lift off the gasket . . .

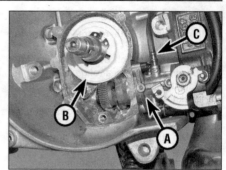

11.15b . . . to access the oil pump (A), drive pinion (B) and oil outlet hose (C)

16 Remove the circlip securing the pump drive pinion, then ease the pinion off the crankshaft **(see illustrations)**. Note which way round the pinion is fitted **(see illustration)**. Note how the pinion drive pin locates in a hole in the shaft

and remove it for safekeeping if it is loose **(see illustration)**. **Note:** *A second circlip may be on the crankshaft behind the drive pinion* **(see illustration)**. *It is not necessary to remove this circlip unless the crankshaft oil seal is going*

to be removed, or if the crankcase halves are going to be separated.

17 Release the clip securing the oil inlet hose from the union on the oil tank and detach the hose – plug the tank union and the open end of the hose to prevent oil loss **(see illustrations 3.9a and b)**. Release the clip securing the oil outlet hose from the union on the carburettor and detach the hose **(see illustration 3.10)**. Feed the hoses through to the oil pump.

18 Undo the screws securing the oil pump, then withdraw the pump **(see illustrations)**.

19 Where fitted, remove the O-ring from the pump body and discard it as a new one must be fitted on reassembly **(see illustration 11.21a)**.

20 Ensure no dirt enters the pump body and clean it using a suitable solvent, then dry the pump thoroughly.

Inspection

21 Follow Steps 9 and 10 to check the condition of the pump **(see illustration)**. Also check the condition of the pump drive and driven pinions and renew them if necessary **(see illustration)**. **Note:** *On the engine photographed the oil pump driven pinion was secured to the pump shaft by a circlip and was available as a separate item. On other engines, the pinion may only be supplied as an integral part of the pump.*

Installation

22 Installation is the reverse of removal, noting the following:

● Where fitted, fit a new O-ring on the pump body and lubricate it with a smear of grease.

11.16a Remove the circlip . . .

11.16b . . . and draw the pinion off the crankshaft

11.16c Note which way round the drive pinion is fitted

11.16d Location of the pinion drive pin

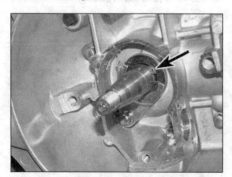

11.16e Note the location of the circlip (arrowed)

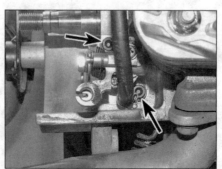

11.18a Undo the screws (arrowed) . . .

11.18b . . . and withdraw the pump

- Ensure the hoses are secured to the pump unions with clips.
- If removed, don't forget to install the drive pinion pin (see Step 16).
- Ensure that the drive pinion is fitted correctly.
- Secure the pump drive pinion with a new circlip.
- Lubricate the drive and driven pinions with high melting-point grease.
- Bleed the pump (see Steps 23 to 25).
- Check the adjustment of the cable (see Chapter 1).

Caution: Accurate cable adjustment is important to ensure that the oil pump delivers the correct amount of oil to the engine and is correctly synchronised with the throttle.

Bleeding

23 Bleeding the pump is the process of removing air from it and allowing it to be filled with oil. First ensure that the inlet hose from the oil tank and the oil filter (where fitted) are completely filled with oil. If necessary, detach the hose from the pump and wait until oil flows from the hose, then reconnect it.

24 Loosen the bleed screw on the pump and wait until oil, without any air mixed with it, flows out the hole, then tighten the screw **(see illustrations)**.

25 Ensure the ignition switch is OFF. Disconnect the oil outlet hose from the carburettor and crank the engine with the kickstarter until oil, without any air mixed with it, flows out the hose, then reconnect the hose and secure it with the clip. Alternatively, fill an auxiliary fuel tank with a 2% (50:1) petrol/two-stroke oil mix and connect it to the carburettor. Disconnect the oil outlet hose from the carburettor, start the engine and run it until oil, without any air mixed with it, flows out the hose, then reconnect the hose and secure it with the clip.

⚠ *Warning: Never run the engine without an oil supply or crank the engine on the electric starter without an oil supply. Never crank the engine with the ignition ON and the spark plug cap disconnected from the spark plug as the ignition system may be damaged.*

11.21a Note the location of the pump body O-ring (arrowed)

11.24a Loosen the bleed screw (arrowed) . . .

12 Crankcase halves 🔧

Note: *To separate the crankcase halves, the engine unit must be removed from the scooter.*

Separation

1 Follow the procedure in Section 3 and remove the engine from the frame.

2 Before the crankcase halves can be separated the following components must be removed:
- Cylinder head (see Section 5)
- Cylinder (see Section 6)
- Alternator (see Section 10)
- Oil pump (see section 11)
- Variator (see Chapter 5)
- Starter motor (see Chapter 9)

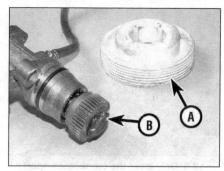

11.21b Oil pump drive gear (A) and driven gear (B)

11.24b . . . but do not remove it to vent air from the system

- Reed valve (see Chapter 3)
- Main stand (Chapter 6)

3 Tape some rag around the connecting rod to prevent it knocking against the cases. Although not essential, it is advisable to remove the piston to avoid damage during this procedure.

4 On some engines, the crankshaft oil seals are held in position by plates on the outside of the crankcases. To remove the seals at this stage, first undo the bolt(s) and remove the plates **(see illustration)**. If required, lever out the oil seals using a flat-bladed screwdriver, taking care not to damage the surface of the crankshaft or the seal housing in the crankcase **(see illustration)**. Alternatively, the seals can be removed once the crankcase halves have been separated.

5 Support the crankcase assembly on the work surface on its left-hand side, then loosen the crankcase bolts evenly, a little at

12.4a Remove the retaining plate . . .

12.4b . . . then lever out the seal carefully

12.5 Loosen the crankcase bolts evenly in a criss-cross sequence

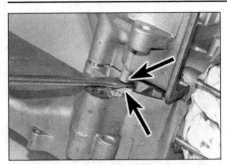

12.6 Only lever the crankcases apart between the pry points – NOT between the mating surfaces

12.7 Drawing the right-hand crankcase half off the crankshaft

12.8a Pressing the crankshaft out of the left-hand crankcase half

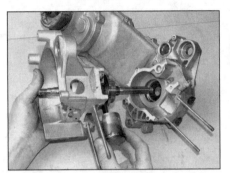

12.8b If the crankshaft remains stuck in the right-hand crankcase . . .

12.8c . . . apply heat and steady pressure with the set-up shown

using the set-up shown **(see illustration)**. Thread the old variator nut onto the end of the crankshaft to protect the threads and make sure the crankshaft assembly is supported to prevent it dropping if it suddenly comes free. **Note:** *On the engine photographed, when the crankcase halves were first separated, the crankshaft remained in the right-hand half* **(see illustration)***. To extract the crankshaft, steady pressure was applied using the set-up shown and considerable heat was required before the crankshaft came free* **(see illustration)**.

9 If fitted, remove the crankcase gasket and discard it as a new one must be used on reassembly.

10 Remove the dowels from either crankcase half for safekeeping if they are loose **(see illustration)**.

11 Clean the mating surfaces of the crankcase halves with a suitable solvent to remove any traces of old gasket or sealant. Take care not to scratch or gouge the soft aluminium.

12 On engines where the oil pump is driven off the crankshaft, remove the pump drive shaft and the shaft bush. If necessary, heat the crankcase around the bush while applying pressure to the shaft.

13 Note the position of the crankshaft oil seals and note which way round the seals are fitted. Before removing the seals, remove any retaining circlips **(see illustration)**. Remove the seals by tapping them gently on one side and then pulling them out with pliers **(see illustration)**. Discard the seals as new ones must be fitted on reassembly.

14 The main bearings will remain in place on

a time and in a criss-cross sequence until they are all finger-tight, then remove them **(see illustration)**. **Note:** *Ensure that all the crankcase bolts have been removed before attempting to separate the cases.*

 HAYNES HINT *Make a cardboard template of the crankcase and punch a hole for each bolt location. This will ensure all bolts are installed correctly on reassembly – this is important as some bolts may be of different lengths.*

6 Lift the right-hand crankcase half off the left-hand half. The cases will be a tight fit on the crankshaft main bearings – apply heat to the right-hand main bearing housing with a hot air gun and carefully lever the cases apart using any pry-points between the cases **(see**

illustration)**. Note:** *Do not try to separate the halves by levering against the mating surfaces as they are easily scored and will not seal correctly afterwards. Do not strike the ends of the crankshaft with a hammer as damage to the end threads or the shaft itself will result.*

7 If the crankcase halves do not separate easily, first ensure all fasteners have been removed, then use a puller arrangement to facilitate the procedure **(see illustration)**. If the puller is placed across the end of the crankshaft, thread the alternator centre nut on first to protect the threads. Take care to ensure that equal pressure is applied on both sides of the puller arrangement at all times and apply heat to the bearing housing.

8 Now apply heat to the left-hand main bearing housing and lift the crankshaft assembly out of the left-hand crankcase half. If necessary, turn the crankcase half over and press the crankshaft assembly out

12.10 Remove the crankcase dowels (arrowed) if they are loose

12.13a Crankshaft oil seal retained by circlip (arrowed)

12.13b Tap the seals with a punch to displace them

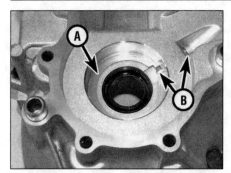

12.22 Inspect the bearing housing (A). Ensure the oilways (B) are clear

12.24 Ensure the new oil seals are installed correctly

12.27 Freezing the main bearing (arrowed) to aid installation

the crankshaft assembly during disassembly. If the main bearings have failed, excessive rumbling and vibration will be felt when the engine is running. Sometimes this may cause the oil seals to fail, resulting in a loss of compression and poor running. Check the condition of the bearings (see *Tools and Workshop Tips* in the *Reference* section) and renew the crankshaft assembly if necessary (see Section 13).

15 If required, remove the transmission assembly from the left-hand crankcase half (see Chapter 5).

Inspection

16 Wash all the components in a suitable solvent and dry them with compressed air. *Caution: Be very careful not to damage the crankcase mating surfaces which may result in loss of crankcase pressure causing poor engine performance. Check both crankcase halves very carefully for cracks and damaged threads.*

17 Small cracks or holes in aluminium castings can be repaired with an epoxy resin adhesive as a temporary measure. Permanent repairs can only be effected by welding, and only a specialist in this process is in a position to advise on the economy or practical aspect of such a repair. On some engines, the crankcase halves can be renewed individually, on others the two halves are only available together as a matching set.

18 Damaged threads can be economically reclaimed by using a thread insert. Most small engineering firms offer a service of this kind. Sheared screws can usually be removed with screw extractors (see *Tools and Workshop Tips* in the *Reference* section). If you are in any doubt about removing a sheared screw, consult an automotive engineer.

19 Always wash the crankcases thoroughly after any repair work to ensure no dirt or metal swarf is trapped inside when the engine is rebuilt.

20 Inspect the engine mounting bushes. If they show signs of deterioration replace them all at the same time. To remove a bush, first note its position in the casing. Heat the casing with a hot air gun, then support the casing and drive the bush out with a hammer and a suitably sized socket. Alternatively, use two

suitably sized sockets to press the bush out in the jaws of a vice. Clean the bush housing with steel wool to remove any corrosion, then reheat the casing and fit the new bush. **Note:** *Always support the casing when removing or fitting bushes to avoid breaking the casing.*

21 On the engine photographed, the front engine mounting passed through two bearings in the crankcase halves. Follow the procedure in *Tools and Workshop Tips* in the *Reference* section to check the bearings.

22 Inspect the bearing housings **(see illustration)**. If a bearing outer race has spun in its housing, the inside of the housing will be damaged. A bearing locking compound can be used to fix the outer race in place on reassembly if the damage is not too severe. **Note:** *If a bearing has spun in its housing the bearing itself is likely to be damaged internally – see Section 13.*

23 Check that the main bearing oilways are clear **(see illustration 12.22)**.

Reassembly

24 Fit the new crankshaft oil seals into the crankcase halves – press them in from the outside using a seal driver or suitably-sized socket . Ensure the seals are fitted the right way round and that they enter the cases squarely **(see illustration)**. Where applicable, secure the seals with new circlips. **Note:** *On the engine photographed, one of the crankcase seals was secured on the outside by a plate (see Step 4). It was found easier to install this seal after the crankcase halves had been joined together.*

12.28a Line-up the crankshaft assembly carefully . . .

25 Support the left-hand crankcase half on the work surface with enough space below it to provide clearance for the end of the crankshaft when it is fully installed.

26 Lubricate the left-hand crankshaft seal and main bearing with the specified two-stroke oil and tape some rag around the connecting rod to prevent it knocking against the cases.

27 Heat the bearing housing in the crankcase with a hot air gun. **Note:** *Avoid applying direct heat onto the crankshaft oil seal.* If required, a freeze spray can be used on the main bearing to aid installation **(see illustration)**.

28 Lower the crankshaft assembly into the crankcase half carefully to avoid damaging the seal. Ensure that the main bearing is aligned with the bearing housing and that the connecting rod is aligned with the crankcase mouth, then press the crankshaft assembly in fully so that the main bearing goes all the way into its housing **(see illustrations)**. If the main bearing does not seat fully, apply more heat around the bearing housing while applying steady pressure to the crankshaft assembly.

29 Allow the case to cool, then wipe the mating surfaces of both crankcase halves with a rag soaked in a suitable solvent and fit the dowels. Fit the crankcase gasket or apply a small amount of suitable sealant to the mating surface of the left-hand case as required **(see illustration)**.

30 Lubricate the right-hand crankshaft seal and main bearing with the specified two-stroke oil.

31 Heat the bearing housing in the crankcase with a hot air gun. **Note:** *Avoid applying direct*

12.28b . . . then press it all the way into the crankcase

12.29 Apply a smear of sealant to the crankcase mating surface

12.32 Installing the right-hand crankcase half

12.33 Use the set-up shown to exert pressure on the right-hand bearing housing

heat onto the crankshaft oil seal. If required, use a freeze spay on the main bearing.

32 Lower the crankcase half over the crankshaft carefully to avoid damaging the seal. Ensure that the two halves of the crankcase are correctly aligned, taking special note of the position of the dowels, and that the main bearing is aligned with the bearing housing in the right-hand case **(see illustration)**.

33 Press the crankcase on fully so that the main bearing goes all the way into its housing. If the main bearing does not seat fully, apply more heat to the area around the bearing housing while applying steady pressure to the crankcase. If necessary, use a large socket, some washers and the old alternator centre nut as shown to exert steady pressure on the bearing housing while heat is being applied **(see illustration)**.

34 Check that the crankcase halves are seated all the way round and that the main bearings are pressed fully into their housings **(see illustration)**. If the casings are not correctly seated, heat the bearing housings while applying firm pressure with the assembly tools used previously. **Note:** *Do not attempt to pull the crankcase halves together using the crankcase bolts as the casing will crack and be ruined.*

35 Clean the threads of the crankcase bolts and install them finger-tight, then tighten them evenly a little at a time in a criss-cross sequence to the torque setting specified in the *Data* section. Support the connecting rod and rotate the crankshaft by hand – if there are any signs of undue stiffness, tight or rough spots, or of any other problem, the fault must be rectified before proceeding further.

36 If necessary, trim the crankcase gasket flush with the mating surface for the cylinder **(see illustration)**.

37 Where fitted, lubricate the oil pump drive shaft and install the shaft and the shaft bush; tap the bush into its seat with a hammer and suitable sized socket **(see illustrations)**. Rotate the crankshaft to ensure the oil pump drive gears are correctly engaged.

38 If applicable, lubricate any remaining crankshaft oil seal with the specified two-stroke oil and fit it over the crankshaft, ensuring that it is the right way round **(see illustration)**. Slide the seal down the shaft carefully to avoid damage and press it firmly into its housing **(see illustration)**. Secure the seal with the plate **(see illustration 12.4a)**.

39 Install the remaining components in the reverse order of removal.

12.34 Ensure crankcase halves are seated all the way round

12.36 Trim off any excess gasket

12.37a Install the oil pump shaft . . .

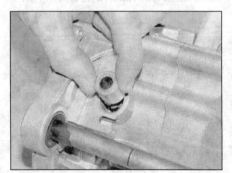

12.37b . . . and shaft bush

12.38a Ensure the seal is the right way round . . .

12.38b . . . and press it into its housing (arrowed)

13 Crankshaft assembly, big-end and main bearings

1 To access the crankshaft and the big-end bearing, the crankcase must be split into two parts (see Section 12).

2 The crankshaft assembly should give many thousands of miles of service. The most likely problems to occur will be a worn small- or big-end bearing due to poor lubrication **(see illustration)**. A worn big-end bearing will produce a pronounced knocking noise, most audible when the engine is under load, and increasing as engine speed rises. This should not be confused with small-end bearing wear, which produces a light metallic rattle (see Section 7).

Inspection

3 To assess the condition of the big-end bearing, hold the crankshaft assembly firmly and push and pull on the connecting rod, checking for any up-and-down freeplay between the two **(see illustration)**. If any freeplay is noted, the bearing is worn and either the bearing or the crankshaft assembly will have to be replaced with a new one. **Note 1:** *A small amount of big-end side clearance (side-to-side movement) is acceptable on the connecting rod.* **Note 2:** *If a new big-end bearing is available, fitting it is a specialist task which should be left to an automotive engineer.*

4 Follow the procedure in *Tools and Workshop Tips* in the *Reference* section and check the main bearings **(see illustration)**. Evidence of extreme heat, such as discoloration or blueing, indicates that lubrication failure has occurred. Be sure to check the oil pump and bearing oilways in the crankcase halves before reassembling the engine.

5 If available, place the crankshaft assembly on V-blocks and check the runout at either end (A and B) using a dial gauge **(see illustration)**. If the crankshaft is out-of-true it will cause excessive engine vibration. If there is any doubt about the condition of the crankshaft have it checked by an automotive engineer. **Note:** *The crankshaft assembly is pressed together and is easily damaged if it is dropped.*

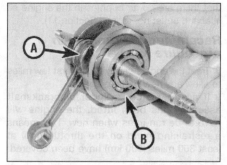

13.2 The crankshaft assembly big-end (A) and main bearings (B)

13.4 Check the main bearings (arrowed) for wear and roughness

6 Inspect the threads on each end of the crankshaft and ensure that the retaining nuts for the alternator rotor and the variator are a good fit. Inspect the splines for the variator pulley on the left-hand end of the shaft **(see illustration)**. Inspect the taper and the slot in the right-hand end of the shaft for the alternator Woodruff key **(see illustration)**. Damage or wear that prevents the rotor from being fitted securely will require a new crankshaft assembly.

7 Where applicable, inspect the oil pump drive gear teeth on the crankshaft and on the pump drive shaft for damage or wear **(see illustration)**. Inspect the ends of the pump drive shaft where it runs in its bearings. Renew any components that are worn or damaged.

Reassembly

8 Follow the procedure in Section 12 to install the crankshaft assembly.

13.3 Any freeplay indicates a worn big-end bearing

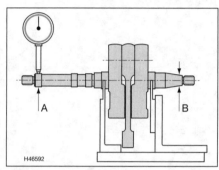

13.5 Check crankshaft runout at points A and B

14 Initial start-up after overhaul/running-in

Initial start-up

1 Make sure the oil tank is at least partly full and the pump has been bled (see Section 11), and that the cable is correctly adjusted (see Chapter 1).

2 Make sure there is fuel in the tank.

3 With the ignition OFF, operate the kickstart to check that the engine turns over easily.

4 Turn the ignition ON, start the engine and allow it to run at a slow idle until it reaches operating temperature. Do not be alarmed if there is a little smoke from the exhaust – this will be due to the oil used to lubricate the engine components during assembly and should subside after a while.

13.6a Inspect the shaft end threads and the variator pulley splines (arrowed)

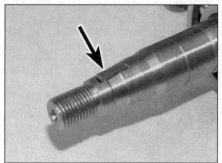

13.6b Inspect the shaft taper and slot (arrowed) for the Woodruff key

13.7 Inspect the oil pump drive gear teeth

5 If the engine proves reluctant to start, remove the spark plug and check that it has not become wet and oily. If it has, clean it and try again. If the engine refuses to start, go through the fault finding charts at the end of this manual to identify the problem.

6 Check carefully that there are no fuel and oil leaks and make sure the transmission and controls, especially the brakes, function properly before road testing the machine.

7 Upon completion of the road test, and after the engine has cooled down completely, check that there are no air bubbles in the engine oil inlet and outlet hoses (see Section 11).

Recommended running-in procedure

8 Treat the engine gently for the first few miles to allow any new parts to bed in.

9 If a new piston, cylinder or crankshaft assembly has been fitted, the engine will have to be run-in as when new. This means a restraining hand on the throttle until at least 300 miles (500 km) have been covered.

There's no point in keeping to any set speed limit – gradually increase performance up to the 600 mile (1000 km) mark. Make sure that the throttle position is varied to vary engine speed, and use full throttle only for short bursts. Experience is the best guide, since it's easy to tell when an engine is running freely.

10 Pay particular attention to the *Pre-ride checks* at the beginning of this manual. Check the tightness of all relevant nuts and bolts.

Chapter 3
Fuel and exhaust systems

Contents

Degrees of difficulty

| Easy, suitable for novice with little experience | 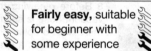 | Fairly easy, suitable for beginner with some experience | | Fairly difficult, suitable for competent DIY mechanic | | Difficult, suitable for experienced DIY mechanic | | Very difficult, suitable for expert DIY or professional | |

1 General information and precautions

The fuel system consists of the fuel tank, fuel tap with filter, carburettor, fuel hoses and control cables. On some scooters, either due to the position of the fuel tank or the use of a fuel header tank in the system, a fuel pump is fitted.

The fuel tap is automatic in operation and is opened by engine vacuum. Generally, the fuel filter is fitted inside the fuel tank and is part of the tap. On some models, an additional fuel filter is fitted in the fuel line.

For cold starting, an electrically-operated automatic choke is fitted in the carburettor. Some models also have an electrically-operated carburettor heater.

Air is drawn into the carburettors via an air filter which is housed next to the drive belt casing.

Several fuel system service procedures are considered routine maintenance items and for that reason are included in Chapter 1.

Note: *On two-stroke engines, lubricating oil is mixed with the fuel in the intake manifold. See Chapter 2B for details of the oil pump.*

Precautions

⚠️ **Warning: Petrol (gasoline) is extremely flammable, so take extra pre-cautions when you work on any part of the fuel system. Don't smoke or allow open flames or bare light bulbs near the work area, and don't work in a garage where a natural gas-type appliance is present. If you spill any fuel on your skin, rinse it off immediately with soap and water. When you perform any kind of work on the fuel system, wear safety glasses and have a fire extinguisher suitable for a class B type fire (flammable liquids) on hand.**

Always perform service procedures in a well-ventilated area to prevent a build-up of fumes.

Never work in a building containing a gas appliance with a pilot light, or any other form of naked flame. Ensure that there are no naked light bulbs or any sources of flame or sparks nearby.

Do not smoke (or allow anyone else to smoke) while in the vicinity of petrol or of components containing it. Remember the possible presence of vapour from these sources and move well clear before smoking.

Check all electrical equipment belonging to the house, garage or workshop where work is being undertaken (see the Safety first! section of this manual). Remember that certain electrical appliances such as drills, cutters etc. create sparks in the normal course of operation and must not be used near petrol or any component containing it. Again, remember the possible presence of fumes before using electrical equipment.

Always mop up any spilt fuel and safely dispose of the rag used.

Any stored fuel that is drained off during servicing work must be kept in sealed containers that are suitable for holding petrol, and clearly marked as such; the containers themselves should be kept in a safe place.

Read the Safety first! section of this manual carefully before starting work.

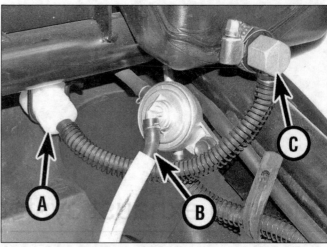

2.1a Fuel tap located on the fuel tank. Note the tank union (A), fuel hose (B) and vacuum hose (C)

2.1b In-line fuel tap. Note the fuel filter (A), vacuum hose (B) and hose union on the tank (C)

2 Fuel tap and filter

Warning: Refer to the precautions given in Section 1 before starting work.

Fuel tap

Check

Note: *Some scooters do not have a separate fuel tap – instead the tap function is controlled by the fuel pump, which will only allow fuel to flow when the engine is turning over. See Section 13 for fuel pump check and renewal. On these machines, the fuel filter is fitted to the fuel supply hose (see Steps 10 to 14).*

1 The fuel tap is located either on the underside of the fuel tank, or in the fuel line between the tank and the carburettor **(see illustrations)**. Remove any body panels as required for access (see Chapter 8). The tap is automatic, operated by a vacuum created when the engine is running which opens a diaphragm inside the tap. If the tap is faulty, it must be renewed – it is a sealed unit for which no individual components are available. The most likely problem is a hole or split in the tap diaphragm.

2 To check the tap, release the clip securing the fuel hose and detach it from the carburettor, being prepared to catch any residual fuel in a rag. Place the open end of the hose in a small container **(see illustration)**. Detach the vacuum hose from the inlet manifold or carburettor, according to model **(see illustrations)**, and apply a vacuum to it (suck on the hose end) – if you are not sure which hose is which on your model, trace the hoses from the tap. Fuel should flow from the tap and into the container **(see illustration)** – if it doesn't, the diaphragm is probably split.

3 Before renewing the tap, check that the vacuum hose is securely attached, and that there are no splits or cracks in the hose. If in doubt, attach a spare hose to the vacuum union on the tap and again apply a vacuum. If fuel still does not flow, remove the tap and fit a new one.

Removal

4 The tap should not be removed unnecessarily from the tank otherwise the O-ring or filter may be damaged.

5 Before removing the tap, connect a drain hose to the fuel hose union and insert its end in a container suitable and large enough for storing the petrol. Apply a vacuum to the vacuum hose (see Step 2) and allow the tank to drain.

6 Release the clips and detach any remaining hoses from the tap, noting where they fit.

7 To remove the tap from the fuel tank, either unscrew the union nut or loosen the clamp securing the tap and withdraw the tap assembly. Be prepared to catch any residual fuel in a rag. Check the condition of the O-ring. If it is in good condition it can be re-used, though it is better to use a new one. If deteriorated or damaged it must be renewed. Allow the gauze filter to dry, then remove all traces of dirt and fuel sediment with a soft brush. Check the gauze for holes. If any are found, a new tap should be fitted as the filter is not available individually.

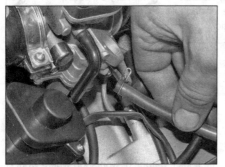

2.2a Detach the fuel hose from the carburettor. Note the hose clip

2.2b Detach the vacuum hose (arrowed) from the manifold . . .

2.2c . . . or the carburettor

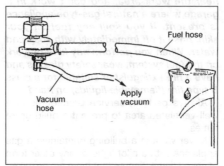

2.2d Place the fuel hose in a container and apply suction to the vacuum hose

2.11 Check the condition of the in-line fuel filter

8 To remove an in-line tap, undo the mounting bolt and lift the tap off, noting which way round it fits.

Installation

9 Installation is the reverse of removal. If the tap is located on the tank, ensure that the union nut or clamp is tightened securely. Fit the fuel and vacuum hoses onto their respective unions and secure them with their clips.

In-line filter

10 Remove any body panels as required for access (see Chapter 8).

11 If the filter has a clear plastic body, check for signs of sediment or a clogged element **(see illustration)**.

12 To remove the filter, first release it from any clips or ties **(see illustrations)**. Loosen the clips securing the fuel hoses to each end of the filter and detach the hoses, being prepared to catch any residual fuel in a rag **(see illustration)**. Note which way round the filter is fitted – an arrow on the filter body indicates the direction of fuel flow **(see illustration)**.

13 The filter is a sealed unit. If it is dirty or clogged, fit a new one.

14 Installation is the reverse of removal. Ensure the filter is the correct way round. Renew the clips on the fuel hoses if the old ones are sprained or corroded.

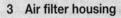

3 Air filter housing

Removal

1 Where applicable, remove the body panels to access the filter housing (see Chapter 8).

2 If the housing is located forward of the drive belt cover, remove the bolts securing it to the engine unit, then release the clip securing the air duct to the carburettor and lift the housing off **(see illustrations)**.

3 On some scooters, a secondary air system (SAS) is fitted (see Section 15). Air is drawn through a hose from the filter housing to the SAS reed valve. Release the clip securing the hose and disconnect it from the union on the

2.12a Release the clip securing the fuel filter

2.12c Detach the fuel hoses from the filter

reed valve **(see illustration)**. Remove the clip for safekeeping.

4 If the filter housing is located above the drive belt cover, first loosen the clamp securing the air duct to the carburettor, then loosen the

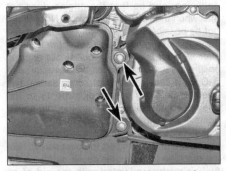

3.2a Undo the filter housing mounting bolts (arrowed) . . .

3.3 Disconnect the air hose from the SAS reed valve (arrowed)

2.12b Release the fuel filter holder (arrowed) from the frame bracket

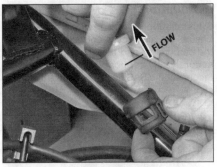

2.12d Arrow indicates direction of fuel flow

clamp and disconnect the air inlet hose from the filter housing **(see illustrations)**.

5 Remove the bolts securing the filter housing to the engine unit, then lift the housing off **(see illustrations)**.

3.2b . . . and release the clip on the air duct (arrowed)

3.4a Loosen the air duct clamp (arrowed) on the carburettor

3.4b Loosen the inlet hose clamp on the filter housing

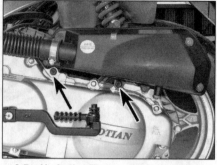

3.5a Undo the filter housing mounting bolts (arrowed) . . .

3.5b . . . and lift the filter housing off

Installation

6 Installation is the reverse of removal. Ensure the air duct is correctly installed on the carburettor and that the clip is tightened securely. If applicable, don't forget to reconnect the SAS hose and secure it with the clip.

4 Fuel/air mixture adjustment – general information

⚠️ **Warning: Adjustment of the pilot screw is made with the engine running. To prevent accidents caused by the rear wheel contacting the ground, ensure that the scooter is on its main stand and if necessary place a support under the scooter to prevent the rear wheel contacting the ground.**

1 Mixture is set using the pilot screw (see illustration 8.1 or 9.1). Adjustment of the pilot screw is not normally necessary and should only be performed if the engine is running roughly, stalls continually, or if a new pilot screw has been fitted.

2 If the pilot screw is removed during a carburettor overhaul, record its current setting by turning the screw it in until it seats lightly, counting the number of turns necessary to achieve this, then unscrew it fully. On installation, turn the screw in until it seats lightly, then back it out the number of turns you've recorded. If fitting a new pilot screw, ideally turn the screw in until it seats, then

back it out the number of turns specified by the scooter manufacturer as the base adjustment setting – setting are given for certain models in the *Data section* at the end of this manual. Alternatively you could use the setting of the original pilot screw as the base position for adjustment.

3 Pilot screw adjustment must be made with the engine running and at normal working temperature. Stop the engine and screw the pilot screw in until it seats lightly, then back it out to the base setting described in Step 2. Start the engine and set the idle speed to the specified amount (see Chapter 1).

4 Now try turning the pilot screw inwards by no more than a ¼ turn, noting its effect on the idle speed, then repeat the process, this time turning the screw outwards.

5 The pilot screw should be set in the position which gives the most consistent, even idle speed without the automatic transmission engaging, and so that the engine does not stall when the twistgrip is opened. **Note:** *It will not be possible to achieve an even idle speed if the spark plug needs adjustment or if the air filter element is dirty. On four stroke engines ensure the valve clearances are correctly set.*

6 Once a satisfactory pilot screw setting has been achieved, further adjustments to the idle speed can be made with the idle speed adjuster screw (see Chapter 1).

7 If it is not possible to achieve a satisfactory idle speed after adjusting the pilot screw, take the machine to a scooter dealer and have the fuel/air mixture adjusted with the aid of an exhaust gas analyser.

5 Automatic choke unit

1 Poor starting or poor engine performance and an increase in fuel consumption are possible signs that the automatic choke is not working properly. After 3 to 5 minutes of the ignition switch being turned on, it should be possible feel the choke unit getting warm.

2 The resistance of the choke should be checked with a multimeter after the engine has been warmed to normal operating temperature and then allowed to cool for ten minutes. Remove the luggage compartment (see Chapter 8) then trace the wiring from the automatic choke unit on the carburettor and disconnect it at the connector (see illustrations).

3 Measure the resistance between the terminals on the choke unit side of the connector with the multimeter set to the ohms scale. Specific figures are not available, but you should get a reading of 20 to 40 ohms if the unit is in good condition.

4 To check that the plunger is not seized in the choke body, first remove the choke unit cover. Undo the screws securing the retaining plate and slide the plate off, then withdraw the choke unit from the carburettor (see illustrations).

5 Measure the protrusion of the plunger from the body (see illustration). Next, use jumper wires to connect a good 12V battery to the

5.2a Location of the automatic choke unit (arrowed). Note the press-on cover

5.2b Release the clip and disconnect the choke unit wiring connector

5.4a Remove the retaining plate . . .

choke unit terminals and measure the protrusion again after 5 minutes. If the measurement has not increased by approximately 3 to 6 mm (depending on the type of carburettor) the unit is faulty and should be renewed.

6 Carburettor overhaul – general information

1 Poor engine performance, difficult starting, stalling, flooding and backfiring are all signs that carburettor maintenance may be required.

2 Keep in mind that many so-called carburettor problems can often be traced to mechanical faults within the engine or ignition system malfunctions. Try to establish for certain that the carburettor is in need of maintenance before beginning a major overhaul.

3 Check the fuel tap and filter, the fuel and vacuum hoses, the fuel pump (where fitted), the intake manifold joints, the air filter, the ignition system and the spark plug before assuming that a carburettor overhaul is required.

4 Most carburettor problems are caused by dirt particles, varnish and other deposits which build up in and eventually block the fuel jets and air passages inside the carburettor. Also, in time, gaskets and O-rings deteriorate and cause fuel and air leaks which lead to poor performance.

5 When overhauling the carburettor, disassemble it completely and clean the parts thoroughly with a carburettor cleaning solvent. If available, blow through the fuel jets and air passages with compressed air to ensure they are clear. Once the cleaning process is complete, reassemble the carburettor using new gaskets and O-rings.

6 Before disassembling the carburettor, make sure you have the correct carburettor gasket set, some carburettor cleaner, a supply of clean rags, some means of blowing out the carburettor passages and a clean place to work.

Note: *Carburettor design differs for 2-stroke and 4-stroke engines. Two-stroke engines use a slide type carburettor, whereas four-stroke*

7.6 Disconnect the vacuum hose from the carburettor union

5.4b . . . then pull out the choke unit. Note the plunger (arrowed)

engines generally use a constant-vacuum (CV) type – ensure that you follow the correct procedure.

7 Carburettor – removal and installation

> ⚠️ **Warning: Refer to the precautions given in Section 1 before starting work.**

Removal

1 Remove the body panels as required on your scooter to access the carburettor (see Chapter 8). Where fitted, remove the carburettor cover, noting how it fits.

2 Remove the air filter housing (see Section 3).

3 Trace the wiring from the automatic choke unit and disconnect it at the connector (see Section 5).

7.4 Disconnect the oil hose from the carburettor union – two-stroke engines

7.7 Location of the float chamber drain screw (arrowed)

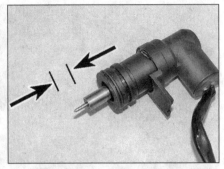

5.5 Measure the protrusion of the plunger from the choke unit body

4 On two-stroke engines, release the clip and disconnect the oil hose from the union on the carburettor **(see illustration)**.

5 Where fitted, disconnect the auto choke wiring connectors **(see illustration)**.

6 If the fuel tap vacuum hose is connected to the carburettor, disconnect it **(see illustration)**.

7 Loosen the drain screw and drain all the fuel from the carburettor float chamber into a suitable container **(see illustration)**.

8 Release the clip and disconnect the fuel hose from the union on the carburettor **(see illustration)**.

9 Where fitted, breather and drain hoses can usually be left attached and withdrawn with the carburettor, as their lower ends are not secured. Note their routing as they are withdrawn.

10 If the throttle cable is attached to a slide inside the carburettor (see Section 8), undo

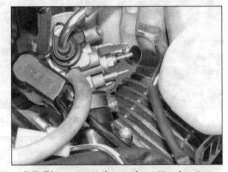

7.5 Disconnect the carburettor heater wiring connectors

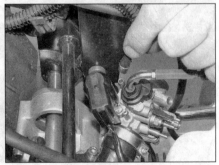

7.8 Disconnect the fuel hose from the carburettor union

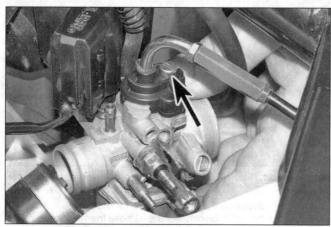

7.10a Remove the screw . . .

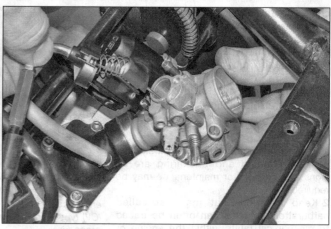

7.10b . . . then withdraw the throttle slide assembly

the screw securing the carburettor top cover, then lift off the cover and withdraw the throttle slide assembly **(see illustrations)**. Secure the cable where the slide assembly will not be damaged. To detach the slide assembly from the cable, see Section 8.

11 If the throttle cable is attached to a pulley on the outside of the carburettor, first detach the outer cable or cable adjuster from its bracket, then detach the inner cable end from the pulley **(see illustrations)**.

12 Note how the lug on the carburettor

locates against the intake manifold, then loosen the clamp securing the carburettor and ease the carburettor off **(see illustrations)**. *Caution: Stuff clean rag into the intake after removing the carburettor to prevent anything from falling inside.*

7.11a Detach the outer cable from the bracket (arrowed)

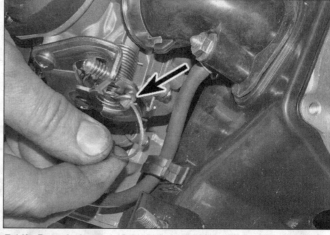

7.11b Detach the end of the inner cable from the pulley (arrowed)

7.12a Note the alignment of the lugs (A). Carburettor clamp screw (B)

7.12b Ease the carburettor off, noting how it fits

7.14a Disconnect the fuel tap vacuum hose (arrowed)

7.14b Undo the nuts (arrowed) . . .

7.14c . . . and lift the manifold off. Note the O-ring seal (arrowed)

13 If required, remove the intake manifold.

14 On four-stroke engines, the manifold is fixed to the cylinder head. If applicable, release the clip securing the fuel tap vacuum hose to the manifold and pull the hose off, then undo the nuts securing the manifold and lift it off **(see illustrations)**. Note the O-ring seal on the manifold. If fitted, lift off the manifold spacer, noting the location of the seal **(see illustrations)**.

15 On two-stroke engines, the manifold is fixed to the upper surface of the crankcase and secures the reed valve assembly (see Section 11).

7.14d Location of the manifold spacer (arrowed)

7.14e Lift off the spacer noting the O-ring seal (arrowed)

Installation

16 Installation is the reverse of removal, noting the following:

● Ensure that the seals and gaskets on the intake manifold are in good condition.

● Make sure the lug on the carburettor is fully engaged with the intake manifold.

● Tighten the clamp screw securely.

● Make sure all hoses are correctly routed and secured and not trapped or kinked.

● Ensure the wiring connectors are secure.

● Follow the procedure in Section 8 to install the throttle slide assembly.

● Reverse the procedure in Step 11 to install the throttle cable on the pulley.

● Check the throttle cable adjustment (see Chapter 1).

● Check the idle speed and adjust as necessary (see Chapter 1).

 8 Slide carburettor overhaul

⚠ *Warning: Refer to the precautions given in Section 1 before starting work.*

Note: *Slide carburettors are generally fitted to two-stroke engines.*

Disassembly

1 Remove the carburettor (see Section 7). Take care when removing components to note their exact locations and any springs or O-rings that may be fitted **(see illustration)**.

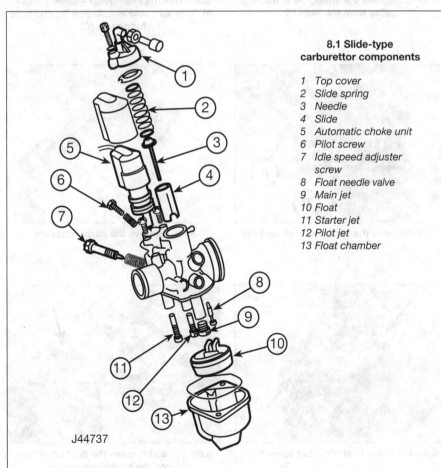

8.1 Slide-type carburettor components

1 *Top cover*
2 *Slide spring*
3 *Needle*
4 *Slide*
5 *Automatic choke unit*
6 *Pilot screw*
7 *Idle speed adjuster screw*
8 *Float needle valve*
9 *Main jet*
10 *Float*
11 *Starter jet*
12 *Pilot jet*
13 *Float chamber*

J44737

8.2a Remove the choke unit cover . . .

8.2b . . . then undo the retaining plate screws (arrowed) . . .

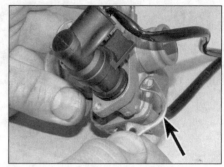

8.2c . . . and remove the retaining plate

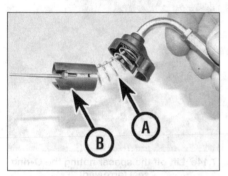

8.3a Compress the spring (A) to free the cable from the slide (B)

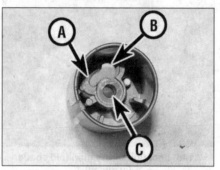

8.3b Throttle slide detail – cable recess (A), hole for cable installation (B) and hole for needle (C)

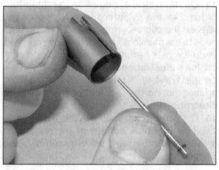

8.4 Remove the needle from the throttle slide

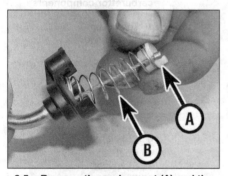

8.5a Remove the spring seat (A) and the spring (B)

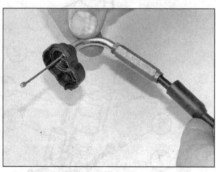

8.5b Remove the carburettor top

2 Where fitted, remove the cover on the automatic choke unit and remove the retaining plate **(see illustrations)**. Withdraw the choke unit from the carburettor body, noting how it fits.

3 To remove the throttle slide assembly from the cable, first compress the slide spring **(see illustration)**. Slot the cable end out of its recess inside the slide, then pull it up through the hole in the bottom of the slide **(see illustration)**.

4 Lift the needle out of the slide **(see illustration)**.

5 Remove the spring seat and the spring from the cable, then pull the carburettor top cover off the cable **(see illustrations)**.

6 Undo the screws securing the float chamber to the base of the carburettor and remove it – note the location of the gasket on the float chamber **(see illustrations)**.

7 Some carburettors are fitted with two removable jets (pilot jet and main jet), some have three removable jets (pilot jet, main jet and starter jet) **(see illustrations)**. Note the location of the jets, then unscrew them. The main jet screws into the base of the atomiser; if the atomiser is slotted, unscrew it if required. The jets will be marked with an identification number or code usually only legible under magnification **(see illustration)**.

8 Withdraw the float pin **(see illustration)**.

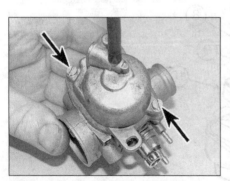

8.6a Undo the float chamber screws . . .

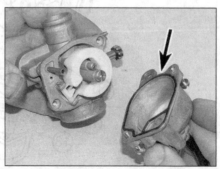

8.6b . . . and remove the float chamber. Note the gasket (arrowed)

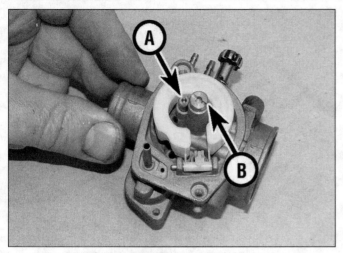

**8.7a Carburettor with two removable jets –
pilot jet (A) and main jet (B)**

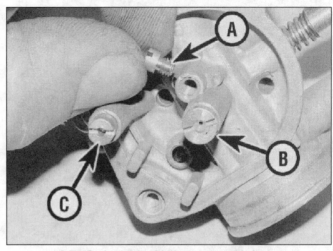

**8.7b Carburettor with three removable jets –
pilot jet (A), main jet (B) and starter jet (C)**

If necessary, displace the pin carefully using a small punch or a nail. **Note:** *On some carburettors, the float pin may be retained by a small screw.*

9 Remove the float and unhook the float needle valve, noting how it fits onto the tab on the float **(see illustrations)**.

10 Where fitted, unscrew the carburettor heater **(see illustration)**.

11 The pilot screw can be removed if required, but note that its setting will be disturbed (see *Haynes Hint*). Unscrew and remove the pilot screw along with its spring and O-ring, where fitted.

8.7c Note the identification number on the jet

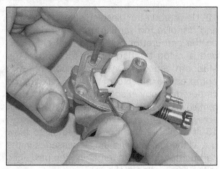

8.8 Remove the float pin

 To record the pilot screw's current setting, turn the screw in until it seats lightly, counting the number of turns necessary to achieve this, then unscrew it fully. On installation, turn the screw in until it seats, then back it out the number of turns you've recorded.

Cleaning

Caution: Use only a petroleum-based solvent for carburettor cleaning. Don't use caustic cleaners.

8.9a Lift out the float. Note the needle valve seat (arrowed)

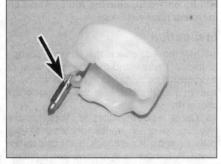

8.9b Note how the float needle valve fits onto the tab (arrowed)

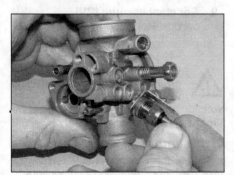

8.10 Remove the carburettor heater

8.11a Note the location of the pilot air screw (arrowed) . . .

8.11b . . . and remove it if required

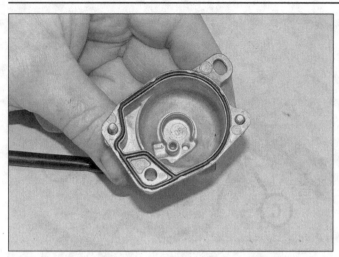

8.27 Ensure that the float chamber gasket is correctly installed

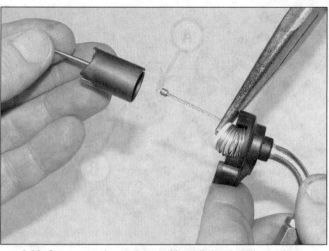

8.32 Compress the spring and install the throttle cable as described

12 Use carburettor cleaning solvent to loosen and dissolve the varnish and other deposits on the carburettor body and float chamber; use a nylon-bristled brush to remove the stubborn deposits. Dry the components with compressed air. **Note:** *Avoid soaking the carburettor body in solvent if any O-ring seals remain inside and remove the gasket and drain screw O-ring from the float chamber.*

13 If available, use compressed air to blow out all the fuel jets and the air passages in the carburettor body, not forgetting the passages in the carburettor intake.

Caution: Never clean the jets or passages with a piece of wire or a drill bit, as they will be enlarged, causing the fuel and air metering rates to be upset.

Inspection

14 If removed, check the tapered portion of the pilot screw and the spring for wear or damage. If necessary, renew the screw or spring. If applicable, fit a new O-ring to the pilot screw.

15 Check the carburettor body, float chamber and top cover for cracks, distorted sealing surfaces and other damage. If any defects are found, renew the faulty component, although a new carburettor will probably be necessary.

16 Insert the throttle slide in the carburettor body and check that it moves up-and-down smoothly. Check the surface of the slide for wear. If it's worn or scored excessively or doesn't move smoothly, renew the components as necessary.

17 The clip on the jet needle enables the needle height within the slide to be altered – usually three grooves are provided and the manufacturer specifies the correct groove for the machine. Remove the clip (noting which groove it's in) and check the needle for straightness by rolling it on a flat surface such as a piece of glass. Fit a new needle if it's bent or if the tip is worn. Refit the clip for safekeeping.

18 Inspect the tip of the float needle valve. If

it has grooves or scratches in it, or is in any way worn, it must be renewed. If the valve seat is damaged, check the availability of new parts, otherwise a new carburettor body will have to be fitted. **Note:** *On scooters with a pumped and pressurised fuel system, a worn or incorrectly sized carburettor float needle valve seat will not be able to shut off the fuel supply sufficiently to prevent carburettor flooding and excessive use of fuel.*

19 Check the float for damage. This will usually be apparent by the presence of fuel inside the float. If the float is damaged, it must be renewed.

20 Inspect the automatic choke unit plunger and needle for signs of wear and renew the unit if necessary. To check the operation of the choke unit see Section 5.

Reassembly

Note: *When reassembling the carburettor, be sure to use new O-rings and gaskets. Do not overtighten the carburettor jets and screws as they are easily damaged.*

21 If removed, install the pilot screw, spring and O-ring; adjust the screw to the setting as noted on removal (see Step 11).

22 If removed, install the carburettor heater **(see illustration 8.10)**.

23 If removed, install the atomiser, then install the main jet **(see illustration 8.7a)**.

24 Install the pilot jet and, if applicable, the starter jet.

25 Hook the float needle valve onto the float tab, then position the float assembly in the carburettor, making sure the needle valve enters its seat **(see illustration 8.9a)**. Install the float pin, making sure it is secure **(see illustration 8.8)**.

26 The carburettor float height should be checked at this point (see Section 10).

27 Fit the gasket onto the float chamber, making sure it is seated properly in its groove **(see illustration)**. Install the float chamber onto the carburettor and tighten the screws securely. Ensure that the O-ring is fitted on the

drain screw and tighten the screw securely.

28 Install the choke unit and secure it with the retaining plate and screws. Install the choke unit cover, if fitted.

29 Install the carburettor (see Section 7).

30 Install the needle in the throttle slide (see Step 4).

31 Install the top cover, spring and spring seat on the cable **(see illustration 8.5a)**. Ensure that the spring seat is fitted so that the protruding lug is facing away from the spring.

32 Compress the spring with the spring seat and hold the spring inside the top cover with needle-nosed pliers, then insert the inner cable end through the installation hole in the slide **(see illustration)**.

33 Locate the cable end in hole (A) **(see illustration 8.3b)**, then release the spring and ensure that the tab on the spring seat locates in hole (B).

34 Install the throttle slide assembly carefully **(see illustration 7.10b)**. Ensure that the needle is aligned with the top of the atomiser and that the slot in the slide is aligned with the lug inside the carburettor body. Hold the top cover in position and secure it with the screw **(see illustration 7.10a)**.

35 Check the throttle cable freeplay and idle speed adjustment (see Chapter 1).

9 Constant vacuum (CV) carburettor overhaul

 Warning: Refer to the precautions given in Section 1 before starting work.

Note: *Constant-vacuum (CV) carburettors are fitted to four-stroke engines.*

Disassembly

1 Remove the carburettor (see Section 7). Take care when removing components to note their exact locations and any springs or O-rings that may be fitted **(see illustration)**.

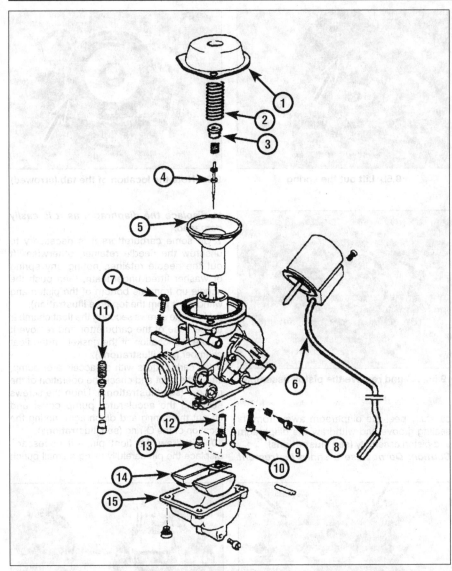

9.3a Undo the screws . . .

9.3b . . . and lift off the throttle cable bracket. Note the cam (arrowed) on the cable pulley

2 Where fitted, remove the cover on the automatic choke unit, then remove the retaining plate securing the choke in the carburettor (Section 5). Withdraw the choke, noting how it fits.

3 If required, undo the screws securing the throttle cable bracket and lift the bracket off – where fitted, note how the accelerator pump lever rests on the cam on the back of the throttle cable pulley **(see illustrations)**.

4 Where fitted, undo the screws securing the air cut-off valve cover, then lift off the cover and remove the spring **(see illustrations)**. Remove the diaphragm, noting which way round it fits, and the O-ring **(see illustration)**.

5 Unscrew and remove the top cover retaining

9.1 Constant vacuum (CV) type carburettor components

1 Top cover	6 Automatic choke unit	11 Accelerator pump
2 Spring	7 Idle speed adjuster	assembly
3 Needle retainer	screw	12 Needle jet
4 Needle	8 Pilot screw	13 Main jet
5 Diaphragm and piston	9 Pilot jet	14 Float
assembly	10 Float needle valve	15 Float chamber

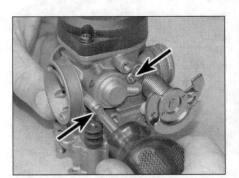

9.4a Undo the screws (arrowed) . . .

9.4b . . . and remove the air cut-off valve cover and spring

9.4c Remove the diaphragm and O-ring (arrowed)

9.5a Undo the top cover retaining screws (arrowed)

9.5b Lift out the spring

9.6a Note the location of the tab (arrowed)

9.6b Lift the diaphragm out carefully . . .

9.6c . . . and remove the piston assembly

to displace the diaphragm as it is easily damaged.

7 On some carburettors it is necessary to unscrew the needle retainer, otherwise lift out the needle retainer, noting any spring or washer fitted underneath, then push the needle up from the bottom of the piston and withdraw it from the top (see illustration).

8 Undo the screws securing the float chamber to the base of the carburettor and remove it – note the location of the gasket on the float chamber (see illustrations).

9 On carburettors with an accelerator pump, lift off the boot and check the operation of the plunger (see illustrations). Undo the screws securing the accelerator pump cover and lift out the spring and diaphragm, noting the location of the O-ring (see illustrations).

10 Withdraw the float pin – if necessary, displace the pin carefully using a small punch

screws, then lift off the cover and remove the spring (see illustrations).

6 Note how the tab on the diaphragm fits in the recess in the carburettor body, then

carefully peel the diaphragm away from its sealing groove and withdraw the diaphragm and piston assembly (see illustrations).
Caution: Do not use a sharp instrument

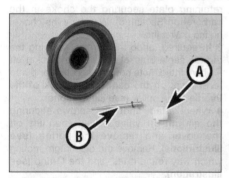

9.7 Lift out the needle retainer (A) and needle (B)

9.8a Undo the float chamber retaining screws (arrowed) . . .

9.8b . . . and lift off the float chamber

9.9a Lift off the accelerator pump boot . . .

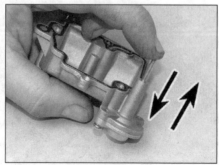

9.9b . . . and check that the plunger moves up and down freely

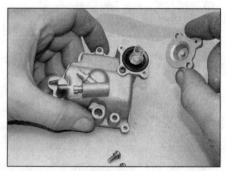

9.9c Remove the accelerator pump cover . . .

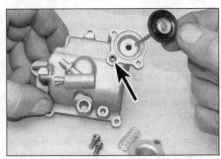

9.9d . . . and remove the spring and diaphragm. Note the location of the O-ring (arrowed)

9.10a Displace the float pin

9.10b Screw (arrowed) secures float pin

or a nail (see illustration). Note that on some carburettors, the float pin may be retained by a small screw (see illustrations). Remove the float and unhook the float needle valve, noting how it fits onto the tab on the float (see illustration).

11 Where fitted, remove the plastic jet cover (see illustration).

12 Note the location of the carburettor jets, then remove them. Unscrew the main jet (see illustration). The main jet screws into the base of the atomiser; if the atomiser is slotted, unscrew it if required (see illustration). Unscrew the pilot jet (see illustration). The jets will be marked with an identification number or code, although you may need a magnifier to read it (see illustration).

13 The pilot screw can be removed if required, but note that its setting will be disturbed (see Haynes Hint). Unscrew and remove the pilot

screw along with its spring and O-ring, where fitted.

> **HAYNES HiNT** *To record the pilot screw's current setting, turn the screw in until it seats lightly, counting the number of turns necessary to achieve this, then unscrew it fully. On installation, turn the screw in until it seats, then back it out the number of turns you've recorded.*

Note: *Do not remove the screws securing the throttle butterfly to the throttle shaft.*

Cleaning

Caution: Use only a petroleum-based solvent for carburettor cleaning. Don't use caustic cleaners.

14 Follow Steps 12 and 13 in Section 8 to clean the carburettor body and jets. If the carburettor has an accelerator pump, pay particular attention to the fuel passage in the float chamber. On some carburettors, the fuel passage is fitted with a one-way valve; blow through the fuel passage with compressed air from the bottom of the pump piston housing. Note: *Avoid soaking the carburettor body in solvent if any O-ring seals remain inside and remove the gasket and drain screw O-ring from the float chamber.*
Caution: Never clean the jets or passages with a piece of wire or a drill bit, as they will be enlarged, causing the fuel and air metering rates to be upset.

Inspection

15 If removed, check the tapered portion of the pilot screw and the spring for wear or

9.10c Note how the needle valve (arrowed) fits on the float tab

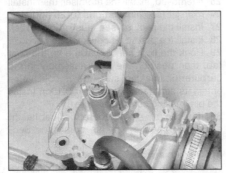

9.11 Remove the jet cover

9.12a Unscrew the main jet . . .

9.12b . . . and the atomiser

9.12c Unscrew the pilot jet

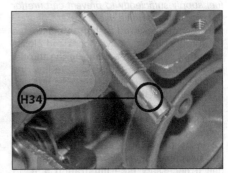

9.12d Note the identification number on the jet

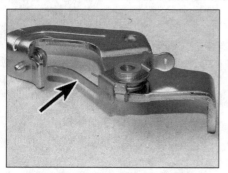

9.23 Check the operation of the accelerator pump lever (arrowed)

9.32 Ensure that the float chamber gasket is correctly installed

damage. If necessary, renew the screw or spring. If applicable, fit a new O-ring to the pilot screw.

16 Check the carburettor body, float chamber and top cover for cracks, distorted sealing surfaces and other damage. If any defects are found, replace the faulty component, although replacement of the entire carburettor will probably be necessary.

17 Inspect the piston diaphragm for splits, holes and general deterioration. Holding it up to a light will help to reveal problems of this nature. Insert the piston in the carburettor body and check that the piston moves up-and-down smoothly. Check the surface of the piston for wear. If it's worn or scored excessively or doesn't move smoothly, replace the components as necessary.

18 Check that the clip is correctly positioned on the needle. **Note:** *On the carburettor used to illustrate this procedure, a washer was fitted below the clip on the needle.* If necessary, remove the clip and check the needle for straightness by rolling it on a flat surface such as a piece of glass. Fit a new needle if it's bent or if the tip is worn. Refit the clip for safekeeping.

19 Inspect the tip of the float needle valve. If it has grooves or scratches in it, or is in any way worn, it must be renewed. If the valve seat is damaged, check the availability of new parts, otherwise a new carburettor body will have to be fitted. **Note:** *On scooters with a pumped and pressurised fuel system, a worn or incorrectly sized carburettor float needle valve seat will not be able to shut off the fuel supply sufficiently to prevent carburettor flooding and excessive use of fuel.*

20 Operate the throttle shaft to make sure the throttle butterfly valve opens and closes smoothly. If it doesn't, cleaning the throttle linkage may help. Otherwise, renew the carburettor.

21 Check the float for damage. This will usually be apparent by the presence of fuel inside the float. If the float is damaged, it must be renewed.

22 Inspect the automatic choke unit plunger and needle for signs of wear and renew the unit if necessary **(see illustration 5.5)**. To check the operation of the choke unit see Section 5.

23 Inspect the accelerator pump diaphragm for splits, holes and general deterioration. Ensure that the spring and the rubber boot are not damaged or deformed and renew them if necessary. Check the operation of the accelerator pump lever **(see illustration)**.

24 Inspect the air cut-off valve diaphragm for splits, holes and general deterioration. Ensure that the spring and the O-ring are not damaged or deformed and renew them if necessary.

Reassembly

Note: *When reassembling the carburettor, be sure to use new O-rings and seals. Do not overtighten the carburettor jets and screws as they are easily damaged.*

25 If removed, install the pilot screw, spring and O-ring; adjust the screw to the setting as noted on removal (see Step 13).

26 If removed, install the atomiser, then install the main jet **(see illustrations 9.12b and a)**.

27 Install the pilot jet **(see illustration 9.12c)**.

28 Install the plastic jet cover where fitted.

29 Hook the float needle valve onto the float tab, then position the float assembly in the carburettor, making sure the needle valve enters its seat **(see illustration 9.10c)**. Install the pin, making sure it is secure.

30 If applicable, the carburettor float height should be checked at this point (see Section 10).

31 On carburettors with an accelerator pump, install the O-ring, pump diaphragm and spring, then fit the cover and tighten the screws securely **(see illustrations 9.9d and c)**. Ensure that the pump plunger operates smoothly, then install the boot **(see illustration 9.9a)**.

32 Fit the gasket onto the float chamber, making sure it is seated properly in its groove **(see illustration)**. Install the float chamber onto the carburettor and tighten the screws securely. Ensure that the O-ring is fitted on the drain screw and tighten the screw securely.

33 If applicable, the carburettor fuel level should be checked at this point (see Section 10).

34 Check that the clip (and washer if applicable) is correctly positioned on the needle, then insert the needle and needle retainer into the piston **(see illustration 9.7)**.

35 Insert the piston assembly into the

carburettor body and push it down lightly, ensuring the needle is correctly aligned with the atomiser **(see illustration 9.6c)**. Align the tab on the diaphragm with the recess in the carburettor body, then press the diaphragm outer edge into its groove, making sure it is correctly seated **(see illustration 9.6a)**. Check the diaphragm is not creased, and that the piston moves smoothly up and down in its bore.

36 Install the spring into the piston and fit the top cover to the carburettor, making sure the spring locates over the raised section on the inside of the cover, then tighten the cover screws securely **(see illustration 9.5b)**.

37 On carburettors with an air cut-off valve, install the O-ring, diaphragm and spring, then fit the cover and tighten the screws securely **(see illustrations 9.4c, b and a)**.

38 If removed, install the throttle cable bracket **(see illustration 9.3a)**. If applicable, ensure that the accelerator pump lever and pulley cam are correctly aligned – check the operation of the lever **(see illustration 9.3b)**.

39 Install the automatic choke unit and secure it with its retaining plate. If fitted, install the choke unit cover.

40 Install the carburettor (see Section 7).

10 Fuel level and float height

1 If the carburettor floods when the scooter is in use, and the float needle valve and the valve seat are good, the fuel level or float height may be incorrect. Adjustment can be made by bending the float tab to change the point at which the float valve shuts off. Note that it is essential to have the fuel level or float height specification relating to your model. This is included for certain models in the *Data* section at the end of this manual.

Fuel level check

2 If not already done, remove the carburettor (see Section 7).

3 Support the carburettor upright in a vice and connect a length of clear fuel hose to the drain union on the base of the float chamber. Secure the hose up against the side of the carburettor and mark it level with the float chamber to carburettor body joint, or the level mark on the side of the carburettor body **(see illustration)**.

4 Carefully pour a small amount of fuel into the carburettor via the fuel hose union, then undo the drain screw in the bottom of the float chamber enough to allow fuel to flow into the clear hose. Continue pouring fuel into the carburettor until the float needle valve shuts off the supply, at which point the level in the clear hose should be at the specified level. Fuel level is generally specified as a distance below the float chamber gasket face.

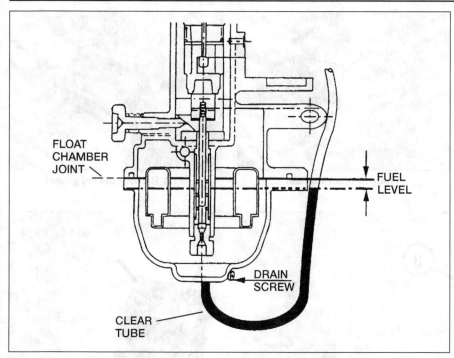

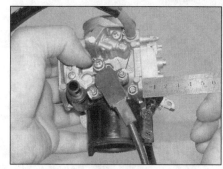

10.7 Measuring the carburettor float height

FLOAT CHAMBER JOINT

FUEL LEVEL

DRAIN SCREW

CLEAR TUBE

10.3 Set-up for measuring the fuel level in the carburettor

valve seat and measure the distance between the float chamber gasket face and the bottom of the float **(see illustration)**.

8 Compare the measurement with the specified height. **Note:** *On some carburettors, it is sufficient that the bottom straight edge of the float should be parallel with the gasket face.*

9 If the float height is incorrect, check the float tab for wear or damage (see Section 8 or 9). If the float tab is metal it can be adjusted carefully to correct the fuel height, otherwise a new float will have to be fitted.

5 If the fuel level is incorrect, remove the float chamber and check the float tab for wear or damage (see Section 8 or 9). If the float tab is metal it can be adjusted carefully to correct the fuel height, otherwise a new float will have to be fitted.

Float height check

6 If not already done, remove the carburettor (see Section 7). Remove the float chamber (see Section 8 or 9).

7 Turn the carburettor upside-down so that the float needle valve is resting against the

11 Reed valve (two-stroke engines)

Removal

1 Remove the carburettor (see Section 7).

2 Undo the screws securing the intake manifold. To undo an anti-tamper shear-head screw (such as shown in the accompanying photo) either hold it firmly with a pair of pliers or, if it is very tight, tap the head round in an anti-clockwise direction with a small chisel or punch **(see illustrations)**. Note that a new shear-head screw will be required on installation **(see illustration)**.

3 Lift the manifold off, noting the seal **(see illustration)**.

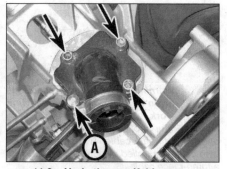

11.2a Undo the manifold screws (arrowed). Note the shear-off head (A)

11.2b Undo the shear screw with pliers . . .

11.2c . . . or tap the head anti-clockwise with a chisel

11.2d Replace the old shear-head screw (A) with a new Allen screw (B)

11.3 Note the seal (arrowed) on the underside of the manifold

11.4a Note the location of the reed valve . . .

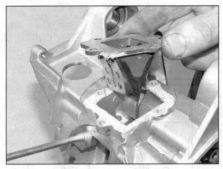

11.4b . . . then lift it out

11.5 Remove the old gasket

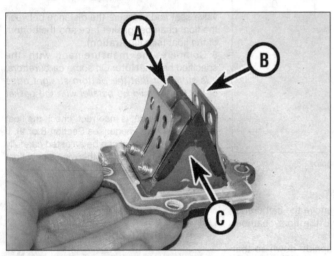

11.7 Reeds (A), stopper plate (B) and valve body (C)

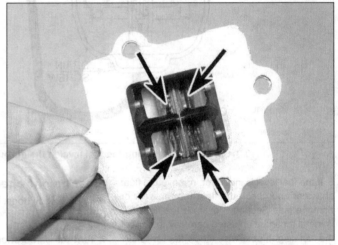

11.8 Check for light between the reeds (arrowed) and the valve body

4 Note the location of the reed valve in the crankcase, then lift it out **(see illustrations)**.
5 Discard any seals or gaskets as new ones must be fitted **(see illustration)**.

Inspection

6 Inspect the reed valve body closely for cracks, distortion and any other damage, particularly around the mating surfaces between the crankcase and the intake manifold – a good seal must be maintained between the components, otherwise crankcase pressure and therefore engine performance will be affected.
7 Check the reeds for cracks, distortion and any other damage. Check also that there are no dirt particles trapped between the reeds and their seats. The reeds should sit flat against the valve body so that a good seal is obtained when the crankcase is under pressure **(see illustration)**. If required, clean the reeds carefully with a suitable solvent to remove any gum.
8 After prolonged use, the reeds tend to become bent and will not therefore seal properly, in which case the assembly should be renewed. A good way to check is to hold the valve up to the light – if light is visible between the reeds and the body they are

not sealing properly **(see illustration)**. If the engine is difficult to start or idles erratically, this could be the problem.
9 Check that the stopper plate retaining screws are tight; do not disassemble the reed valve as individual components are not available.

Installation

10 Installation is the reverse of removal, noting the following:
● Ensure all mating surfaces are clean and perfectly smooth.
● Use new gaskets where applicable

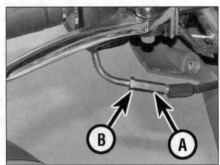

12.2 Throttle cable adjuster (A) and locknut (B)

12 Throttle cable and twistgrip

 Warning: Refer to the precautions given in Section 1 before starting work.

Note: *All four-stroke engines are fitted with a one-piece throttle cable. Two-stroke engines with cable-controlled oil pumps are fitted with a three-piece cable.*

Four-stroke engines

Removal

1 Remove the body panels as required on your scooter to access the carburettor and the throttle twistgrip on the handlebar (see Chapter 8). If applicable, remove the mirror (see Chapter 8). Note that the cable run between the handlebar and the carburettor may require removal of the front panel or belly panel for access to ties securing the cable.
2 Loosen the cable adjuster locknut and thread the adjuster fully in to slacken the cable at the twistgrip end **(see illustration)**.
3 Undo the twistgrip housing screws and separate the two halves of the housing **(see**

12.3 Twistgrip housing screws (arrowed)

12.4a Draw the twistgrip off . . .

12.4b . . . then disconnect the inner cable end (arrowed)

illustration). Lift off the rear half of the housing, noting the location of the switch gear.

4 Draw the twistgrip off the handlebar, then detach the inner cable end from the twistgrip pulley **(see illustrations)**.

5 Where fitted, undo the screw securing the cable elbow to the twistgrip housing, then draw the cable out of the housing **(see illustrations)**.

6 Detach the cable from the throttle slide (see Section 8) or the carburettor pulley (see Section 9).

7 Ensure the cable is free from any clips or guides, then withdraw it from the machine, noting the correct routing.

> *When fitting a new cable, tape the lower end of the new cable to the upper end of the old cable before removing it from the machine. Slowly pull the lower end of the old cable out, guiding the new cable down into position. Using this method will ensure the cable is routed correctly and unless the cable gets caught up when passing through any guides or ties, it should avoid removal of the body panels.*

Installation

8 Installation is the reverse of removal, noting the following:

● Lubricate the upper end of the cable with grease before fitting it into the twistgrip.

● Locate the tab on the twistgrip housing with the hole in the handlebar.

● Ensure the cable is correctly routed and clipped into place – it must not interfere with any other component and should not be kinked or bent sharply.

● Adjust the cable freeplay (see Chapter 1).

● Check the cable operation before riding the scooter.

Two-stroke engines fitted with a cable controlled oil pump

Removal

9 The throttle cable consists of three sections – the main cable from the twistgrip goes into a splitter, with separate cables from this going to

12.5a Detach the cable elbow from the housing . . .

the carburettor and oil pump (see Chapter 1, Section 13).

10 If a cable problem is diagnosed, check the availability of replacement parts – on some scooters it is possible to renew individual cables rather than the whole assembly.

11 Remove the body panels as required on your scooter to access the carburettor, the oil pump and the throttle twistgrip on the handlebar (see Chapter 8). If applicable, remove the mirror (see Chapter 8). Note that the cable run between components will require removal of the front panel or belly panel for access to the splitter and to ties securing the cable.

12 Disconnect the cable from the twistgrip (see Steps 2 to 5).

13 Detach the cable from the throttle slide assembly and the carburettor top cover (see Section 8).

14 Follow the procedure in Chapter 1, Section 17, to access the oil pump.

12.15 Detach the inner cable from the oil pump pulley

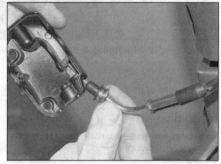

12.5b . . . then draw out the inner cable

15 Loosen the cable adjuster locknut and thread the adjuster fully in to slacken the cable at the oil pump end, then detach the outer cable from its bracket and detach the cable end from the pump pulley **(see illustration)**.

16 If the complete cable assembly is being removed, ensure the cables are free from any clips or guides, then withdraw the assembly from the machine, noting the correct routing.

17 If an individual cable is being removed, first detach the cable from the twistgrip, carburettor or oil pump as applicable, then detach the cable from the splitter as follows.

18 Locate the splitter either behind the front panel or the belly panel **(see illustration)**.

19 Undo the screw securing the cover and lift it off – note the location of the three cables on the pulley, then detach the appropriate cable **(see illustrations)**.

Caution: Before removing a cable, make a

12.18 Location of the cable assembly splitter

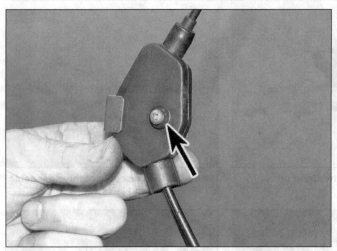

12.19a Remove the cover screw (arrowed)

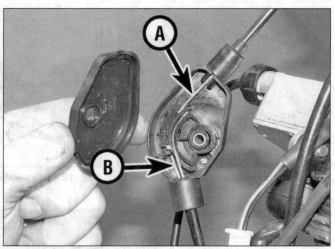

12.19b Location of the cable from the twistgrip (A) and from the carburettor and oil pump (B)

careful note of its routing to ensure correct installation.

Installation

20 Installation is the reverse of removal, noting the following:
● Lubricate the upper end of the cable with grease before fitting it into the twistgrip.
● Locate the tab on the twistgrip housing with the hole in the handlebar.
● Lubricate the cable ends and splitter pulley with grease.
● Ensure the cables are correctly routed and clipped into place – they must not interfere with any other component and should not be kinked or bent sharply.
● Adjust the cable freeplay and check the oil pump setting (see Chapter 1).
● Check the cable operation before riding the scooter.

13 Fuel pump

Warning: Refer to the precautions given in Section 1 before starting work.

Check

1 When the engine is running, the alternating vacuum and pressure in the crankcase opens and closes a diaphragm in the pump. Generally, the pump supplies fuel direct to the carburettor, but on some scooters, the pump supplies fuel to a header tank which ensures an immediate supply of fuel to the carburettor when the scooter has been standing unused.
2 The most likely cause of pump failure will be a split in the pump diaphragm.
3 The fuel pump is usually mounted on the frame alongside the fuel tank **(see illustration)**. Remove the body panels as required on your scooter to access the pump (see Chapter 8).
4 To check whether the pump is operating,

release the clip securing the fuel supply hose to the carburettor, or header tank as applicable, and detach the hose. Place the open end in a container suitable for storing petrol. Turn the engine over on the starter motor and check whether fuel flows from the hose into the container. If fuel flows, the pump is working correctly.
5 If no fuel flows from the pump, first check that this is not due to a blocked filter or fuel hose, or due to a split in the vacuum hose from the crankcase, before renewing the pump **(see illustration)**. Check all the hoses for splits, cracks and kinks, and check that they are securely connected on each end by a good clip. Check that any air vent for the fuel tank is not blocked. If the filter and hoses are good, renew the pump.

Renewal

6 Release the clips securing the fuel and vacuum hoses and detach them from the pump, noting which fits where. Be prepared to catch any residue fuel in a suitable container. The fuel hoses should be clamped to prevent fuel leaks using any of the methods shown in *Tools and Workshop Tips* in the *Reference* section.
7 Undo the pump fixings and remove the pump, noting which way up it fits.

13.3 Location of the fuel pump. Note the clips (arrowed) securing the hoses

8 Install the new pump, making sure the hoses are correctly attached and secured with the clips. If the old clips are corroded or deformed, fit new ones.

14 Exhaust system

Warning: If the engine has been running the exhaust system will be very hot. Allow the system to cool before carrying out any work.

Silencer removal

Note: *Some scooters are fitted with a one-piece exhaust system. Follow the procedure for removing the complete system.*
1 Undo the fixing securing the silencer to the downpipe, then loosen the mounting bolts securing the silencer, or silencer bracket, to the engine **(see illustration)**.
2 Support the silencer, then withdraw the mounting bolts and lift the silencer off.
3 Where fitted, remove the gasket from the silencer-to-downpipe joint and discard it as a new one must be used. If required, undo the mounting nuts and separate the silencer from its bracket.

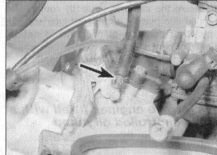

13.5 Check the vacuum hose (arrowed) from the crankcase

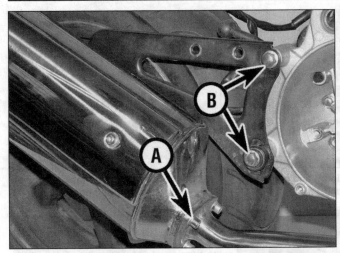

14.1 Undo the fixings (A) and loosen the mounting bolts (B)

14.6a Exhaust downpipe is located on the underside of the scooter

14.6b Downpipe fixings may require spraying with penetrating oil

14.7 Location of silencer mounting bolts on one-piece exhaust system

Complete system removal

4 Remove the body panels as required on your scooter to access the exhaust system and cylinder head (see Chapter 8).

5 On two-stroke machines fitted with a secondary air system (see Section 15), loosen the clip securing the air hose to the reed valve housing on the exhaust downpipe and disconnect the hose.

6 Undo the nuts or bolts securing the downpipe to the exhaust port **(see illustrations)**.

> *Exhaust system fixings tend to become corroded and seized. It is advisable to spray them with penetrating oil before attempting to loosen them.*

7 Loosen the bolts securing the silencer, or silencer bracket, then support the exhaust system and remove the bolts **(see illustration)**. Lower the downpipe clear of the frame and bodywork, then lift the complete exhaust system off the scooter.

8 Remove the exhaust port-to-pipe gasket and discard it as a new one must be used **(see illustration)**.

9 The exhaust system of some restricted 50 cc two-stroke machines is fitted with a resonator tube **(see illustration)**. If your scooter has been de-restricted and the resonator tube has been removed, check around the welded patch on the exhaust for gas leaks. De-restricting requires a number of modifications to the engine and should only be undertaken by a scooter specialist.

Installation

10 Installation is the reverse of removal, noting the following:

● Clean the exhaust port studs or bolts and lubricate them with a suitable copper-based grease before reassembly.

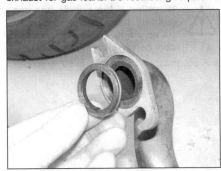

14.8 Remove the gasket from the exhaust port-to-pipe joint

14.9 Resonator tube on restricted 50 cc exhaust system

15.1 Location of the secondary air system reed valve housing

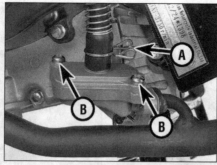

15.3a Air hose clip (A) and cover screws (B)

15.3b Note the alignment tabs (arrowed) on the cover and housing

15.4a Lift out the reed valve, noting the reed on the underside

15.4b Note the seal (arrowed) around the top edge of the reed valve body

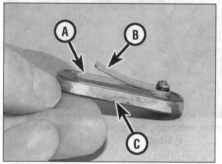

15.5 Reed (A), stopper plate (B) and valve body (C)

15.6 Check for light between the reed (arrowed) and the valve body

● Clean the jointing surfaces of the exhaust port and the pipe.
● Use new gaskets.
● Smear the port gasket with grease to hold it in place while fitting the exhaust system.
● Leave all fixings finger-tight until the system has been installed and correctly aligned, then tighten the exhaust port fixings first.
● Run the engine and check that there are no exhaust gas leaks.

15 Secondary air system

> ⚠️ **Warning: If the engine has been running the exhaust system will be very hot. Allow the system to cool before carrying out any work.**

1 A secondary air system is fitted to scooters with a catalytic converter in the exhaust **(see illustration)**. The system sucks fresh air into the exhaust pipe via a reed valve to promote the burning of unburnt gases. This reduces the emission of hydrocarbons and raises the temperature inside the exhaust so that the catalytic converter works at optimum efficiency.

2 Remove any body panels as necessary to access the secondary air system (see Chapter 8).

3 Release the clip securing the air hose to the reed valve housing and disconnect the hose, then undo the screws securing the cover and lift it off, noting how it fits **(see illustrations)**.

4 Lift out the reed valve noting which way round it fits – note the seal around the top edge of the body **(see illustrations)**.

5 Check the reed for cracks, distortion and any other damage. Check also that there are no dirt particles trapped between the reed and its seat. The reed should sit flat against the valve body so that a good seal is obtained against back pressure in the exhaust **(see illustration)**. If required, clean the reed carefully with a suitable solvent to remove any gum.

6 After prolonged use, the reed tends to become bent and will not therefore seal properly, in which case the assembly should be renewed. A good way to check is to hold the valve up to the light – if light is visible between the reed and the body it is not sealing properly **(see illustration)**.

7 Check that the stopper plate retaining screws are tight; do not disassemble the reed valve as individual components are not available.

8 Installation is the reverse of removal. Ensure that the components are fitted the correct way round **(see illustrations 15.4a, 4b and 3b)**. Inspect the air hose for cracks and splits and renew it if necessary.

Chapter 4
Ignition systems

Contents

Degrees of difficulty

Easy, suitable for novice with little experience

Fairly easy, suitable for beginner with some experience

Fairly difficult, suitable for competent DIY mechanic

Difficult, suitable for experienced DIY mechanic

Very difficult, suitable for expert DIY or professional

1 General information

All scooters covered by this manual are fitted with an electronic capacitor discharge ignition system, known commonly as CDI.

The components which make up the CDI system are the alternator ignition source coil, ignition trigger, pulse generator coil, ignition control unit (ICU), HT coil and spark plug **(see illustration)**. On some models the HT coil is integral with the ignition control unit **(see illustration)**.

The ignition trigger, which is on the outside surface of the alternator rotor, activates the pulse generator coil as the crankshaft rotates, sending a signal to the ICU which in turn supplies the HT coil with the power necessary to produce a spark at the plug. The ignition source coil produces the power for the ignition system when the engine is running, and on most machines the battery provides the power for initial starting.

The ICU incorporates an ignition advance system controlled by signals from the pulse generator coil. This varies the timing of the ignition spark depending on engine speed.

There is no provision for adjusting the ignition timing.

Depending upon the model specification, most ignition systems incorporate a safety circuit which prevents the engine from being started unless one of the brake levers is pulled in and/or the side stand is up (refer to your scooter handbook or wiring diagram for details). For security, many scooters are fitted with an ignition immobiliser (see Section 4).

Due to their lack of mechanical parts, the components of the ignition system are totally maintenance-free. If ignition system troubles occur, and the faulty component can be isolated by a series of checks, the only cure is to replace it with a new one. Keep in mind that most electrical parts, once purchased, cannot be returned. To avoid unnecessary expense, make sure the faulty component has been positively identified before buying a replacement.

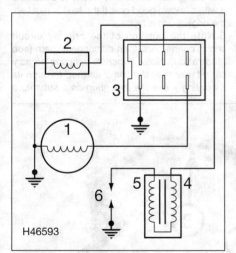

1.1a Wiring diagram for a typical ignition system with separate ignition control unit and ignition coil

1   *Ignition source coil*
2   *Ignition pick-up coil*
3   *Ignition control unit*
4   *HT coil primary winding*
5   *HT coil secondary winding*
6   *Spark plug*

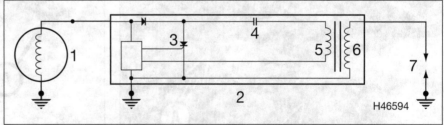

1.1b Wiring diagram for a typical ignition system with combined ignition control unit and ignition coil

1   *Ignition source coil*
2   *Combined ignition control unit and HT coil*
3   *SCR*
4   *Capacitor*
5   *HT coil primary winding*
6   *HT coil secondary winding*
7   *Spark plug*

2.2 Earth the spark plug and operate the starter

2 Ignition system – checking

⚠️ **Warning: The energy levels in electronic systems can be very high. On no account should the ignition be switched on whilst the plug or plug cap is being held – shocks from the HT circuit can be most unpleasant. Secondly, it is vital that the engine is not turned over with the plug cap removed, and that the plug is soundly earthed when the system is checked for sparking. The ignition system components can be seriously damaged if the HT circuit becomes isolated.**

1 As no means of adjustment is available, any failure of the system can be traced to failure of a system component or a simple wiring fault. Of the two possibilities, the latter is by far the most likely. In the event of failure, check the system in a logical fashion, as described below.

2 Disconnect the HT lead from the spark plug. Connect the lead to a new plug of the correct specification and lay the plug on the engine with the thread earthed **(see illustration)**. If necessary, hold the spark plug with an insulated tool.

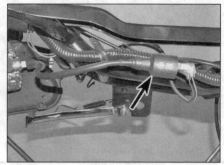

3.2a Location of the ignition coil behind the belly panel

⚠️ **Warning: Do not remove the spark plug from the engine to perform this check – atomised fuel being pumped out of the open spark plug hole could ignite, causing severe injury!**

3 Having observed the above precautions, turn the ignition switch ON and turn the engine over on the starter motor. If the system is in good condition a regular, fat blue spark should be evident between the plug electrodes. If the spark appears thin or yellowish, or is non-existent, further investigation will be necessary. Before proceeding further, turn the ignition OFF.

Caution: Some ignition systems are designed for the combined resistance of the spark plug and spark plug cap. To avoid the risk of damaging the ICU, a spark testing tool should not be used.

4 Ignition faults can be divided into two categories, namely those where the ignition system has failed completely, and those which are due to a partial failure. The likely faults are listed below, starting with the most probable source of failure. Work through the list systematically, referring to the subsequent sections for full details of the necessary checks and tests. **Note:** *Before checking the following items ensure that the battery is fully charged and that the fuse is in good condition.*

Loose, corroded or damaged wiring connections, broken or shorted wiring between any of the component parts of the ignition system (see illustration 1.1)
Faulty spark plug with dirty, worn or corroded plug electrodes, or incorrect gap between electrodes (see Chapter 1)
Faulty HT coil or spark plug cap
Faulty ignition switch (see Chapter 9)
Faulty immobiliser (where fitted)
Faulty ignition source coil
Faulty pulse generator coil
Faulty ICU

5 If the above checks don't reveal the cause of the problem, have the ignition system tested by a scooter dealer.

3 HT coil and spark plug cap

Check

1 Disconnect the battery negative (-ve) lead (see Chapter 9).

2 Trace the HT lead back from the spark plug cap to the HT coil **(see illustrations)**. Remove any body panels as required for access to the coil (see Chapter 8).

3 Pull the spark plug cap off the plug and inspect the cap, HT lead and coil for cracks and other damage **(see illustration)**.

4 The condition of the coil primary and secondary windings can be checked with a multimeter. Note: If no specifications are available in the Data section to confirm the results of the following tests, the only way to determine conclusively that the ignition coil is defective is to substitute it with a known good one. If the fault is rectified, the original unit is faulty.

5 Note the position of the primary circuit wiring connectors, then disconnect them **(see illustration)**. **Note:** *If there is only one primary circuit wire then the coil is earthed through its mounting – use the mounting as a substitute*

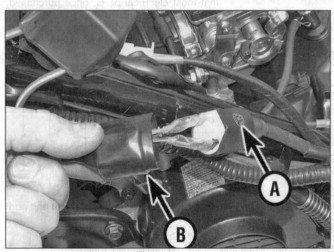

3.2b Location of the ignition coil (A) behind the side panel. Note the protective boot (B)

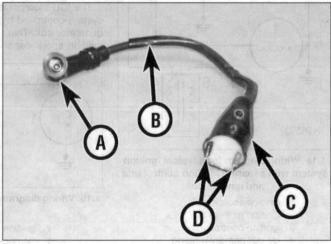

3.3 Spark plug cap (A), HT lead (B), coil (C) and primary circuit wiring terminals (D)

3.5a Disconnect the primary circuit connectors from the coil

3.5b HT coil primary winding check

for the earth wire terminal in this check. Set the multimeter to the appropriate ohms scale and connect the meter probes to the primary circuit wiring terminals **(see illustration)**. This will give a resistance reading for the coil primary windings which should be consistent with the specifications in the *Data* section. If the reading is outside the specified range, it is likely the coil is defective.

6 Set the multimeter to the K-ohms scale and connect the meter probes to the earth primary circuit wiring terminal and the spark plug terminal inside the plug cap **(see illustration)**. This will give a resistance reading for the coil secondary windings. If the reading is not within the specified range, unscrew the plug cap from the HT lead and connect the probes to the earth primary circuit wiring terminal and the core of the lead. If the reading is now as specified, the plug cap is suspect. If the reading is still outside the specified range, it is likely that the coil is defective.

7 Should any of the above checks not produce the expected result, have your

findings confirmed by a scooter specialist wherever possible. If the coil is confirmed to be faulty, it must be renewed – the coil is a sealed unit and cannot be repaired.

8 To check the condition of the spark plug cap, set the multimeter to the appropriate ohms scale and connect the meter probes to the HT lead and plug terminals inside the cap **(see illustration)**. If the reading is outside the specified range, the cap is defective and a new one must be fitted. **Note:** *In many cases, the resistance rating of the cap, such as 5 K-ohms, will be marked on the outside.* If the reading is as specified, the cap connection may have been faulty. Remake the connection between the cap and the HT lead and check the resistance reading for the coil secondary windings again (see Step 6).

Removal

9 Disconnect the battery negative (-ve) lead (see Chapter 9).
10 Remove any body panels as required for access (see Step 2).
11 Note the position of the primary circuit

wiring connectors, then disconnect them **(see illustration 3.5a)**. Disconnect the HT lead from the spark plug.
12 Unscrew the fixings securing the coil to the frame and remove it.

Installation

13 Installation is the reverse of removal. If the coil is earthed through its mounting, ensure the mounting is clean and free from corrosion. Make sure the wiring connectors and HT lead are securely connected.

4 Immobiliser system

General information

Caution: The use of the correct, resistor type, spark plug and suppresser cap is essential to prevent interference with the immobiliser system and possible loss of key programming.

3.6 HT coil secondary winding check

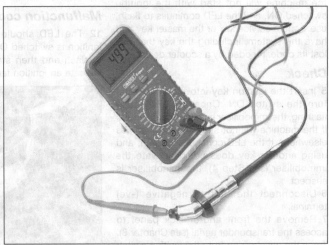

3.8 Measuring the resistance of the spark plug cap

4.7a Transponder aerial (arrowed) is clipped to the ignition switch

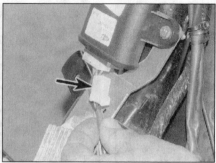

4.7b Disconnect the aerial wiring connector from the immobiliser

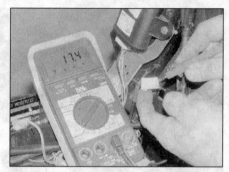

4.7c Measuring the resistance in the transponder aerial

1 The system comprises a security coded ignition key with integral transponder, the immobiliser and transponder aerial. When the key is inserted into the ignition switch the security code is transmitted from the key to the immobiliser via the aerial which is located around the switch. The code deactivates the immobiliser and the warning LED on the instrument panel stops flashing. When the key is removed, the immobiliser is activated and the warning LED starts flashing. **Note:** *To minimise battery discharging, the warning LED goes out after a period of time although the immobiliser system remains active. Disconnecting the battery does not deactivate the immobiliser system.*

2 One master key and several ignition service keys are supplied with each machine when new. The keys and the immobiliser are encoded by the factory. The master key should be kept in a safe place and not used on a day-to-day basis.

3 If an ignition key is lost, obtain a replacement from a scooter dealer and have the system recoded. The dealer will require the master key for this purpose. Once the system is recoded the lost key will not deactivate the immobiliser.

4 The ignition keys can lose their code. If the machine will not start with the ignition switched ON, and the LED continues to flash, use a spare service key or the master key and have the system, including the key that has lost its code, recoded by a scooter dealer.

Check

5 Insert the ignition key into the switch and turn the switch ON. Once the LED stops flashing, the immobiliser has been deactivated; if the machine will not start, the problem lies elsewhere. If the LED continues to flash, and using another key does not deactivate the immobiliser (see Step 4), the immobiliser is suspect.

6 Disconnect the battery negative (-ve) terminal.

7 Remove the front and/or kick panel to access the transponder aerial (see Chapter 8). Trace the aerial wiring from the ignition switch to the immobiliser and disconnect the wiring **(see illustrations)**. Check the resistance

in the aerial with a multimeter set to the appropriate ohms scale, connecting the meter probes to the terminals in the connector **(see illustration)**. A reading of 5 to 20 ohms can be expected; if infinite resistance is shown, the aerial is most likely damaged.

8 If the machine still will not start, the immobiliser should be checked by a specialist. **Note:** *It is not possible to substitute an immobiliser from another machine, or a second-hand immobiliser, as this will not recognise the security code from your ignition key.*

9 When a new (uncoded) immobiliser is fitted, check that it is working before encoding it. Turn the ignition ON and start the engine; the engine should run but will not rev freely. If the engine runs, the immobiliser can be encoded using the master key. **Note:** *Encoding the immobiliser is irreversible – only encode a new immobiliser once you are sure the system is working correctly.*

10 If the engine does not start, the problem lies elsewhere.

11 To check the LED, remove the instrument cluster (see Chapter 9) and test for continuity between the LED terminals. There should be continuity in one direction only. If there is no continuity, or continuity in both directions, replace the LED with a new one.

Malfunction codes

12 The LED should flash once when the ignition is switched ON. If the LED continues to flash and then stays on permanently to indicate an ignition fault, try using the master

5.3 Trace the wiring back to the connectors

key to turn the ignition ON. If this works, the service key has lost its programme. If the fault persists, refer to your scooter handbook or immobiliser data sheet for details of malfunction codes.

5 Source coil and pulse generator coil

1 To check the condition of the ignition source coil and the pulse generator coil it is first necessary to identify the wiring for the individual components. Remove the body panels (see Chapter 8) and alternator fan cowling (see Chapter 2A or 2B) as required according to model.

2 Disconnect the battery negative (-ve) lead.

3 Trace the source coil and pulse generator coil wiring from the back of the alternator housing and disconnect it at the connectors **(see illustration)**. If available, use your scooter's wiring diagram to identify the appropriate wires. Alternatively, check the colour coding of the wires at the source coil (on the alternator stator) and the pulse generator coil adjacent to the alternator rotor.

4 Using a multimeter set to the appropriate ohms scale, measure the source coil resistance by connecting the meter probes between the coil wire terminal on the alternator side of the connector and earth (ground). Now reset the multimeter and measure the pulse generator coil resistance by connecting the meter probes between the pulse generator wire terminal on the alternator side of the connector and earth (ground).

5 Where coil values are given in the *Data* section at the end of this manual it will be possible to compare your readings to establish whether the coils are faulty. If the readings obtained differ greatly from those given, particularly if the meter indicates a short circuit (no measurable resistance) or an open circuit (infinite, or very high resistance), the alternator stator and pulse generator coil assembly must be renewed. However, first check that the fault is not due to a damaged or broken wire from the coil to the connector; pinched or broken wires can usually be repaired.

6 The source coil and pulse generator coil

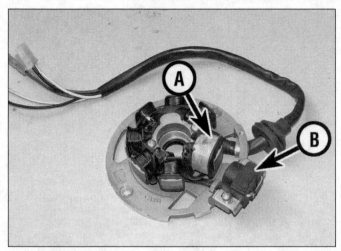

5.6 Alternator stator assembly with ignition source coil (A) and pulse generator coil (B)

6.3a Location of the ICU behind the luggage compartment

are integral with the alternator stator **(see illustration)**. Refer to the relevant Section of Chapter 2A or 2B for the removal and installation procedure.

6	Ignition control unit (ICU)

Check

1 If the tests shown in the preceding sections have failed to isolate the cause of an ignition fault, it is possible that the ICU itself is faulty. In order to determine conclusively that the unit is defective, it should be substituted with a known good one. If the fault is rectified, the original unit is faulty. **Note:** *The ICU unit will be damaged if a non-resistor type spark plug or spark plug cap are fitted. When fitting a new ICU unit, always ensure the spark plug and cap are of the correct specification before starting the engine.*

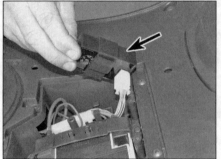

6.3b Location of the ICU inside the battery compartment

Removal and installation

2 Disconnect the battery negative (-ve) lead (see Chapter 9).
3 Refer to the wiring diagram for your scooter, then trace the wiring from both the alternator and the ignition coil to the ICU **(see illustrations)**. Remove the luggage

6.4 Disconnect the ICU wiring connector

compartment or any body panels as required for access to the ICU (see Chapter 8).
4 If applicable, unclip the ICU from the frame, then release the catch on the wiring connector and disconnect it **(see illustration)**.
5 Installation is the reverse of removal. Make sure the wiring connector is correctly and securely connected.

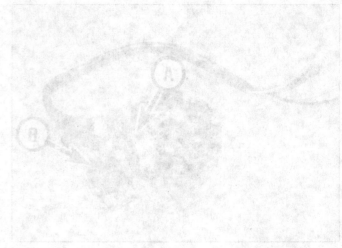

Chapter 5
Transmission: Drive components and gearbox

Contents

Degrees of difficulty

Easy, suitable for novice with little experience	**Fairly easy,** suitable for beginner with some experience	**Fairly difficult,** suitable for competent DIY mechanic	**Difficult,** suitable for experienced DIY mechanic	**Very difficult,** suitable for expert DIY or professional

---

1 General information

The transmission is fully automatic in operation. Power is transmitted from the engine to the rear wheel by belt, via a variable size drive pulley (the variator), an automatic clutch on the driven pulley, and a reduction gearbox. The variator and the automatic clutch both work on the principal of centrifugal force.

The transmission can be worked on with the engine in the scooter.

Note: *On some scooters the internal components of the transmission may differ slightly to those described or shown. When dismantling, always note the fitted position,* order and way round of each component as it is removed.

2 Drive belt cover

Removal

1 Remove any body panels as required for access to the transmission casing (see Chapter 8). If required, remove the air filter housing (see Chapter 3).
2 Release the rear brake cable and any wiring from the clips secured by the drive belt cover bolts **(see illustrations).** Some scooters are fitted with a rev limiter sensor inside the drive belt cover. Trace the wiring from the casing and disconnect it at the connector – on the machine photographed, the storage compartment had to be removed to locate the wiring connector. Free the wiring from any clips or ties and feed it back to the cover.
3 Where fitted, detach the air cooling duct from the front of the cover **(see illustration).** If applicable, follow the procedure in Section 3 and remove the kickstart lever. **Note:** *If the kickstart mechanism is mounted inside the drive belt cover it is not necessary to remove the lever before removing the cover. However, if the mechanism is located in the back of the casing, as on the 152/157QMI units covered in Chapter 2B, the lever must be removed to allow the cover to be pulled off. If the location of the mechanism is not known, remove the lever as a precaution.*
4 Working in a criss-cross pattern, loosen the

2.2a **Release the rear brake cable (arrowed) . . .**

2.2b **. . . and any wiring from the clips (arrowed)**

2.3 **Release the clip (arrowed) and detach the air cooling duct**

2.4a Note the location of the brake cable clip . . .

2.4b . . . and any wiring clips secured by the cover screws

2.5 Remove the cover gasket, noting the location of any dowels (arrowed)

2.7 Location for outer end of starter motor pinion (arrowed)

2.8 Location of the rev limiter sensor (arrowed)

2.10 Locate the gasket over the dowels (arrowed) in the case

drive belt cover retaining bolts and remove the bolts noting the position of any clips **(see illustrations)**.

 Make a cardboard template of the cover and punch a hole for each bolt location. This will ensure all bolts are installed correctly on reassembly – this is important as some bolts may be of different lengths.

5 Lift off the cover. **Note:** *Sealant should not be used on the cover, but if it will not lift away easily, tap it gently around the edge with a soft-faced hammer.* If necessary, lift off the cover gasket – if the gasket is damaged, discard it and fit a new one on reassembly **(see illustration)**. Note that on scooters equipped with a cover mounted kickstart mechanism (Type 2), a gasket of the same thickness as

the original must be fitted. Note the location of any dowels and remove them for safekeeping if they are loose.

6 If the kickstart mechanism is located inside the cover, note the position of the kickstart quadrant and the engaging pinion **(see illustration 3.6)**.

7 If the starter motor engages with the variator, note how the outer end of the starter motor pinion assembly locates in the cover **(see illustration)**.

8 If fitted, note the location of the rev limiter sensor **(see illustration)**.

9 Clean any dust or dirt from the inside of the casing with a suitable solvent, taking care to avoid contact with the belt and the drive faces of the pulleys. Any evidence of oil inside the casing suggests a worn seal either on the crankshaft or the gearbox input shaft which must be rectified. Evidence of grease inside the casing suggests worn seals in the clutch centre which should also be rectified.

Installation

10 Installation is the reverse of removal, noting the following:

● If removed, fit the dowels in the case; apply a smear of grease to the gasket to hold it in place and fit the gasket over the dowels **(see illustration)**.

● If required, apply a smear of grease to the end of the starter motor pinion and to the threads of the cover bolts.

● If applicable, ensure the kickstart quadrant and engaging pinion are correctly located in the cover **(see illustration 3.6)**.

● Don't forget to fit any clips to the cover bolts **(see illustration 2.4a or b)**.

● Tighten the cover bolts evenly in a criss-cross pattern.

● Install the kickstart lever, then operate the lever to ensure the mechanism engages correctly with the kickstart driven gear and that the lever returns to its proper rest position afterwards.

3 Kickstart mechanism

Kickstart lever

1 Before removing the kickstart lever, note the rest position – if necessary, mark the end of the shaft next to the slot in the lever with a dab of paint **(see illustration)**.

2 Undo the lever pinch bolt and pull the lever off **(see illustration)**.

3 Inspect the splines on the end of the kickstart shaft and the splines on the kickstart lever for

3.1 Mark the kickstart shaft with a dab of paint

3.2 Undo the lever pinch bolt and pull the lever off

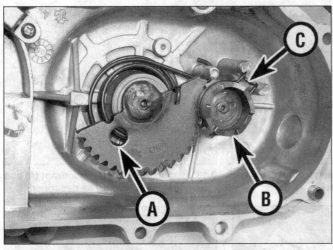

3.6 Kickstart quadrant (A), engaging pinion (B) and location of pinion spring (C)

3.7a Hold the kickstart lever and withdraw the pinion

damage **(see illustration 3.14)**. If necessary, remove the drive belt cover (see Section 2) and renew any damaged components.

4 Installation is the reverse of removal. Fit the lever in the rest position (see Step 1) and tighten the pinch bolt securely. Operate the lever to check that it turns smoothly and returns to its rest position under spring pressure.

Kickstart mechanism

Note: *The kickstart mechanism is either mounted inside the drive belt cover or in the back of the drive belt casing. Follow the appropriate procedure to remove, inspect and install the mechanism.*

Cover mounted mechanism

5 Remove the drive belt cover (see Section 2). Note the layout of the kickstart mechanism – if the kickstart quadrant and engaging pinion are located inside the cover, follow Steps 6 to 24 (Type 1). If the kickstart quadrant engages on a pinion located on the end of the variator pulley, follow the procedure in Steps 25 to 41 (Type 2).

Type 1

6 Note the position of the kickstart quadrant and how it engages with the engaging pinion, and note how the spring on the engaging pinion locates in the cover **(see illustration)**.

7 If the kickstart lever has been removed, fit

it onto its shaft temporarily. Apply light hand pressure on the kickstart lever, then pull the engaging pinion out of its recess in the cover, noting the washer on the pinion shaft **(see illustrations)**. Release the kickstart lever slowly and allow the quadrant to rest against the stop inside the cover **(see illustration)**.

8 Remove the circlip and washer (if fitted) from the kickstart shaft on the outside of the cover **(see illustrations)**.

9 Ease the kickstart shaft out of the cover and release the tension on the kickstart return spring. Unhook the spring from the kickstart quadrant and withdraw the shaft, noting the location of the sleeve **(see illustrations)**.

3.7b Note the washer (arrowed) on the pinion shaft

3.7c Allow the quadrant to rest against the stop (arrowed)

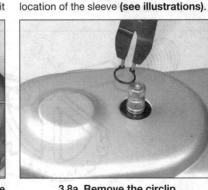

3.8a Remove the circlip . . .

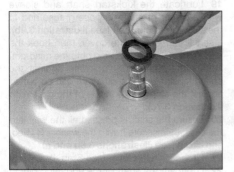

3.8b . . . and the washer

3.9a Remove the kickstart shaft . . .

3.9b . . . noting the location of the sleeve

3.10 Remove the thrust washer

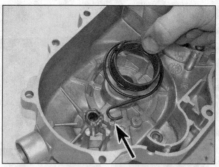

3.11 Unhook the spring from the post (arrowed)

3.13 Inspect the kickstart quadrant (A) and engaging pinion (B) as described

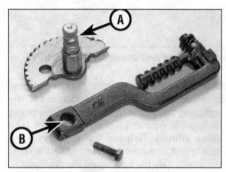

3.14 Inspect the splines on the shaft (A) and on the kickstart lever (B)

3.15 Dogs (arrowed) on the kickstart driven gear

3.23 Install the engaging pinion as described

10 If fitted, lift off the thrust washer **(see illustration)**.

11 Note how the return spring locates inside the cover and how one end is hooked around the post, then remove the spring **(see illustration)**.

12 Clean all the components with a suitable solvent.

13 Inspect the teeth on the kickstart quadrant and the teeth on the engaging pinion for wear and damage **(see illustration)**. Check the shafts of the engaging pinion, the kickstart shaft and the shaft sleeve, for signs of wear.

14 Inspect the splines on the end of the kickstart shaft and the splines on the kickstart

lever for damage **(see illustration)**.

15 Check the dogs on the end of the engaging pinion **(see illustration 3.13)** and the corresponding dogs on the kickstart driven gear **(see illustration)**.

16 If any components are worn or damaged they should be renewed. **Note:** *To renew the kickstart driven gear, follow the procedure in Section 4.*

17 Ensure the spring on the engaging pinion is a firm fit and inspect the kickstart return spring for cracks and wear at each end. When fitted, the return spring should return the kickstart lever to the rest position and hold it there; if not, it has sagged and should be replaced with a new one.

18 Install the return spring with its long end innermost. Hook the long end around the post on the inside of the cover **(see illustration 3.11)**. If applicable, install the thrust washer **(see illustration 3.10)**.

19 Lubricate the kickstart shaft and sleeve with a smear of multi-purpose grease and fit the sleeve onto the shaft **(see illustration 3.9b)**. Insert the shaft into the cover, then hook the outer end of the return spring onto the quadrant. Rotate the shaft anti-clockwise against the spring tension until the quadrant can be butted against the stop on the inside of the case **(see illustration 3.7c)**.

20 Ensure the shaft is pressed all the way into the case, then secure it with the washer (if fitted) and circlip **(see illustrations 3.8b and a)**.

21 Fit the kickstart lever (see Step 4).

22 Lubricate the shaft of the engaging pinion with a smear of grease and install the washer **(see illustrations 3.7b)**.

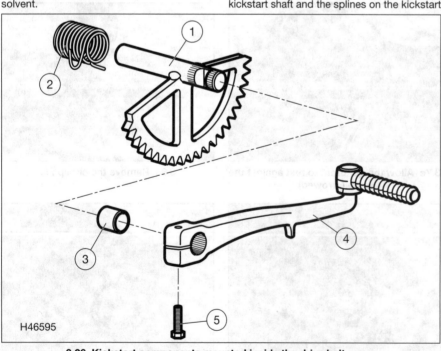

H46595

3.26 Kickstart components mounted inside the drive belt cover

1 Kickstart quadrant	*3 Bush*	*5 Pinch bolt*
2 Return spring	*4 Kickstart lever*	

23 To fit the pinion into the case, align the spring with the detent in the case, then turn the kickstart quadrant against spring pressure and engage it with the engaging pinion – movement of the quadrant will draw the pinion into the case **(see illustration)**. Check the operation of the mechanism.

24 Refit the drive belt cover (see Section 2).

Type 2

25 If not already done, remove the kickstart lever (see Steps 1 and 2).

26 Note the position of the kickstart quadrant and how the return spring locates inside the cover **(see illustration)**.

27 Carefully ease the return spring off the kickstart shaft and unhook it from the post inside the cover.

28 Withdraw the kickstart shaft from the cover, noting the location of the bush **(see illustration 3.26)**. **Note:** *The bush should be a press fit in the cover – do not remove it unless it is loose or in need of renewal.*

29 The kickstart driven pinion is located on the end of the variator pulley **(see illustration)**.

30 Undo the screws securing the driven pinion assembly and lift the assembly off, noting the location of the components inside the housing.

31 Clean all the components with a suitable solvent, then lay them out in the order of assembly for inspection

32 Inspect the splines on the end of the kickstart shaft and the splines on the kickstart lever for damage.

33 Inspect the teeth on the kickstart quadrant and the teeth on the driven pinion for wear and damage. Check the kickstart shaft and the shaft bush for signs of wear.

34 Check the dogs on the inner end of the driven pinion and the corresponding dogs on the variator centre nut.

35 Inspect the kickstart return spring for cracks and wear at each end. When fitted, the return spring should return the kickstart lever to the rest position and hold it there; if not, it has sagged and should be replaced with a new one. Check that the spring in the driven pinion assembly is not damaged and that it holds the driven pinion in position when the components are assembled.

36 If any components are worn or damaged they should be renewed.

 Warning: On scooters with this kickstart mechanism, the variator centre nut has a LEFT-HAND thread. To undo the nut, follow the procedure in Section 4 to hold the variator, then turn the nut CLOCKWISE.

37 Lubricate the kickstart shaft and bush with a smear of multi-purpose grease, then insert the shaft into the cover. Install the return spring – ensure the lower end is located against the kickstart quadrant, then hook the upper end around the post inside the cover.

38 Fit the kickstart lever (see Step 4).

39 If the variator centre nut has been renewed, follow the procedure in Section 4 and tighten it securely.

40 Assemble the components of the driven pinion as noted on removal **(see illustration 3.29)**, then install the assembly onto the variator centre nut and secure it with the screws. Check that the pinion is free to rotate in a clockwise direction and locks when turned anti-clockwise.

41 Lubricate the inner end of the kickstart shaft with a smear of grease, then refit the drive belt cover using the appropriate thickness cover gasket (see Section 2).

Casing mounted mechanism

42 Follow the procedure in Steps 1 and 2 and remove the kickstart lever.

43 Remove the drive belt cover (see Section 2). Note the location of the washer on the outer end of the kickstart shaft.

44 Remove the variator (see Section 4).

45 Note the position of the kickstart quadrant and how it engages with the engaging pinion, which in turn engages with the driven gear on the crankshaft **(see illustration)**. There

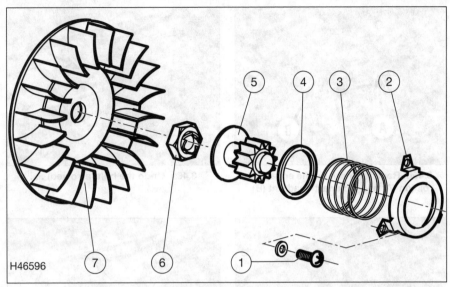

3.29 Kickstart driven pinion components

1 Screw	3 Spring	6 Variator centre nut
2 Assembly housing	4 Thrust washer	7 Variator pulley – outer half
	5 Driven pinion	

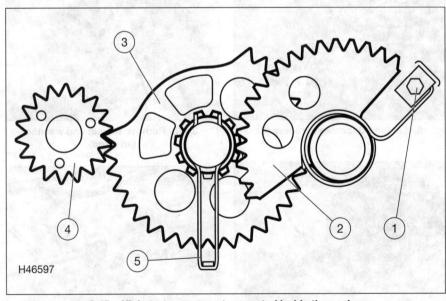

3.45a Kickstart components mounted inside the casing

1 Return spring plate bolt	4 Driven gear
2 Kickstart quadrant	5 Engaging pinion spring clip
3 Engaging pinion	

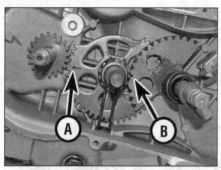

3.45b Register mark on the engaging pinion (A) and kickstart quadrant (B)

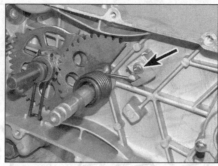

3.46a Undo the bolt (arrowed) . . .

3.46b . . . and remove the plate

3.46c Use pliers to ease out the spring

3.47a Remove the kickstart shaft assembly

3.47b Return spring locates on peg (arrowed)

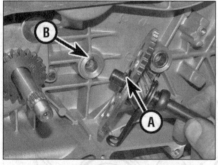

3.48a Pin (A) locates in recess (B)

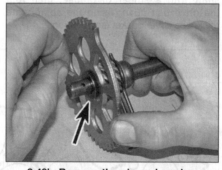

3.48b Remove the pin and washer (arrowed)

3.48c Slide off the pinion, noting the spring (arrowed)

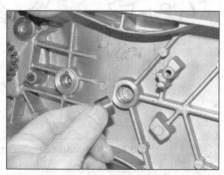

3.50 Kickstart shaft bush is located in the casing

should be register marks on the teeth of the kickstart quadrant and the engaging pinion to aid installation – if not, make your own with a

dab of paint **(see illustration)**. Note how the closed end of the spring clip on the engaging pinion locates in the casing.

46 Undo the kickstart return spring plate bolt and remove the plate **(see illustrations)**. Ease the long end of the spring out from the stop in the casing with care – the spring is under tension **(see illustration)**.

47 Withdraw the kickstart shaft assembly **(see illustration)**. Slide off the washer and the return spring, noting how the short end of the spring locates around the peg on the shaft **(see illustration)**.

48 Withdraw the engaging pinion noting how the pin behind the pinion locates in the recess in the casing **(see illustration)**. Compress the spring on the pinion shaft, withdraw the pin and remove the washer, then slide the pinion off the shaft noting the location of the spring **(see illustrations)**.

49 Clean all the components in a suitable solvent.

50 Inspect the teeth on the kickstart quadrant, the engaging pinion and the driven gear for wear and damage **(see illustration 3.45a)**. Check the shafts of the engaging pinion and the kickstart quadrant for signs of wear. If a sleeve or bush is fitted on the kickstart shaft, inspect that also **(see illustration)**.

51 Inspect the splines on the end of the kickshaft shaft and the splines in the kickstart lever for damage.

52 If any components are worn or damaged they should be renewed.

53 To remove the kickstart driven gear, use a suitable puller to draw it off the taper on the

3.53a Draw the driven gear off with a puller

3.53b Ensure both tapers (arrowed) are clean

crankshaft **(see illustration)**. Temporarily install the variator centre nut to avoid damaging the threads on the end of the crankshaft. If the gear is a tight fit, heat it with a hot air gun. Once the gear has been removed, note the location of any Woodruff key on the crankshaft and ensure it is a tight fit in its slot before installing the gear on reassembly. To install the driven gear, clean the taper on the crankshaft and inside the gear with a suitable solvent **(see illustration)**. Fit the gear onto the crankshaft, then temporarily assemble the variator centre sleeve and outer pulley half and tighten the centre nut to press the driven gear firmly onto its taper. The gear should remain in position once the variator components have been removed.

54 Assemble the spring and engaging pinion on the pinion shaft, then compress the spring and install the washer and pin **(see illustrations 3.48c and b)**. Lubricate the ends

of the engaging pinion shaft with a smear of multi-purpose grease and install the engaging pinion. Align the pin behind the pinion with the recess in the casing **(see illustration 3.48a)**. Ensure the pinion teeth align with the driven gear on the crankshaft and align the closed end of the spring clip with the detent in the case **(see illustrations 3.45a and b)**.

55 Install the bush for the kickstart shaft **(see illustration 3.50)**. Fit the return spring and washer on the shaft **(see illustration 3.47b)**. Lubricate the shaft with a smear of grease, then install the shaft, ensuring that the register marks on the kickstart quadrant and the engaging pinion align (see Step 45).

56 Turn the long end of the return spring clockwise to tension the spring and locate the cranked end against the stop in the casing **(see illustration 3.46c)**. Secure the spring with the plate and tighten the bolt securely.

57 Install the variator (see Section 4).
58 Install the drive belt cover (see Section 2).
59 Follow the procedure in Step 4 and install the kickstart lever.

4 Variator

Removal

1 Remove the drive belt cover (see Section 2).
2 To remove the variator centre nut, the crankshaft must be locked to stop it turning. On some engines, the outer half of the variator pulley acts as the kickstart driven gear and a proprietary tool which locks onto the toothed edge of the pulley is required to hold the crankshaft **(see illustration)**. Ensure that the tool is locked firmly in place to prevent damage to the gear teeth and apply steady pressure to the centre nut to loosen it **(see illustration)**. On other engines, either hold the variator with a strap wrench, or locate a suitable holding tool in the holes provided in the pulley **(see illustrations)**. A holding tool can be made from two strips of steel (see *Tool Tip*). Note: *The variator centre nut is tight – to avoid damage, ensure the variator pulley is held firmly before attempting to undo the nut.*

⚠️ *Warning: On scooters with the 'Type 2' kickstart mechanism (Section 3), the variator centre nut has a LEFT-HAND thread. To undo the nut, turn it CLOCKWISE.*

4.2a Holding the variator with a proprietary tool . . .

4.2b . . . apply steady pressure to loosen the centre nut

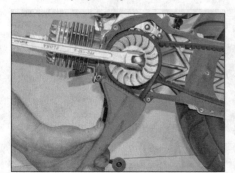

4.2c Holding the variator with a strap wrench

4.2d Using the holding tool to undo the variator centre nut

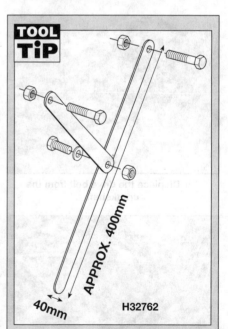

TOOL TiP

APPROX. 400mm

40mm

H32762

A holding tool can be made using two strips of steel bolted together in the middle, and with a nut and bolt through each end which locate into the holes in the pulley.

4.3a Note the location of the kickstart driven gear (arrowed)

4.3b Lift off the kickstart driven gear and cooling fan . . .

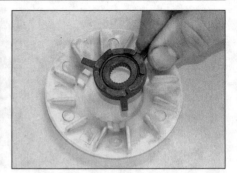

4.3c . . . then separate the gear from the fan

4.4a Lift off the splined plate . . .

4.4b . . . then lift off the outer half of the pulley

4.4c Note the splined centre (arrowed)

3 Remove the variator centre nut and washer. On some scooters, the kickstart driven gear is held in place by the nut – note how the splined centre of the gear locates on the crankshaft,

or how the gear and cooling fan are fitted as an assembly **(see illustrations)**.
4 Remove the outer half of the variator pulley – on some scooters the drive from the

crankshaft is transmitted to the pulley via a splined plate, on others the centre of the pulley itself is splined **(see illustrations)**.
5 Move the drive belt aside – unless you are removing the clutch assembly, leave the belt on the clutch pulley **(see illustration)**. Mark the belt with a directional arrow if it is removed so that it can be refitted the correct way round.
6 If fitted, remove the washer and spacer from the crankshaft **(see illustrations)**.
7 The variator assembly comprises a centre sleeve, ramp plate and variator body – grip the assembly so that the ramp plate at the back is held into the variator body, then draw the complete assembly off the shaft **(see illustrations)**.
8 Withdraw the centre sleeve and lift out the ramp plate, noting how it fits **(see

4.5 Displace the drive belt from the crankshaft

4.6a Remove the washer . . .

4.6b . . . and spacer if fitted

4.7a Pull off the variator assembly

4.7b On some scooters, note the location of the starter (one-way) clutch (arrowed)

4.8a Withdraw the centre sleeve . . .

4.8b . . . and lift out the ramp plate

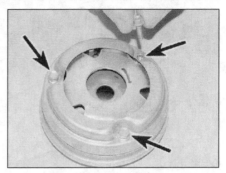

4.8c Undo the screws . . .

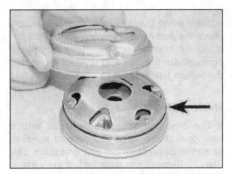

4.8d . . . and lift off the cover. Note the location of the O-ring

4.9a Remove the ramp guides

4.9b Lift out the rollers

illustrations). On some scooters, the variator is fitted with a cover – undo the screws securing the cover and lift it off, noting the location of the O-ring (see illustrations). On these scooters, the rollers are lubricated with high melting-point grease.

9 Remove the ramp guides and lift out the rollers, noting which way round they fit (see illustrations).

10 Clean all the components using a suitable solvent.

Inspection

11 Measure the diameter of each roller; they should all be the same size (see illustration). Inspect the surface of each roller for flat spots. Renew all the rollers as a set. **Note:** *Variator rollers are not interchangeable between different models. Always specify the year*

and model of your scooter when buying new rollers.

12 Inspect the surface of the ramps in the variator body and the ramp plate for wear or damage (see illustration). Check the slots in the ramp guides where they fit in the variator body and fit new components as necessary.

13 Inspect the surface of the variator sleeve for wear and fit a new one if necessary. Measure the outside diameter (OD) of the sleeve and the internal diameter (ID) of the variator body (see illustration), then compare the results with the specifications in the *Data* section. Renew any component worn beyond the service limit.

14 Check the condition of the splines in the centre of the outer half of the variator pulley or in the splined plate (see illustration 4.4a or c). Inspect the inner face of the pulley for

signs of overheating or blueing, caused by the pulley running out of alignment. Renew the pulley half if it is damaged.

Installation

15 If required, lubricate the rollers and the ramps with high melting point grease, then fit the rollers into the variator body (see illustration 4.9b). **Note:** *Too much grease in the variator will make it to run out of balance and cause vibration. If new rollers are fitted, check with your supplier as to whether they need greasing or not.*

16 Check that the ramp guides are correctly fitted on the ramp plate and install the plate (see illustrations 4.9a and 8b).

17 Where fitted, install the cover, taking care not to dislodge the O-ring, and tighten the

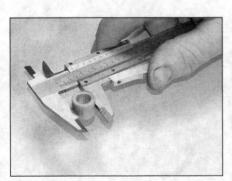

4.11 Measure the diameter of each roller

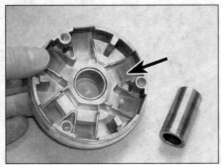

4.12 Inspect the variator ramps (arrowed) for wear

4.13 Measuring the ID of the variator body

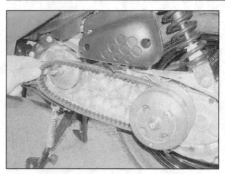

4.19 Press the belt into the clutch pulley and fit it onto the variator pulley

4.24 Check by measuring that the pulley is not skewed

4.25 Ease the belt into place between the two pulleys

cover screws securely **(see illustrations 4.8d and c)**.

18 Grip the variator so that the ramp plate is held into the body and install the assembly and the centre sleeve onto the crankshaft (see Step 7). **Note:** *If the ramp plate moves and the rollers are dislodged, disassemble the variator and reposition the rollers correctly.*

19 Clean both inner faces of the variator pulley with a suitable solvent, then compress the clutch pulley centre spring and press the drive belt into the clutch pulley to facilitate fitting it over the variator pulley **(see illustration)**.

20 If fitted, install the washer and spacer on the crankshaft **(see illustrations 4.6b and a)**.

21 Install the outer half of the variator pulley – if applicable, install the splined plate **(see illustrations 4.4b, a and c)**. Ensure that the splines align with the crankshaft.

22 If fitted, install the kickstart driven gear (see Step 3). Fit the washer and centre nut finger-tight. **Note:** *Many manufacturers recommend fitting a new centre nut.* Make sure the outer pulley half butts against the centre sleeve and is not skewed by the belt.

23 Install the locking tool used on removal (see Step 2) and tighten the centre nut to the specified torque setting.

24 Measure the distance between the crankcase face and the edge of the outer pulley half, then rotate the crankshaft and repeat the measuring procedure several times to ensure the outer pulley half is not skewed **(see illustration)**.

25 Ease the drive belt out of the clutch pulley to reduce the slack in the belt **(see illustration)**, then fit the cover (see Section 2).

5 Drive belt

Inspection

1 Most manufacturers specify service intervals for drive belt inspection and service limits for the width of the belt, but it is good practice to check the condition of the belt whenever the cover is removed (see Section 2).

2 Check along the entire length of the belt for cracks, splits, fraying and damaged teeth and renew the belt if any such damage is found **(see illustration)**. Measure the belt width and compare the result with the specification in the *Data* section at the end of this manual. Where no data is given for your model, the only real way to check is to compare the width of the existing belt with that of a new one.

3 The belt will wear during the normal course of use and dust will accumulate inside the cover. However, a large amount of dust or debris inside the cover is an indication of abnormal wear and the cause, such as high spots on the pulleys or pulley misalignment, should be investigated. **Note:** *Drive belts are not interchangeable between different models. Always specify the year and model of your*

scooter when buying a new belt. If in doubt, check the part number marked on the belt.

4 Oil or grease inside the casing will contaminate the belt and prevent it gripping the pulleys (see Section 2).

Renewal

5 The drive belt must be replaced with a new one at the specified service interval, or earlier dependent on belt condition (see Step 2). Remove the outer half of the variator pulley (see Section 4) and lift the belt off the crankshaft and the clutch pulley without disturbing the variator assembly.

6 Fit the new belt, making sure any directional arrows point in the direction of normal rotation, then install the variator outer pulley half (see Section 4).

6 Clutch and clutch pulley

Removal

1 Remove the drive belt (see Section 5).

2 To remove the clutch centre nut it is necessary to hold the clutch to prevent it turning. On some scooters, a holding tool that locates in the holes in the clutch drum can be used (see Section 4 ***Tool Tip***); alternatively you can use a strap wrench **(see illustrations)**.

5.2 Check the belt for wear and damage

6.2a Prevent the clutch from turning with a home-made tool . . .

6.2b . . . or a strap wrench

6.3 Remove the clutch drum . . .

6.4 . . . then pull the clutch and pulley off the shaft

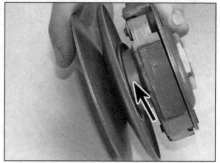

6.5a Compress the centre spring (arrowed) . . .

3 Remove the clutch drum **(see illustration)**.
4 Draw the clutch and pulley assembly off the gearbox input shaft **(see illustration)**.
5 To remove the large clutch assembly nut it is necessary to hold the clutch to prevent it turning (see Step 2). The clutch and pulley is assembled under pressure from the centre spring – take care when undoing the assembly nut and maintain downwards pressure on the clutch shoes backplate to avoid damage to the threads of the nut **(see illustrations)**.
6 On machines with an engine size greater than 100 cc it is advisable to clamp the assembly to take the spring pressure off the nut. Use the set-up shown, ensuring no pressure is applied to the rim of the pulley and that there is adequate room to undo the nut **(see illustrations)**. Fit a strap wrench around the clutch shoes to hold the assembly while the nut is undone, then

6.5b . . . while undoing the clutch assembly nut

6.5c Using the home-made holding tool

release the spring pressure gradually by undoing the clamp.
7 Remove the clutch shoes and backplate, then remove the spring seat and spring **(see illustrations)**.

Inspection

8 Check the inner surface of the clutch drum for damage and scoring and inspect the splines in the centre; renew it if necessary **(see illustration)**. Measure the internal diameter of the

6.6a A home-made clamp for disassembling the clutch

6.6b Ensure the clamp does not rest on the rim (arrowed) of the pulley

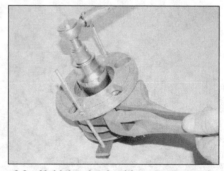

6.6c Hold the clutch with a strap wrench and undo the nut

6.7a Remove the clutch shoes and backplate (arrowed)

6.7b Lift off the spring seat (A) and spring (B)

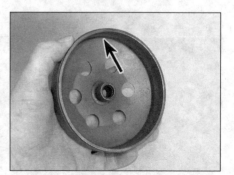

6.8a Examine the inner surface of the clutch drum (arrowed)

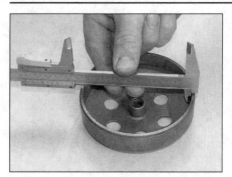

6.8b Measure the internal diameter of the drum as described

6.9 Check the clutch friction material (arrowed)

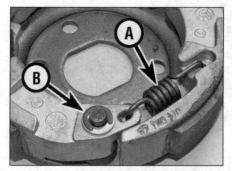

6.10 Inspect the shoe springs (A) and retaining clips (B)

6.11 Measure the spring free length

6.12 Inspect the inner faces of the clutch pulley (arrowed)

drum at several points to determine if it is worn or out-of-round **(see illustration)**. If it is worn or out-of-round, replace it with a new one.

9 Check the amount of friction material remaining on the clutch shoes **(see** illustration**)**. If the friction material has worn to the service limit specified in the *Data* section – around 2 mm where no information is available, or the shoes are worn unevenly, fit a new shoe assembly.

10 Inspect the shoe springs for wear, cracks and stretching **(see illustration)**. Ensure that the shoes are not seized on their pivot pins and that the retaining circlips, where fitted, are secure on the ends of the pins. If any parts are worn or damaged, fit a new shoe backplate assembly.

11 Check the condition of the centre spring. If it is bent or appears weak, renew it. Where a spring free length is given in the *Data* section measure the spring length to check if it has sagged **(see illustration)**. Fit a new spring if it has worn to less than the service limit.

12 Inspect the inner faces of the clutch pulley for signs of overheating or blueing, caused by the pulley running out of alignment **(see illustration)**.

13 On most scooters, two bearings are fitted in the hub of the pulley **(see illustrations)**. Inspect the rollers of the inner bearing for flat spots and ensure the outer sealed ball bearing turns smoothly (see *Tools and Workshop Tips* in the *Reference* section). If any of the clutch pulley internal components are worn or damaged, fit a new clutch pulley assembly. **Note:** *Lubricating grease for the bearings should be sealed inside by O-rings. If grease has worked its way past the O-rings onto the pulley a new assembly should be fitted.*

14 On some clutches, such as the ones fitted to the 152/157QMI engine units covered in Chapter 2B, it is possible to disassemble the pulley for further inspection. Pull off the centre sleeve, noting the location of the O-rings **(see illustration)**. Check that the outer face of the pulley moves up-and-down the hub smoothly, sliding around the rollers on the guide pins **(see illustration)**. Pull out the guide pins

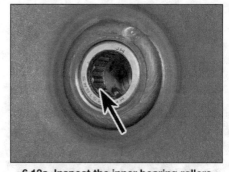

6.13a Inspect the inner bearing rollers (arrowed) . . .

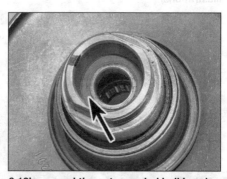

6.13b . . . and the outer sealed ball bearing

6.14a Location of clutch pulley O-rings

6.14b Pulley should move smoothly on guide pin rollers (arrowed)

6.14c Pull out the guide pins . . .

6.14d . . . and separate the pulley halves

6.15a Measure the OD of the inner pulley hub . . .

6.15b . . . and the ID of the outer pulley hub. Note outer grease seal (arrowed)

6.19 Locate the shoe backplate on the spring seat and install the assembly nut

noting how the rollers fit, then separate the two halves of the pulley **(see illustrations)**.

15 Clean off any old grease then measure the OD of the inner pulley hub and the ID of the outer pulley hub and compare the results with the specifications in the *Data* section **(see illustrations)**. Compare the results with the specifications in the *Data* section. Renew any component worn beyond the service limit.

16 If grease from the centre of the clutch hub has contaminated the outside of the assembly renew the seals and O-rings.

17 Lubricate the pulley hub, guide pins and rollers with molybdenum disulphide grease, then reassemble the clutch pulley in the reverse order of disassembly

Installation

18 Clean any grease off the faces of the clutch pulley with suitable solvent, then install the centre spring and spring seat **(see illustration 6.7b)**.

19 Position the shoe assembly on the spring seat, ensuring the flats on the shoe backplate are aligned with the pulley hub. Compress the spring using the same method as for disassembly (see Steps 5 and 6) and install the large assembly nut finger-tight **(see illustration)**. Hold the clutch to prevent it turning and tighten the nut securely – apply the torque setting specified in the *Data* section where given for your model **(see illustration**

6.5c or 6.6c). If applicable, release the clamp.

20 Lubricate the needle bearing in the hub of the pulley with molybdenum disulphide grease and install the clutch and pulley assembly on the gearbox input shaft **(see illustration 6.4)**.

21 Install the clutch drum, ensuring the splines align with the shaft **(see illustration 6.3)**. Hold the clutch to prevent it turning and tighten the nut (see Step 2).

22 Install the remaining components in the reverse order of removal.

7 Gearbox

Note: *The internal components of the gearbox are either located inside a separate housing bolted onto the right-hand side of the transmission casing (Type 1) or inside an extension of the transmission casing (Type 2). The Type 2 gearbox is fitted to the 152/157QMI engine units covered in Chapter 2B.*

Type 1

Removal

1 Remove the clutch and clutch pulley (see Section 6).

2 Remove the rear wheel and brake shoes (see Chapter 7).

3 If a drain plug is fitted to the machine, drain the gearbox oil **(see illustration)**. **Note:** *Remove the filler plug to assist oil drainage.*

4 Unscrew the bolts securing the gearbox to the drive belt casing **(see illustrations)**.

> **HAYNES HiNT**
>
> *Make a cardboard template of the gearbox cover and punch a hole for each bolt location. This will ensure all bolts are installed correctly on reassembly – this is important as some bolts may be of different lengths.*

5 Support the casing on a block of wood, then carefully ease the gearbox away from

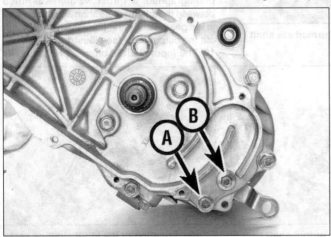

7.3 Gearbox drain plug (A) and filler plug (B)

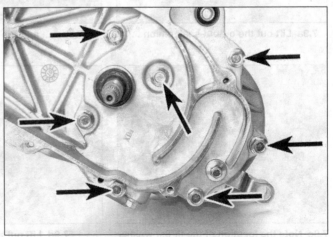

7.4a Undo the gearbox bolts (arrowed) . . .

7.4b . . . noting their different lengths and locations

7.5a Support the casing . . .

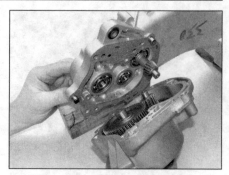

7.5b . . . then lift away the gearbox

7.6 Discard the gasket. Note the position of the dowels (arrowed)

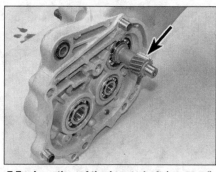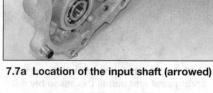

7.7a Location of the input shaft (arrowed)

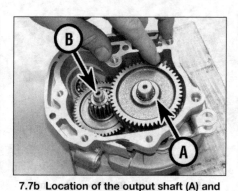

7.7b Location of the output shaft (A) and intermediate shaft (B)

the casing and remove it (see illustrations). If the gearbox is stuck, tap around the joint face between the cover and the box with a soft-faced mallet to free it. Do not try to lever the gearbox off as this may damage the sealing surfaces. **Note:** *On gearboxes*

not fitted with a drain plug, position a tray to catch the oil when the box is removed.

6 Discard the gasket as a new one must be fitted on reassembly (see illustration). Note the position of any dowels on the casing

or gearbox housing and remove them for safekeeping if they are loose.

7 There are three gearbox shafts – the input shaft which carries the clutch, the output shaft which carries the rear wheel, and an intermediate shaft. The input shaft will remain in its bearing in the casing and the intermediate and output shafts will remain in the gearbox housing (see illustrations). Note how the gear pinions mesh together.

8 Check the shafts for any thrust washers and remove them, noting where they fit. Check carefully – sometimes the washers will stick to the shaft bearings.

9 Lift out the output shaft pinion, then lift out the intermediate shaft – on the model photographed, a thrust washer was fitted between the intermediate shaft and the bearing in the gearbox housing (see illustrations). Lift out the output shaft (see illustration).

10 The input shaft is often a press fit in its

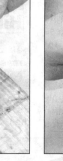

7.9a Lift out the output shaft pinion . . .

7.9b . . . and the intermediate shaft

7.9c Note the location of the thrust washer

7.9d Lift out the output shaft

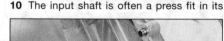

7.10a Location of the input shaft oil seal (arrowed)

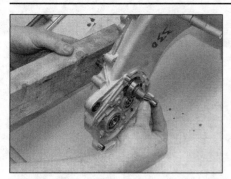

7.10b Remove the input shaft as described

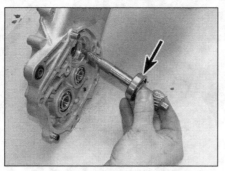

7.10c Note the location of the input shaft bearing (arrowed)

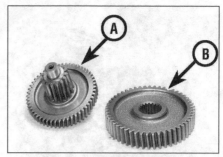

7.14 Inspect the teeth on the pinions – intermediate shaft (A) and output shaft pinion (B)

bearing and should not be removed unless the shaft, the bearing or the oil seal is to be renewed **(see illustration)**. To remove the shaft, first fit the clutch centre nut to protect the threads, then drive the shaft out using a soft-faced mallet or a block of wood on the clutch end – if necessary, heat the casing with a hot air gun to aid removal **(see illustrations)**. The bearing will come out with the shaft.

11 Check the casing and gearbox housing for any remaining washers and remove them, noting where they fit.

12 Do not remove the gear pinions from the shafts unnecessarily – they should only be removed if components are being renewed.

Inspection

13 Clean all traces of old gasket material from the case and gearbox mating surfaces, taking

care not to scratch or gouge the soft aluminium. Wash all the components in a suitable solvent and dry them with compressed air.

14 Check the pinion teeth for cracking, chipping, pitting and other obvious wear or damage **(see illustration)**. Check for signs of scoring or blueing on the pinions and shafts caused by overheating due to inadequate lubrication.

15 Ensure that all the pinions are a tight fit on their shafts **(see illustration)**.

16 Inspect the splines and threads on the input and output shafts **(see illustrations)**.

17 Renew any damaged or worn components. In some cases, the pinions are a press fit on the shafts, or are retained by circlips allowing components to be renewed individually. Some pinions are an integral part of the shaft and on some scooters shafts are only supplied as matched items.

18 Check the condition of the input and output shaft oil seals. Any loss of gearbox oil must be remedied immediately to avoid expensive damage or seizure. If the input shaft oil seal fails, oil will run into the drive belt case behind the clutch. If either of the shafts has been removed, it is good practice to fit a new seal prior to installation (see *Tools and Workshop Tips* in the *Reference* section). Lever the input shaft seal out from the clutch side of the casing; lever the output shaft seal out from the inside of the gearbox housing **(see illustrations)**.

19 Inspect the bearings (see *Tools and Workshop Tips* in the *Reference* section). If the bearings need renewing, the output shaft bearing can be driven out using a bearing driver or suitably-sized socket **(see illustration)**. Bearings that are fitted into blind holes require an internal bearing puller

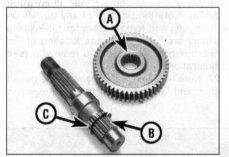

7.15 Check for wear on the pinion splines (A) and on the shafts (B). Note the circlip (C) – output shaft shown

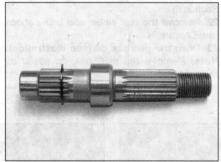

7.16a Inspect the output shaft for wear and damage

7.16b Inspect the input shaft for wear and damage

7.18a Levering out the input shaft oil seal

7.18b Levering out the output shaft oil seal

7.19a Driving out the output shaft bearing

7.19b Using an internal bearing puller with slide-hammer attachment

7.19c Using a hot air gun to heat the bearing housing

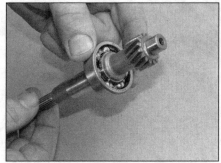

7.19d Check the condition of the input shaft bearing

and slide-hammer to extract them without damaging the case **(see illustration)**. Always heat the bearing housing first to aid removal and fitting **(see illustration)**. Don't forget to check the bearing on the input shaft **(see illustration)**. If specialist tools are not available consult an automotive engineer.

Installation

20 Installation is the reverse of removal, noting the following:

7.23 Gearbox drain plug (A) and filler plug (B)

● Ensure any washers are fitted to the shafts before assembly.
● Lubricate both ends of the intermediate shaft with molybdenum disulphide grease before installation.
● Fit any dowels into the cover.
● Use a new cover gasket.
● Smear the inside of the oil seals with grease before installing the shafts.
● Tighten the gearbox bolts evenly and in a criss-cross pattern.
● If a gearbox drain plug is fitted, fit a new sealing washer.
● Fill the gearbox with the specified amount and type of oil (see Chapter 1).

Type 2

Removal

21 Remove the clutch and clutch pulley (see Section 6).
22 Remove the rear wheel and brake shoes (see Chapter 7).
23 Drain the gearbox oil **(see illustration)**. **Note:** *Remove the filler plug to assist oil drainage.*
24 Unscrew the bolts securing the

gearbox cover to the drive belt casing **(see illustration)**.

> **HAYNES HINT** *Make a cardboard template of the gearbox cover and punch a hole for each bolt location. This will ensure all bolts are installed correctly on reassembly – this is important as some bolts may be of different lengths.*

25 Carefully ease the cover together with the input shaft away from the casing **(see illustration)**. If the cover is stuck, tap around the joint face between the cover and the casing with a soft-faced mallet to free it. Do not try to lever the cover off as this may damage the sealing surfaces.
26 Discard the gasket as a new one must be fitted on reassembly **(see illustration 7.37a)**. Note the position of any dowels on the casing and remove them for safekeeping if they are loose. Note the location of the gearbox breather hose and remove it **(see illustration)**.
27 Note how the gear pinions on the output shaft and intermediate shaft mesh together.

7.24 Undo the gearbox bolts (arrowed)

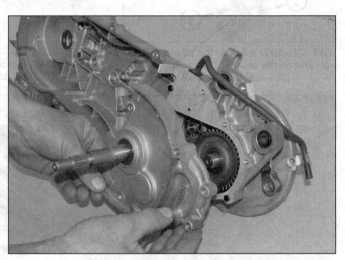

7.25 Remove the gearbox cover

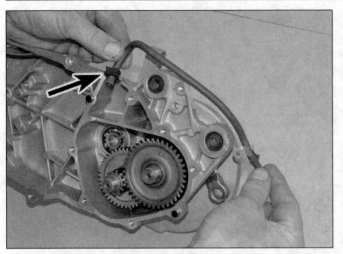

7.26 Remove the breather hose noting the position of the seal (arrowed)

7.28a Lift out the output shaft pinion . . .

As they are removed, check the shafts for any thrust washers and remove them, noting where they fit. Check carefully – sometimes the washers will stick to the shaft bearings.

28 Lift out the output shaft pinion, then lift out the intermediate shaft **(see illustrations)**.

29 Withdraw the output shaft **(see illustration)**. Note the location of the circlip on the shaft.

30 The input shaft is often a press fit in its bearing and should not be removed unless the shaft, the bearing or the oil seal is to be renewed **(see illustration)**. To remove the shaft, first fit the clutch centre nut to protect the threads, then drive the shaft out using a soft-faced mallet or a block of wood on the clutch end – if necessary, heat the casing with a hot air gun to aid removal. The bearing will come out with the shaft.

Inspection

31 Clean all traces of old gasket material from the gearbox mating surfaces, taking care not to scratch or gouge the soft aluminium.

7.28b . . . and the intermediate shaft

Wash all the components in a suitable solvent and dry them with compressed air.

32 Check the pinion teeth for cracking, chipping, pitting and other obvious wear or damage **(see illustration)**. Check for signs of scoring or blueing on the pinions and shafts caused by overheating due to inadequate lubrication.

7.29 Location of circlip on output shaft

33 Inspect the splines and threads on the input and output shafts.

34 Renew any damaged or worn components. Some pinions are an integral part of the shaft and on some scooters shafts are only supplied as matched items.

35 Check the condition of the input and output shaft oil seals. Any loss of gearbox

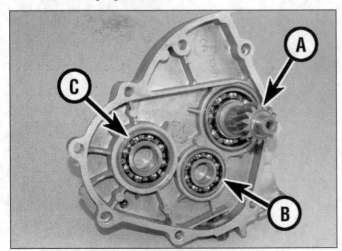

7.30 Location of the input shaft (A). Note bearings for the intermediate shaft (B) and output shaft (C)

7.32 Check for damage to the pinion teeth and shafts

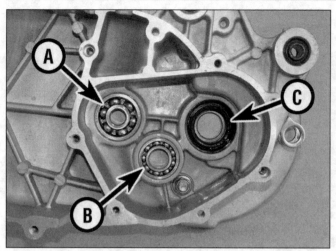

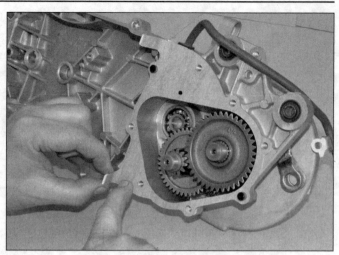

7.36 Input shaft (A) and intermediate shaft (B) bearings. Output shaft oil seal and bearing (C)

7.37a Fold the tabs on the gasket over . . .

7.37b . . . to seal against the ends of the belt casing (arrowed)

oil must be remedied immediately to avoid expensive damage or seizure. If the input shaft oil seal fails, oil will run into the drive belt case behind the clutch. If either of the shafts has been removed, it is good practice to fit a new seal prior to installation (see *Tools and Workshop Tips* in the *Reference* section). Lever the input shaft seal out from the clutch side of the casing; lever the output shaft seal out from the inside of the gearbox housing.

36 Inspect the bearings in the casing and the gearbox cover (see *Tools and Workshop Tips* in the *Reference* section). If the bearings need renewing, the output shaft bearing can be driven out using a bearing driver or suitably-sized socket **(see illustration)**. Bearings that are fitted into blind holes require an internal bearing puller and slide-hammer to extract them without damaging the case. Always heat the bearing housing first to aid removal and fitting. Don't forget to check the bearing on the input shaft **(see illustration 7.30)**. If specialist tools are not available consult an automotive engineer.

Installation

37 Installation is the reverse of removal, noting the following:

- Smear the inside of the oil seals with grease before installing the shafts.
- Ensure any washers are fitted to the shafts before assembly.
- Lubricate both ends of the intermediate shaft with molybdenum disulphide grease before installation.
- Fit any dowels into the cover.
- Use a new cover gasket **(see illustrations)**.
- Tighten the gearbox bolts evenly and in a criss-cross pattern to the specified torque (see Chapter 2B Specifications).
- Fit a new sealing washer on the gearbox drain plug.
- Fill the gearbox with the specified amount and type of oil (see Chapter 1).

Chapter 6
Frame and suspension

Contents

Degrees of difficulty

Easy, suitable for novice with little experience	**Fairly easy,** suitable for beginner with some experience	**Fairly difficult,** suitable for competent DIY mechanic	**Difficult,** suitable for experienced DIY mechanic	**Very difficult,** suitable for expert DIY or professional

1 General information

All scooters covered by this manual are fitted with a tubular and pressed steel one-piece frame.

The engine/transmission unit is linked to the frame by a pivoting assembly at the front and by the shock absorber at the rear, making the unit an integral part of the rear suspension.

Front suspension is by conventional telescopic forks or a trailing link arrangement with either a single or twin shock absorbers.

Ancillary items such as stands and handle-bars are covered in this Chapter.

2 Frame

1 The frame should not require attention unless accident damage has occurred. In most cases, frame renewal is the only satisfactory remedy for such damage. A few frame specialists have the jigs and other equipment necessary for straightening the frame to the required standard of accuracy, but even then there is no simple way of assessing to

what extent the frame may have been over-stressed.

2 After a high mileage, the frame should be examined closely for signs of cracking or splitting at the welded joints. Loose engine mount and suspension bolts can cause ovaling or fracturing of the mounting points. Minor damage can often be repaired by specialist welding, depending on the extent and nature of the damage.

3 Remember that a frame which is out of alignment will cause handling problems. If misalignment is suspected as the result of an accident, it will be necessary to strip the machine completely so the frame can be thoroughly checked.

3.2 Location of the main stand. Note the stand springs (arrowed)

3.3 Prise the springs off carefully to avoid damage or injury

3.4a Remove the split pin . . .

3.4b . . . and the washer . . .

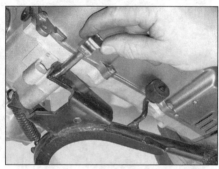

3.4c . . . then withdraw the pivot pin

3.5 Ease the stand off. Note the location of the spring (arrowed)

3 Stands

Main stand

1 Support the scooter securely in an upright position using an auxiliary stand. **Note:** *Do not rest the weight of the machine on the bodywork – if necessary, remove the belly panel to expose the frame (see Chapter 8).*
2 On most scooters covered in this manual, the main stand is fixed directly to the underside of the engine cases **(see illustration)**.

3 The stand is held in position by one or two springs – take great care when removing the springs as they are under considerable tension **(see illustration)**. **Note:** *On some scooters, the single spring can be left in position and removed with the stand (see Step 5).*
4 Remove the split pin and washer securing the pivot pin, then withdraw the pivot pin **(see illustrations)**.
5 Ease the stand off – if the spring is still attached, unhook it from the lug on the crankcase **(see illustration)**.
6 Thoroughly clean the stand and remove all road dirt and old grease. Inspect the pivot pin and the pivot holes in the bracket for wear and renew

them if necessary **(see illustration)**. Inspect the spring; if it is sagged or is cracked a new spring must be fitted. Inspect the rubber stop on the stand and renew it if it is worn or perished.
7 Installation is the reverse of removal, noting the following:
● Apply grease to the pivot pin and all pivot points.
● Secure the pivot pin with a new split pin **(see illustration)**.
● Ensure that the spring holds the stand up securely when it is not in use – an accident is almost certain to occur if the stand extends while the machine is in motion. If necessary, fit a new spring.

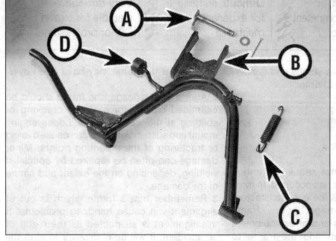

3.6 Main stand components. Pivot pin (A), bracket (B), spring (C) and stop (D)

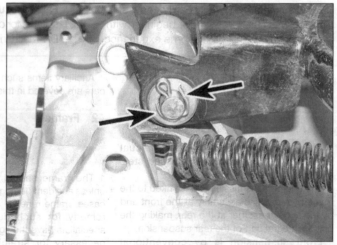

3.7 Bend the ends of the split pin (arrowed) as shown

3.10a Unhook the stand spring (arrowed)

3.10b Note the location of the spring plate (arrowed)

3.11 Location of the pivot bolt (A) and stand switch (B)

Side stand

8 Support the scooter on its main stand (see Step 1).

9 If necessary, remove the belly panel to access the stand pivot bolt (see Chapter 8).

10 Unhook the stand spring, noting how it fits **(see illustrations)**. If applicable, note the location of the spring plate.

11 Unscrew the stand pivot bolt and remove the bolt, washer and stand **(see illustration)**. If applicable, note the location of the stand switch.

12 Installation is the reverse of removal, noting the following:

● Apply grease to the pivot bolt.

● Ensure that the stand contact plate actuates the stand switch when the stand is lowered.

● Check the spring tension – it must hold the stand up when it is not in use. If necessary, fit a new spring.

● Check the operation of the sidestand switch (see Chapter 9, Section 7).

4 Handlebars

Removal

1 Remove the handlebar covers and any body panels as necessary to access the steering stem (see Chapter 8). Note that on some scooters, the rear cover cannot be removed until the handlebars have been displaced.

2 If required, the handlebars can be displaced from the steering stem for access to the bearings without having to detach any cables, hoses or main wiring looms, or remove the switches, brake levers or master cylinders. If this is the case, ignore the Steps which do not apply.

3 Where fitted, loosen the centre screws for the bar end weights and withdraw the weights from the handlebars. Take care not to undo the screws too far and lose the nuts on the end of the screws **(see illustration)**.

4 Undo the throttle twistgrip housing screws and slide the twistgrip off the end of the handlebar (see Chapter 3).

5 Disconnect the wiring from each brake light switch **(see illustration)**.

6 Undo the left-hand handlebar switch housing screws and displace the housing (see Chapter 9). **Note:** *On most scooters, the switch housing incorporates the rear brake*

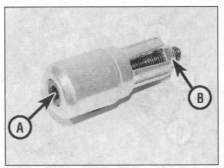

4.3 Loosen bar end weight centre screw (A) to release nut (B)

lever bracket. If required, disconnect the rear brake cable (see Chapter 7).

7 Check that no other electrical components are mounted on the handlebars and detach them as necessary.

8 Unscrew the front brake master cylinder assembly clamp bolts and position the assembly clear of the handlebar, making sure no strain is placed on the hydraulic hose (see Chapter 7). Keep the master cylinder reservoir upright to prevent air entering the system.

9 Remove the left-hand grip; peel the grip off the end of the bar, or if necessary cut it off.

10 On scooters with the handlebars secured by a stem bolt, remove the nut and washer, then withdraw the bolt noting the shaped spacer **(see illustrations)**. Support the handlebars and withdraw the bolt, then lift the bars off the steering stem **(see illustration)**.

11 On scooters with the handlebars secured

4.5 Disconnect the brake light switch wiring connectors (arrowed)

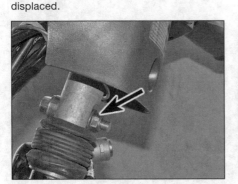

4.10a Undo the nut (arrowed) on the stem bolt . . .

4.10b . . . then withdraw the bolt, noting the shaped spacer (arrowed)

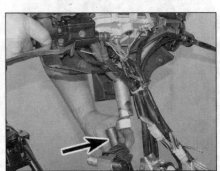

4.10c Lift the handlebars off the steering stem (arrowed)

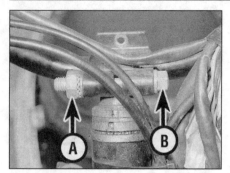

4.11 Undo the nut (A) and withdraw the pinch bolt (B)

by a clamp and pinch bolt, undo the nut and bolt, then lift off the bars **(see illustration)**.

12 If the handlebar components have been left attached, position the bars so that no strain is placed on any of the cables, brake hose or wiring, and protect the body panels to prevent scratching.

Installation

13 Installation is the reverse of removal, noting the following:

● Tighten the handlebar stem bolt securely. Torque settings are given for certain models in the Data section.

● Use a suitable adhesive to secure the left-hand grip on the handlebar.

● Don't forget to reconnect the brake light switch wiring connectors.

● Check the operation of the brakes and lights before riding the scooter.

5 Steering head bearings – adjustment

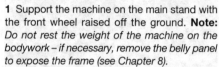

1 Support the machine on the main stand with the front wheel raised off the ground. **Note:** *Do not rest the weight of the machine on the bodywork – if necessary, remove the belly panel to expose the frame (see Chapter 8).*

2 Remove the handlebar covers and any body panels as necessary to access the steering stem (see Chapter 8).

3 If required, displace the handlebars (see Section 4). Where fitted, lift off the protective boot **(see illustration)**.

4 Some scooters are fitted with one locknut above the bearing adjuster nut, others have two locknuts. The locknut and the adjuster nut are usually held in place with a lock washer **(see illustration)**. Check carefully which arrangement you have.

5 If the lock washer has tabs which locate in notches in the locknut, first prise the tabs out of the notches. **Note:** *A tabbed lock washer should not be re-used; remove the locknut and fit a new washer after adjusting the bearings.*

6 If one locknut is fitted, hold the adjuster nut and loosen the locknut using a suitable spanner, C-spanner or grips **(see illustration)**.

7 If two locknuts are fitted, unscrew the top nut then lift the tab washer off the remaining two nuts, noting how it fits **(see illustration)**. Unscrew the second locknut. A rubber washer is fitted between the second locknut and the adjuster nut. Discard it if it is crushed or

damaged and fit a new one on reassembly.

8 Using either a spanner, C-spanner or grips, loosen the adjuster nut slightly to take pressure off the bearing then tighten the nut until all freeplay is removed **(see illustration)**. Check that the steering still turns freely from side-to-side with no front-to-rear movement (see Chapter 1, Section 33). The object is to set the adjuster nut so that the bearings are under a very light loading, just enough to remove any freeplay **(see illustration)**.

Caution: Take great care not to apply excessive pressure because this will cause premature failure of the bearings.

9 With the bearings correctly adjusted, the adjuster nut must be held to prevent it from moving while the locknut is tightened. Where necessary, first install a new lockwasher ensuring the tabs locate correctly in the adjuster nut.

10 Where one locknut is fitted, tighten the locknut securely, then bend the remaining lockwasher tabs up to secure the locknut. **Note:** *Some manufacturers specify a torque setting for the locknut (given in the Data section for certain models). However to apply this a service tool or a suitable fabricated tool (see illustration 5.11a) is required and the handlebars must be displaced (see Section 4).*

11 Where two locknuts are fitted, install the rubber washer and then the second locknut, tightening it finger-tight. Hold the adjuster nut to prevent it turning, then tighten the second locknut only enough to align its notches with the notches in the adjuster nut and install the tab washer **(see illustration 5.7)**. Install

5.3 Lift off the protective boot

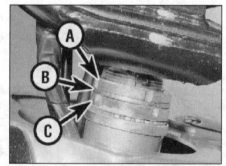

5.4 Locknut (A), washer (B), adjuster nut (C)

5.6 Loosen the locknut as described

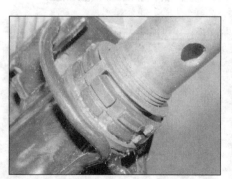

5.7 Location of the tab washer

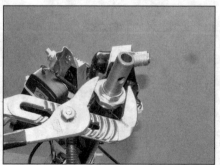

5.8a Adjusting the steering head bearings with slip-joint pliers

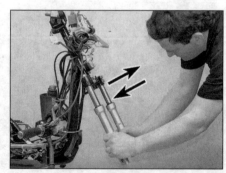

5.8b Checking for front-to-rear movement in the steering head bearings

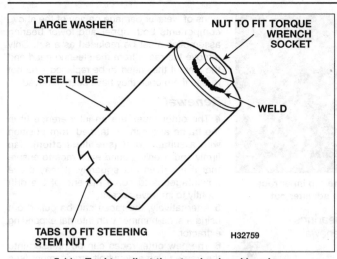

5.11a Tool to adjust the steering head bearings

LARGE WASHER
NUT TO FIT TORQUE WRENCH SOCKET
STEEL TUBE
WELD
TABS TO FIT STEERING STEM NUT
H32759

5.11b Hold the adjuster nut and tighten the locknut with the special tool

the top locknut, then hold the adjuster nut to prevent it turning and tighten the top locknut securely. If the special tool is available, tighten the locknut to the specified torque setting **(see illustrations)**.

12 Check the bearing adjustment and re-adjust if necessary, then install the remaining components in the reverse order of

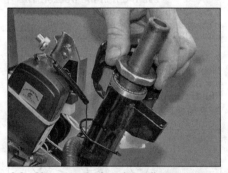

6.6a Unscrew the bearing adjuster nut . . .

removal. Don't forget to install the protective boot **(see illustration 5.3)**.

6 Steering stem

Removal

1 Displace the brake caliper and remove the front wheel (see Chapter 7).

2 If the front mudguard or mudguard liner are mounted on the front suspension, remove them (see Chapter 8).

3 If required, remove the front suspension (see Section 8).

4 Remove the handlebars (see Section 4).

5 Remove the bearing adjuster locknut(s) and washer as applicable (see Section 5).

6 Support the steering stem, then unscrew the bearing adjuster nut and carefully lower the stem out of the steering head **(see illustrations)**. Note which way round the

adjuster nut fits – on some scooters, the inner race of the top steering head bearing is integral with the adjuster nut **(see illustration 6.12)**. **Note:** *Place a clean rag on the floor beneath the steering head to catch the ball bearings if they are loose when the steering stem is removed.*

7 The ball bearings in the lower race will either fall out of the race or stick to the lower inner race on the steering stem **(see illustration)**. The top bearing, and, if it is separate from the adjuster nut, the top inner race, will remain in the top of the steering head.

8 If not already done, lift out the top inner race and the top bearing **(see illustration)**. **Note:** *The balls of the top bearing may be loose or they may be housed in a cage.*

9 Remove all traces of old grease from the ball bearings and races and inspect them for wear or damage (see Section 7). **Note:** *Do not attempt to remove the outer races from the steering head or the lower bearing inner race from the steering stem unless they are to be renewed.*

6.6b . . . and lower the steering stem out of the steering head

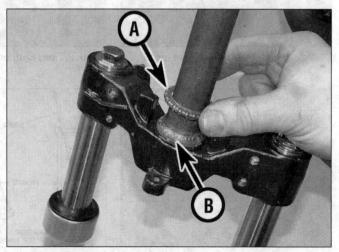

6.7 Location of the lower bearing (A) and lower inner race (B)

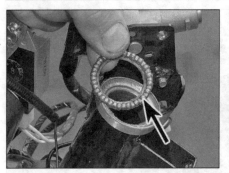

6.8 Top bearing (arrowed) is housed in a cage

Installation

10 Apply a liberal quantity of grease to the bearing inner and outer races and install the top bearing **(see illustration 6.8)**.

11 Assemble the lower race ball bearings on the lower inner race on the steering stem; if they are a loose assembly they will be retained by the grease.

12 Carefully lift the steering stem up through the steering head, ensuring the lower race ball bearings remain in place. Either thread the combined top inner bearing race/adjuster nut onto the stem or install the inner race and thread the adjuster nut onto the stem **(see illustration)**. Ensure the adjuster nut is fitted the right way round.

13 Follow the procedure in Section 5 to adjust the steering head bearings, then install the remaining components in the reverse order of removal.

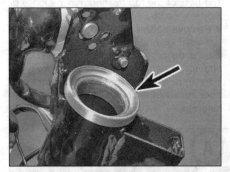

7.3a Inspect the races in the top . . .

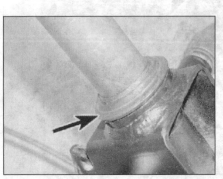

7.3c Lower inner race on the steering stem

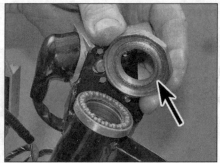

6.12 Location of the top inner race (arrowed) on the adjuster nut

---

7 Steering head bearings – inspection and renewal

Inspection

1 Remove the steering stem (see Section 6).

2 Remove all traces of old grease from the bearings and races and check them for wear or damage.

3 The races should be polished and free from indentations. The outer races are in the steering head, the top inner race is either integral with the bearing adjuster nut or it rests on top of the top bearing, and the lower inner race is on the steering stem **(see illustrations)**. Inspect the ball bearings for signs of wear, pitting or corrosion, and, where fitted, examine the bearing retainer cage for signs of cracks or splits. If there are any

7.3b . . . and bottom of the steering head

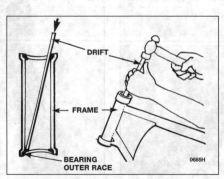

7.4 Drive the bearing outer races out with a brass drift as shown

signs of wear or damage on any of the above components both upper and lower bearing assemblies must be replaced as a set. Only remove the races from the steering head and the stem if they need to be replaced – do not re-use them once they have been removed.

Renewal

4 The outer races are an interference fit in the frame and can be tapped from position with a suitable drift **(see illustration)**. Tap firmly and evenly around each race to ensure that it is driven out squarely. It may prove advantageous to curve the end of the drift slightly to improve access.

5 Alternatively, the races can be pulled out using a slide-hammer with internal expanding extractor.

6 The new outer races can be pressed into the frame using a drawbolt arrangement **(see illustration)**, or by using a large diameter tubular drift which bears only on the outer edge of the race. Ensure that the drawbolt washer or drift (as applicable) bears only on the outer edge of the race and does not contact the working surface.

> **HAYNES HINT** *Installation of new bearing outer races is made much easier if the races are left overnight in the freezer. This causes them to contract slightly making them a looser fit.*

7 To remove the lower inner race from the steering stem, first drive a chisel between the base of the race and the fork yoke **(see illustration)**. Work the chisel around the race to ensure it lifts squarely. Once there is

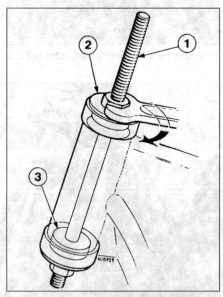

7.6 Using a drawbolt to fit the outer races in the steering head

1 Long bolt or threaded bar
2 Thick washer
3 Guide for lower race

clearance beneath the race, use two levers placed on opposite sides of the race to work it free, using blocks of wood to improve leverage and protect the yoke. If the race is firmly in place it can be split using an angle grinder – take great care not to nick or gouge the steering stem **(see illustration)**.

8 Fit the new lower inner race onto the steering stem. A length of tubing with an internal diameter slightly larger than the steering stem will be needed to tap the new bearing into position. Ensure that the drift bears only on the inner edge of the race and does not contact its working surface.

9 Install the steering stem (see Section 6).

8 Front suspension

General information

1 Two types of front suspension are fitted to the scooters covered in this manual. Most scooters have motorcycle-type telescopic forks where the fork legs can be removed individually for disassembly **(see illustration 8.13)**. Others are equipped with trailing link suspension with twin shock absorbers **(see illustration 8.47)**.

2 Some suspension assemblies use self-locking nuts which should be discarded after use. Always use new self-locking nuts when reassembling the suspension.

Telescopic fork suspension

Note: *Always dismantle the fork legs*

7.7a Using a chisel to remove the lower inner race

separately to avoid interchanging parts. Check the availability of replacement parts and the type and quantity of fork oil required before disassembling the forks. Note that on some scooters, individual parts are not available – if the fork legs are damaged or worn, new leg assemblies will have to be fitted.

Removal

3 Displace the brake caliper and remove the front wheel (see Chapter 7).

4 Follow the procedure in Chapter 8 to remove the front mudguard and any body panels as required to access the fork top bolts and clamp bolts **(see illustrations 8.5 and 7a)**.

5 Note the position of the fork top bolt in relation to the top surface of the fork yoke **(see illustration)**.

6 If the fork leg is going to be disassembled or the fork oil is going to be changed, loosen the fork top bolt while the leg is still clamped in the fork yoke **(see illustration 8.5)**. To do this,

7.7b Using an angle grinder to split the lower inner race

first undo the fork leg clamp bolt(s) and push the leg a short distance up through the yoke, then temporarily tighten the clamp bolt(s). Now loosen the top bolt. **Note 1:** *Some fork legs have a location groove for one of the clamp bolts – remove the bolt before attempting to move the leg* **(see illustration 8.7c)**. **Note 2:** *On one of the scooters used to illustrate this procedure, the fork top bolts had to be removed completely before the legs could be withdrawn from the yoke* **(see illustration 8.7d)**.

7 Undo the fork clamp bolt(s) and remove the fork leg by twisting it and pulling it downwards **(see illustrations)**.

> **HAYNES HiNT** *If the fork legs are seized in the yokes, spray the area with penetrating oil and allow time for it to soak in before trying again.*

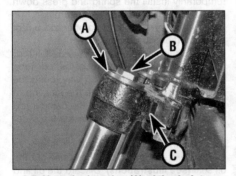

8.5 Note the location (A) of the fork top bolt (B) against the yoke (C)

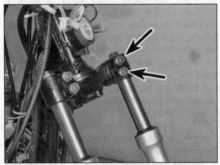

8.7a Loosen the clamp bolts (arrowed) . . .

8.7b . . . then withdraw the fork leg

8.7c Note the groove (arrowed) for the clamp bolt, where applicable

8.7d If necessary, remove the top bolt . . .

8.7e . . . then undo the clamp bolt to free the leg

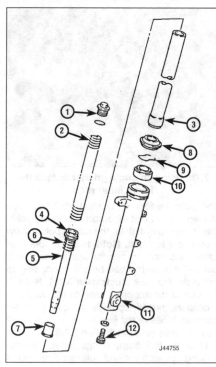

8.13 Typical telescopic fork leg components

1	Top bolt	7	Spring seat
2	Spring	8	Dust seal
3	Fork tube	9	Circlip
4	Sealing ring	10	Oil seal
5	Damper	11	Fork slider
6	Rebound spring	12	Damper bolt

8 If the top bolts have been removed, temporarily install them to prevent accidental loss of fork oil.

Installation

9 Remove all traces of corrosion from the fork tubes and the yokes. Install each fork leg individually. Slide the leg up through the yoke until the top edge of the fork tube is level with the top edge of the yoke. Where applicable, ensure the location groove for the clamp bolt is correctly aligned.

10 If the top bolt has been loosened, or if it has been removed to allow for installation of the leg, temporarily clamp the leg in the yoke and tighten the top bolt (see Step 6).

8.18 Ease off the dust seal

8.16 Note the location of the top bolt O-ring (arrowed)

11 With the fork leg correctly positioned in the yoke, tighten the clamp bolt(s). Torque settings are given for certain models in the *Data section* at the end of this manual.

12 Install the remaining components in the reverse order of removal. Check the operation of the front forks and brake before riding the scooter.

Disassembly

13 Remove the fork leg (see Steps 3 to 7). Always dismantle the fork legs separately to avoid interchanging parts **(see illustration)**. Store all components in separate, clearly marked containers.

14 The damper bolt should be loosened at this stage. Invert the fork leg and compress the fork tube in the slider so that the spring exerts maximum pressure on the damper, then loosen the bolt in the base of the fork slider **(see illustration 8.20)**.

15 If the fork top bolt was not loosened with the fork on the scooter, carefully clamp the fork tube in a vice equipped with soft jaws, taking care not to overtighten or score the tube's surface, and loosen the top bolt.

16 Unscrew the top bolt from the top of the fork tube. Note any O-ring fitted to the top bolt; if it is damaged, fit a new one on reassembly **(see illustration)**.

⚠ *Warning: The fork spring is pressing on the fork top bolt with considerable pressure. Unscrew the bolt very carefully, keeping a downward pressure on it and release it slowly as it is likely to spring clear. It is advisable to wear some form of eye and*

8.20 Remove the damper bolt and sealing washer (arrowed)

8.17 Withdraw the fork spring

face protection when carrying out this operation.

17 Slide the fork tube down into the slider and withdraw the spring **(see illustration)**. Note which way up the spring is fitted. **Note:** *On the model photographed, the spring was fitted with its closer wound coils uppermost.*

18 Carefully prise out the dust seal from the top of the slider **(see illustration)**.

19 Invert the fork leg over a measuring vessel and pump the fork vigorously to expel as much fork oil as possible. It is important to record how much oil is drained from each fork because this can then be used as a guide to refilling.

20 Remove the previously loosened damper bolt and its sealing washer from the bottom of the slider **(see illustration)**. Discard the sealing washer as a new one must be used on reassembly. If the damper bolt was not loosened before dismantling the fork, temporarily install the spring and press down on it to prevent the damper from turning.

21 Pull the fork tube and damper rod out of the slider **(see illustration)**.

22 Withdraw the damper rod and, if fitted, the rebound spring from inside the fork tube **(see illustration)**. Note which way round the rebound spring is fitted. Note the location of the spring seat on the end of the damper rod – the spring seat may be left inside the slider **(see illustration 8.29)**.

23 Prise the retaining clip out of its groove in the top of the fork slider, then prise out the oil seal **(see illustrations)**. Discard the oil and dust seals as a new ones must be used on reassembly.

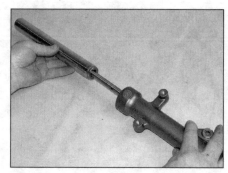

8.21 Pull out the fork tube and damper

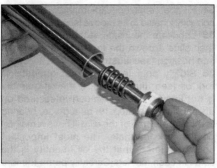

8.22 Withdraw the damper and rebound spring

8.23a Note the location of the retaining clip . . .

8.23b . . . then remove the clip . . .

8.23c . . . and prise out the oil seal

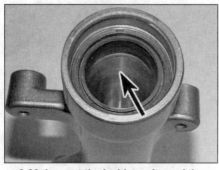

8.26 Inspect the inside surface of the sliders (arrowed) for wear

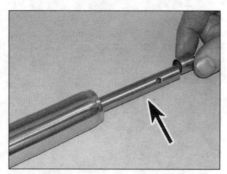

8.29 Fit the spring seat on the bottom of the damper (arrowed)

Inspection

24 Clean all parts in a suitable solvent and dry them with compressed air, if available.

25 Inspect the fork tubes for score marks, pitting or flaking of the chrome finish and excessive or abnormal wear. Check the straightness of the tubes with a straight-edge. If either of the tubes is damaged, worn or bent, renew both fork tubes – never have fork tubes straightened.

26 If the fork tubes are worn or pitted, it is likely that the inside bearing surface of the sliders will be damaged also. If the surface is scored or pitted, renew the sliders **(see illustration)**.

27 Inspect the springs for cracks, sagging and other damage. Measure the spring free length – the spring in both forks must be the same length. If one spring is defective, renew the springs as a pair.

28 Where fitted, check the condition of the

rebound spring as well as the main spring, and inspect the sealing ring on the damper for wear and damage **(see illustration 8.22)**. **Note:** *Do not remove the sealing ring from the damper unless it requires renewal.*

Reassembly

29 Where fitted, slide the rebound spring onto the damper, ensuring it is the correct way round. Insert the damper into the top of the fork tube and slide it down so that it protrudes out from the bottom of the tube, then fit the spring seat **(see illustration)**.

30 Insert the spring into the fork tube, ensuring it is the correct way round (see Step 17).

31 Lubricate the fork tube with the specified fork oil, then compress the spring to hold the damper in position and invert the slider over the damper and fork tube assembly **(see illustration)**.

32 Fit a new sealing washer onto the damper

bolt and apply a few drops of a suitable, non-permanent thread-locking compound, then install the bolt into the bottom of the slider **(see illustration)**. If the damper rotates inside the tube, press the slider down to hold the damper under spring pressure.

33 Push the fork tube fully into the slider and remove the spring, then lubricate the inside of the new oil seal with fork oil and slide it over the tube with its markings facing upwards **(see illustration)**. Press the seal into place in the slider. If necessary, use a suitable piece of tubing to tap the seal carefully into place; the tubing must be slightly larger in diameter than the fork tube and slightly smaller in diameter than the seal recess in the slider. Take care not to scratch the fork tube during this operation; if the fork tube is pushed fully into the slider any accidental scratching is confined to the area above the seal.

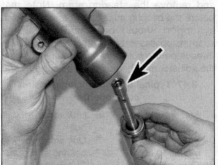

8.31 Install the slider over the fork tube. Note the spring seat (arrowed)

8.32 Use a new sealing washer and thread-locking compound on the damper bolt

8.33 Install the oil seal with its markings facing up

8.34 Fit the oil seal retaining clip . . .

8.35 . . . and then the dust seal

8.36a Pour in the specified quantity of fork oil

8.36b Measure the oil level from the top of the fork tube

34 Fit the retaining clip, making sure it is correctly located in its groove (**see illustration**).
35 Lubricate the inside of the new dust seal then slide it down the fork tube and press it into position (**see illustration**).
36 Slowly pour in the correct quantity of fork oil (**see illustration**). If the oil quantity is not known, use the amount measured on dismantling (see Step 19) as a guide, bearing in mind that some of the oil will have remained on the fork internals. The most important consideration is that the oil quantity is the same in each fork leg. Carefully pump the fork to distribute the oil evenly, then compress the fork tube fully into its slider and use a ruler to measure the oil level from the top of each tube (**see illustration**). Add or remove oil until the level is the same in each leg, ensuring you don't stray too far from the original quantity. Fork oils are available in varing viscosities, light (5W), medium (10W) or heavy (20W).
37 Pull the fork tube out of the slider to its full extension and install the spring, ensuring it is the correct way round (**see illustration 8.17**).
38 If necessary, fit a new O-ring to the fork top bolt (**see illustration 8.16**). If the top bolt can be fitted at this stage, keep the fork leg fully extended and press down on the spring whilst threading the bolt into the top of the fork tube. Turn the bolt carefully to ensure it is not cross-threaded. **Note:** *The top bolt can be tightened when the fork has been installed and is securely held in the yoke.*

⚠ *Warning: It will be necessary to compress the spring by pressing it down with the top bolt in order to engage the threads of the top bolt with the fork tube. This is a potentially dangerous operation and should be performed with care, using an assistant if necessary. Wipe off any excess oil before starting to prevent the possibility of slipping.*
39 Install the fork leg (see Steps 9 to 12).

Trailing link suspension

Removal and installation

40 Displace the brake caliper and remove the front wheel (see Chapter 7).
41 Follow the procedure in Chapter 8 to remove the front mudguard.
42 To remove the complete front suspension assembly, follow the procedure in Section 6 and remove the steering stem. Note that before the bearing adjuster nut is unscrewed, a support should be placed under the suspension assembly to avoid straining the threads on the nut or steering stem. Unscrew the adjuster nut, then remove the support and

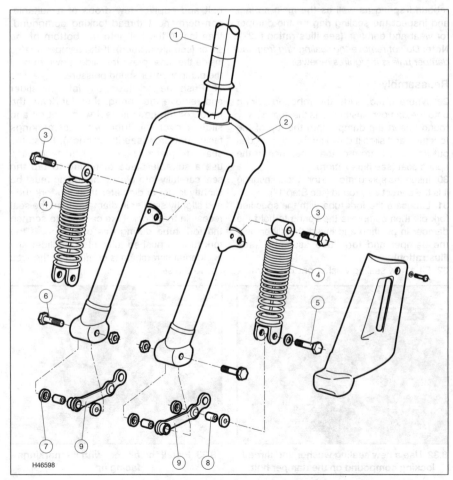

8.47 Typical trailing link suspension components

1 *Steering stem*	6 *Link arm pivot*
2 *Fork yoke*	*bolt*
3 *Shock upper*	7 *Link arm pivot*
mounting bolt	*bearing and seals*
4 *Shock absorber*	8 *Shock pivot*
5 *Shock lower*	*bearing and seals*
mounting bolt	9 *Link arm*

H46598

draw the steering stem down through the steering head.

43 Installation is the reverse of removal. Note that the suspension assembly should be supported once the stem has been located in the steering head. The adjuster nut can then be installed without danger of damaging the threads on the nut or steering stem.

Disassembly

44 Displace the brake calliper and remove the front wheel (see Chapter 7).

45 Follow the procedure in Chapter 8 to remove the front mudguard.

46 The trailing link assembly can be disassembled without having to remove the front fork and steering stem.

47 Remove the suspension cover and the trailing link trim **(see illustration opposite)**.

48 Working on one side at a time, undo the shock absorber lower mounting bolt and separate the link arm from the shock – note the location of the seals on both sides of the link arm **(see illustration 8.47)**. Undo the shock absorber upper mounting bolt and lift the shock off.

49 Before separating the each link arm from the fork leg, check the condition of the pivot bearing by moving the arm laterally against the leg. If any play is felt, the bearing or pivot bolt is worn. Also move the arm up and down. If any roughness is felt or the arm does not move smoothly and freely, the bearing or pivot is damaged. If any components are worn or damaged, new link arms will have to be fitted – individual parts are not available.

50 To remove the link arm, first loosen the link arm pivot bolt, then support the arm and withdraw the bolt. Lift the link arm off, noting the location of the seals on both sides of the pivot bearing. Note which way round the link arms are fitted.

51 Check for any play in the bearings between the brake caliper mounting bracket, torque arm and fork leg **(see illustration)**. If there is play, a new bracket or torque arm will have to be fitted – individual parts are not available. To remove the assembly, undo the nut and bolt securing the torque arm to the fork leg and lift the assembly off, noting the location of the seals.

Inspection

52 Clean all components thoroughly, removing all traces of dirt, corrosion and grease. Inspect all components closely, looking for obvious signs of wear such as heavy scoring, or for damage such as cracks or distortion.

53 Insert the pivot bolts into their respective bearings and check for lateral freeplay. If there is freeplay, new link arms will have to be fitted – individual parts are not available.

54 Inspect the shock absorbers for obvious physical damage and the shock springs for looseness, cracks or signs of fatigue.

55 Inspect the damper rods for signs of bending, pitting and oil leaks **(see illustration)**.

56 Inspect the mountings at the top and bottom of the shock for wear or damage.

Reassembly

57 Working on one side at a time, lubricate the pivot bolts and bearings with a smear of grease before installation. Ensure that the seals are installed on both sides of the link arm bearing, then align the arm with the fork leg, ensuring it is the right way round, and install the bolt. If applicable, thread a new self-locking nut onto the bolt (see Step 2) and tighten the nut securely.

58 Install the shock absorber and tighten the nuts and bolts – don't forget to install the seals on both sides of the link arm.

59 If removed, assemble the seals and torque arm onto the caliper bracket, install the torque arm-to-caliper bracket bolt and tighten the nut securely. Align the assembly with the mounting bracket on the fork leg and install the pivot bolt and nut – don't forget to install the seals on both sides of the torque arm bearing.

60 Install the suspension cover and the trailing link trim.

61 Install the remaining components in the reverse order of removal. Check the operation of the front suspension and brake before riding the scooter.

9 Rear shock absorber

Removal

1 Support the machine on its main stand and position a support under the rear wheel so that the engine does not drop when the shock absorber is removed, but also making sure that the weight of the machine is off the rear suspension so that the shock is not compressed.

2 The shock absorber is secured to the frame at the top and the transmission casing at the bottom. To access the upper mounting bolt, remove the luggage compartment or body panels as necessary according to model (see Chapter 8). If necessary, remove the air filter housing to access the lower mounting bolt (see Chapter 3).

3 Undo and remove the nut, or the nut and bolt, securing the top of the shock absorber to the frame **(see illustration)**.

9.3 Upper rear suspension mounting (arrowed)

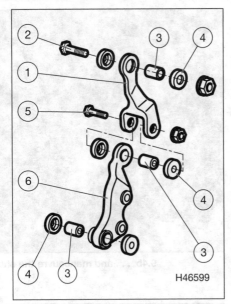

8.51 Torque arm and brake caliper bracket assembly

1	*Torque arm*	*5*	*Torque arm to*
2	*Torque arm pivot*		*caliper bracket*
	bolt		*bolt*
3	*Pivot bearing*	*6*	*Caliper*
4	*Seal*		*bracket*

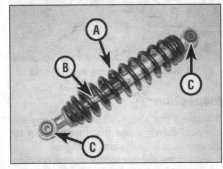

8.55 Inspect the shock spring (A), damper rod (B) and mountings (C)

4 Undo the nut and bolt securing the bottom of the shock absorber to the transmission casing; support the shock and remove the bolt, then manoeuvre the shock away from the machine **(see illustrations)**.

9.4a Undo the lower rear suspension mounting . . .

9.4b . . . and manoeuvre the shock out

9.6 Check the shock mountings (arrowed) for wear

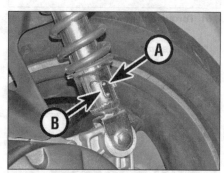

9.8 Rear shock spring seat (A) and adjustment stopper (B)

Inspection

5 Inspect the shock absorber for obvious physical damage and the shock spring for looseness, cracks or signs of fatigue.
6 Inspect the damper rod for signs of bending,

pitting and oil leaks **(see illustration 8.55)**. Check the mountings at the top and bottom of the shock, and the mounting bolts, for wear or damage **(see illustration)**.

Installation

7 Installation is the reverse of removal. Tighten the shock absorber mounting bolts securely; torque settings are given in the *Data* section at the end of this manual for certain models.

Adjustment

8 On some scooters, the rear shock absorber is adjustable for spring pre-load. Adjustment is made using a suitable C-spanner (one is provided in the toolkit) to turn the spring seat on the bottom of the shock absorber **(see illustration)**.
9 Support the scooter on the main stand with no load on the rear suspension. To increase the pre-load (stiffen the suspension), turn

the spring seat to a higher position on the adjustment stopper. To decrease the pre-load (soften the suspension), turn the spring seat to a lower position on the adjustment stopper. **Note:** *Always use the correct tool to adjust the spring pre-load to avoid damaging the spring seat.*

10 Front engine mounting bracket

1 On some scooters the front engine mounting bracket is bolted to the front, lower edge of the crankcase, on others it is bolted to the top of the crankcase **(see illustrations)**. In all cases, the mounting bracket employs rubber-in-torsion 'silentbloc' bushes and damping rubbers to restrict movement.

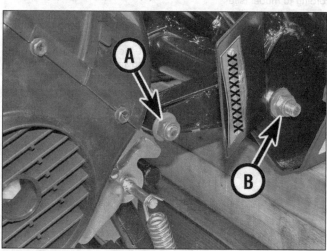

10.1a Engine-to-mounting bolt (A) and mounting-to-frame bolt (B)

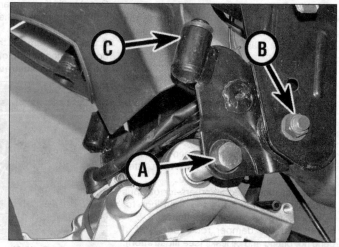

10.1b Engine-to-mounting bolt (A) and mounting-to-frame bolt (B). Note the rubber bump stop (C)

10.3a Undo the self-locking nut . . .

10.3b . . . then withdraw the bolt . . .

10.3c . . . and lift off the mounting bracket

Removal

2 Remove the engine/transmission unit (see Chapter 2A, 2B or 2C).
3 Counterhold the mounting bracket bolt and undo the self-locking nut, then withdraw the bolt and remove the mounting bracket **(see illustrations)**. Where fitted, note the location of the rubber damper **(see illustration)**.

Inspection

4 Thoroughly clean all components, removing all traces of dirt, corrosion and grease.
5 Inspect the silentbloc bushes closely, looking for obvious signs of deterioration such as compression and cracks, or distortion due

to accident damage **(see illustration)**. The bushes are generally a very tight fit and a drawbolt tool will be required to press the old ones out and to press the new ones in.
6 Where the mounting bracket bolts to the front edge of the crankcase it should be necessary to compress the rubber damper in order to install the bracket-to-frame bolt **(see illustration 10.3d)**. If the bracket is not a tight fit, renew the rubber damper.
7 On the hanger bracket type mounting, check for wear on the rubber bump stops **(see illustration 10.1b)**. If the rubbers have worn, allowing metal-to-metal contact, renew them.
8 Check the bracket and engine mounting

bolts for wear. Check the holes in the engine bracket for wear. If the bolts are not a precise fit in the bracket the components must be replaced with new ones.
9 Refer to Chapter 2A, 2B or 2C as applicable and check the bushes or bearings in the crankcase mounting lugs.

Installation

10 Installation is the reverse of removal. Smear some grease on the bracket and engine mounting bolts before installation. If applicable, use new self-locking nuts. Tighten all mounting bolts to the torque setting specified in the *Data* section at the end of this manual.

10.3d Note the location of the damper (arrowed)

10.5 Silentbloc bushes are fitted in both ends of the mounting bracket

Notes

Chapter 7
Brakes, wheels and tyres

Contents

Degrees of difficulty

Easy, suitable for novice with little experience		**Fairly easy,** suitable for beginner with some experience		**Fairly difficult,** suitable for competent DIY mechanic		**Difficult,** suitable for experienced DIY mechanic		**Very difficult,** suitable for expert DIY or professional	

1 General information

An hydraulic disc brake is fitted at the front and a cable-operated drum brake at the rear.

The master cylinder for the front brake is integral with the brake lever, although it may be necessary to remove one of the handlebar covers to access the brake fluid reservoir. Many models are fitted with an ABS unit on the caliper which controls brake fluid pressure in the event of hard or sudden brake operation, thus preventing front wheel lock up.

Cast wheels, fitted with tubeless tyres are used on all models. The tyre information label on the scooter will give tyre size information and recommended pressures.

Caution: Disc brake components rarely require disassembly. Do not disassemble components unless absolutely necessary. If an hydraulic brake hose is loosened, the entire system must be disassembled, drained, cleaned and then properly filled and bled upon reassembly. Do not use solvents on internal brake components. Solvents will cause the seals to swell and distort. Use only clean brake fluid, a dedicated brake cleaner or denatured alcohol for cleaning. Use care when working with brake fluid as it can injure your eyes; it will also damage painted surfaces and plastic parts.

2 Front brake pads

Warning: The dust created by the brake system may contain asbestos, which is harmful to your health. Never blow it out with compressed air and don't inhale any of it. An approved filtering mask should be worn when working on the brakes.

1 To remove the brake pads, first displace the brake caliper. You will probably find that there is insufficient space between the caliper and the wheel rim to remove the caliper on its own – undo the caliper bracket bolts and

2.1a Undo the bracket mounting bolts (arrowed) . . .

2.1b . . . and slide the caliper off the disc

2.3a Undo the pad pins . . .

2.3b . . . and draw the pads out

2.3c Note the location of the pad spring (arrowed)

3 If the pads are retained by pins, undo the pins and draw the pads out **(see illustrations)**. Note the location of the single pad spring inside the caliper **(see illustration)**.

4 If the pads are retained by springs, loosen the caliper slider pin before displacing the caliper, then remove the slider pin once the caliper is off the disc **(see illustrations)**. Rotate the caliper around the fixed slider pin until it is clear of the caliper bracket, then draw the caliper off the pin **(see illustrations)**. The pads are retained in the bracket by springs at both ends **(see illustration)**. Note how the springs are located in the bracket, then lift the pads out carefully.

5 Inspect the surface of each pad for contamination and check if the pads are worn **(see illustration)**. If either pad is worn down to, or beyond, the service limit (see Chapter 1,

slide the caliper and bracket assembly off **(see illustrations)**. **Note 1:** *If it is necessary to remove the caliper slider pin before the pads are removed, loosen the pin before displacing the caliper (see Step 4).* **Note 2:** *Do not operate the brake lever while the caliper is off the disc.*

2 Two different methods are used to retain the brake pads in the caliper – pad pins and pad springs.

2.4a Loosen the caliper slider pin (arrowed) . . .

2.4b . . . then remove it once the caliper is displaced

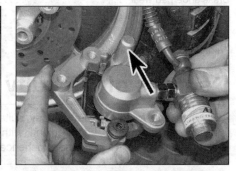

2.4c Rotate the caliper around the fixed pin (arrowed) . . .

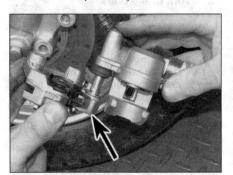

2.4d . . . until it is clear of the bracket (arrowed) . . .

2.4e . . . then draw the caliper off the pin

2.4f The brake pads are retained by two springs (arrowed)

Section 10), is fouled with oil or grease, or heavily scored or damaged, both pads must be renewed. **Note:** *It is not possible to degrease the friction material; if the pads are contaminated in any way they must be renewed.*

6 If the pads are in good condition, clean them carefully using a fine wire brush which is completely free of oil and grease to remove all traces of road dirt and corrosion. Spray the caliper with a dedicated brake cleaner to remove any dust and remove any traces of corrosion which might cause sticking of the caliper/pad operation.

7 Remove all traces of corrosion from the pad pins **(see illustration 2.3a)**. Inspect the pins for wear and damage and renew them if necessary. Prior to reassembly, smear the pins with copper-based grease.

8 Clean all old grease off the caliper slider pins and inspect them for wear **(see illustrations 2.4b and e)**. If the pins are corroded, check the seals on the caliper and bracket for damage and renew then if new components are available. Prior to reassembly, smear the pins with copper-based grease.

9 Remove all traces of corrosion from the pad springs **(see illustrations 2.3c and 4f)**. If the springs are badly worn or damaged, fit new springs.

10 Check the condition of the brake disc (see Section 4).

11 If new pads are being installed, slowly push the piston as far back into the caliper as possible using hand pressure or a piece of wood for leverage. This will displace brake fluid back into the hydraulic reservoir, so it may be necessary to remove the reservoir cap, plate and diaphragm and siphon out some fluid (depending on how much fluid was in there in the first place and how far the piston has to be pushed in). If the piston is difficult to push back, attach a length of clear hose to the bleed valve and place the open end in a suitable container, then open the valve and try again. Take great care not to draw any air into the system and don't forget to tighten the valve once the piston has been sufficiently displaced. If in doubt, bleed the brakes afterwards (see Section 7).

Caution: Never lever the caliper against the brake disc to push a piston back into the caliper as damage to the disc will result.

12 Smear the backs of the pads with copper-based grease, making sure that none gets on the front or sides of the pads.

13 Installation is the reverse of removal, noting the following:
● If applicable, ensure any pad springs are in place inside the caliper.
● Fit the pads into the caliper or caliper bracket so that the friction material faces the disc.
● Ensure there is sufficient space between the pads to slide the caliper assembly onto the disc **(see illustration)**.
● Tighten the caliper mounting bolts securely.
● Operate the brake lever several times to bring the pads into contact with the disc

2.5 Measure the amount of friction material on each pad

● Check the brake fluid level and top-up if necessary (see *Pre-ride checks*)

14 Check the operation of the brake before riding the scooter.

3 Front brake caliper

⚠️ **Warning: If a caliper indicates the need for renewal (usually due to leaking fluid or sticky operation), all old brake fluid should be flushed from the system at the same time. Also, the dust created by the brake system may contain asbestos, which is harmful to your health. Never blow it out with compressed air and don't inhale any of it. An approved filtering mask should be worn when working on the brakes. Do not, under any circumstances, use petroleum-based solvents to clean brake parts. Use a dedicated brake cleaner or denatured alcohol only, as described. To prevent damage from spilled brake fluid, always cover paintwork when working on the braking system.**

Removal

1 If the caliper is being removed from the scooter, first loosen and then lightly tighten the brake hose banjo bolt **(see illustration)**. If the machine is equipped with ABS, support the ABS valve to avoid straining the connection to the caliper while loosening the bolt.

2 Unscrew the caliper bracket bolts and slide the caliper off the disc **(see illustrations 2.1a**

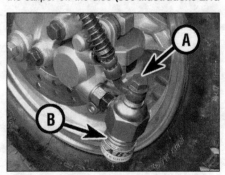

3.1 Brake hose banjo bolt (A). Note the ABS valve (B)

2.13 Allow space between the pads for installation on the disc

and b). **Note:** *Do not operate the brake lever while the caliper is off the disc.*

3 If the caliper is just being displaced, the brake pads can be left in place. Support the caliper with a cable-tie to ensure no strain is placed on the hydraulic hose.

4 If the caliper is being cleaned and inspected, remove the brake pads and note the location of the pad spring(s) (see Section 2). **Note:** *It is not necessary to disconnect the brake hose to clean and inspect the caliper.* Clean the exterior of the caliper with denatured alcohol or brake system cleaner. Inspect the caliper for signs of damage, especially around the mounting lugs and the bleed screw and renew it if necessary.

5 If brake fluid is leaking from around the edge of the piston, the internal piston seal has failed **(see illustration)**. If new seals are available the caliper can be overhauled, otherwise a new caliper will have to be fitted.

6 To remove the caliper from the machine, first note the alignment of the banjo fitting on the caliper, then unscrew the banjo bolt and separate the hose from the caliper **(see illustration)**. Discard the sealing washers as new ones must be used on installation. Wrap a plastic bag tightly around the end of the hose to prevent dirt entering the system and secure the hose in an upright position to minimise fluid loss. **Note:** *If you are planning to overhaul the caliper and do not have a source of compressed air to blow out the piston, just loosen the banjo bolt at this stage and retighten it lightly. The hydraulic system can then be used to force the piston out of the*

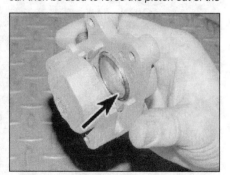

3.5 Fluid leaks indicate a failed seal

3.6 Unscrew the banjo bolt to detach the brake hose

3.7a Unscrew the slider pin . . .

3.7b . . . then separate the caliper from its bracket. Note the fixed pin (arrowed)

3.8a Using compressed air to displace the piston

3.8b Once the piston (arrowed) has reached the end of its bore . . .

3.8c . . . it can be removed by hand

caliper. *Disconnect the hose once the piston has been sufficiently displaced.*

Overhaul

Caution: Disassembly, overhaul and reassembly of the brake caliper must be done in a spotlessly clean work area to avoid contamination and possible failure of the brake hydraulic system components. To prevent damage from spilled brake fluid, always cover painted components and bodywork.

7 If not already done, separate the caliper from the caliper bracket – it may be necessary to unscrew the slider pin before pulling the caliper off the fixed pin **(see illustrations)**.

8 Displace the piston from its bore using either compressed air or by carefully operating the front brake lever to pump it out. If the piston is being displaced hydraulically, it may be necessary to top-up the brake fluid

reservoir during the procedure. Also, have some clean rag ready to catch any spilled fluid when the piston reaches the end of the bore. If the compressed air method is used, direct the air into the fluid inlet on the caliper and prevent the piston being ejected forcibly with a piece of wood **(see illustrations)**. **Note:** *Use only low pressure to ease the piston out – if the air pressure is too high and the piston is forced out, the caliper and/or piston may be damaged.*

⚠️ *Warning: Never place your fingers in front of a piston in an attempt to catch or protect it when applying compressed air, as serious injury could result.*

9 If the piston sticks in its bore, try to displace it with compressed air (see Step 8). If the stuck piston cannot be displaced, a new caliper will have to be fitted.

Caution: Do not try to remove a piston by

levering it out, or by using pliers or any other grips.
10 Remove the dust seal and the piston seal from the piston bore, taking care to avoid scratching the bore **(see illustration)**. Discard the seals as new ones must be fitted.
11 Clean the piston and bore with clean brake fluid or brake system cleaner. If compressed air is available, blow it through the fluid galleries in the caliper to ensure they are clear and use it to dry the parts thoroughly (make sure it is filtered and unlubricated).
Caution: Do not, under any circumstances, use a petroleum-based solvent to clean brake parts.
12 Inspect the bore and piston for signs of corrosion, nicks and burrs and loss of plating. If surface defects are present, the caliper assembly must be renewed. If the caliper is in bad shape the master cylinder should also be checked.
13 Lubricate the new piston seal with clean brake fluid and install it in the groove in the caliper bore **(see illustration)**.
14 Lubricate the new dust seal with clean brake fluid and install it in the groove in the caliper bore.
15 Lubricate the piston with clean brake fluid and install it, closed-end first, into the caliper bore **(see illustrations)**. Using your thumbs, push the piston all the way in, making sure it enters the bore squarely.

Installation

16 If the brake pads have been removed, install the pads (see Section 2). If the caliper

3.10 Remove the seals carefully

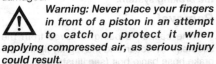

3.13 Lubricate the dust seal (A), piston seal (B) and piston (C) with clean brake fluid

has just been displaced, install the caliper on the brake disc **(see illustration 2.1b)**.

17 Install the caliper mounting bolts, and tighten them securely. If applicable, also tighten the caliper slider pin.

18 If the caliper was removed from the machine, or a new caliper is being fitted, connect the brake hose to the caliper, using new sealing washers on both sides of the banjo fitting. Align the banjo fitting as noted on removal. Tighten the banjo bolt to the specified torque setting and top-up the brake fluid reservoir (see *Pre-ride checks*). Bleed the brake system (see Section 7).

19 Check for fluid leaks and check the operation of the brake before riding the scooter.

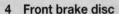
4 Front brake disc

Inspection

1 Inspect the surface of the disc for score marks and other damage **(see illustration)**. Light scratches are normal after use and won't affect brake operation, but deep grooves and heavy score marks will reduce braking efficiency and accelerate pad wear. If a disc is badly grooved it must be machined or renewed.

2 The disc must not be machined or allowed to wear down to a thickness less than the minimum stamped on the disc **(see illustration 4.1)**. Check the thickness of the disc with a micrometer and renew it if necessary **(see illustration)**.

3 To check disc warpage, position the machine upright so that the wheel is raised off the ground. Attach a dial gauge to the suspension with the tip of the gauge touching the surface of the disc about 10 mm from the outer edge. Rotate the wheel and watch the gauge needle; a small amount of movement is acceptable. If excessive movement is indicated, first check the wheel bearings for play (see Section 15). If the bearings are good, the disc is warped and should be replaced with a new one.

Removal

4 Remove the front wheel (see Section 13).
Caution: Do not lay the wheel down and allow it to rest on the disc – the disc could become warped.

5 If you are not replacing the disc with a new one, mark the relationship of the disc to the wheel so that it can be installed in the same position. Unscrew the disc retaining bolts, loosening them a little at a time to avoid distorting the disc, then remove the disc **(see illustration)**.

Installation

6 Before installing the disc, make sure there is no dirt or corrosion where the disc seats on

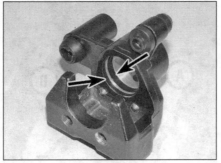

3.15a Once the seals (arrowed) have been installed . . .

the hub. If the disc does not sit flat when it is bolted down, it will appear to be warped when checked or when the front brake is used.

7 Install the disc, making sure that the minimum thickness information is facing up, or that the directional arrow, if applicable, points in the direction of normal wheel rotation **(see illustration)**. Align the previously applied register marks, if you are reinstalling the original disc. Install the bolts and tighten them evenly and a little at a time in a criss-cross sequence.

8 Clean the disc using acetone or brake system cleaner. If a new brake disc has been installed, remove any protective coating from its working surfaces.

9 Install the front wheel (see Section 13).

10 Operate the brake lever several times to bring the pads into contact with the disc. Check the operation of the brake before riding the scooter.

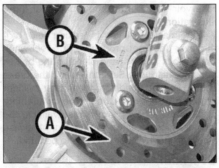

4.1 Inspect the surface of the disc (A) for damage. Note the minimum thickness (B)

4.5 Unscrew the bolts (arrowed) to remove the disc

3.15b . . . press the piston in, closed-end first

5 Front brake master cylinder

Removal

1 Remove the handlebar covers for access (see Chapter 8).

2 If the master cylinder is just being displaced, ensure the fluid reservoir cover is secure. Unscrew the master cylinder clamp bolts and remove the back of the clamp **(see illustration)**. Note the UP mark on the clamp. Position the assembly clear of the handlebar, making sure no strain is placed on the brake hose and the brake light switch wiring. Keep the fluid reservoir upright to prevent air entering the hydraulic system.

4.2 Measuring the thickness of the disc with a micrometer

4.7 Brake disc directional arrow

5.2 Unscrew the clamp bolts (arrowed).
Note the UP mark

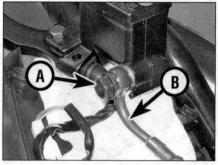

5.4 Brake hose banjo bolt (A) and banjo
fitting (B)

5.6 Lift off the master cylinder//fluid
reservoir assembly

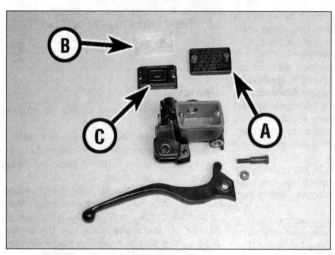

5.9 Master cylinder cover (A), diaphragm plate (B) and
diaphragm (C)

5.10 Remove the brake light switch. Note the retaining tab
(arrowed)

3 If the master cylinder is being removed, first disconnect the brake light switch wiring connector (see Chapter 9).

4 Unscrew the brake hose banjo bolt and detach the banjo fitting, noting its alignment with the master cylinder **(see illustration)**.

5 Once disconnected, secure the hose in an upright position to minimise fluid loss. Wrap a clean plastic bag tightly around the end to prevent dirt entering the system. Discard the sealing washers as new ones must be fitted on reassembly.

6 Undo the master cylinder clamp bolts and remove the back of the clamp **(see illustration 5.2)**. Lift the master cylinder and reservoir away from the handlebar **(see illustration)**.

7 If the master cylinder is leaking fluid, or if the lever does not produce a firm feel when the brake is applied, and bleeding the brakes does not help (see Section 7), and the brake hose is in good condition, the master cylinder requires attention. Check the availability of parts – if a new piston kit is available the master cylinder can be overhauled, otherwise a new master cylinder will have to be fitted.

Overhaul

8 Before disassembling the master cylinder, read through the entire procedure and make sure that you have obtained all the new parts required including some new DOT 4 brake fluid, some clean rags and internal circlip pliers.

Caution: Overhaul of the brake master cylinder must be done in a spotlessly clean work area to avoid contamination and possible failure of the brake hydraulic system components. To prevent damage from spilled brake fluid, always cover painted components and bodywork.

9 Undo the reservoir cover retaining screws and lift off the cover, the diaphragm plate and the diaphragm **(see illustration)**. Drain the brake fluid from the reservoir into a suitable container. Wipe any remaining fluid out of the reservoir with a clean rag.

10 Remove the brake light switch – the switch is either secured to the underside of the lever bracket by a screw, or retained by a tab **(see illustration)**. If required, remove the brake lever (see Section 10).

11 Carefully remove the dust boot from the master cylinder to reveal the pushrod retaining circlip **(see illustrations)**.

12 Depress the piston and use circlip pliers to remove the circlip, then slide out the piston assembly and the spring, noting how they fit **(see illustrations)**. If the piston is difficult to remove, apply low pressure compressed air to the fluid outlet. Lay the parts out in the

5.11a Remove the dust boot . . .

5.11b . . . to access the pushrod circlip
(arrowed)

proper order as an aid to reassembly **(see illustration)**.

13 Clean the master cylinder and fluid reservoir with clean brake fluid or brake system cleaner. If compressed air is available, blow it through the fluid galleries to ensure they are clear and use it to dry the parts thoroughly (make sure the air is filtered and unlubricated).

Caution: Do not, under any circumstances, use a petroleum-based solvent to clean brake parts.

14 Check the bore inside the master cylinder for corrosion, scratches, nicks and score marks. If damage or wear is evident, the master cylinder must be replaced with a new one. If the master cylinder is in poor condition, then the caliper should be checked as well.

15 The dust boot, circlip, piston assembly and spring are included in the master cylinder rebuild kit **(see illustration 5.12c)**. Use all of the new parts, regardless of the apparent condition of the old ones. Fit them according to the layout of the old piston assembly.

16 Install the spring on the inner end of the piston and lubricate the piston assembly with clean brake fluid **(see illustration)**. Install the components in the master cylinder in the reverse order of disassembly. Depress the piston and install the new circlip, making sure it is properly located in the groove **(see illustrations 5.12a and 11b)**.

17 Fit the dust boot, making sure the lip is seated properly in the groove.

18 Inspect the fluid reservoir cover, diaphragm plate and diaphragm and renew any parts if they are damaged or deteriorated.

Installation

19 Installation is the reverse of removal, noting the following:
● Ensure the back of the master cylinder clamp is correctly fitted **(see illustration 5.2)**.
● Ensure the brake light wiring is connected securely.
● Connect the brake hose to the master cylinder, using new sealing washers on both sides of the banjo fitting.
● Align the banjo fitting as noted on removal.
● Fill the fluid reservoir with new brake fluid (see *Pre-ride checks*).
● Bleed the air from the system (see Section 7).
● Ensure the reservoir diaphragm is correctly seated and that the cover screws are tightened securely.

20 Check the operation of the brake and the brake light before riding the scooter.

6 Brake hoses and fittings

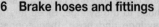

Inspection

1 Brake hose condition should be checked

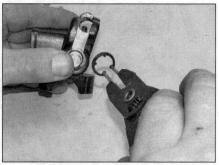

5.12a Remove the circlip . . .

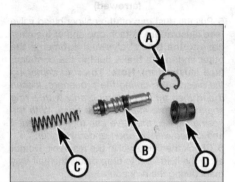

5.12c Typical front brake master cylinder components. Circlip (A), piston and seals (B), spring (C) and dust boot (D)

regularly and the hose replaced at the specified interval (see Chapter 1).

2 Remove the front body panels as necessary to inspect the full length of the hose (see Chapter 8).

3 Twist and flex the hose while looking for cracks, bulges and seeping fluid. Check extra carefully where the hose connects to the banjo fittings, as this is a common area for hose failure **(see illustration)**.

4 Inspect the banjo fittings – if they are rusted, cracked or damaged, fit new hoses.

Renewal

Caution: To prevent damage from spilled brake fluid while renewing the brake hose, always cover painted components and bodywork.

5 Most brake hoses have banjo fittings on both ends. Unscrew the banjo bolts carefully,

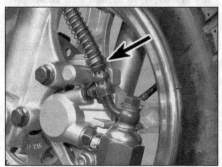

6.3 Inspect the hose connection to the banjo fitting carefully

5.12b . . . and remove the piston and spring

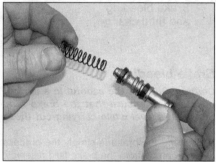

5.16 Install the spring on the piston assembly

noting the alignment of the fittings with the master cylinder or brake caliper **(see illustrations 5.4 and 6.3)**.

6 Free the hose from any clips or guides and remove it, noting its routing. Discard the sealing washers. **Note:** *Do not operate the brake lever while a brake hose is disconnected.*

7 Position the new hose, making sure it is not twisted or otherwise strained, and ensure that it is correctly routed through any clips or guides and is clear of all moving components.

8 Check that the fittings align correctly, then install the banjo bolts, using new sealing washers on both sides of the fittings **(see illustration)**. Tighten the banjo bolts securely.

9 Flush the old brake fluid from the system, refill with new brake fluid and bleed the air from the system (see Section 7).

10 Check the operation of the brakes before riding the scooter.

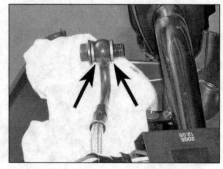

6.8 Always use new sealing washers (arrowed) on both sides of the banjo fittings

7.4 Check for air bubbles in the bottom of the fluid reservoir

7 Brake bleeding and fluid change

Brake bleeding

Caution: Support the scooter in a upright position and ensure that the brake fluid reservoir is level while carrying-out these procedures.

1 Bleeding the brake is simply the process of removing air from the brake fluid reservoir, master cylinder, the hose and the brake caliper. Bleeding is necessary whenever a brake system connection is loosened, or when a component is replaced or renewed. Leaks in the system may also allow air to enter, but leaking brake fluid will reveal their presence and warn you of the need for repair.

2 To bleed the brake, you will need some new DOT 4 brake fluid, a small container partially filled with new brake fluid, a length of clear vinyl or plastic hose, some rags and a spanner to fit the brake caliper bleed valve.

3 If necessary, remove the handlebar cover for access to the fluid reservoir (see Chapter 8).

Caution: To prevent damage from spilled brake fluid while bleeding the brake, always cover painted components and bodywork.

4 Remove the reservoir cover, diaphragm plate and diaphragm and slowly pump the brake lever a few times, until no air bubbles can be seen floating up from the holes in the bottom of the reservoir **(see illustration)**. This bleeds air from the master cylinder end of the system. Temporarily refit the reservoir cover.

7.7 Check for air bubbles (arrowed) in the fluid leaving the caliper

7.5a Location of the caliper bleed valve (arrowed)

5 Pull the dust cap off the caliper bleed valve **(see illustration)**. Attach one end of the clear hose to the bleed valve and submerge the other end in the brake fluid in the container **(see illustration)**. **Note:** *To avoid damaging the bleed valve during the procedure, loosen it and then tighten it temporarily with a ring spanner before attaching the hose. With the hose attached, the valve can then be opened and closed with an open-ended spanner.*

6 Check the fluid level in the reservoir. Do not allow the fluid level to drop below the half-way mark during the procedure.

7 Carefully pump the brake lever three or four times and hold it in while opening the caliper bleed valve. When the valve is opened, brake fluid will flow out of the caliper into the clear hose and the lever will move toward the handlebar **(see illustration)**.

8 Tighten the bleed valve, then release the brake lever gradually. Repeat the process until no air bubbles are visible in the brake fluid leaving the caliper and the lever is firm when applied. On completion, disconnect the hose, ensure the bleed valve is tightened securely and fit the dust cap.

9 Top-up the reservoir, install the diaphragm, diaphragm plate and cover, and wipe up any spilled brake fluid. Check the entire system for fluid leaks.

If it's not possible to produce a firm feel to the lever the fluid may be aerated. Let the brake fluid in the system stabilise for a few hours and then repeat the procedure when the tiny bubbles in the system have settled out. To speed this process up, tie the brake lever to the handlebar so that the system is pressurised.

Fluid change

Note: *Some manufacturers recommend back-filling the hydraulic system with a syringe to avoid troublesome air locks (see Steps 16 to 22).*

10 Changing the brake fluid is a similar process to bleeding the brakes and requires the same materials plus a suitable tool for siphoning the fluid out of the hydraulic reservoir. Also ensure that the container is

7.5b Set-up for bleeding the hydraulic brake system

large enough to take all the old fluid when it is flushed out of the system.

11 Follow the procedure in Step 5, then remove the reservoir cover, diaphragm plate and diaphragm and siphon the old fluid out of the reservoir. Fill the reservoir with new brake fluid, then follow the procedure in Step 7.

12 Tighten the bleed valve, then release the brake lever gradually. Keep the reservoir topped-up with new fluid at all times or air may enter the system and greatly increase the length of the task. Repeat the process until new fluid can be seen emerging from the bleed valve.

Old brake fluid is invariably much darker in colour than new fluid, making it easy to see when all old fluid has been expelled from the system.

13 Disconnect the hose, ensure the bleed valve is tightened securely and install the dust cap.

14 Top-up the reservoir, install the diaphragm, diaphragm plate and cover, and wipe up any spilled brake fluid. Check the entire system for fluid leaks.

15 Check the operation of the brake before riding the scooter.

16 If, after changing the brake fluid, it proves impossible to obtain a firm feel at the brake lever, it may be necessary to back-fill the system. To back-fill the hydraulic system, remove the reservoir cover, diaphragm plate and diaphragm and siphon the old fluid out of the reservoir. Temporarily refit the reservoir cover but do not tighten the fixing screws.

17 Remove the brake caliper and slowly push the piston as far back into the caliper as possible using hand pressure or a piece of wood for leverage, then siphon any residual fluid from the reservoir. Leave the cover off the reservoir. Refit the brake caliper.

18 Fill a suitable syringe with approximately 40 ml of new brake fluid and connect a short length of hose to the syringe. Bleed any air from the syringe and hose, then connect the hose to the caliper bleed valve. **Note:** *To avoid damaging the bleed valve during the procedure, loosen it and then tighten it temporarily with a ring spanner before attaching the hose. With the hose attached,*

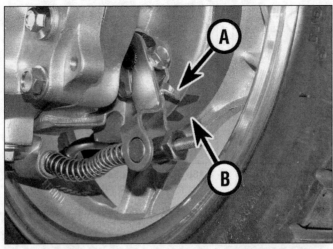

8.1 Brake wear indicator (A) and index mark (B)

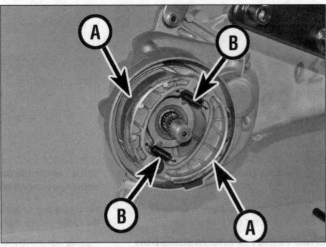

8.2 Check the friction material (A) and springs (B)

the valve can then be opened and closed with an open-ended spanner.

19 Open the bleed valve and carefully inject fluid into the system until the level in the reservoir is up to the half-way mark. Tighten the bleed valve, disconnect the hose and refit the dust cap.

20 Operate the brake lever carefully several times to bring the pads into contact with the disc, then check the fluid level in the reservoir and top-up if necessary (see *Pre-ride checks*).

21 Install the diaphragm, diaphragm plate and cover, and wipe up any spilled brake fluid. Check the system for fluid leaks.

22 Check the operation of the brake before riding the scooter.

8 Rear drum brake

⚠️ **Warning: The dust created by the brake system may contain asbestos, which is harmful to your health. Never blow it out with compressed air and don't inhale any of it. An approved filtering mask should be worn when working on the brakes.**

Inspection

1 Some scooters are fitted with a brake wear indicator – if the wear indicator aligns with the index mark when the brake is applied, the shoes should be renewed **(see illustration)**.

2 Alternatively, remove the wheel (see Section 14). Check the amount of friction material on the brake shoes and compare the result with the specification in the *Data* section at the end of this manual **(see illustration)**. If the friction material has worn down to the minimum thickness (see Chapter 1, Section 11), fit new brake shoes.

3 Inspect the friction material for contamination. If it is fouled with oil or grease, or heavily scored or damaged, both shoes must be renewed as a set. Note that it is not possible to degrease the friction material; if the shoes are contaminated in any way they must be renewed. **Note:** *Any evidence of oil inside the rear brake suggests a worn seal on the gearbox output shaft which must be rectified (see Chapter 5).*

4 If the shoes are in good condition, clean them carefully using a fine wire brush which is completely free of oil and grease to remove all traces of dust and corrosion.

5 Check the condition of the brake shoe springs; they should hold the shoes tightly in place against the operating cam and pivot post **(see illustration 8.2)**. Remove the shoes (see Steps 10 to 12) and renew the springs if they appear weak or are obviously deformed or damaged.

6 Clean the surface of the brake drum using brake system cleaner. Examine the surface for scoring and excessive wear **(see illustration)**. While light scratches are to be expected, any heavy scoring will impair braking and there is no satisfactory way of removing them; in this event the wheel should be renewed, although you could consult a specialist engineer who might be able to skim the surface.

7 If available, measure the internal diameter of the brake drum with a Vernier caliper – take several measurements to ensure the drum has not worn out-of-round. If the drum is out-of-round, fit a new wheel. **Note:** *A brake drum that is out-of-round will cause the brake lever to pulse when the brake is applied.*

8 To check and lubricate the brake cam, first remove the brake shoes (see Steps 11 to 12). Note the position of the brake arm, then loosen the brake arm pinch bolt and pull the cam out of the backplate or casing **(see illustrations)**. Clean all traces of old grease off the cam and shaft. If the bearing surfaces of the cam or shaft are worn the cam should be renewed.

9 Lubricate the shaft of the cam with a smear of copper-based grease. Position the brake arm as noted on removal, then install the cam in the backplate or casing, ensuring it locates fully into the brake arm. Tighten the pinch bolt securely **(see illustration 8.8a)**. Lubricate the

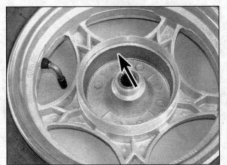

8.6 Check the surface of the brake drum (arrowed)

8.8a Loosen of the brake arm pinch bolt (arrowed) . . .

8.8b . . . then pull out the brake cam (A). Note the pivot post (B)

8.12 Fold the shoes inwards to release the spring tension

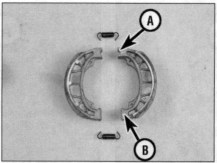

8.13a Assemble the shoes and springs as shown – rounded ends (A) and flat ends (B)

8.13b Fold the shoes down over the cam and pivot post

cam and the pivot post with a smear of copper grease and install the brake shoes.

Shoe removal and installation

10 Remove the wheel (see Section 14).

11 If the shoes are not going to be renewed they must be installed in their original positions – mark them to aid reassembly. Note how the springs are fitted.

12 Grasp the outer edge of each shoe and fold them inwards towards each other to release the spring tension and remove the shoes **(see illustration)**. Remove the springs from the shoes.

13 To install the shoes, first lubricate the cam and the pivot post with a smear of copper grease and hook the springs into the shoes **(see illustration)**. Position the shoes in a V on the cam and pivot post, then fold them down into position **(see illustration)**. Operate the brake arm to check that the cam and shoes work correctly.

14 Install the wheel and test the operation of the brake before riding the scooter.

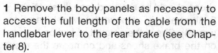

9 Brake cable

1 Remove the body panels as necessary to access the full length of the cable from the handlebar lever to the rear brake (see Chapter 8).

2 Fully unscrew the adjuster on the lower end of the cable and release the cable from the brake arm **(see illustration)**. Note the location of the return spring on the cable, if fitted **(see illustration)**.

3 Release the cable from the stop on the underside of the transmission casing and any clips retained by the belt cover screws **(see illustration)**.

4 Where fitted, displace the cover on the handlebar lever, then pull the outer cable out of the lever bracket and free the inner cable end from its socket in the underside of the lever **(see illustrations)**.

5 Withdraw the cable from the scooter, noting its routing.

HAYNES HiNT *When fitting a new cable, tape the lower end of the new cable to the upper end of the old cable before removing it from the machine. Slowly pull the lower end of the old cable out, guiding the new cable down into position. Using this method will ensure the cable is routed correctly and will avoid having to remove any of the body panels.*

9.2a Unscrew the adjuster and release the cable from the brake arm

9.2b Note the location of the return spring (arrowed)

9.3 Release the brake cable from any clips (arrowed)

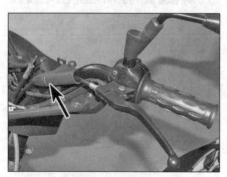

9.4a Displace the handlebar lever cover (arrowed)

9.4b Pull the cable out of the handlebar bracket . . .

9.4c . . . and release the inner cable end from the lever

6 Installation is the reverse of removal. Make sure the cable is correctly routed and clipped into place. Lubricate the cable trunnion at the handlebar end with grease before fitting it into the lever and adjust the cable freeplay (see Chapter 1).
7 Check the operation of the brake before riding the scooter.

10 Brake levers

Removal

1 Remove the body panels as necessary to access the brake lever bracket on the handlebar (see Chapter 8).
2 Where fitted, displace the cover on the handlebar lever (see illustration 9.4a).
3 When removing the rear brake lever, first unscrew the adjuster on the lower end of the cable to slacken the cable.
4 To remove either the front or rear brake lever, unscrew the lever pivot bolt locknut on the underside of the lever, then withdraw the pivot bolt and remove the lever from its bracket (see illustration).
5 When removing the front brake lever, note how the lever locates against the master cylinder pushrod and the brake light switch (see Section 5). The lever bracket is integral with the front brake master cylinder (see Section 5).
6 When removing the rear brake lever, note how the lever locates against the brake light switch and free the inner end of the brake cable from its socket in the underside of the

lever (see Section 9). The lever bracket is integral with the handlebar switch unit (see Chapter 9).

Installation

7 Installation is the reverse of removal. Apply grease to the pivot bolt shank and the contact areas between the lever and its bracket.
8 When installing the rear brake lever, lubricate the cable trunnion at the handlebar end with grease before fitting it into the lever and adjust the cable freeplay (see Chapter 1).
9 Check the operation of the brakes and the brake light before riding the scooter.

11 Wheels – inspection and repair

1 In order to carry out a proper inspection of the wheels, it is necessary to support the scooter upright so that the wheel being inspected is raised off the ground. Clean the wheels thoroughly to remove mud and dirt that may interfere with the inspection procedure or mask defects. Make a general check of the wheels (see Chapter 1) and tyres (see *Pre-ride checks*).
2 If available, attach a dial gauge to the suspension (front) or the transmission casing (rear) with the tip of the gauge touching the side of the rim. Spin the wheel slowly and check the axial (side-to-side) runout of the rim (see illustration).
3 In order to accurately check radial (out-of-round) runout with the dial gauge, the wheel should be removed from the machine, and the tyre from the wheel. With the axle clamped in a vice or jig and the dial gauge positioned on the top of the rim, the wheel can be rotated to check the runout.
4 An easier, though slightly less accurate, method is to attach a stiff wire pointer to the front suspension or transmission casing with the end of the pointer a fraction of an inch from the edge of the wheel rim where the wheel and tyre join. If the wheel is true, the distance from the pointer to the rim will be constant as the wheel is rotated. **Note:** *If wheel runout is excessive, check the wheel bearings very carefully before renewing the wheel (see Section 16).*
5 The wheels should also be visually inspected for cracks, flat spots on the rim and other damage. Look very closely for dents

in the area where the tyre bead contacts the rim. Dents in this area may prevent complete sealing of the tyre against the rim, which leads to deflation of the tyre over a period of time. If damage is evident, or if runout is excessive, the wheel will have to be replaced with a new one. Never attempt to repair a damaged cast alloy wheel.

12 Wheels – alignment check

1 Misalignment of the wheels can cause strange and potentially serious handling problems and will most likely be due to bent frame or suspension components as the result of an accident. If the frame or suspension are at fault, repair by a frame specialist or replacement with new parts are the only options.
2 To check wheel alignment you will need an assistant, a length of string or a perfectly straight piece of wood and a ruler. A plumb bob or spirit level for checking that the wheels are vertical will also be required. Support the scooter in an upright position on its main stand.
3 If a string is used, have your assistant hold one end of it about halfway between the floor and the centre of the rear wheel, with the string touching the back edge of the rear tyre sidewall.
4 Run the other end of the string forward and pull it tight so that it is roughly parallel to the floor. Slowly bring the string into contact with the front sidewall of the rear tyre, then turn the front wheel until it is parallel with the string. Measure the distance (offset) from the front tyre sidewall to the string (see illustration). **Note:** *Where the same size tyre is fitted front and rear, there should be no offset.*

10.4 Brake lever pivot bolt locknut

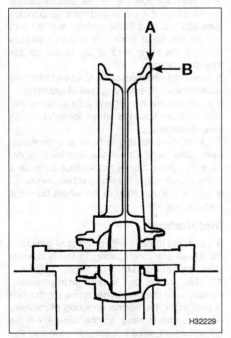

11.2 Check the wheel for radial (out-of-round) runout (A) and axial (side-to-side) runout (B)

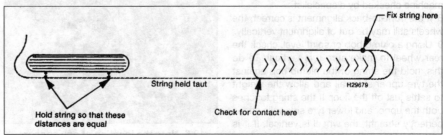

12.4 Wheel alignment check using string

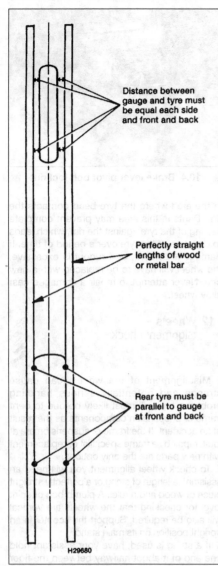

Distance between gauge and tyre must be equal each side and front and back

Perfectly straight lengths of wood or metal bar

Rear tyre must be parallel to gauge at front and back

H29680

12.6 Wheel alignment check using a straight-edge

5 Repeat the procedure on the other side of the machine. The distance from the front tyre side-wall to the string should be equal on both sides.
6 As previously mentioned, a perfectly straight length of wood or metal bar may be substituted for the string (see illustration).
7 If the distance between the string and tyre is greater on one side, or if the rear wheel appears to be out of alignment, have your machine checked by a specialist.
8 If the front-to-back alignment is correct, the wheels still may be out of alignment vertically.
9 Using a plumb bob or spirit level, check the rear wheel to make sure it is vertical. To do this, hold the string of the plumb bob against the tyre upper sidewall and allow the weight to settle just off the floor. If the string touches both the upper and lower tyre sidewalls, the wheel is perfectly straight. If it is not, adjust the main stand until it is.
10 Once the rear wheel is vertical, check the

13.3 Disconnect the speedometer cable

13.4b . . . and withdraw the axle

front wheel in the same manner. If both wheels are not perfectly vertical, the frame and/or major suspension components are bent.

13 Front wheel

Removal

Caution: Don't lay the wheel down and allow it to rest on the brake disc – it could become warped. Set the wheel on wood blocks so the disc doesn't support the weight of the wheel.
1 Support the scooter in an upright position on its main stand with the front wheel off the ground.
2 Unscrew the brake caliper mounting bolts and displace the caliper (see Section 3). **Note:** *Do not operate the brake lever while the caliper*

13.6 Note the location of any spacers

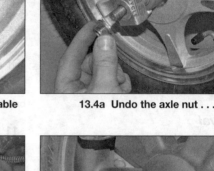

13.4a Undo the axle nut . . .

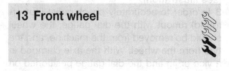

13.5 Lift off the speedometer drive housing

is off the disc. If required for access, remove the front section of the front mudguard (see Chapter 8).
3 Unscrew the knurled ring and disconnect the speedometer cable from the speedometer drive housing (see illustration).
4 Counterhold the axle and undo the axle nut, then support the wheel and withdraw the axle from the wheel and front suspension (see illustrations). If the scooter is fitted with trailing link forks, note how the axle passes through the lower end of the brake caliper mounting bracket.
5 Lower the wheel out of the forks and lift off the speedometer drive housing (see illustration).
6 Note the position of any axle spacers and remove them from the wheel for safekeeping (see illustration).
7 Clean the axle and remove any corrosion using steel wool. Check the axle for straight-ness by rolling it on a flat surface such as a piece of plate glass. If the axle is bent, renew it.
8 Check the condition of the wheel bearings (see Section 15).

Installation

9 Lubricate the axle with a smear of grease.
10 Install any axle spacers in the hub seals (see illustration 13.6).
11 Manoeuvre the wheel into position, making sure the directional arrow on the tyre is pointing in the normal direction of rotation. Apply some grease to the inside of the speedometer drive housing, then install the housing, ensuring it locates correctly on the wheel hub (see illustration).
12 Lift the wheel into place. Check that

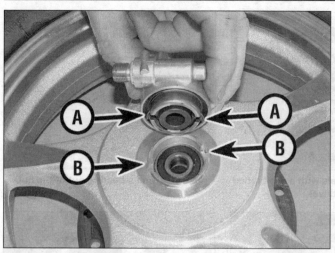

13.11 Note how the tabs (A) locate in the slots (B) in the hub

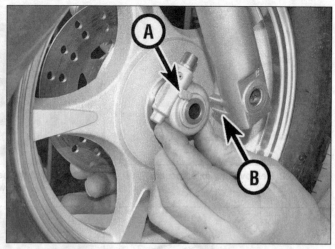

13.12 Note how the tab (A) locates against the stop (B)

the speedometer drive housing is located correctly against the inside of the fork or link arm **(see illustration)**. On scooters fitted with trailing link forks, ensure that the brake caliper bracket is correctly positioned between the link arm and the wheel hub.

13 Slide the axle in carefully ensuring all the components remain in alignment.

14 Install the axle nut and tighten it securely. Apply the torque setting if one is given for your model in the *Data section* .

15 Connect the speedometer cable.

16 Install the brake caliper, making sure the pads sit squarely on each side of the disc (see Section 3).

14.3 Lever off the centre cover

14.5 Lift off the wheel

17 Move the scooter off its stand, apply the front brake and pump the suspension a few times to settle all components in position.

18 Check the operation of the front brake before riding the scooter.

14 Rear wheel

Removal

Note: *It may not be possible to remove the rear wheel with the exhaust system in place.*

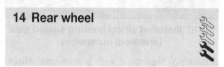

14.4 Undo the centre nut

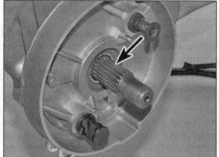

14.6a Inspect the splines (arrowed) on the axle . . .

If necessary, remove the complete system – do not remove the exhaust system mounting bolts and attempt to lever the wheel behind the silencer with the exhaust manifold still connected – damage to the manifold studs and cylinder will result.

1 Support the scooter in an upright position on its main stand with the rear wheel off the ground.

2 If necessary, remove the exhaust system (see Chapter 3).

3 If fitted, lever the centre cover off with a small flat-bladed screwdriver **(see illustration)**.

4 Have an assistant apply the rear brake, then unscrew the hub centre nut and remove the nut and washer **(see illustration)**.

5 Slide the wheel off the axle and manoeuvre it out of the back of the machine **(see illustration)**.

6 Inspect the splines on the axle and on the inside of the hub for wear and damage **(see illustrations)**. If the splines are worn, both components should be replaced with new ones. To replace the axle the gearbox must first be disassembled (see Chapter 5).

Installation

7 Installation is the reverse of removal – slide the wheel onto the axle carefully to avoid disturbing the alignment of the brake shoes. Tighten the hub centre nut securely. Apply the

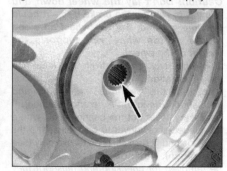

14.6b . . . and on the inside of the hub

15.2 Remove any axle spacers

15.3 Lever out the seals with a flat-bladed screwdriver

15.6a Driving a bearing out of the hub

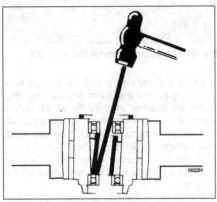
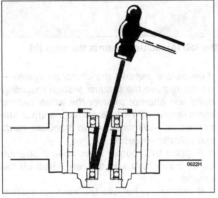

15.6b Locate the rod as shown when driving out a bearing

torque setting if one is given for your models in the *Data section* at the end of this manual.

8 Check the operation of the rear brake before riding the scooter.

15 Front wheel bearings

Note: *The front wheel bearings are located inside the wheel hub. There are no rear wheel bearings as such, the rear axle/gearbox output shaft bearings are located inside the gearbox (see Chapter 5).*

Check

1 Remove the front wheel (see Section 13). **Caution: Don't lay the wheel down and allow it to rest on the brake disc – it could become warped. Set the wheel on wood blocks so the wheel rim supports the weight of the wheel.**

2 Remove any spacers from the wheel hub **(see illustration)**.

3 Inspect the bearings (see *Tools and Workshop Tips* in the *Reference* section). If necessary, lever out the bearing seals with a flat-bladed screwdriver to gain access to the bearings and fit new seals on reassembly **(see illustration)**. **Note:** *Caged ball bearings can be removed for checking and reused if they are good.*

4 If there is any doubt about the condition of

15.10 Installed wheel bearing sealed side (arrowed) outermost

a bearing, replace it with a new one. **Note:** *Always renew the wheel bearings in sets, never individually.*

Renewal

5 If not already done, lever out the bearing seal. Check for any retaining circlips and remove them.

6 To remove the bearings from the hub, support the wheel on wooden blocks to allow the bearings to be driven out **(see illustrations)**. Note the position of the bearings before removing them. **Caution: Don't support the wheel on the brake disc when driving out the bearings.**

7 To remove a caged ball bearing, use a metal rod (preferably a brass drift punch) inserted through the centre of the bearing on one side of the wheel hub or hub assembly, to tap evenly around the outer race of the bearing on the other side. The bearing spacer (if fitted) will come out with the bearing.

8 Turn the hub over and remove the remaining bearing using the same procedure.

9 Thoroughly clean the bearing housings with a suitable solvent and inspect them for scoring and wear. If a housing is damaged, indicating that the bearing has seized and spun in use, it may be possible to secure the new bearing in place with a suitable bearing locking solution.

10 Install a new bearing into its seat in one side of the hub, with the marked or sealed side facing outwards (see *Tools and Workshop Tips* in the *Reference* section), then turn the hub over, install the bearing spacer and install the other new bearing **(see illustration)**.

15.12 Driving in a new seal with a socket

11 If applicable, secure the bearing with the circlip and ensure the circlip is properly located in its groove.

12 Install new bearing seals – if necessary, drive the seals in carefully using a suitably-sized socket that bears on the outer edge of the seal **(see illustration)**.

13 Lubricate the inner edge of the seals with a smear of grease, then install the wheel (see Section 13).

16 Tyre fitting

1 When selecting new tyres, refer to the tyre information label on the scooter or the information given in the owners handbook. Ensure that front and rear tyre types are compatible, the correct size and correct speed rating **(see illustration)**. If necessary seek advice from a tyre fitting specialist.

2 It is recommended that tyres are fitted by a tyre specialist rather than attempted in the home workshop. This is particularly relevant in the case of tubeless tyres because the force required to break the seal between the wheel rim and tyre bead is substantial, and is usually beyond the capabilities of an individual working with normal tyre levers. Additionally, the specialist will be able to balance the wheel after tyre fitting.

3 Note that although punctured tubeless tyres can in some cases be repaired, some manufacturers do not recommend the use of repaired tyres.

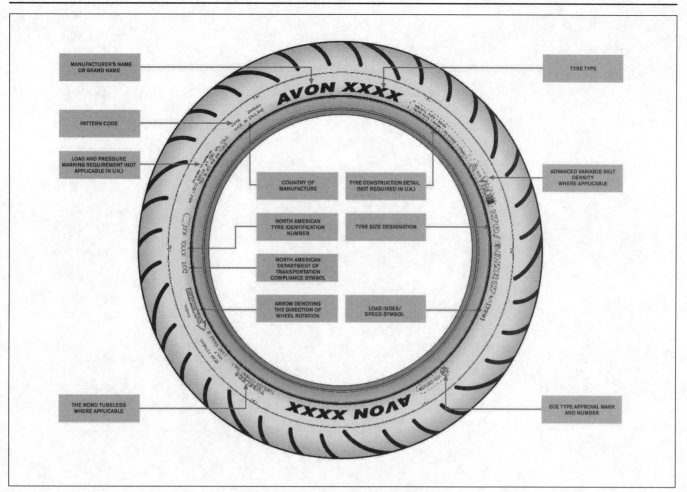

16.1 Common tyre sidewall markings

Chapter 8
Bodywork

Contents

Degrees of difficulty

Easy, suitable for novice with little experience	Fairly easy, suitable for beginner with some experience	Fairly difficult, suitable for competent DIY mechanic	Difficult, suitable for experienced DIY mechanic	Very difficult, suitable for expert DIY or professional

1 General information

Almost all the functional components are enclosed by body panels, making removal of relevant panels a necessary part of most servicing and maintenance procedures. Panel removal is straightforward, and as well as facilitating access to mechanical components, it avoids the risk of accidental damage to the panels.

Most panels are retained by screws and inter-locking tabs, although in some cases trim clips are used (see Section 5). Always check the details in your scooter handbook and follow the advice given at the beginning of Section 8 before removing the panels.

2 Mirrors

1 If the mirror stem is covered by a rubber boot, pull back the lower end of the boot to expose the top of the fixing. Where the mirror threads into a housing, slacken the locknut then unscrew the mirror (see illustrations). **Note:** *To remove the housing, follow the procedure in Chapter 3 to remove the throttle twistgrip (right-hand side), or in Chapter 9 to remove the handlebar switch (left-hand side).*
2 Where the mirror passes through a bore and is secured by a nut, unscrew the nut from the underside and remove the mirror (see illustration).
3 Installation is the reverse of removal. Position the mirror as required, then hold it in place and tighten the nut.

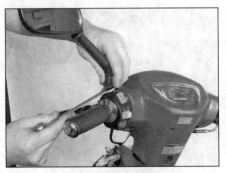

2.1a Slacken the nut . . .

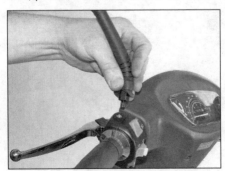

2.1b . . . then unscrew the mirror

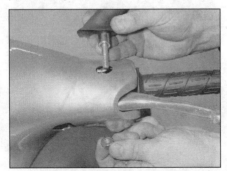

2.2 Undo the nut from the bottom of the stem and remove the mirror

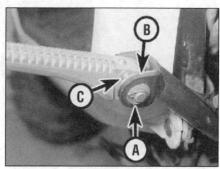

3.1 Remove the split pin (A) to release the pivot pin. Note the detent plate (B) and ball (C)

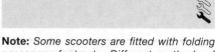

3 Passenger footrests

Note: *Some scooters are fitted with folding passenger footrests. Different methods of securing the footrests are employed – study the design before attempting to remove the footrest.*

Removal

1 If applicable, remove the split pin and washer or spring clip from the bottom of the footrest pivot pin, then withdraw the pivot pin and remove the footrest **(see illustration)**. Some footrests are held in position with a detent plate, ball and spring; note how they are fitted and take care that they do not spring out when removing the footrest.

2 Where the footrest is secured by a pivot bolt, counterhold the bolt and undo the nut on the underside of the footrest **(see illustration)**. **Note:** *It may be necessary to remove a cover or lift a floor mat to access the bolt.* Withdraw the bolt and slide the footrest out of the bracket.

Installation

3 Installation is the reverse of removal. Apply a smear of grease to the pivot pin or bolt and ensure any washers or spacers are fitted on the bolt before it is installed. If applicable, tighten the nut enough to allow the footrest to pivot without binding in the bracket. Alternatively, install the spring clip, ensuring it is a firm fit, or fit a new split pin.

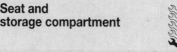

4 Seat and storage compartment

Seat

1 Release the seat catch and swing the seat upright.

2 The seat is retained by the hinge at the front of the seat base. Support the seat and undo the hinge screws, then lift the seat away **(see illustration)**.

3 The seat latch mechanism is actuated by a cable from the seat lock or ignition switch **(see illustrations)**.

4 To remove the seat lock, first remove the storage compartment (see Steps 9 to 11). Unclip the cable from the cable stop on the

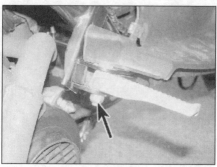

3.2 Undo the nut to remove the footrest

back of the side panel, and from the lock **(see illustration)**, then remove the side panel or seat cowling (see Section 8). The lock is retained in a recess in the panel by a spring clip. Pull off the spring clip, note how the lock locates in the panel recess, then remove the lock **(see illustration)**.

5 To remove the ignition switch, first unscrew the cap on the seat cable mechanism and disconnect the inner cable end from the mechanism **(see illustration)**. Follow the procedure in Chapter 9 to remove the switch assembly.

6 To remove the latch mechanism, first disconnect the cable from the lock, then disconnect it from the latch. Undo the bolts securing the latch mechanism to the frame and lift it off **(see illustration)**.

7 Installation is the reverse of removal.

8 Check the operation of the latch mechanism and lubricate it with a smear of grease. If

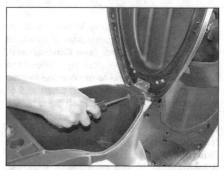

4.2 Undo the hinge screws to remove the seat

4.3a Latch mechanism is actuated either by a separate lock . . .

4.3b . . . or by the ignition switch (arrowed)

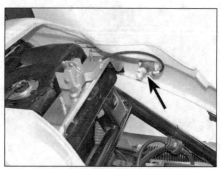

4.4a Unclip the cable from the back of the lock (arrowed)

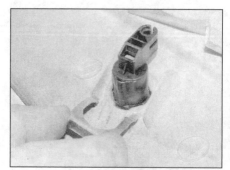

4.4b Pull off the spring clip to remove the lock

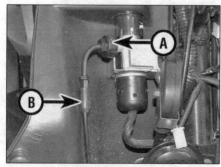

4.5 Unscrew the cap (A) to disconnect the seat cable. Note the adjuster (B)

4.6 Seat latch is secured by two bolts (arrowed)

4.9a Lifting the access panel (arrowed) . . .

4.9b . . . allows access to the engine and carburettor

applicable, adjust the freeplay in the cable (see illustration 4.5).

> ⚠️ **Warning: Ensure the actuating cable is properly connected to the lock before closing the seat, otherwise you will have no way of releasing the latch.**

Storage compartment

9 Unlock the seat and swing it upright. Generally, an engine access panel is fitted in the bottom of the compartment, although this offers limited access to the engine **(see illustrations)**. For better access remove the storage compartment as follows. **Note:** *On most scooters, the storage compartment can be removed with the seat attached.*

10 Undo the screws, bolts or flange nuts securing the storage compartment to the frame **(see illustrations)**. Note that on some scooters, the screws also secure some body panels.

11 Check that no electrical components such as relays or fuseboxes are clipped to the compartment, then lift it out **(see illustration)**.

12 Installation is the reverse of removal.

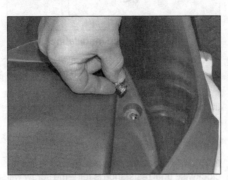

4.10a Undo the fixings in the bottom of the storage compartment . . .

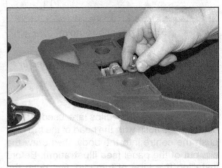

4.10b . . . and on the top edge – note the nut and washer

4.10c Remove the bolt fixings on compartment upper edge . . .

4.11 . . . then lift the storage compartment out

| 5 | Panel fasteners | |

1 Before removing any body panel, study it closely, noting the position of the fasteners and associated fittings.

2 Once the evident fasteners have been removed, try to remove the panel but DO NOT FORCE IT – if it will not release, check that all fasteners have been removed. On some panels, fasteners are located behind trim panels or underneath the floor mat **(see illustrations)**. **Note:** *Adjacent panels are often joined together by tabs and slots (see Step 16).*

3 Note all the fasteners and associated fittings removed with the panel to be sure of returning everything to its correct place on installation.

 HAYNES HiNT *Make a cardboard template of the panel and punch a hole for each fastener location. This will ensure all fasteners are installed correctly on reassembly – this is important as some fasteners may be of different sizes or lengths.*

4 Before installing a panel, check that all fasteners and fittings are in good condition and renew any that are damaged.

5 Tighten the fasteners securely, but be careful not to overtighten any of them or the panel may

5.2a Fixings for main body panels may be hidden behind trim panels . . .

break (not always immediately) due to uneven stress. Take particular care when tightening self-tapping screws into plastic lugs on the backs of panels – if the lugs break the panel will have to be replaced with a new one.

5.2b . . . or underneath the floor mat

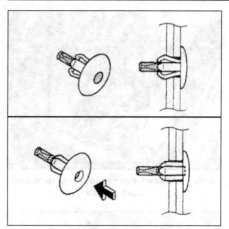

5.6a Trim clip removal

Top   *Clip installed*
Bottom *Clip with centre pin pushed in
           ready for removal*

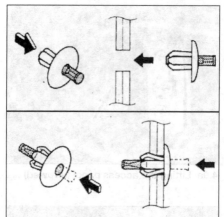

5.6b Trim clip installation

Top   *Clip ready for installation*
Bottom *Clip being secured in panel*

Trim clips

6 Two types of trim clips are used. If the centre pin is flush with the head of the trip clip, push the centre into the body, then draw the clip out of the panel **(see illustration)**. Before installing this type of trim clip, first push the centre back out so that it protrudes from the top of the clip **(see illustration)**. Fit the clip into its hole, then push the centre in so that it is flush with the top of the clip.

7 Alternatively, if the centre pin has a raised head, pull the pin out, then draw the clip out of the panel **(see illustration)**. To install the clip, fit the clip into its hole, then push the centre in until it clicks into place.

Quick release screws

8 To undo a quick-release screw, turn it anti-clockwise until resistance is felt – the screw will normally turn between 90° and 180°. As the panel is removed, note the alignment between the screw and its retaining mechanism.

9 To install a quick-release screw, first ensure it is correctly aligned, then turn it clockwise until resistance is felt – the screw should now be locked.

Self-tapping screws

10 When the panel is removed, note the location of the screws. If they engage in plastic lugs on an adjacent panel, check the condition of each lug and ensure it is not split or the thread stripped **(see illustration)**. If necessary, repair a damaged lug with a proprietary repair kit (see Section 6).

11 If the screws engage in U-clips, check that the clips are a firm fit on the mounting lug and that they are not sprained **(see illustration)**. If necessary, fit new U-clips.

Spacers and bushes

12 Some bolts and screws are designed to retain a panel in conjunction with a washer, rubber bush and spacer **(see illustration)**. Note the order of the components on removal, and ensure they are in place before installing the fixing, or the panel will not be held firmly.

Wellnuts

13 Wellnuts are sometimes used to secure windscreens, where excessive pressure will crack the screen. Wellnuts have a metal thread retained inside a rubber bush which is a firm press fit in the windscreen **(see illustration)**. Avoid overtightening the screw, otherwise the bush will twist and damage the locating hole.

Peg and grommet

14 Ease the panel back and exert firm, even pressure to pull the peg out of the rubber grommet **(see illustration)**. If the peg is a tight fit, use a lubricating spray to release it. Do not rock the panel as the peg may snap.

5.7 Pull out the centre pin to remove the clip

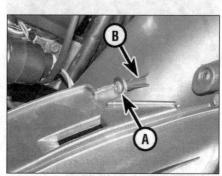

5.10 Self-tapping screw (A) secured in lug (B)

5.11 U-clips (arrowed) should be a firm push fit

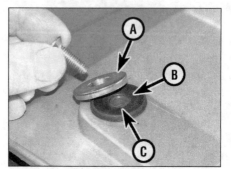

5.12 Note the order of the washer (A), bush (B) and spacer (C)

5.13 Wellnut threads are retained inside a rubber bush

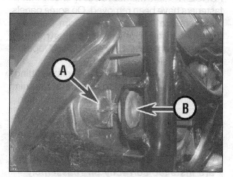

5.14 Peg (A) is secured in rubber grommet (B)

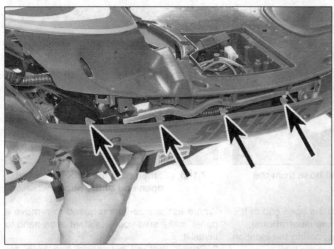

5.16 Row of hooked tabs (arrowed) engage in slots in the adjacent panel

6.2 Typical repair kit for plastic panels

15 If the grommet has split or hardened with age, replace it with a new one.

Note that a small amount of lubricant (liquid soap or similar) applied to rubber mounting grommets will assist the lugs to engage without the need for undue pressure.

Tab and slot

16 The edges of adjacent panels are often joined by tabs and slots – once all the fixing screws have been removed, slide these panels apart rather than pull them **(see illustration)**.

6 Panel repair

1 In the case of damage to the body panels, it is usually necessary to remove the broken panel and replace it with a new (or used) one. There are however some shops that specialise in 'plastic welding', so it may be worthwhile seeking the advice of one of these specialists before scrapping an expensive component.
2 Proprietary repair kits can be obtained for repair of small components **(see illustration)**.

7 Fuel and oil tanks

Warning: Refer to the precautions given in Chapter 3, Section 1 before proceeding.

Fuel tank

1 Generally, the fuel tank is located underneath the seat, although on some scooters the tank is underneath the floor panel. The location of the fuel filler is a good guide to the location of the tank.

2 Remove the body panels as necessary to access the tank (see Section 8).
3 Disconnect the battery negative (-ve) lead and the fuel gauge sender wiring connector (see Chapter 9).
4 If the tank is located underneath the seat, fuel flow to the carburettor will be controlled by a tap, either on the underside of the tank or in the fuel line to the carburettor (see Chapter 3). If required, follow the procedure in Chapter 3, Section 2, and drain any fuel in the tank into a suitable container. Disconnect the tap vacuum hose.
5 If the tank is located underneath the floor panel, fuel flow to the carburettor will be

7.6 Remove the collar (arrowed) from around the fuel filler neck

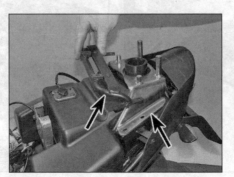
7.7b . . . and lift off the fuel tank brackets (arrowed)

controlled by a pump mounted on the frame alongside the fuel tank. Disconnect the fuel hose between the tank and the pump at the pump, and drain any residual fuel in the tank into a suitable container.
6 Temporarily remove the fuel tank cap, then remove any collar around the filler neck **(see illustration)**.
7 Undo the fixings securing the tank support bracket(s) to the frame and remove the bracket(s) **(see illustrations)**.
8 Re-install the fuel tank cap.
9 Note the location of any drain or vent hoses and disconnect them if necessary **(see illustration)**.

7.7a Undo the fixings (arrowed) on both sides . . .

7.9 Release the clip and disconnect the vent hose (arrowed)

7.10 Lift out the fuel tank

7.14a Detach the oil hose from the tank . . .

7.14b . . . then plug the tank union and open end of the hose

10 Lift the fuel tank out **(see illustration)**.

⚠ *Warning: If the fuel tank is removed from the scooter, it should not be placed in an area where sparks or open flames could ignite the fumes coming out of the tank. Be especially careful inside garages where a natural gas-type appliance is located, because the pilot light could cause an explosion.*

11 Installation is the reverse of removal, noting the following:
● Ensure no wiring is trapped between the tank and the frame.
● Tighten the fixings securely.
● Ensure the fuel and vacuum hoses are a tight fit on their unions.
● Ensure any vent or drain hoses are correctly routed.

Oil tank (two-stroke engines)

12 Generally, the oil tank is located underneath the seat or in front of the engine unit. Remove any body panels as necessary to access the oil tank and, if necessary, remove the fuel tank (see above).

13 Disconnect the oil level warning light sensor wiring connector (see Chapter 9).

14 Release the clip securing the oil hose to the union on the oil tank and detach the hose

– plug the tank union and the open end of the hose to prevent oil loss **(see illustrations)**.

15 Undo the tank fixings, noting the location of any washers, then lift out the tank.

16 Installation is the reverse of removal, noting the following:
● Ensure no wiring is trapped between the tank and the frame.
● Tighten the fixings securely.
● Ensure the oil hose is pushed fully onto the union on the tank and secure it with the clip.
● Bleed any air trapped in the hose (see Chapter 2C, Section 11).

8 Body panels

1 In most cases, adjacent body panels are linked together with some form of fixing and it is usually necessary to remove panels in a specific order – if available, refer to your scooter handbook for details. Removing trim panels, floor mats, rear carriers and the under seat storage compartment often allows access to concealed panel fixings.

2 In some cases the aid of an assistant will be required when removing panels to avoid the risk of straining tabs or damaging paintwork.

Where assistance was required to remove a panel, make sure your assistant is on hand to install it.

3 Check that all mounting brackets are straight and repair or renew them if necessary before attempting to install the panel.

4 The following information is intended as a general guide to panel removal.

Handlebar covers

5 Remove the handlebar covers to gain access to the instrument cluster, brake master cylinder and, where applicable, the headlight unit.

6 First, if necessary, remove the mirrors (see Section 2).

7 The covers are usually in two sections, screwed and clipped together. There will either be an upper and lower section, or a front and rear section. Either remove the screws along the outside edge, then ease the halves apart, or remove the screws securing the rear section to the front section and ease the front section off **(see illustrations)**. Do not force the covers apart – if a cover will not come free, ensure that all the screws have been removed. Don't forget that wiring for the headlight or the instrument cluster, and the speedometer cable, will restrict how far a cover will become displaced.

8 If the instrument cluster is located in the top

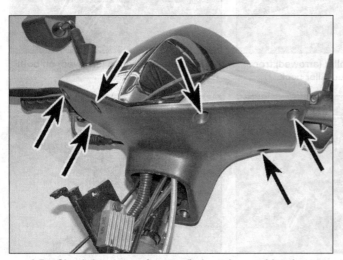

8.7a Check for screws (arrowed) along the outside edges

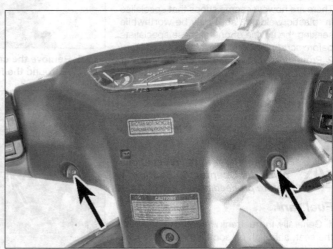

8.7b Check for screws (arrowed) on the rear cover . . .

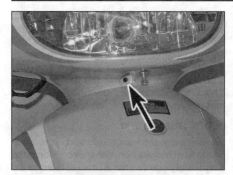

8.7c . . . and hidden underneath the headlight (arrowed)

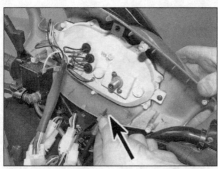

8.8 Disconnect the speedometer cable (arrowed) and wiring connectors

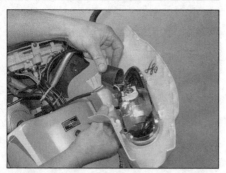

8.9a Disconnect the headlight wiring connectors

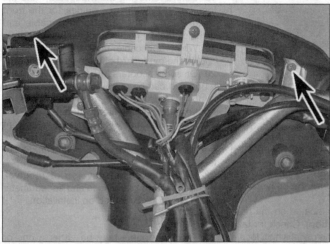

8.9b Rear cover is secured by screws (arrowed) on the inside . . .

8.9c . . . and the outside of the cover

cover, ease the cover up, then unscrew the knurled ring securing the speedometer cable and disconnect the wiring connectors before removing the cover **(see illustration)**.

9 If the headlight unit is located in the front cover, disconnect the wiring connectors before removing the cover **(see illustration)**. Note that the rear cover, containing the instrument cluster, will be secured to the handlebars by

additional screws **(see illustrations)**.

10 Note any cut-out in the covers for the throttle cable.

11 On some scooters, the handlebars must be removed in order to remove the lower cover (see Chapter 6).

12 Installation is the reverse of removal. Check the operation of the instruments and/or headlight before riding the scooter.

Front panel

13 Generally, the front panel is secured by fixings through the kick panel and the front panel itself **(see illustrations)**. Also check for fixings along the bottom edge of the panel, between the front panel and the floor panel or belly panel **(see illustrations)**.

14 If the headlight unit is located in the front

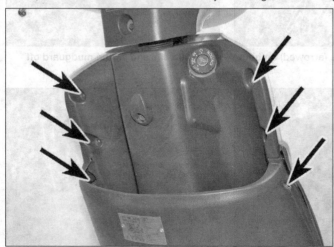

8.13a Front panel fixings (arrowed) in the kick panel . . .

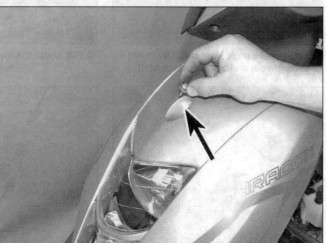

8.13b . . . and in the front panel

8.13c Check for fixings along the lower edge

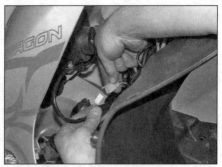

8.14 Take care not to strain the headlight wiring connector

8.15a Lifting off the upper panel. Note the tabs (arrowed)

8.15b Lifting off the lower panel. Note the fixing point (arrowed) with the belly panel

along the bottom edge **(see illustration)**. Note any electrical connections when removing this panel.

16 Installation is the reverse of removal. Ensure that any tabs or clips are correctly located before installing the fixing screws. Check the operation of the headlight and/or turn signals before riding the scooter.

Front mudguard

17 Generally, the front mudguard is mounted on the front suspension, either directly onto the suspension legs or onto a bracket fixed to the underside of the fork yoke. On some scooters it is secured to the front body panels.

18 Before removing the mudguard, note the location of any clips or guides for the front brake hose or the speedometer cable and displace them if necessary **(see illustration)**.

19 Where applicable, undo the fixing screws and lift the mudguard off **(see illustrations)**.

20 On some scooters, the front section of the mudguard can be removed to facilitate wheel removal. Undo the fixing screws and draw the front section off **(see illustrations)**.

21 If the mudguard is secured to the front body panels it may be necessary to remove the front wheel before removing the mudguard (see Chapter 7).

22 Installation is the reverse of removal. Ensure the front brake hose and speedometer cable are correctly routed on installation.

Belly panel

23 The belly panel may be either a one or two-piece assembly. Check along the centre of the panel underneath the scooter for a join.

panel, ease the panel forward and disconnect the light wiring connectors before removing the panel **(see illustration)**.

15 Some scooters are fitted with a two-piece front panel – the upper section allows access

to electrical components located on the front of the frame **(see illustration)**. Check for tabs along the lower edge of the panel which locate in slots in the lower panel. The lower section is secured by fixings through the kick panel and

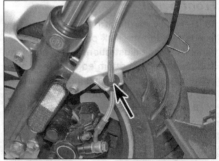

8.18 Brake hose is secured by guide (arrowed) on the front mudguard

8.19a Undo the fixings (arrowed) on both sides . . .

8.19b . . . and lift the mudguard off

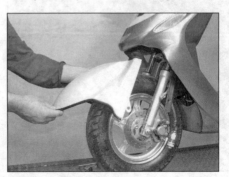

8.20a Removing the front section of the mudguard

8.20b Note how the tabs (arrowed) on the mudguard . . .

8.20c . . . locate in the bracket on the fork yoke

24 Generally, the front of the belly panel is secured to the front panel, kick panel or to the frame **(see illustration)**. Remove the front panel (see Steps 13 to 15) for access to hidden fixings

25 On some scooters, the belly panel is secured by screws through the floor panel **(see illustration)**.

26 When all the fixings have been removed, carefully ease the belly panel off **(see illustration)**.

27 On some scooters, the belly panel is comprised of the lower part of the front panel, and the left and right-hand side panels **(see illustration)**. Undo the fixings along the length of the side panel, then ease the panel off, noting any tabs that secure it to slots in adjacent panels – take care to avoid breaking the tabs **(see illustrations)**.

28 Installation is the reverse of removal. Ensure that any tabs or clips are correctly located before installing the fixing screws.

Underseat panel

29 Remove the seat and storage compartment (see Section 4).

30 Where fitted, remove the floor mat, then undo any fixings on the lower edge of the panel **(see illustration)**.

31 Remove any fixings between the upper edge of the panel, the side panels and the frame **(see illustration)**.

32 Ease off the underseat panel, noting the location of the tabs **(see illustration)**. On

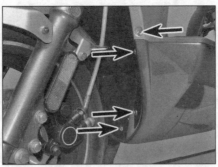

8.24 Screws (arrowed) secure front of belly panel

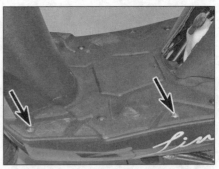

8.25 Screws (arrowed) secure top edge of belly panel

8.26 Ease the belly panel off. Note the location of the side stand

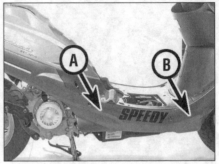

8.27a Side panel (A) and front panel (B)

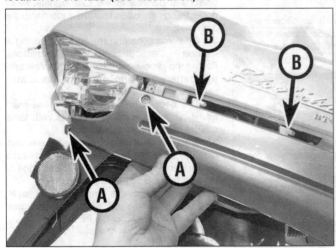

8.27b Check for fixings (A) and tabs (B) . . .

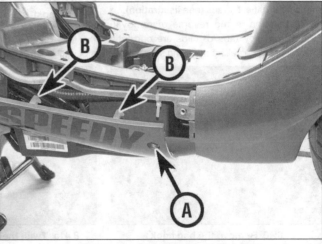

8.27c . . . along the length of the panel

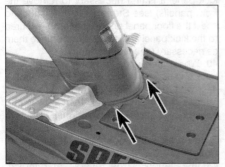

8.30 Remove the fixings (arrowed) on the lower edge of the panel

8.31 Remove the fixings (arrowed) between the side panel and the underseat panel

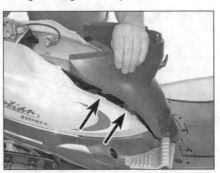

8.32a Ease off the underseat panel, noting the tabs

8.32b Tabs (arrowed) secure underseat panel to floor panel

8.35 Location of the battery housing in the floor panel

8.36 Undo the bolts securing the floor panel

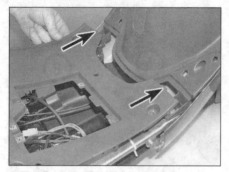

8.37a Ease the floor panel back to release any tabs (arrowed) . . .

8.37b . . . then lift it off the machine

8.39 Screw (arrowed) secures kick panel to floor panel

some scooters, the underseat panel is secured to the floor panel by tabs (see illustration).

33 Installation is the reverse of removal. Ensure that any tabs or clips are correctly located before installing the fixing screws.

Floor panel

34 On most scooters, it is necessary to remove some of the adjacent panels before the floor panel will lift off. Check for tab and slot fixings to the kick panel, belly panel,

underseat panel and the side panels. Floor panel fixings are often located underneath the floor mat.

35 On some scooters, the battery housing is located in the floor panel (see illustration). Follow the procedure in Chapter 9 to remove the battery housing and any associated electrical components.

36 The floor panel is secured to the main frame tube and support brackets with large screws or bolts (see illustration).

37 When all the fixings have been removed, carefully ease the floor panel off – note tabs on the panel may locate in the lower edge of the kick panel (see illustrations).

38 Installation is the reverse of removal. Ensure no cables or wiring are trapped between the panel and the frame.

Kick panel

39 On most scooters, before removing the kick panel it is first necessary to remove the front panel(s) (see Steps 13 to 15). Check to see if the floor panel or belly panel are secured to the kick panel and remove or displace them as necessary (see illustration).

40 Where fitted, undo the bolt securing the bag hook and remove the hook (see illustration).

41 Twist the ignition switch surround to release it from the panel, then pull it out, noting how it fits (see illustrations).

42 When all the fixings have been removed, carefully ease the kick panel off (see illustration).

43 Installation is the reverse of removal. Ensure no cables or wiring are trapped between the panel and the frame.

8.40 Remove the bag hook

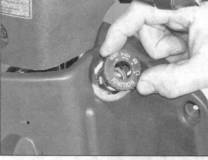

8.41a Twist the switch surround . . .

8.41b . . . then pull it out of the panel

8.42 Ease the kick panel off

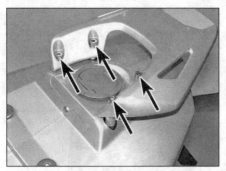

8.44a Undo the mounting bolts (arrowed) . . .

8.44b . . . and lift off the rear carrier

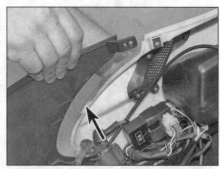

8.49a Ease the panels apart carefully, noting any tabs (arrowed) . . .

8.49b . . . then lift the seat cowling off

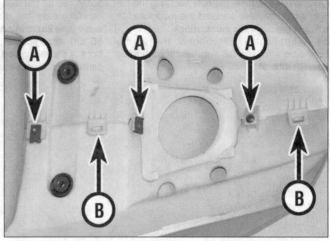

8.50 Screw fixings (A) and tabs (B) securing the halves of the seat cowling

Seat cowling

44 If fitted, undo the bolts securing the rear carrier and lift the carrier off **(see illustrations)**.

45 Remove the seat and storage compartment (see Section 4).

46 If applicable, disconnect the seat latch cable from the cable stop on the back of the cowling panel, and from the lock **(see illustration 4.4a)**.

47 If applicable, undo any fixings securing the cowling to the side panels or, if necessary, remove the side panels **(see illustration 8.27b)**.

48 Undo any bolts or screws securing the cowling to the frame , noting the location of any bushes and spacers **(see illustration 5.12)**.

49 When all the fixings have been removed, carefully ease the cowling away from adjacent panels, noting any tabs, and lift it off **(see illustrations)**. Note that it may be necessary to temporarily remove the fuel filler cap in order to remove the cowling. Don't forget to install the cap once the cowling has been removed.

50 On most scooters, the seat cowling is a two-piece assembly. If necessary, undo the fixings and release the tabs holding the two halves together **(see illustration)**.

51 Installation is the reverse of removal. Take care to ensure that the cowling is correctly positioned around the tail light lens and that

any tabs are aligned with adjacent panels before installing the fixing screws.

Rear mudguard

52 On most scooters the mudguard is secured to the rear of the frame underneath the side panels or seat cowling. The mudguard assembly may include the mounting for the tail light and the rear turn signals.

53 Remove the panels as necessary to access the mudguard fixings **(see illustration)**. On one of the models photographed, the mudguard was retained on two studs also used to secure the tail light assembly, and a bracket underneath the fuel tank **(see illustrations)**.

8.53a Mudguard fixings (arrowed) located behind seat cowling

8.53b Mudguard is supported on studs (arrowed) . . .

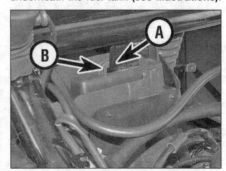

8.53c . . . and frame tab (A) locates in slot (B) on the mudguard

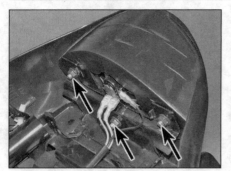

8.53d Nuts (arrowed) secure tail light and mudguard assembly

8.55a Removing the rear mudguard

8.55b Removing the rear mudguard, tail light and turn signals assembly

On another machine, the nuts securing the tail light assembly also secured the mudguard to a frame bracket **(see illustration)**.

54 If applicable, disconnect the wiring connectors for the tail light and turn signals (see Chapter 9).

55 When all the fixings have been removed, carefully ease the rear mudguard assembly away **(see illustrations)**.

56 On some scooters, a mud flap is fitted in front of the rear wheel to keep road dirt off the carburettor. If necessary, follow the procedure

in Chapter 3 to remove the exhaust system, then undo the mounting bolts and remove the mud flap.

57 Installation is the reverse of removal. If applicable, check the operation of the tail light and/or turn signals before riding the scooter.

Chapter 9
Electrical systems

Contents

Degrees of difficulty

Easy, suitable for novice with little experience	**Fairly easy,** suitable for beginner with some experience	**Fairly difficult,** suitable for competent DIY mechanic	**Difficult,** suitable for experienced DIY mechanic	**Very difficult,** suitable for expert DIY or professional

1 General information

All models have 12-volt electrical systems charged by a three-phase alternator with a separate regulator/rectifier. The regulator maintains the charging system output within a specified range to prevent overcharging, and the rectifier converts the AC (alternating current) output of the alternator to DC (direct current) to power the lights and other components and to charge the battery.

The location of electrical components such as relays, resistors and diodes varies enormously. Refer to the wiring diagram in your handbook and trace the wiring to the component, removing any body panels as necessary to gain access (see Chapter 8).

A wiring diagram is useful when tracing electrical faults, if only to identify which are the power supply and earth wires leading from components. You may find a wiring diagram is provided in the owners manual supplied with the scooter. Several typical wiring diagrams are provided at the end of this Chapter.

Note: *Keep in mind that electrical parts, once purchased, cannot be returned. To avoid unnecessary expense, make very sure the faulty component has been positively identified before buying a replacement part.*

2 Electrical systems – fault finding

 Warning: To prevent the risk of short circuits, the ignition switch must always be OFF and the battery negative (-ve) terminal should be disconnected before any of the scooter's other electrical components are disturbed. Don't forget to reconnect the terminal securely once work is finished or if battery power is needed for circuit testing.

1 A typical electrical circuit consists of an electrical component, the switches, relays, etc, related to that component and the wiring and connectors that link the component to the battery and the frame.

2 Before tackling any troublesome electrical circuit, first study the wiring diagram thoroughly to get a complete picture of what makes up that individual circuit. Trouble spots, for instance, can often be narrowed down by noting if other components related to that circuit are operating properly or not. If several components or circuits fail at one time, chances are the fault lies either in the fuse or in the common earth (ground) connection, as several circuits are often routed through the same fuse and earth (ground) connections.

3 Electrical problems often stem from simple causes, such as loose or corroded connections or a blown fuse. Prior to any electrical fault finding, always visually check the condition of the fuse, wires and connections in the problem circuit. Intermittent failures can be especially frustrating, since you can't always duplicate the failure when it's convenient to test. In such situations, a good practice is to clean all connections in the affected circuit, whether or not they appear to be good. All of the connections and wires should also be wiggled to check for looseness which can cause intermittent failure.

4 If you don't have a multimeter it is highly advisable to obtain one – they are not expensive and will enable a full range of electrical tests to be made. Go for a modern digital one with LCD display as they are easier to use. A continuity tester and/or test light are useful for certain electrical checks as an alternative, though are limited in their

2.4a A digital multimeter can be used for all electrical tests

2.4b A battery powered continuity tester

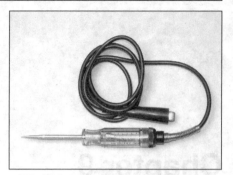

2.4c A simple test light can be used for voltage checks

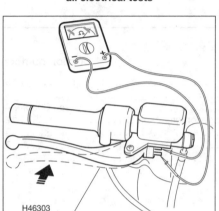

2.10 Testing a brake light switch for continuity

usefulness compared to a multimeter **(see illustrations)**.

Continuity checks

5 The term continuity describes the uninterrupted flow of electricity through an electrical circuit. Continuity can be checked with a multimeter set either to its continuity function (a beep is emitted when continuity is found), or to the resistance (ohms / Ω) function, or with a dedicated continuity tester. Both instruments are powered by an internal battery, therefore the checks are made with the ignition OFF. As a safety precaution, always disconnect the battery negative (-) lead before making continuity checks, particularly if ignition system checks are being made.

6 If using a multimeter, select the continuity

function if it has one, or the resistance (ohms) function. Touch the meter probes together and check that a beep is emitted or the meter reads zero, which indicates continuity. If there is no continuity there will be no beep or the meter will show infinite resistance. After using the meter, always switch it OFF to conserve its battery.

7 A continuity tester can be used in the same way – its light should come on or it should beep to indicate continuity in the switch ON position, but should be off or silent in the OFF position.

8 Note that the polarity of the test probes doesn't matter for continuity checks, although care should be taken to follow specific test procedures if a diode or solid-state component is being checked.

Switch continuity checks

9 If a switch is at fault, trace its wiring to the wiring connectors. Separate the connectors and inspect them for security and condition. A build-up of dirt or corrosion here will most likely be the cause of the problem – clean up and apply a water dispersant such as WD-40, or alternatively use a dedicated contact cleaner and protection spray.

10 If using a multimeter, select the continuity function if it has one, or the resistance (ohms) function, and connect its probes to the terminals in the connector **(see illustration)**. Simple ON/OFF type switches, such as brake light switches, only have two wires whereas combination switches, like the handlebar switches, have many wires. Study the wiring diagram to ensure that you are connecting to the correct pair of wires. Continuity should be indicated with the switch ON and no continuity with it OFF.

Wiring continuity checks

11 Many electrical faults are caused by damaged wiring, often due to incorrect routing or chaffing on frame components. Loose, wet or corroded wire connectors can also be the cause of electrical problems.

12 A continuity check can be made on a single length of wire by disconnecting it at each end and connecting the meter or continuity tester probes to each end of the wire **(see illustration)**. Continuity should be indicated if the wire is good. If no continuity is shown, suspect a broken wire.

13 To check for continuity to earth in any earth wire connect one probe of your meter or tester to the earth wire terminal in the connector and the other to the frame, engine, or battery earth (-) terminal. Continuity should be indicated if the wire is good. If no continuity is shown, suspect a broken wire or corroded or loose earth point (see below).

Voltage checks

14 A voltage check can determine whether power is reaching a component. Use a multimeter set to the dc (direct current) voltage scale to check for power from the battery or regulator/rectifier, or set to the ac (alternating current) voltage scale to check for power from the alternator. A test light can be used to check for dc voltage. The test light is the cheaper component, but the meter has the advantage of being able to give a voltage reading.

15 Connect the meter or test light in parallel, i.e. across the load **(see illustration)**.

16 First identify the relevant wiring circuit by

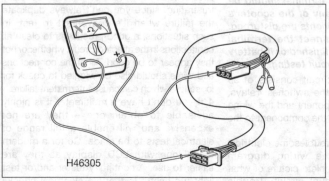

2.12 Testing for continuity in a wiring loom

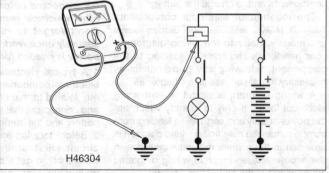

2.15 Connect the multimeter in parallel, or across the load, as shown

referring to the wiring diagram at the end of this manual. If other electrical components share the same wiring circuit, take note whether they are working correctly – this is useful information in deciding where to start checking the circuit.

17 If using a meter, check first that the meter leads are plugged into the correct terminals on the meter (red to positive (+), black to negative (-). Set the meter to the appropriate volts function (dc or ac), where necessary at a range suitable for the battery voltage – 0 to 20 vdc. Connect the meter red probe (+) to the power supply wire and the black probe to a good metal earth (ground) on the scooter's frame or directly to the battery negative terminal. Battery voltage, or the specified voltage, should be shown on the meter with the ignition switch, and if necessary any other relevant switch, ON.

18 If using a test light **(see illustration 2.4c)**, connect its positive (+) probe to the power supply terminal and its negative (-) probe to a good earth (ground) on the scooter's frame. With the switch, and if necessary any other relevant switch, ON, the test light should illuminate.

19 If no voltage is indicated, work back towards the power source continuing to check for voltage. When you reach a point where there is voltage, you know the problem lies between that point and your last check point.

Earth (ground) checks

20 Earth connections are made either directly to the engine or frame (such as the starter motor or ignition coil which only have a positive feed) or by a separate wire into the earth circuit of the wiring harness. Alternatively a short earth wire is sometimes run from the component directly to the scooter's frame.

21 Corrosion is a common cause of a poor earth connection, as is a loose earth terminal fastener.

22 If total or multiple component failure is experienced, check the security of the main earth lead from the negative (-) terminal of the battery, the earth lead bolted to the engine, and the main earth point(s) on the frame. If corroded, dismantle the connection and clean all surfaces back to bare metal. Remake the connection and prevent further corrosion from forming by smearing battery terminal grease over the connection.

23 To check the earthing of a component, use an insulated jumper wire to temporarily bypass its earth connection **(see illustration)** – connect one end of the jumper wire to the earth terminal or metal body of the component and the other end to the scooter's frame. If the circuit works with the jumper wire installed, the earth circuit is faulty.

24 To check an earth wire first check for corroded or loose connections, then check the wiring for continuity (Step 13) between each connector in the circuit in turn, and then to its earth point, to locate the break.

 Remember that all electrical circuits are designed to conduct electricity from the battery, through the wires, switches, relays, etc. to the electrical component (light bulb, starter motor, etc). From there it is directed to the frame (earth) where it is passed back to the battery. Electrical problems are basically an interruption in the flow of electricity from the battery or back to it.

3 Battery

 Warning: Be extremely careful when handling or working around the battery. Do not allow electrolyte to come in contact with your skin or painted or plastic surfaces of the scooter. Rinse off any spills immediately with plenty of water. Check with the local authorities about disposing of an old battery. Many communities will have collection centres which will see that batteries are disposed of safely.

Removal and installation

1 Refer to your scooter handbook and remove the battery access panel.
2 Where fitted, remove the battery strap. Undo the negative (-ve) terminal screw first and disconnect the lead from the battery, then undo the positive (+ve) terminal screw and disconnect the lead **(see illustrations)**.
3 Lift the battery from its holder.
4 Before installation, clean the battery terminals, terminal screws, nuts and lead ends with a wire brush, knife or steel wool to ensure a good electrical connection.
5 Install the battery, then reconnect the leads, connecting the positive (+ve) lead first, and secure the battery strap.

 Battery corrosion can be kept to a minimum by applying a layer of petroleum jelly to the terminals after the cables have been connected.

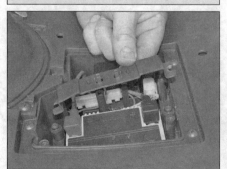

3.2a Remove the battery strap

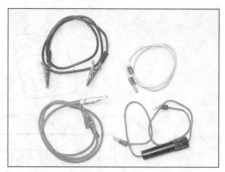

2.23 A selection of jumper wires for making earth (ground) checks

6 Fit the battery access panel.

Inspection and maintenance

7 All the scooters covered in this manual are fitted with a sealed, maintenance-free (MF) battery. **Note:** *Do not attempt to open the battery as resulting damage will mean that it will be unfit for further use.*

8 Check the battery terminals and leads for tightness and corrosion. If corrosion is evident, undo the terminal screws and wash the terminals and lead ends in a solution of baking soda and hot water, then dry them thoroughly. Reconnect the leads and apply a thin coat of petroleum jelly or battery terminal grease to the connections to prevent further corrosion.

9 The battery case should be kept clean to prevent current leakage, which can discharge the battery over a period of time (especially when it sits unused). Wash the outside of the case with a solution of baking soda and water. Rinse the battery thoroughly, then dry it.

10 Look for cracks in the case and renew the battery if any are found. If acid has been spilled on the battery holder or surrounding bodywork, neutralise it with a baking soda and water solution, dry it thoroughly, then touch up any damaged paint.

11 If the machine is not used for long periods of time, disconnect the leads from the battery terminals and charge the battery once every month to six weeks.

12 The condition of the battery can be assessed by measuring the voltage present at the battery terminals with a multimeter. Connect the meter positive (+ve) probe to

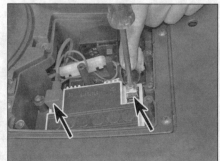

3.2b Disconnect the negative (-ve) lead first, then the positive (+ve) lead (arrowed)

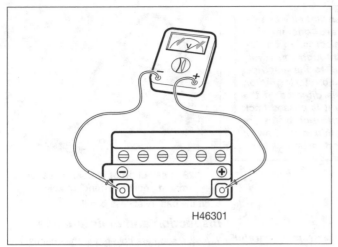

3.12 Measuring battery open-circuit voltage

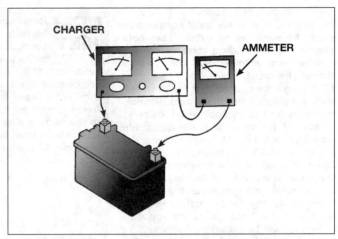

3.16a If the charger has no built-in ammeter, connect one in series as shown. DO NOT connect the ammeter between the battery terminals or it will be ruined

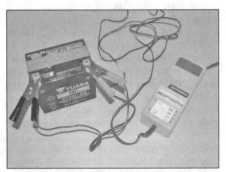

3.16b These battery chargers monitor battery condition and charge at a safe rate

the battery positive (+ve) terminal, and the negative (-ve) probe to the battery negative (-ve) terminal **(see illustration)**. A fully charged battery should have a terminal voltage of between 12.8 and 13.0V. Compare the reading with the specifications given in the *Data* section at the end of this manual. If the voltage falls below 12 volts the battery must be removed and recharged as described below. **Note:** *Before taking the measurement, wait at least 30 minutes after any charging has taken place (including running the engine).*

13 If battery condition is suspect, connect the multimeter to the battery terminals as before (see Step 12), turn the ignition ON and press

the starter button. If the meter reading drops below 8V a new battery is required.

Battery charging

Caution: Be extremely careful when handling or working around the battery. The electrolyte is very caustic and an explosive gas (hydrogen) is given off when the battery is charging.

14 Ensure the charger is suitable for charging a 12V battery. When charging a maintenance free battery, make sure that you use a regulated battery charger.

15 Remove the battery (see Steps 1 to 3). Connect the charger to the battery **BEFORE** switching the charger ON. Make sure that the positive (+ve) lead on the charger is connected to the positive (+ve) terminal on the battery, and the negative (-ve) lead is connected to the negative (-ve) terminal.

16 Refer to the markings on the battery for the recommended charge rate – manufacturers generally recommend a rate of no more than 0.5 amps for 5 to 10 hrs, or a quick charge rate of 5A for 30 minutes. Exceeding this figure can cause the battery to overheat, buckling the plates and rendering it useless. Few owners will have access to an expensive current controlled charger, so if a normal domestic charger is used check that after a possible

initial peak, the charge rate falls to a safe level **(see illustration)**. If the battery becomes hot during charging **STOP**. Further charging will cause damage. Use of one of the dedicated motorcycle battery chargers is recommended **(see illustration)**.

17 If the recharged battery discharges rapidly when left disconnected it is likely that an internal short caused by physical damage or sulphation has occurred. A new battery will be required. A sound battery will tend to lose its charge at about 1% per day.

18 Install the battery (see Steps 4 to 6).

4 Fuse

1 The electrical system is protected by a main fuse, usually mounted near the battery. On higher spec models some individual electrical circuits are protected by their own (secondary) fuses. Refer to your scooter's handbook for details of fuse location.

2 Two types of fuse are fitted – the glass cartridge type and the flat-bladed type **(see illustrations)**. A blown fuse is easily identified by a break in the element – pull the fuse out of its holder to check it visually **(see illustration)**.

4.2a Checking a glass cartridge fuse

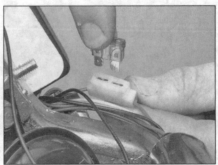

4.2b Checking a flat-bladed fuse

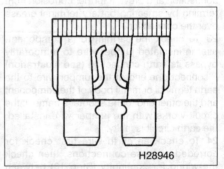

4.2c A blown fuse can be identified by a break in the element

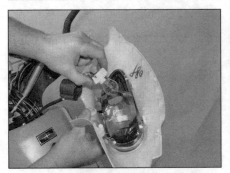

5.3a Remove the bulbholder from the headlight unit . . .

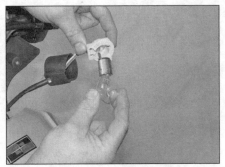

5.3b . . . then twist and withdraw the bulb

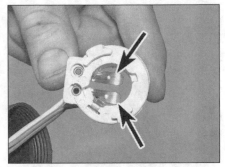

5.3c Make sure the bulb terminals (arrowed) are clean

5.3d Remove the tail light lens . . .

5.3e . . . then twist and withdraw the bulb

5.3f Note the terminals (arrowed) for the combined brake and tail light bulb

Note: *If the break in the element is not obvious, use a multimeter and check across the fuse ends for continuity (see Section 2).*

3 The fuse will be clearly marked with its rating and must only be replaced by a fuse of the correct rating. It is advisable to carry spare fuses on the scooter at all times.

⚠️ **Warning: Never put in a fuse of a higher rating or bridge the terminals with any other substitute, however temporary it may be. Serious damage may be done to the circuit, or a fire may start.**

4 If the fuse blows, be sure to check the wiring circuit very carefully for evidence of a short-circuit. Look for bare wires and chafed, melted or burned insulation. If a new fuse is fitted before the cause is located, it will blow immediately.

5 Occasionally the fuse will blow or cause an open-circuit for no obvious reason. Corrosion of the fuse ends and fuse holder terminals may occur and cause poor fuse contact. If this happens, remove the corrosion with a wire brush or steel wool, then spray the fuse ends and fuse holder terminals with electrical contact cleaner.

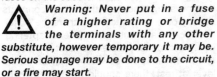

5 Lighting system

1 The lighting system consists of the headlight, sidelight (on certain models), tail light, turn signals, brake light, instrument panel lights, handlebar switches and fuse.

2 On most of the scooters covered by this manual, the engine must be running for any of the lights to work. If none of the lights work, always check the fuse (where fitted) and alternator lighting coil before proceeding (see Section 8). If applicable, check the condition of the lighting resistor (see Step 11).

Lights

Note: *Access to the headlight and tail light bulbs varies from model to model. For precise details, refer to your scooter handbook. If body panels need removing, refer to Chapter 8.*

3 If a light fails to work, first check the bulb and the terminals in the bulbholder or the bulb wiring connector **(see illustrations)**.

Caution: If the headlight bulb is of the quartz-halogen type, do not touch the bulb glass as skin acids will shorten the bulb's service life. If the bulb is accidentally touched, it should be wiped carefully when cold with a rag soaked in methylated spirit and dried before fitting.

4 Next check for voltage on the supply side of the bulbholder or wiring connector with a test light or multimeter with the light switch ON. Don't forget that the engine may have to be running to do this check (see Step 2). When checking the headlight, select either high or low beam at the handlebar switch. When checking the brake light, pull either brake lever in.

5 If no voltage is indicated, check the wiring between the bulbholder and the light switch, then check the switch (see Steps 12 to 16).

6 If voltage is indicated, check for continuity between the earth wire terminal and an earth

point on the scooter frame. If there is no continuity, check the earth circuit for a broken or poor connection.

Instrument panel lights

Note: *On some scooters, the panel is illuminated with LEDs. Although unlikely, if an LED fails, it may be necessary to renew the complete panel circuit – check the availability of parts with a scooter dealer.*

7 If one light fails to work, check the bulb and the bulb terminals **(see illustrations)**. If none of the lights work, refer to the wiring diagram in your scooter handbook, then check for voltage on the supply side of the instrument cluster wiring connector, if necessary with the engine running and light switch ON **(see illustration)**.

8 If no voltage is indicated, check the wiring between the connector, the light switch and the ignition switch, then check the switches themselves.

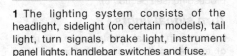

5.7a Pull the bulbholder out of the instrument cluster . . .

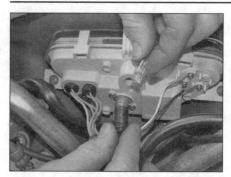

5.7b . . . then pull the panel bulb out of its holder

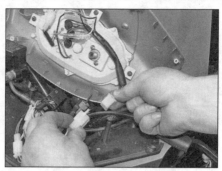

5.7c Check for voltage on the supply side (arrowed) of the connector

5.11 A typical lighting system resistor

5.14 Trace the switch wiring to the connector (arrowed)

5.15a Undo the switch housing screws (arrowed) . . .

5.15b . . . and separate the two halves of the housing. Note the switch gear (arrowed)

9 If voltage is indicated, check for continuity between the power supply wire terminal on the instrument cluster side of the connector and the corresponding terminal in the bulbholder; no continuity indicates a break in the circuit.

10 If continuity is present, check for continuity between the earth wire terminal in the wiring connector and an earth point on the scooter frame. If there is no continuity, check the earth circuit for a broken or poor connection.

Lighting system resistor

11 On some scooters, the lighting system is protected by a resistor **(see illustration)**. To test the resistor, substitute it with a known good one or have the resistance checked by a scooter specialist.

Handlebar switches

12 Generally speaking, the switches are reliable and trouble-free. Most problems,

5.18 Brake light switch wiring connectors (arrowed)

when they do occur, are caused by dirty or corroded contacts, but wear and breakage of internal parts is a possibility that should not be overlooked when tracing a fault. If breakage does occur, the entire switch and related wiring harness will have to be renewed as individual parts are not available.

13 The switches can be checked for continuity using a multimeter or test light and battery. Always disconnect the battery negative (-ve) lead, which will prevent the possibility of a short circuit, before making the checks.

14 Remove the body panels as necessary to trace the wiring from the switch in question back to its connector (see Chapter 8). Disconnect the relevant wiring connector **(see illustration)**. Refer to the wiring diagram in your scooter handbook and check for continuity between the terminals of the switch wiring with the switch in the various positions (i.e. switch OFF – no continuity, switch ON – continuity).

15 If the checks indicate a problem exists, undo the screws securing the two halves of the housing and separate them **(see illustrations)**. Note the location of the housing screws – they are often different lengths. Note that on most scooters, the right-hand housing is integral with the throttle twistgrip (see Chapter 3).

16 Spray the switch contacts with electrical contact cleaner. If they are accessible, the contacts can be scraped clean carefully with a knife or polished with crocus cloth. If switch components are damaged or broken, it will be obvious when the switch is disassembled.

17 Clean the inside of the switch body

thoroughly and smear the contacts with suitable grease before reassembly.

Brake light switches

18 If necessary, remove the handlebar cover (see Chapter 8), then disconnect the switch wiring connectors **(see illustration)**. Note that on some scooters the wiring connects directly onto the switch, on others the switch connects via a sub-loom (see Chapter 7). Using a continuity tester, connect a probe to each terminal on the switch. With the brake lever at rest, there should be no continuity. Pull the brake lever in – there should now be continuity. If not, fit a new switch.

19 If the switch is good, refer the wiring diagram in your scooter handbook to check the brake light circuit using a multimeter or test light (see Section 2).

6 Turn signal system

1 The turn signal system consists of the turn signal lights, instrument panel light, handlebar switch, relay and fuse.

2 On most models, the engine must be running for the turn signal lights to work. If none of the lights work, always check the fuse (where fitted) and alternator lighting coil before proceeding (see Section 8).

Turn signal lights

3 Most turn signal problems are the result of a failed bulb or corroded socket **(see**

illustrations). This is especially true when the turn signals function properly in one direction, but not in the other. Follow the procedures described in Section 5 to check the bulbs and the sockets, the operation of the turn signal switch and the turn signal warning light in the instrument cluster.

Turn signal relay

4 If the bulbs and sockets are good, test the power supply to the signal relay **(see illustration)**. Disconnect the relay wiring connector and check for voltage at the input wire terminal in the connector with the engine running, using a multimeter or test light connected to a good earth. Turn the engine OFF. If there is no voltage, use the wiring diagram in your scooter handbook to check the supply circuit.

5 If there is voltage, reconnect the wiring connector to the relay and use a test light to check for voltage on the output side of the relay wiring connector with the engine running. The light should flash; if it does not, fit a new relay.

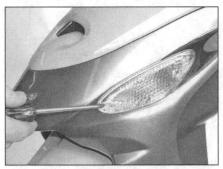
6.3a Undo the screw securing the turn signal lens

6.3b Twist and withdraw the bulb

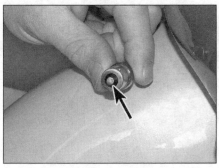
6.3c Note the single terminal contact (arrowed) on the turn signal bulb

6.4 A typical turn signal relay (arrowed)

7 Starter system

1 The starter system consists of the starter switch, starter motor, battery, relay and fuse **(see illustration)**. On some scooters, one or both of the brake light switches and, where fitted, the side stand switch, are part of a safety circuit which prevents the engine starting unless the brake is held on and the side stand is up. Refer to Section 5 to check the brake light switch. On two-stroke scooters, the oil level sensor and diode are also part of the safety circuit.

2 If the starter circuit is faulty, first check the fuse (see Section 5). Also check that the battery is fully-charged (see Section 3). If, after testing, the starter system is good, check the starter pinion assembly and starter clutch (see Chapter 2A, 2B or 2C as applicable).

Starter relay

3 To locate the starter relay, either trace the lead from the positive terminal of the battery to the relay, or trace the lead back from the starter motor to the relay **(see illustrations)**.

4 Disconnect the starter motor lead from the relay **(see illustration)**. With the ignition switch ON, press the starter switch. The relay should be heard to click. Switch the ignition OFF. If the relay doesn't click it can be tested on the workbench as follows.

5 Disconnect the battery terminals, remembering to disconnect the negative (-ve) terminal first.

6 Disconnect both leads from the starter relay, making a careful note of which lead fits on which terminal (the terminals are usually numbered). Trace the wiring from the relay and disconnect it at the connector. Remove the relay.

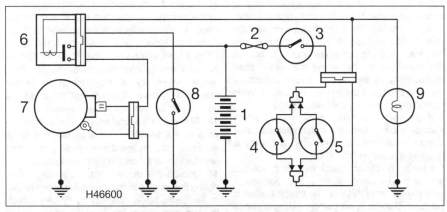
7.1 Wiring diagram for a typical starter system

1 Battery	4 Front brake light switch	7 Starter motor
2 Fuse	5 Rear brake light switch	8 Starter switch
3 Ignition switch	6 Starter relay	9 Brake light

7.3a Trace the lead (arrowed) from the starter motor . . .

7.3b . . . to the starter relay. Note the terminals (arrowed)

7.4 Undo the nut and disconnect the starter motor lead

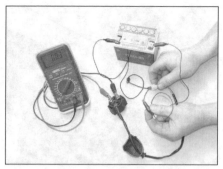

7.7 Set-up for testing the starter relay

7.11a Disconnect the wiring connector . . .

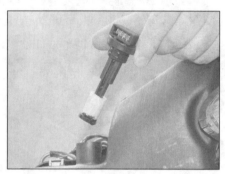

7.11b . . . and withdraw the sensor from the tank

7.15a Location of the side stand switch (arrowed)

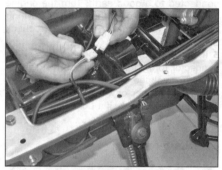

7.15b Disconnect the side stand switch wiring connector

7 Set a multimeter to the ohms x 1 scale and connect it across the relay's battery and starter motor terminals – there should be no continuity. Using a fully-charged 12 volt battery and two insulated jumper wires, connect across the terminals of the wiring connector **(see illustration)**. At this point the relay should be heard to click and the multimeter read 0 ohms (continuity) indicating the relay is good.

8 If the relay does not click when battery voltage is applied and the multimeter indicates infinite resistance (no continuity), the relay is faulty and must be renewed.

9 If the relay is good, check for battery voltage across the terminals of the wiring connector with the ignition ON when the starter button is pressed. If there is no battery voltage, check the other components and wiring in the starter circuit as described in Step 1.

Oil level sensor and diode (two-stroke engines)

10 The oil level warning light in the instrument cluster should come on temporarily when the ignition is first turned on as a check of the warning circuit. If the light fails to come on, first check the bulb (see Section 5), then check the wiring between the instrument cluster and the sensor.

11 To test the sensor, disconnect the wiring connector and withdraw the sensor from the oil tank **(see illustrations)**. Note the location of the seal and fit a new one on reassembly if it is damaged or deformed.

 Warning: Block the opening in the tank to prevent anything falling inside.

12 Connect a multimeter or continuity tester to the terminals on the top of the sensor and check for continuity with the sensor float UP (tank full). Now slowly lower the float to the DOWN (tank empty) position. There should be no continuity (infinite resistance) until the float nears the empty position, when continuity should be shown. If this is not the case the sensor is faulty and must be renewed.

13 The diode should only allow current to pass in one direction. This is usually shown as an arrowhead on the diode housing and may also be indicated on the wiring diagram.

14 Unplug the diode from the wiring loom, noting the wire locations. Using a multimeter set to the ohms scale, connect its probes across the two terminals of the diode. Continuity (zero resistance) should be shown in one direction and no continuity (infinite resistance) should be shown in the opposite direction. If it doesn't behave as stated, fit a new diode.

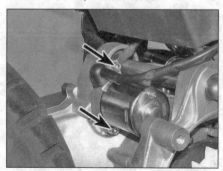

7.19 Undo the two bolts (arrowed), noting the earth cable where fitted

Side stand switch

15 The side stand switch is mounted on the stand bracket **(see illustration)**. To test the switch, trace the wiring back to the connector and disconnect it **(see illustration)**. **Note:** *It may be necessary to remove the belly panel or floor panel to access the wiring connector.*

16 Connect a multimeter or continuity tester to the terminals on the switch side of the connector. With the side stand up there should be continuity (zero resistance) between the terminals, with the stand down there should be no continuity (infinite resistance).

17 If the switch does not work as expected, check that the fault is not caused by a sticking switch plunger due to the ingress of road dirt. If required, follow the procedure in Chapter 6 and remove the stand, then spray the switch with a water dispersant aerosol. If the switch still does not work it is defective and must be renewed.

Starter motor

Removal and installation

18 To remove the starter motor, first disconnect the battery negative (-ve) lead. If accessible, disconnect the lead from the starter motor terminal **(see illustration 7.3a)**. Alternatively, trace the lead from the starter motor terminal and disconnect it at the connector or the starter relay (see Step 4).

19 Unscrew the two bolts securing the starter motor to the crankcase, noting any earth wire secured by the bolts **(see illustration)**.

20 Withdraw the starter motor **(see illustration)**. If not already done, disconnect

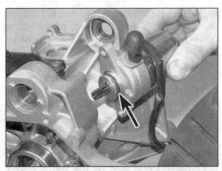

7.20 Note the O-ring (arrowed) fitted to the starter motor body

7.24a Undo the screws (arrowed)

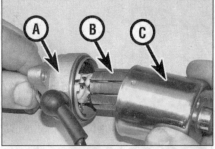

7.24b Hold the shaft so that the armature (B) remains in the end cover (A) while the housing (C) is removed

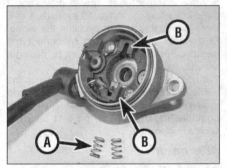

7.26 Springs (A) fit in holders (B) for the carbon brushes

7.27a Measuring the length of the starter motor brushes

7.27b Brushes mounted on separate brush plate

the lead from the motor terminal. Inspect the O-ring on the end of the motor body and fit a new one on reassembly if it is damaged or deformed.

21 Installation is the reverse of removal. Apply a smear of engine oil to the body O-ring and secure the earth wire with one of the mounting bolts.

Overhaul

22 The parts of the starter motor that are most likely to wear are the brushes, the commutator and the bearings. If the motor is suspect, it can be inspected as follows. **Note:** *A number of different starter motors are fitted across the range of scooters covered by this manual. Before disassembling the motor, check the availability of new parts. If parts are not available it may be worthwhile consulting an auto electrician before buying a new motor, as sometimes, depending on the nature of the fault, they can be repaired. When disassembling the motor, carefully note the correct fitted position of each component before removing it, as the procedure given below is general and does not cover the specific components of each type of motor.*

23 Remove the starter motor (see Steps 18 to 20).

24 Undo the screws or bolts securing the housing to the end cover and draw the housing off, leaving the armature in place in the cover **(see illustrations)**. Note the position of any housing seals and remove them carefully. **Note:** *If there is oil inside the starter motor the internal cover seal has failed – check the availability of a new seal or cover assembly.*

25 Withdraw the armature from the cover, noting any shims or washers on either or both ends of the armature shaft, and noting how the carbon brushes locate onto the commutator.

26 Slide the brushes out from their holders; note the position of the brush springs and remove them for safekeeping if they are loose **(see illustration)**.

27 Check that the brushes are firmly attached to their terminals. If the brushes are excessively worn, cracked or chipped, they should be renewed, otherwise a new starter motor must be fitted. Some manufacturers specify a service limit for the brushes (see *Data section*) **(see illustration)**. Note that some starter motors are fitted with a separate brush plate **(see illustration)**.

28 Inspect the commutator bars on the armature for scoring, scratches and discoloration **(see illustration)**. The commutator can be cleaned and polished with crocus cloth, but

do not use sandpaper or emery paper. After cleaning, wipe away any residue with a cloth soaked in electrical system cleaner or denatured alcohol.

29 Using an multimeter or test light and battery, check for continuity between the commutator bars **(see illustration)**. Continuity (zero resistance) should exist between each bar and all of the others.

30 Also, check for continuity between the commutator bars and the armature shaft **(see illustration)**. There should be no continuity (infinite resistance) between the commutator and the shaft. If the checks indicate otherwise, the armature is defective.

31 Check the front end of the armature shaft for worn or chipped teeth **(see illustration 7.28)**. Check the condition of the bearing which may be either on the armature or in the motor cover.

32 Reassemble the starter motor in the

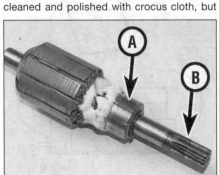

7.28 Inspect the commutator bars (A). Note the drive teeth (B)

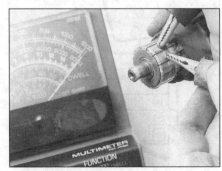

7.29 Continuity should exist between the commutator bars

7.30 There should be no continuity between the commutator bars and the armature shaft

reverse order of disassembly, noting the following:

● Press the brushes into their holders against the pressure of their springs, then fit the armature into the end cover carefully to avoid damaging the seal.

● Ensure each brush is pressed against the commutator by its spring and is free to move easily in its holder.

● Lubricate the bush in the end of the housing with a smear of grease.

8 Charging system

1 If the performance of the charging system is suspect, the system as a whole should be checked first, followed by testing of the individual components and circuits (see illustration). **Note:** *Before beginning the checks, make sure the battery is fully charged and that all circuit connections are clean and tight.*

2 Checking the output of the charging system and the performance of the various components within the charging system requires the use of a multimeter – if a multimeter is not available, have the system tested a scooter specialist or auto electrician.

3 When making the checks, follow the procedures carefully to prevent incorrect connections or short circuits, as irreparable damage to electrical system components may result if short circuits occur.

Leakage test

4 Disconnect the battery negative (-ve) terminal.

5 Set the multimeter to the Amps function and connect its negative (-ve) probe to the battery negative (-ve) terminal, and positive (+ve) probe to the disconnected negative (-ve) lead (see illustration). Always set the meter to a high Amps range initially and then bring it down to the mA (milli Amps) range; if there is a high current flow in the circuit it may blow the meter's fuse.

Caution: Always connect an ammeter in series, never in parallel with the battery, otherwise it will be damaged. Do not turn the ignition ON or operate the starter motor when the meter is connected – a sudden surge in current will blow the meter's fuse.

6 While manufacturers figures may vary, if the current leakage indicated exceeds 1 mA, there is probably a short circuit in the wiring. Disconnect the meter and reconnect the negative (-ve) lead to the battery, tightening it securely,

7 If current leakage is indicated, refer to the wiring diagram in your scooter handbook and systematically disconnect individual electrical components and repeat the test until the source is identified.

Alternator

Regulated output test

8 Start the engine and warm it up to normal operating temperature, then stop the engine and turn the ignition OFF.

9 Support the scooter on its main stand with the rear wheel clear of the ground.

10 To check the regulated voltage output, set the multimeter to the 0 – 50 volts DCV scale (voltmeter). Connect the meter positive (+ve) probe to the battery positive (+ve) terminal, and the negative (-ve) probe to the battery negative (-ve) terminal (see illustration).

11 Start the engine and slowly increase the engine speed to a fast idle; the regulated voltage should be between 13 to 16 volts, or as specified in the *Data section* at the end of this manual for your model. Now turn the headlight ON and note the reading – there should be no significant change in the output voltage.

12 If the voltage is not within these limits, there is a fault either in the regulator/rectifier or the alternator itself. If available, substitute the regulator/rectifier with a known good one and test again (see Steps 19 to 21). If the voltage is still outside the specified limits, check the alternator coil resistance (see Steps 14 to 17).

13 Some manufacturers only specify an unregulated alternator output. This check requires a wiring diagram and test details specific to your scooter, and is best undertaken by a scooter specialist or auto-electrician.

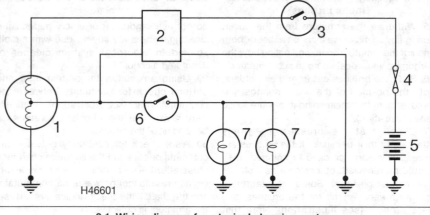

H46601

8.1 Wiring diagram for a typical charging system

1 *Charging/lighting*	2 *Regulator/rectifier*	4 *Fuse*	6 *Lighting switch*
coil	3 *Ignition switch*	5 *Battery*	7 *Bulbs*

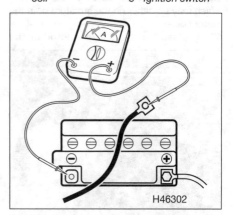

H46302

8.5 Checking the charging system leakage rate - connect the meter as shown

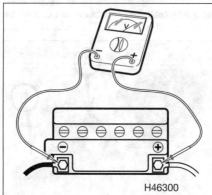

H46300

8.10 Checking the charging system regulated voltage - connect the meter as shown

 Clues to a faulty regulator are constantly blowing bulbs, with brightness varying considerably with engine speed, and battery overheating.

Coils resistance test

14 Disconnect the battery negative (-ve) terminal. Trace the wiring from the alternator cover on the right-hand side of the engine and disconnect it at the connector **(see illustration)**.

15 Refer to the wiring diagram in your scooter handbook and identify the wire terminals for the charging coil and lighting coil in the alternator side of the connector. **Note:** *For alternators with three charging coil wires of the same colour code, see Step 16.* Set the multimeter to the ohms x 1 scale and connect the meter probes to the charging coil wire terminal and to earth, and then to the lighting coil terminal and earth. This will give resistance readings for the coils which should be consistent with the specifications in the *Data* section **(see illustration)**.

16 Alternatively, set the multimeter to the ohms x 1 scale and check the resistance between one pair of wire terminals at a time and note the three readings obtained. Also check for continuity between each terminal and earth. The readings should be consistent with the specifications in the *Data* section and there should be no continuity (infinite resistance) between any of the terminals and earth.

17 If the readings obtained differ greatly from those specified, particularly if the meter indicates a short circuit (no measurable resistance) or an open circuit (infinite, or very high resistance), the alternator stator assembly must be renewed. However, first check that the fault is not due to a damaged or broken wire from the alternator to the connector; pinched or broken wires can usually be repaired.

18 Refer to the procedure in Chapter 2A, 2B or 2C, as applicable, for details of alternator removal and installation.

Regulator/rectifier

19 On most scooters, the regulator/rectifier is located at the front of the machine **(see illustration)** – remove any body panels as required for access (see Chapter 8).

20 Undo the bolt securing the unit, then disconnect the wiring connector and lift it off **(see illustration)**.

21 Installation is the reverse of removal.

9.2a Wiring connector (arrowed) is located inside boot

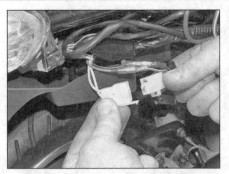

8.14 Disconnect the alternator wiring connector

8.19 Location of the regulator/rectifier (arrowed)

Ensure that there is a clean earth connection between the unit and its mounting and that any earthing wire is secured by the mounting bolt.

9 Ignition switch

Warning: To prevent the risk of short circuits, disconnect the battery negative (-ve) lead before making any ignition switch checks.

Check

1 Remove any body panels as required for access (see Chapter 8).

2 Ensure the battery negative (-ve) lead is disconnected. Either pull back the boot on the switch wiring connector and disconnect the connector, or disconnect the connector

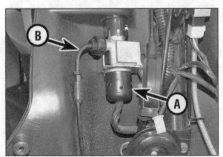

9.2b Disconnect wiring connector (A) from the switch assembly. Note the seat lock cable (B)

8.15 Checking the resistance in the alternator coils

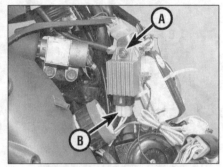

8.20 Undo the bolt (A) and disconnect the connector (B)

directly from the underside of the switch **(see illustrations)**.

3 Refer to the wiring diagram in your scooter handbook, then using a multimeter or continuity tester, check the continuity of the switch or connector terminal pairs. Continuity should exist between the connected terminals when the switch is in the indicated position.

4 If the switch fails any of the tests, replace it with a new one.

Removal

5 Disconnect the battery negative (-ve) lead and the switch wiring connector (see Step 2). If applicable, unclip the immobiliser transponder aerial from the front of the switch **(see illustration)**.

6 If applicable, unscrew the cap on the seat lock cable mechanism and disconnect the inner cable end from the mechanism **(see illustration 9.2b)**.

9.5 Where fitted, unclip the immobiliser ring

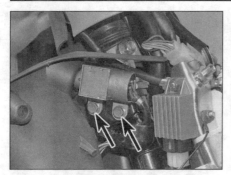

9.7a Bolts (arrowed) secure switch assembly to frame

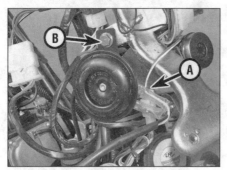

10.2 Horn wiring connectors (A) and mounting bolt (B)

7 The switch is secured to the frame either by normal bolts or shear-head bolts **(see illustrations)**. To remove a shear-head bolt, drill off the bolt head, then remove the switch. The threaded section of the shear-head bolt can then be unscrewed with pliers.

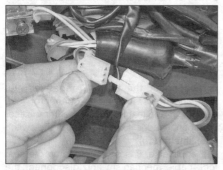

11.2 Disconnect the fuel level sensor wiring connector

11.4b . . . noting the position of any tabs (arrowed) . . .

9.7b Switch assembly secured by shear-head bolt (arrowed)

Installation

8 Installation is the reverse of removal. Tighten the bolt(s) finger-tight, then operate the key to ensure the steering lock mechanism is correctly aligned with the frame and steering stem. Now tighten the bolt(s) securely – when tightening the shear-head bolt, turn it until the head snaps off.
9 Reconnect the battery negative (-ve) lead once all electrical connections have been made to the switch.

10 Horn

Check

1 Remove any body panels as required for access to the horn (see Chapter 8).

11.4a Release the sensor from the fuel tank . . .

11.4c . . . then lift the unit and float out

2 Disconnect the wiring connectors from the horn and ensure that the contacts are clean and free from corrosion **(see illustration)**.
3 To test the horn, use jumper wires to connect one of the horn terminals to the battery positive (+ve) terminal and the other horn terminal to the battery negative (-ve) terminal. If the horn sounds, check the handlebar switch (see Section 5) and the wiring between the switch and the horn.
4 If the horn doesn't sound, replace it with a new one.

Renewal

5 Disconnect the wiring connectors from the horn, then unscrew the bolt securing the horn and remove it.
6 Install the horn and tighten the mounting bolt securely. Connect the wiring connectors and test the horn.

11 Fuel gauge and level sensor

⚠️ *Warning: Petrol (gasoline) is extremely flammable, so take extra precautions when you work on any part of the fuel system. Don't smoke or allow open flames or bare light bulbs near the work area, and don't work in a garage where a natural gas-type appliance is present. If you spill any fuel on your skin, rinse it off immediately with soap and water. When you perform any kind of work on the fuel system, wear safety glasses and have a fire extinguisher suitable for a class B type fire (flammable liquids) on hand.*

Fuel gauge

1 Remove any body panels as required for access to the top of the fuel tank (see Chapter 8).
2 Either disconnect the wiring connector from the top of the fuel level sensor, or trace the wiring to the connector and disconnect it **(see illustration)**.
3 Connect a jumper wire between the terminals on the wiring loom side of the connector. With the ignition switched ON, the fuel gauge should read FULL. If it doesn't, check the wiring between the connector and the gauge. If the wiring is good, then the gauge is confirmed faulty. **Note:** *On most scooters, the fuel gauge is integral with the instrument cluster, for which no individual parts are available. If the fuel gauge is faulty, the entire cluster must be renewed (see Section 12).*

Fuel level sensor

4 Disconnect the wiring connector from the fuel level sensor (see Steps 1 and 2). Release the sensor from the tank, noting the location of any locking tabs, then manoeuvre the unit out, noting how it fits **(see illustrations)**. **Note:** *On some scooters the sensor is retained by a locking ring. Note the location of the seal and*

11.4d Note the location of the seal

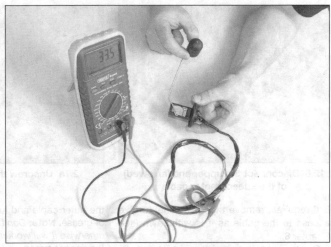

11.6 Set-up for testing the fuel level sensor

fit a new one on reassembly if it is damaged or deformed

 Warning: Block the opening in the tank to prevent the escape of petrol fumes and accidental fuel spillage.

5 Check the operation of the sensor – the arm should move freely without binding. Also check that the float is held securely on the arm and that it is not damaged. This will usually be apparent by the presence of fuel inside the float. If any of the component parts are faulty or damaged, fit a new sensor.

6 Check the operation of the sensor using a multimeter set to the ohms x 100 scale. Connect the probes to the terminals in the wiring connector with the float UP (tank full), then slowly lower the float to the DOWN (tank empty) position (see illustration).

7 As a general rule, when the tank is full a low resistance reading should be obtained, and when the tank is empty a higher reading should be obtained. If this is not the case the sensor is faulty and must be renewed.

8 If the sensor is good, check the wiring between the sensor and the gauge.

9 Check the condition of the sensor seal and fit a new one if it is deformed or perished. Insert the sensor carefully into the tank, then lock it in position.

12 Instrument cluster and speedometer cable

Instrument cluster

1 Special instruments are required to check the operation of the speedometer. If it is believed to be faulty, take the machine to a scooter specialist for assessment, although check first that the drive cable is not broken (see below).

2 Refer to Section 11 to check the fuel gauge and Section 5 to check the warning lights. Individual components are not available, so if an instrument or panel display is faulty, the entire cluster must be renewed.

3 Follow the procedure in Chapter 8, Section 8, to remove one or both of the handlebar covers – the instrument cluster is mounted in either the top or rear cover (see illustrations). Remove the screws securing the instrument cluster to the cover and lift it off.

4 Installation is the reverse of removal. Make sure that the speedometer cable and wiring connectors are correctly routed and secured.

Speedometer cable

Removal

5 Follow the procedure in Chapter 8, Section 8, to displace one or both of the handlebar covers to gain access to the upper end of the cable.

6 Unscrew the knurled ring securing the speedometer cable and disconnect it from the instrument cluster (see illustration).

7 Unscrew the knurled ring securing the lower end of the speedometer cable and pull the inner cable out of the drive housing (see illustrations). Note the forked end of the inner cable which locates over a tab inside the drive housing.

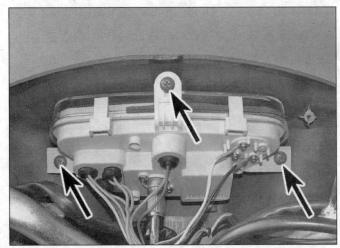

12.3a Instrument cluster is retained by screws (arrowed)

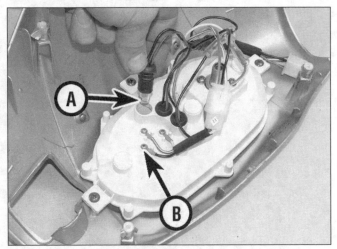

12.3b Note the location of the warning lights (A) and fuel gauge wiring terminals (B)

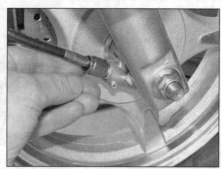

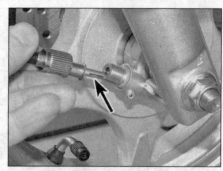

12.6 Disconnect the upper end (arrowed) of the speedometer cable

12.7a Unscrew the knurled ring . . .

12.7b . . . and withdraw the forked end (arrowed) of the inner cable

8 If required, remove the front panel to give access to the cable as it is withdrawn (see Chapter 8).

9 Pull the cable out carefully, releasing it from any guides and noting its correct routing.

10 If required, follow the procedure in Chapter 7, Section 13, to remove the speedometer drive housing.

Installation

11 If required, draw the inner cable out from the outer cable and lubricate it with a smear of grease. **Note:** *Don't apply too much grease otherwise it will work its way up the cable into the speedometer.*

12 Route the cable up through the any guides on the front suspension and inside the bodywork to the instrument cluster and connect the upper end securely to the speedometer **(see illustration 12.6)**.

13 Connect the lower end to the drive housing, ensuring that the inner cable is correctly installed, then tighten the knurled ring securely **(see illustrations 12.7b and a)**. Raise the front wheel clear of the ground and rotate it by hand to ensue the inner cable is correctly located.

14 Check that the cable doesn't restrict steering movement or interfere with any other components.

15 Install the remaining components in the reverse order of removal.

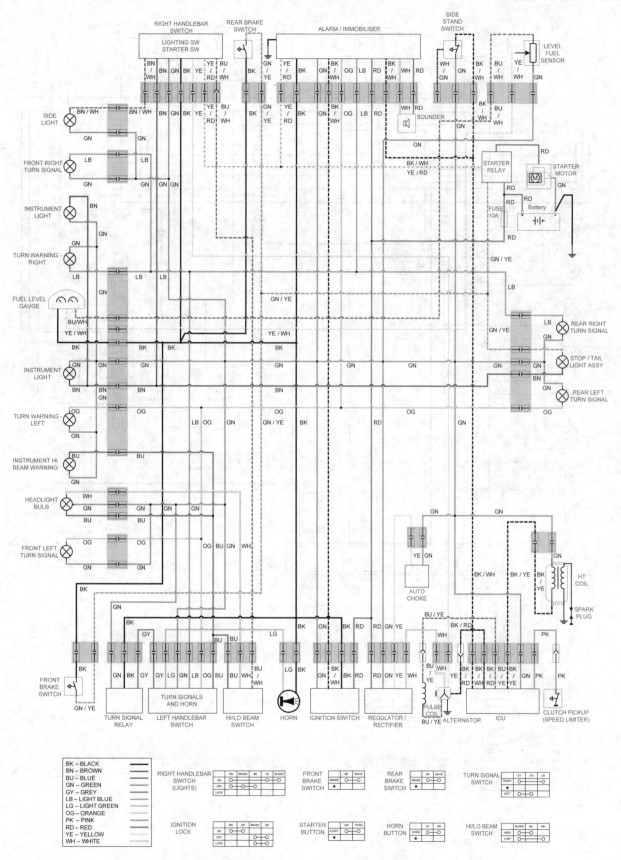

Wiring diagram – 50cc four-stroke models

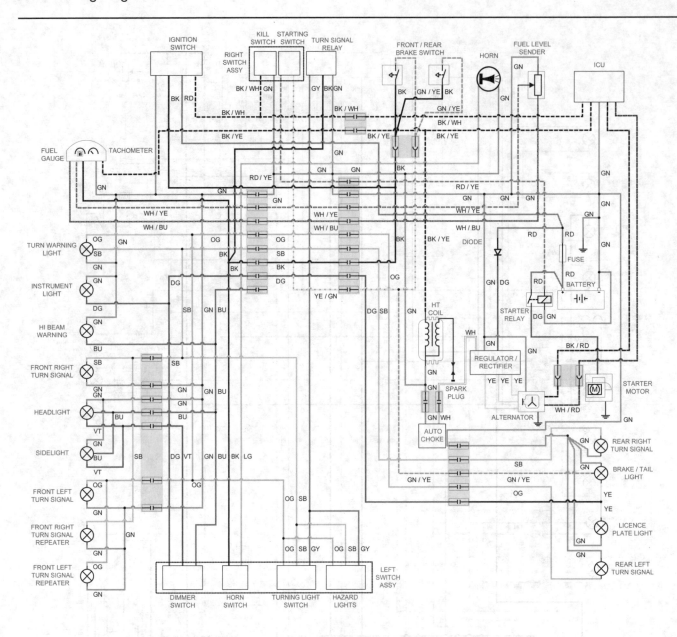

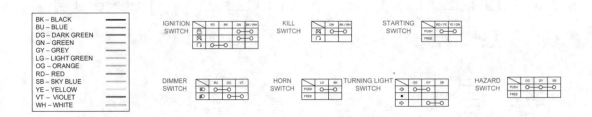

Wiring diagram – 125/150cc models

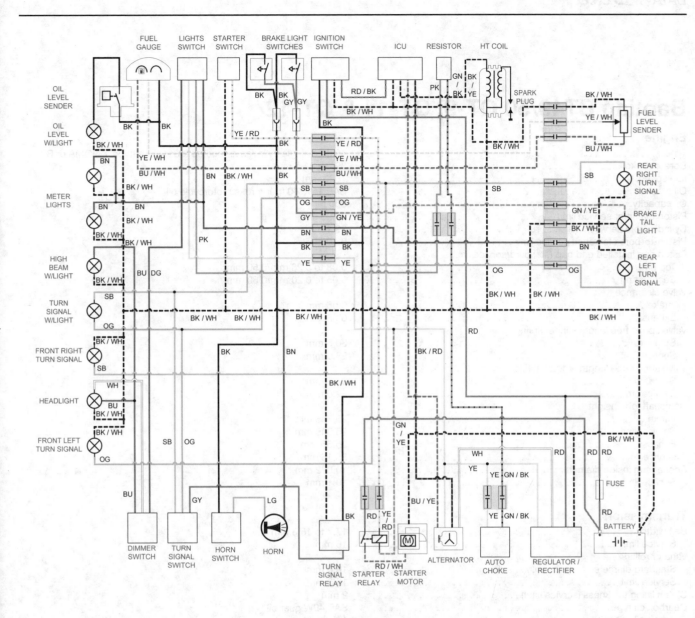

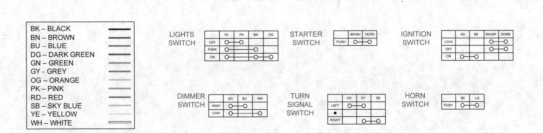

Wiring diagram – 50cc two-stroke models

Baotian BT49/50 QT-9, QT-11 & QT-12

Engine

Type	49.5 cc single cylinder, air-cooled four-stroke (type 139QMA or B)
Bore x stroke	39.0 x 41.5 mm
Idle speed.	1800 rpm
Oil type.	SAE 15W/40 four-stroke motorcycle oil
Oil capacity.	800 ml
Piston diameter service limit	38.93 mm
Cylinder bore service limit	39.1 mm
Piston-to-bore clearance service limit	0.10 mm
Piston ring installed end gap (standard/service limit)	
Top ring.	0.08 to 0.20 mm/0.50 mm
Second ring	0.05 to 0.20 mm/0.50 mm
Valve clearance	
Intake	0.06 mm
Exhaust	0.08 mm
Valve spring free length – inner spring	
Standard.	30.5 mm
Service limit	28.5 mm
Valve spring free length – outer spring	
Standard.	34.1 mm
Service limit	32.0 mm
Camshaft lobe height	
Intake	25.745 mm
Service limit	25.345 mm
Exhaust.	25.55 mm
service limit	25.15 mm
Rocker arm inside diameter	10.022 mm
Service limit	10.1 mm

Transmission

Belt width	17.7 to 18.3 mm
Service limit	16 mm
Variator rollers	
Standard diameter	16.0 mm
Service limit	15.5 mm
Clutch lining thickness (service limit)	2 mm
Gearbox oil type.	SAE 40W gear oil
Gearbox oil capacity	110 ml

Fuel system

Fuel tank capacity	6.5 litres
Carburettor type.	PZ18J
Pilot screw setting	2 ± 1/2 turns out
Throttle cable freeplay	2 to 6 mm

Ignition system

Spark plug type	NGK C7HSA
Electrode gap.	0.6 to 0.7 mm
Timing	
At 1700 rpm	13° BTDC (F mark aligned)
At 3800 rpm (full advance)	28° BTDC
Pulse generator coil resistance	50 to 200 ohms
HT coil primary resistance	0.2 to 0.3 ohm
HT coil secondary resistance	
with plug cap	8 to 12 K-ohms
without plug cap.	3 to 5 K-ohms

Brakes

Disc brake fluid type.	DOT 4
Drum brake lever freeplay	10 to 20 mm at lever ball end

Tyres

Sizes	
QT-9 and QT-11	3.50-10
QT-12	120/70-12
Pressures	
Front	29 psi (2.0 Bar)
Rear	33 psi (2.3 Bar)

Electrical system

Battery	YTX5L-BS
Capacity	12V, 4Ah
Voltage (fully charged)	13.1V
Alternator	
Output (regulated).	14 to 15V (DC)
Charging coil resistance.	0.2 to 1.0 ohm
Lighting coil resistance.	0.1 to 0.8 ohm
Fuse	10A
Bulbs	
Headlight	35W (halogen on QT-12 Tanco and Rocky)
Brake/tail light.	21/8W
Turn signal lights.	10W
Instrument and warning lights	5W

Torque wrench settings

Cylinder head nuts	17 Nm
Engine mounting nut	45 Nm
Flywheel nut	40 Nm
Variator centre nut	55 Nm
Clutch centre nut	40 Nm
Rear shock absorber lower bolt.	40 Nm
Rear shock absorber upper bolt	25 Nm
Steering head bearing locknut	70 Nm
Handlebar bolt and nut.	45 Nm
Front axle nut	60 Nm
Rear hub nut.	120 Nm

Daelim Cordi

Engine

Type	49.5 cc single-cylinder two-stroke
Cooling system	Air-cooled
Fuel system	Slide piston carburetor
Ignition system	CDI
Transmission	Variable speed automatic, belt driven
Suspension	Telescopic front, swingarm with single shock rear
Brakes	Disc front, drum rear
Tires (front and rear)	90/90-10-50J
Wheelbase	1227 mm
Weight (dry)	76.5 kg
Fuel tank capacity	4.8 litres

Engine

Spark plug type	
Standard	NGK BP6HS or BPR6HS
Low speed riding	NGK B46HSA or BR46HSA
High speed riding	NGK BP7HS or BPR7HS
Electrode gap	0.6 to 0.7 mm
Idle speed (rpm)	1800 to 2000 rpm
Engine oil type	2-stroke oil
Engine oil capacity	1.2 litres
Bore x stroke	40 x 39.4 mm
Piston diameter	
ID mark A	39.955 to 39.960 mm
No ID mark	39.960 to 39.965 mm
ID mark B	39.965 to 39.970 mm
Service limit, all grade marks	39.90 mm
Piston to bore clearance	
Standard	0.40 to 0.55 mm
Service limit	0.13 mm
Piston ring installed end gap (top and second)	0.15 to 0.30 mm

Fuel system

Throttle twistgrip freeplay	2 to 6 mm
Main jet	77
Slow jet	38
Needle type/position	Not specified
Air screw setting	1-1/2 turns out
Float level	8 mm

Ignition system

Ignition coil peak primary voltage	300 volts minimum
Ignition pulse generator peak voltage	2.8 volts minimum
Ignition pulse generator resistance	400 to 800 ohms
Exciter coil resistance	50 to 200 ohms
Ignition coil primary resistance	0.1 to 0.5 ohm
Ignition coil secondary resistance (cap installed)	6.3 to 10.3 K-ohms

Transmission

Belt width (service limit)	15.5 mm
Weight roller outer diameter	
Standard	15.920 to 16.080 mm
Service limit	15.4 mm
Clutch lining thickness (service limit)	2.0 mm
Clutch spring free length	98.1 mm

Brakes

Brake fluid	DOT 4
Disc thickness (limit)	2.5 mm
Pad wear limit	To wear line
Brake lever freeplay (front and rear)	10 to 20 mm
Rear brake shoe wear limit	When wear indicator marks align or 2.0 mm
Rear brake drum diameter (limit)	95.5 mm

Tyre pressures

Front	25 psi
Rear	29 psi

Electrical system

Battery	
Capacity	12V-3Ah
Voltage (fully charged)	13.0 to 13.2 volts
Alternator	
Output (regulated)	13.0 to 15.0 volts
Charging coil resistance	0.4 to 1.0 ohms
Fuse	7 amps

Torque wrench settings

Transmission oil check bolt	13 Nm
Cylinder head nuts	10 Nm
Drive pulley nut	54 Nm
Clutch driven face nut	54 Nm
Clutch outer nut	39 Nm
Alternator rotor nut	39 Nm
Crankcase bolts	10 Nm
Engine hanger bracket nut	
To engine	49 Nm
To frame	72 Nm
Front axle nut	59 Nm
Rear axle nut	108 Nm
Handlebar to steering stem post nut	49 Nm
Handlebar to steering stem bolt	49 Nm
Steering stem bearing adjustment nut	
First step	10 Nm
Second step	Loosen 1/8 turn
Steering stem locknut	68 Nm
Steering stem to fork bolt	34 to 44 Nm
Front fork damper rod bolts	20 Nm
Front fork to triple clamp bolts	40 Nm
Rear shock bolts (upper and lower)	40 Nm
Swingarm mounting bolts	49 Nm
Front brake bolts	
Caliper bracket bolts	27 Nm
Caliper pad pins	18 Nm
Caliper slide pins	23 Nm
Brake hose union bolts	35 Nm
Rear brake arm bolt	6 Nm

Daelim Delfino

Engine	99.7 cc single-cylinder two-stroke
Cooling system.	Air-cooled
Fuel system	Slide piston carburetor
Ignition system	CDI
Transmission.	Variable speed automatic, belt driven
Suspension	Telescopic front, swingarm with single shock rear
Brakes	Disc front, drum rear
Tires (front and rear)	100/90-10 56J
Wheelbase	1290 mm
Weight (dry)	220 kg
Fuel tank capacity	7.2 litres

Engine

Spark plug type	NGK BR8HS
Electrode gap	0.6 to 0.7-mm
Idle speed (rpm)	1800 rpm
Engine oil type	2-stroke oil (DMC Ultra or equivalent)
Engine oil capacity	1.2 litres
Bore x stroke	50.6 x 49.6 mm
Piston diameter (3 mm up from bottom of skirt)	
ID mark B	50.565 to 50.569 mm
ID mark A	50.570 to 50.574 mm
No ID mark	50.575 to 50.579 mm
Piston to bore clearance (limit)	0.10 mm
Piston ring installed end gap	
Top - standard	0.15 to 0.35 mm
Service limit	0.60 mm
Second - standard	0.15 to 0.35 mm
Service limit	0.40 mm

Fuel system

Throttle twistgrip freeplay	2 to 6 mm
Main jet	88
Slow jet	38
Needle type/position	Not specified
Airscrew setting	1-1/8 turns out
Float level	8 mm

Ignition system

Ignition pulse generator resistance	50 to 200 ohms
Ignition coil primary resistance.	0.1 to 0.3 ohm
Ignition coil secondary resistance (cap installed)	7.5 to 8.6 K-ohms
Ignition coil secondary resistance (without cap)	2.7 to 3.5 K-ohms

Transmission

Belt width (service limit)	16.5 mm
Weight roller outer diameter	
Standard	15.920 to 16.080 mm
Limit	15.4 mm
Clutch lining thickness (service limit)	2.0 mm
Clutch spring free length (limit).	137.5 mm

Brakes

Brake fluid	DOT 4
Disc thickness (limit).	3.0 mm
Pad wear limit.	To wear line
Rear brake lever freeplay	10 to 20 mm
Rear brake shoe wear limit.	When wear indicator marks align or 2.0 mm
Rear brake drum diameter (limit)	111 mm

Tire pressures

Front.	22 psi
Rear	
Rider only	25 psi
Rider and passenger	32 psi

Electrical system

Battery	
Capacity	12V-3Ah
Voltage (fully charged)	13.0 to 13.2 volts
Alternator	
Output (regulated).	13.0 to 15.0 volts
Charging coil resistance	0.3 to 1.2 ohms
Fuse	7 amps

Torque wrench settings

Transmission oil check bolt	18 Nm
Cylinder head bolts	10 Nm
Drive pulley nut.	44 Nm
Clutch driven face nut	54 Nm
Clutch outer nut	39 Nm
Alternator rotor nut.	39 Nm
Crankcase bolts	Not specified
Engine hanger bracket nut	70 Nm
Front axle nut	58 Nm
Rear axle nut	117 Nm
Steering stem locknut	68 Nm
Handlebar to steering stem bolt.	44 Nm
Steering stem bearing adjustment nut	
First step	10 Nm
Second step	Loosen 1/8 turn
Rear shock bolts	
Upper	39 Nm
Lower	25 Nm
Swingarm mounting bolts	48 Nm
Front brake bolts	
Caliper bracket bolts	28 Nm
Caliper pad pins	18 Nm
Caliper slide pins	23 Nm
Brake hose union bolts	34 Nm
Rear brake arm bolt	6 Nm

Daelim E-FIVE, S-FIVE

Engine . . . . 49.5 cc single-cylinder two-stroke
Cooling system. . . . . Air-cooled
Fuel system . . . . Piston valve carburetor
Ignition system . . . . CDI
Transmission. . . . . Variable speed automatic, belt driven
Suspension . . . . Telescopic front, swingarm with single shock rear
Brakes . . . . Disc front, drum rear
Tires 130/90-10 61J
Wheelbase . . . . 1260 mm
Weight (dry)
    E-FIVE . . . . 86 kg
    S-FIVE . . . . 94 kg
Fuel tank capacity . . . . 6 litres

Engine

Spark plug type
    E-FIVE NGKB7HS
    S-FIVE NGKB8HSA
Electrode gap . . . . 0.6 to 0.7 mm
Idle speed (rpm) . . . . 1800 ± 100 rpm
Engine oil type . . . . 2-stroke oil
Engine oil capacity. . . . . 1.2 litres
Bore x stroke . . . . 39.0 x 41.1 mm
Piston diameter (service limit, all grade marks) . . . . 38.9 mm
Piston to bore clearance (service limit). . . . . 0.10 mm
Piston ring installed end gap (top and second)
    Standard . . . . 0.10 to 0.25 mm
    Service limit . . . . 0.40 mm

Fuel system

Throttle twistgrip freeplay. . . . . 2 to 6 mm
Main jet 75
Slow jet 38
Needle type/position . . . . Not specified
Air screw setting. . . . . 1-1/4 turns out
Float level . . . . 8 mm

Ignition system

Ignition coil peak primary voltage . . . . 120 volts minimum
Ignition pulse generator peak voltage . . . . 1.5 volts minimum
Ignition pulse generator resistance . . . . 100 ohms ± 20%
Ignition coil primary resistance. . . . . 0.1 to 0.5 ohm
Ignition coil secondary resistance (cap installed). . . . . 6.5 to 9.5 K-ohms

Transmission

Belt width (service limit) . . . . 16.5 mm
Weight roller outer diameter
    Standard . . . . 15.920 to 16.080 mm
    Service limit . . . . 15.4 mm
Clutch lining thickness (service limit) . . . . 2.0 mm
Clutch spring free length (service limit) . . . . 98.1 mm

Brakes

Brake fluid . . . . DOT 4
Disc thickness (limit). . . . . 3.0 mm
Pad wear limit. . . . . To wear line
Brake lever freeplay (front and rear) . . . . 10 to 20 mm
Rear brake shoe wear limit. . . . . When wear indicator marks align or 2.0 mm
Rear brake drum diameter (limit) . . . . 111 mm

Tyre pressures

Front . . . . 25 psi
Rear . . . . 29 psi

Electrical system

Battery
  Capacity 12V-3Ah
  Voltage (fully charged) . . . . 13.0 to 13.2 volts
Alternator
  Output (regulated). . . . . 14.0 to 15.0 volts
  Charging coil resistance . . . . 0.8 ohms ± 20%
Fuse . . . . 7 amps

Torque wrench settings

Transmission oil check bolt . . . . 13 Nm
Cylinder head nuts . . . . 10 Nm
Clutch driven face nut . . . . 54 Nm
Drive face nut . . . . 39 Nm
Clutch outer nut . . . . 39 Nm
Alternator rotor nut . . . . 39 Nm
Starter clutch Allen bolts . . . . 28 Nm
Crankcase bolts . . . . 10 Nm
Engine hanger bracket nut
  To engine. . . . . 49 Nm
  To frame . . . . 72 Nm
Front axle nut . . . . 59 Nm
Rear axle nut. . . . . Not specified
Handlebar to steering stem bolt. . . . . 49 Nm
Steering stem bearing adjustment nut
  First step . . . . 10 Nm
  Second step . . . . Loosen 1/8 turn
Steering stem locknut . . . . 68 Nm
Steering stem to fork bolt. . . . . 34 to 44 Nm
Front fork damper rod bolts . . . . 20 Nm
Front fork to triple clamp bolts. . . . . Not specified
Rear shock bolts (upper and lower) . . . . 39 Nm
Swingarm mounting bolts . . . . 48 Nm
Front brake bolts
  Caliper bracket bolts . . . . 26 Nm
  Caliper pin bolt . . . . Not specified
  Caliper pad pins . . . . 18 Nm
  Caliper brake hose union bolt . . . . 34 Nm
Rear brake arm bolt . . . . Not specified

Keeway Hurricane, Matrix, F-act (Focus) & Flash 50

Engine
Type . . . . 49.8 cc single cylinder air-cooled two-stroke
Bore x stroke . . . . 40.0 x 39.2 mm
Idle speed. . . . . 1800 ± 100 rpm
Oil type. . . . . Two-stroke (2T) motorcycle oil
Oil tank capacity. . . . . 1.0 litre
Piston diameter service limit . . . . 39.885 mm
Cylinder bore service limit . . . . 40.075 mm
Piston to bore clearance service limit . . . . 0.12 mm
Piston ring installed end gap . . . . 0.75 mm
Piston ring free end gap. . . . . 3.6 mm

Transmission
Belt width service limit . . . . 16 mm
Clutch lining thickness service limit . . . . 1.2 mm
Clutch drum ID service limit . . . . 112.5 mm
Clutch spring free length
    Standard . . . . 69 mm
    Service limit . . . . 64.5 mm
Gearbox oil . . . . SAE85W/90 gear oil
Gearbox oil capacity . . . . 100 ml

Fuel system
Fuel tank capacity
    Hurricane, Flash . . . . 5 litres
    Matrix, F-act (Focus) . . . . 4.8 litres
Throttle cable freeplay . . . . 0.5 to 1 mm
Carburettor type. . . . . PZ19JB slide type
    Main jet. 80
    Pilot jet 57.5
    Needle clip position . . . . 3rd groove from top
    Pilot screw setting . . . . 1 1/2 ± 1/2 turns out
    Float height. . . . . 13 ± 1 mm

Ignition system
Spark plug type
    Hurricane . . . . NGK BPR7BHS
    Matrix . . . . NGK BR8HSA
    Flash, F-act (Focus) . . . . NGK BR7ES
Electrode gap. . . . . 0.6 to 0.7 mm
Timing. . . . . 15° BTDC
HT coil secondary winding resistance . . . . 12 to 18 K-ohms with plug cap

Brakes
Disc brake
    Fluid type . . . . DOT 4
    Pad minimum thickness . . . . To wear limit indicator
    Disc thickness (service limit). . . . . 3.5 mm
Drum brake
    Drum internal diameter (service limit). . . . . 110.7 mm
    Shoe lining minimum thickness . . . . 1.5 mm
    Brake lever freeplay . . . . 15 to 25 mm at lever ball end

Tyres

Sizes
Hurricane 3.50-10
F-act (Focus), Matrix . . . . 120/70-12 front, 130/70-12 rear
Flash . . . . 3.00-10 or 3.50-10
Pressures
Hurricane . . . . 22 psi (1.5 Bar) front, 25 psi (1.75 Bar) rear
F-act (Focus), Matrix . . . . 32 psi (2.2 Bar)
Flash . . . . 36 psi (2.5 Bar)

Electrical system

Battery
Hurricane, Matrix, F-act (Focus) 12V 4Ah
Flash 12V 3Ah
Alternator
Output (regulated) . . . . 13 to 16V (DC) @ 5000 rpm
Charging coil resistance . . . . 0.5 to 1.1 ohms
Starter motor brush service limit . . . . 3.5 mm
Fuse 10A
Bulbs
Headlight (main/dipped) 35/35W
Brake/tail light 21/5W
Turn signal lights 10W

Torque wrench settings

Spark plug . . . . 15 to 18 Nm
Cylinder head nuts . . . . 18 to 28 Nm
Oil pump bolts . . . . 3 to 5 Nm
Engine mounting bolts . . . . 37 to 44 Nm
Exhaust manifold nuts . . . . 8 to 12 Nm
Exhaust system mounting bolts . . . . 18 to 28 Nm
Alternator rotor nut . . . . 35 to 45 Nm
Stator plate screws . . . . 10 to 12 Nm
Variator centre nut . . . . 40 to 60 Nm
Clutch assembly nut . . . . 40 to 60 Nm
Gearbox oil filler/level plug . . . . 9 to15 Nm
Rear shock absorber lower bolt . . . . 22 to 29 Nm
Rear shock absorber upper bolt . . . . 37 to 44 Nm
Steering head bearing locknut . . . . 37 to 44 Nm
Handlebar stem bolt . . . . 37 to 44 Nm
Front axle nut . . . . 37 to 44 Nm
Rear hub nut . . . . 85 to 98 Nm

Keeway ARN, Matrix & F-act (Focus) 125

Engine

Type	124.6 cc single cylinder air-cooled four-stroke
Bore x stroke	52.4 x 57.8 mm
Idle speed	1600 ± 100 rpm
Oil type	SAE 10W/40 four-stroke motorcycle oil
Oil capacity	1.0 litre
Piston diameter	
Size code A	52.370 to 52.375 mm
Size code B	52.375 to 52.380 mm
Cylinder bore diameter	
Size code A	52.400 to 52.405 mm
Size code B	52.405 to 52.410 mm
Piston-to-bore clearance	0.025 to 0.035 mm
Piston ring installed end gap	
Top and second rings	0.1 to 0.2 mm
Oil control ring	0.3 to 0.4 mm
Valve clearance	0.12 to 0.16 mm
Valve spring free length	
Inner spring	32.3 ± 0.05 mm
Outer spring	35.0 ± 0.05 mm
Camshaft lobe height	
Intake	29.625 ± 0.05 mm
Exhaust	29.038 ± 0.05 mm
Cylinder compression service limit	174 psi (12 Bars)

Transmission

Gearbox oil	SAE85W/90 gear oil
Gearbox oil capacity	
ARN	220 ml
Matrix, Focus	100 ml

Fuel system

Fuel tank capacity	5.2 litres
Carburettor type	PD24JC CV type
Main jet	179
Pilot jet	30
Pilot screw setting	1 to 2 turns out
Float height	13 ± 1 mm

Ignition system

Spark plug type . . . . NGK C7HSA
Electrode gap . . . . 0.6 to 0.7 mm
Timing
    At 1700 rpm (F mark aligned) . . . . 15° BTDC
    At full advance (4000 rpm) . . . . 28° BTDC
Pulse generator coil resistance . . . . 100 to 180 ohms
HT primary resistance . . . . 0.25 ± 0.05 ohm
HT coil secondary resistance
    with plug cap . . . . 7.5 ± 1 K-ohms
    without plug cap . . . . 3.4 ± 0.3 K-ohms

Brakes

Disc brake
    Fluid type . . . . DOT 4
    Pad minimum thickness . . . . To wear limit indicator
    Disc thickness . . . . 4 mm
Drum brake
    Drum internal diameter . . . . 130 mm
    Shoe lining thickness . . . . 6 mm
    Brake lever freeplay . . . . 15 to 25 mm at lever ball end

Tyres

Size . . . . 120/70 x 12 front, 130/70 x 12 rear
Pressure
    ARN . . . . 25 psi (1.75 Bar) front, 29 psi (2.0 Bar) rear
    Matrix, F-act (Focus) . . . . 32 psi (2.2 Bar)

Electrical system

Battery 12V 6Ah
Alternator
    Output (regulated) . . . . 14.4 ± 0.4V (DC)
    Charging and lighting coil resistance . . . . less than 2 ohms
Fuse
    ARN, Matrix 15A
    Focus 8A
Bulbs
    Headlight (main/dipped) 35/35W
    Brake/tail light 21/5W
    Turn signal lights 10W

Torque wrench settings

Valve cover bolts . . . . 10 to 12 Nm
Spark plug . . . . 10 to 15 Nm
Engine mounting bolts . . . . 45 to 58 Nm
Alternator rotor nut . . . . 45 to 55 Nm
Stator coil screws . . . . 6 to 8 Nm
Oil pump bolts . . . . 10 to 12 Nm
Handlebar stem bolt . . . . 37 to 44 Nm
Front axle nut . . . . 55 to 62 Nm

Kymco Super 8 50

Engine

Type	49.5 cc single cylinder, air-cooled four-stroke
Bore x stroke	39.0 x 41.4 mm
Idle speed	1900 ± 100 rpm
Oil type	SAE 15W/40 API SF four-stroke motorcycle oil
Oil capacity	700 ml
Piston-to-bore clearance service limit	0.10 mm
Piston ring installed end gap service limit	0.45 mm
Cylinder compression pressure	228 psi (16 Bars)
Valve clearance	0.04 mm
Valve spring free length – inner spring	
Standard	31.1 mm
Service limit	30.1 mm
Valve spring free length – outer spring	
Standard	34.3 mm
Service limit	33.3 mm
Camshaft lobe height service limit	
Intake	26.038 mm
Exhaust	25.407 mm
Rocker arm inside diameter	10.000 to 10.015 mm
Service limit	10.1 mm

Transmission

Belt width	17.5 mm
Service limit	16.5 mm
Variator rollers	
Standard diameter	15.920 to 16.080 mm
Service limit	15.4 mm
Clutch drum diameter service limit	107.5 mm
Clutch lining thickness service limit	1.5 mm
Spring free length service limit	97 mm
Gearbox oil type	SAE 90W gear oil
Gearbox oil capacity	180 ml

Fuel system

Fuel tank capacity	6 litres
Carburettor type	CVK 18.5 mm
Main jet	80
Pilot jet	35
Pilot screw setting	2 ± 1/2 turns out
Float height	10 mm
Automatic choke resistance	10 ohms
Throttle cable freeplay	2 to 6 mm

Ignition system

Spark plug type	NGK CR7HSA
Electrode gap	0.6 to 0.7 mm
Timing	
At idle (F mark)	13° BTDC @ 1700 rpm
At full advance	28° BTDC @ 4000 rpm
Pulse generator coil resistance	40 to 300 ohms
HT coil primary resistance	0.1 to 1.0 ohm
HT coil secondary resistance	
with plug cap	7 to 12 K-ohms
without plug cap	3 to 5 K-ohms

Brakes

Disc brake
  Fluid type . . . . DOT 4
  Disc thickness service limit . . . . 3 mm
Drum brake
  Drum diameter service limit . . . . 131 mm
  Shoe lining service limit . . . . 2 mm
  Brake lever freeplay . . . . 10 to 20 mm at lever ball end

Tyres

Sizes
  Front 100/80-14
  Rear 120/80-14
Pressures
  Front . . . . 22 psi (1.5 Bars)
  Rear . . . . 29 psi (2.0 Bars)

Electrical system

Battery 12V, 4Ah
  Voltage – fully charged 13.1V
  Voltage – undercharged 12.3V
Alternator
  Output (regulated). . . . . 14.5 ± 0.5V (DC)
  Charging coil resistance . . . . 0.1 to 1.0 ohm
Fuse 7A, 10A, 10A
Starter motor brush length service limit . . . . 8.5 mm

Torque wrench settings

Spark plug . . . . 10 to 14 Nm
Cylinder head cover bolts . . . . 8 to 12 Nm
Cylinder head nuts . . . . 18 to 22 Nm
Crankcase bolts . . . . 8 to 12 Nm
Exhaust manifold nuts . . . . 10 to 14 Nm
Exhaust mounting bolts . . . . 30 to 36 Nm
Oil filter screen cap. . . . . 10 to 20 Nm
Oil drain bolt . . . . 11 to 15 Nm
Oil pump bolts . . . . 1 to 3 Nm
Engine mounting nut . . . . 45 to 50 Nm
Alternator nut . . . . 35 to 45 Nm
Alternator stator bolts. . . . . 8 to 12 Nm
Variator centre nut . . . . 35 to 40 Nm
Clutch assembly nut. . . . . 50 to 60 Nm
Clutch centre nut . . . . 35 to 40 Nm
Rear shock absorber lower bolt . . . . 24 to 30 Nm
Rear shock absorber upper bolt . . . . 35 to 45 Nm
Steering head bearing locknut . . . . 60 to 80 Nm
Handlebar bolt and nut. . . . . 45 to 55 Nm
Front axle nut . . . . 50 to 70 Nm
Rear hub nut . . . . 110 to 130 Nm

Kymco Super 8 125

Engine

Type	124.6 cc single cylinder, air-cooled four-stroke
Bore x stroke	52.4 x 57.8 mm
Idle speed	1700 ± 100 rpm
Oil type	SAE 15W/40 API SF four-stroke motorcycle oil
Oil capacity	800 ml
Piston diameter service limit	52.3 mm
Cylinder bore diameter service limit	52.5 mm
Piston-to-bore clearance service limit	0.10 mm
Piston ring installed end gap service limit	0.5 mm
Cylinder compression pressure	184 psi (13 Bars)
Valve clearance	0.12 mm
Valve spring free length service limit	
Inner spring	32.3 mm
Outer spring	35.0 mm
Camshaft lobe height service limit	
Intake	29.40 mm
Exhaust	29.16 mm
Rocker arm inside diameter	10.000 to 10.015 mm
Service limit	10.1 mm

Transmission

Belt width	17.5 mm
Service limit	16.5 mm
Variator rollers	
Standard diameter	15.920 to 16.080 mm
Service limit	15.4 mm
Clutch lining thickness service limit	1.5 mm
Clutch drum diameter service limit	125.5 mm
Spring free length service limit	147.6 mm
Gearbox oil type	SAE 90W gear oil
Gearbox oil capacity	180 ml

Fuel system

Fuel tank capacity	6 litres
Carburettor type	CVK 26 mm
Main jet	104
Pilot jet	35
Pilot screw setting	3 ± 1/2 turns out
Float height	17 mm
Automatic choke resistance	10 ohms
Throttle cable freeplay	2 to 6 mm

Ignition system

Spark plug type	NGK CR7HSA
Electrode gap	0.6 to 0.7 mm
Timing	
At idle (F mark)	13° BTDC @ 1700 rpm
At full advance	27° BTDC @ 4000 rpm
Pulse generator coil resistance	40 to 300 ohms
HT coil primary resistance	0.1 to 1.0 ohm
HT coil secondary resistance	
with plug cap	7 to 12 K-ohms
without plug cap	3 to 5 K-ohms

Brakes

Disc brake
    Fluid type . . . . DOT 4
    Disc thickness service limit . . . . 3 mm
Rear drum brake
    Drum diameter service limit . . . . 131 mm
    Shoe lining service limit . . . . 1.5 mm
    Brake lever freeplay . . . . 10 to 20 mm at lever ball end

Tyres

Sizes
    Front 100/80-14
    Rear 120/80-14
Pressures
    Front . . . . 22 psi (1.5 Bar)
    Rear . . . . 29 psi (2.0 Bar)

Electrical system

Battery 12V, 7Ah
    Voltage – fully charged 13.1V
    Voltage – undercharged 12.3V
Alternator
    Output (regulated). . . . . 14.5 ± 0.5V (DC)
    Charging coil resistance . . . . 0.1 to 1.0 ohm
Fuse 7A, 10A, 10A
Starter motor brush length service limit . . . . 8.5 mm

Torque wrench settings

Spark plug . . . . 10 to 14 Nm
Cylinder head nuts . . . . 20 Nm
Crankcase bolts . . . . 8 to 12 Nm
Exhaust manifold nuts . . . . 10 to 14 Nm
Exhaust mounting bolts . . . . 30 to 36 Nm
Oil filter screen cap. . . . . 10 to 20 Nm
Oil drain bolt . . . . 11 to 15 Nm
Oil pump bolts . . . . 1 to 3 Nm
Alternator nut . . . . 35 to 45 Nm
Alternator stator bolts. . . . . 8 to 12 Nm
Variator centre nut . . . . 35 to 40 Nm
Clutch assembly nut. . . . . 50 to 60 Nm
Clutch centre nut . . . . 35 to 40 Nm
Rear shock absorber lower bolt . . . . 24 to 30 Nm
Rear shock absorber upper bolt . . . . 35 to 45 Nm
Steering head bearing locknut . . . . 60 to 80 Nm
Handlebar bolt and nut. . . . . 45 to 55 Nm
Front axle nut . . . . 50 to 70 Nm
Rear hub nut. . . . . 110 to 130 Nm

Kymco ZX50

Engine

Type	49.4 cc single cylinder air-cooled two-stroke
Bore x stroke	39.0 x 41.4 mm
Idle speed.	2100 ± 100 rpm
Oil type	Two-stroke (2T) motorcycle oil to JASO FC
Oil tank capacity.	800 ml
Compression pressure	164 psi (11.5 Bars)
Piston diameter service limit	38.90 mm
Cylinder bore service limit	39.05 mm
Piston-to-bore clearance service limit	0.10 mm
Piston ring installed end gap service limit	0.40 mm

Transmission

Belt width service limit	17 mm
Clutch lining thickness service limit	2 mm
Clutch drum ID service limit	107.5 mm
Clutch roller diameter service limit	12.4 mm
Clutch spring free length service limit	82.6 mm
Gearbox oil.	SAE90W gear oil
Gearbox oil capacity	100 ml

Fuel system

Fuel tank capacity	4.9 litres
Throttle cable freeplay	2 to 6 mm
Carburettor type.	Slide type 14 mm
Main jet	80
Pilot jet	35.5
Needle clip position	1st groove from top
Pilot screw setting	1 ± 1/4 turn out
Float height.	5 mm
Automatic choke resistance.	5 ohms

Ignition system

Spark plug type	NGK BR8HSA
Electrode gap.	0.6 to 0.7 mm
Timing.	15.5 ± 2° BTDC
HT coil primary winding resistance	0.15 to 0.19 ohms
HT coil secondary winding resistance	
with plug cap	7 to 10 K-ohms
without plug cap.	3.2 to 4 K-ohms
Pulse generator coil resistance	80 to 160 ohms

Brakes

Disc brake

    Fluid type . . . . DOT 4

    Pad minimum thickness . . . . 2 mm

    Disc thickness service limit . . . . 3.0 mm

Drum brake

    Drum internal diameter service limit . . . . 111 mm

    Shoe lining minimum thickness . . . . 2 mm

Rear brake lever freeplay . . . . 10 to 20 mm at lever ball end

Tyres

Size 120/70-12

Pressures

    Front . . . . 22 psi (1.5 Bar)

    Rear . . . . 25 psi (1.75 Bar)

Electrical system

Battery 12V 3Ah

Battery terminal voltage . . . . 12.8V minimum

Alternator

    Output (regulated) . . . . 14.5 ± 0.5V (DC) @ 8000 rpm

    Charging coil resistance . . . . 0.2 to 1.2 ohm

    Lighting coil resistance . . . . 0.3 to 1.0 ohm

Fuse 7A

Torque wrench settings

Spark plug . . . . 11 to 17 Nm

Cylinder head bolts . . . . 15 to 17 Nm

Exhaust manifold nuts . . . . 10 to 14 Nm

Exhaust system mounting bolts . . . . 30 to 36 Nm

Engine mounting bracket-to-frame bolt . . . . 35 to 45 Nm

Engine mounting bracket-to-engine bolt . . . . 45 to 55 Nm

Alternator rotor nut . . . . 35 to 40 Nm

Stator plate screws . . . . 8 to 12 Nm

Variator centre nut . . . . 35 to 40 Nm

Clutch assembly nut . . . . 50 to 60 Nm

Clutch centre nut . . . . 35 to 45 Nm

Gearbox oil level plug . . . . 10 to15 Nm

Rear shock absorber lower bolt . . . . 24 to 30 Nm

Rear shock absorber upper bolt . . . . 35 to 45 Nm

Steering head bearing locknut . . . . 45 Nm

Handlebar nut . . . . 33 Nm

Front axle nut . . . . 50 to 70 Nm

Rear hub nut . . . . 110 to 130 Nm

Kymco YUP 50

Engine

Type	49.4 cc single cylinder air-cooled two-stroke
Bore x stroke	39.0 x 41.4 mm
Idle speed.	2100 ± 100 rpm
Oil type.	Two-stroke (2T) motorcycle oil to JASO FC
Oil tank capacity.	800 ml
Compression pressure	164 psi (11.5 Bars)
Piston diameter service limit	38.90 mm
Cylinder bore service limit	39.05 mm
Piston-to-bore clearance service limit	0.10 mm
Piston ring installed end gap service limit	0.40 mm

Transmission

Belt width service limit	17 mm
Clutch lining thickness service limit	2 mm
Clutch drum ID service limit	107.5 mm
Clutch roller diameter service limit.	15.4 mm
Clutch spring free length service limit	82.6 mm
Gearbox oil.	SAE90W gear oil
Gearbox oil capacity	80 ml

Fuel system

Fuel tank capacity	5.3 litres
Throttle cable freeplay	2 to 6 mm
Carburettor type.	Slide type 14 mm PB058
Main jet.	75
Pilot jet	35
Needle clip position	1st groove from top
Pilot screw setting	1 ± 1/4 turn out
Float height.	8.6 mm
Automatic choke resistance.	5 ohms

Ignition system

Spark plug type	NGK BR8HSA
Electrode gap.	0.6 to 0.7 mm
Timing.	13.5 ± 1.5° BTDC
HT coil primary winding resistance	0.15 to 0.19 ohms
HT coil secondary winding resistance	
with plug cap	7 to 10 K-ohms
without plug cap.	3.2 to 4 K-ohms
Pulse generator coil resistance	80 to 160 ohms

Brakes

Disc brake
    Fluid type . . . . DOT 4
    Pad minimum thickness. . . . . 2 mm or to wear indicator
    Disc thickness service limit . . . . 3.0 mm
Drum brake
    Drum internal diameter service limit. . . . . 111 mm
    Shoe lining minimum thickness . . . . 2 mm
Rear brake lever freeplay . . . . 10 to 20 mm at lever ball end

Tyres

Size
    Front. 120/70-12
    Rear 130/70-12
Pressures
    Front. . . . . 22 psi (1.5 Bar)
    Rear . . . . 25 psi (1.75 Bar)

Electrical system

Battery 12V 3Ah
Battery terminal voltage
    Fully charged . . . . 13 to 13.2V
    Minimum charge. 12.3V
Alternator
    Charging coil resistance. . . . . 0.2 to 8.0 ohm
    Lighting coil resistance. . . . . 0.3 to 5.0 ohm
Fuse 7A

Torque wrench settings

Spark plug . . . . 11 to 17 Nm
Cylinder head bolts . . . . 15 to 17 Nm
Crankcase bolts . . . . 8 to 12 Nm
Exhaust manifold nuts . . . . 10 to 14 Nm
Exhaust system mounting bolts . . . . 30 to 36 Nm
Engine mounting bracket-to-frame bolt. . . . . 35 to 45 Nm
Engine mounting bracket-to-engine bolt . . . . 45 to 55 Nm
Alternator rotor nut. . . . . 35 to 40 Nm
Stator plate screws. . . . . 8 to 12 Nm
Variator centre nut . . . . 35 to 40 Nm
Clutch assembly nut. . . . . 50 to 60 Nm
Clutch centre nut . . . . 35 to 45 Nm
Rear shock absorber lower bolt. . . . . 24 to 30 Nm
Rear shock absorber upper bolt . . . . 35 to 45 Nm
Steering head bearing locknut. . . . . 60 to 80 Nm
Handlebar nut. . . . . 45 to 50 Nm
Front axle nut . . . . 50 to 70 Nm
Rear hub nut. . . . . 110 to 130 Nm

Kymco People S 50

Engine

Type	49.5 cc single cylinder, air-cooled four-stroke
Bore x stroke	39.0 x 41.4 mm
Idle speed	1900 ± 100 rpm
Oil type	SAE 15W/40 API SF four-stroke motorcycle oil
Oil capacity	700 ml
Piston diameter service limit	38.9 mm
Cylinder bore diameter service limit	39.1 mm
Piston-to-bore clearance service limit	0.10 mm
Piston ring installed end gap service limit	0.50 mm
Cylinder compression pressure	256 psi (18 Bars)
Valve clearance	0.04 mm
Valve spring free length service limit	
Inner spring	31.2 mm
Outer spring	34.1 mm
Camshaft lobe height service limit	
Intake	25.3 mm
Exhaust	25.2 mm
Rocker arm inside diameter	10.000 to 10.015 mm
Service limit	10.1 mm

Transmission

Belt width	18 mm
Service limit	17 mm
Variator roller diameter service limit	15.4 mm
Clutch lining thickness service limit	1.5 mm
Clutch drum diameter service limit	112.5 mm
Spring free length service limit	154.6 mm
Gearbox oil type	SAE 90W gear oil
Gearbox oil capacity	180 ml

Fuel system

Fuel tank capacity	5 litres
Carburettor type	CVK 20 mm
Main jet	80
Pilot jet	35
Pilot screw setting	1 ± 3/4 turns out
Float height	19 mm
Automatic choke resistance	5 ohms
Throttle cable freeplay	2 to 6 mm

Ignition system

Spark plug type	NGK CR7HSA
Electrode gap	0.6 to 0.7 mm
Timing	
At idle (F mark)	15° BTDC @ 1700 rpm
At full advance	28° BTDC @ 4000 rpm
HT coil primary resistance	0.1 to 1.0 ohm
HT coil secondary resistance	
with plug cap	7 to 12 K-ohms
without plug cap	2 to 4 K-ohms

Brakes

Disc brake
    Fluid type . . . . DOT 4
    Pad service limit . . . . 2.75 mm
    Disc thickness service limit . . . . 3 mm
Drum brake
    Drum diameter service limit . . . . 131 mm
    Shoe lining service limit . . . . 2.1 mm
    Brake lever freeplay . . . . 10 to 20 mm at lever ball end

Tyres

Sizes
    Front 100/80-16
    Rear 120/80-16
Pressures
    Front . . . . 25 psi (1.75 Bar)
    Rear . . . . 29 psi (2.0 Bar)

Electrical system

Battery 12V, 6Ah
    Voltage – fully charged 13.1V
    Voltage – undercharged 12.3V
Alternator
    Output (regulated). . . . . 13.5 to 15.5V (DC) @ 5000 rpm
    Charging coil resistance . . . . 0.2 to 1.2 ohm
Fuse . . . . 7A x 2
Starter motor brush length service limit . . . . 8.5 mm

Torque wrench settings

Spark plug . . . . 12 Nm
Cylinder head nuts . . . . 20 Nm
Crankcase bolts . . . . 9 Nm
Exhaust manifold nuts . . . . 22 Nm
Exhaust mounting bolts . . . . 33 Nm
Oil filter screen cap. . . . . 15 Nm
Oil drain bolt . . . . 10 Nm
Alternator nut . . . . 55 Nm
Alternator stator bolts. . . . . 9 Nm
Variator centre nut . . . . 55 Nm
Clutch assembly nut. . . . . 55 Nm
Clutch centre nut . . . . 55 Nm
Rear shock absorber lower bolt . . . . 24 to 30 Nm
Rear shock absorber upper bolt . . . . 35 to 45 Nm
Steering head bearing locknut . . . . 70 to 80 Nm
Handlebar bolt and nut. . . . . 45 to 55 Nm
Front axle nut . . . . 50 to 70 Nm
Rear hub nut . . . . 110 to 130 Nm

Kymco People S 125 & 200

Engine

Type	124.6/163 cc single cylinder, air-cooled four-stroke
Bore x stroke	
125 cc.	52.4 x 57.8 mm
200 cc.	60.0 x 57.8 mm
Idle speed.	1700 ± 100 rpm
Oil type	SAE 15W/40 API SF four-stroke motorcycle oil
Oil capacity.	800 ml
Piston diameter service limit	
125 cc.	52.3 mm
200 cc.	59.9 mm
Cylinder bore diameter service limit	
125 cc.	52.5 mm
200 cc.	60.1 mm
Piston-to-bore clearance service limit	0.10 mm
Piston ring installed end gap service limit	0.5 mm
Cylinder compression pressure	
125 cc.	184 psi (13 Bars)
200 cc.	213 psi (15 Bars)
Valve clearance	0.12 mm
Valve spring free length service limit	
Inner spring.	31.2 mm
Outer spring	34.1 mm
Camshaft lobe height service limit	
Intake (125 cc)	29.30 mm
Intake (200 cc)	29.40 mm
Exhaust (125 cc).	29.15 mm
Exhaust (200 cc)	29.05 mm
Rocker arm inside diameter.	10.000 to 10.015 mm
Service limit	10.1 mm

Transmission

Belt width	20 to 21 mm
Service limit	19 mm
Variator rollers	
Standard diameter	17.920 to 18.080 mm
Service limit	17.4 mm
Clutch lining thickness service limit	1.5 mm
Clutch drum diameter service limit.	125.5 mm
Spring free length service limit.	163.7 mm
Gearbox oil type.	SAE 90W gear oil
Gearbox oil capacity	180 ml

Fuel system

Fuel tank capacity	6.8 litres
Carburettor type.	CVK 24 mm
Main jet.	114
Pilot jet	35
Pilot screw setting	2 3/8 ± 3/4 turns out
Float height.	19 mm
Automatic choke resistance.	15 ohms
Throttle cable freeplay	2 to 6 mm

Ignition system

Spark plug type . . . . NGK CR7HSA
Electrode gap . . . . 0.6 to 0.7 mm
Timing
   At idle (F mark) . . . . 15° BTDC @ 1700 rpm
   At full advance . . . . 28° BTDC @ 4000 rpm
Pulse generator coil resistance . . . . 70 to 130 ohms
HT coil primary resistance . . . . 0.1 to 1.0 ohm
HT coil secondary resistance
   with plug cap . . . . 7 to 12 K-ohms
   without plug cap . . . . 2 to 4 K-ohms

Brakes

Disc brake
   Fluid type . . . . DOT 4
   Pad service limit . . . . 2.75 mm
   Disc thickness service limit . . . . 3 mm
Drum brake
   Drum diameter service limit . . . . 131 mm
   Shoe lining service limit . . . . 2.1 mm
   Brake lever freeplay . . . . 10 to 20 mm at lever ball end

Tyres

Sizes
   Front 100/80-16
   Rear 120/80-16
Pressures
   Front . . . . 25 psi (1.75 Bar)
   Rear . . . . 29 psi (2.0 Bar)

Electrical system

Battery 12V, 6Ah
   Voltage – fully charged 13.1V
   Voltage – undercharged 12.3V
Alternator
   Output (regulated). . . . . 13.5 to 15.5V (DC) @ 5000 rpm
   Charging coil resistance . . . . 0.2 to 1.2 ohm
   Lighting coil resistance . . . . 0.1 to 1.0 ohm
Fuse 10A, 15A
Starter motor brush length service limit . . . . 8.5 mm

Torque wrench settings

Spark plug . . . . 12 Nm
Cylinder head nuts . . . . 20 Nm
Crankcase bolts . . . . 9 Nm
Exhaust manifold nuts . . . . 22 Nm
Exhaust mounting bolts . . . . 35 Nm
Oil drain bolt . . . . 13 Nm
Alternator nut . . . . 55 Nm
Alternator stator bolts . . . . 9 Nm
Variator centre nut . . . . 55 Nm
Clutch assembly nut . . . . 55 Nm
Clutch centre nut . . . . 55 Nm
Rear shock absorber lower bolt . . . . 27 Nm
Rear shock absorber upper bolt . . . . 40 Nm
Steering head bearing locknut . . . . 70 to 80 Nm
Handlebar bolt and nut . . . . 40 to 50 Nm
Front axle nut . . . . 60 Nm
Rear hub nut . . . . 110 Nm

Kymco Agility 50

Engine

Type	49.5 cc single cylinder, air-cooled four-stroke
Bore x stroke	39.0 x 41.4 mm
Idle speed	1900 ± 100 rpm
Oil type	SAE 15W/40 API SF four-stroke motorcycle oil
Oil capacity	700 ml
Piston-to-bore clearance service limit	0.10 mm
Piston ring installed end gap service limit	0.45 mm
Cylinder compression pressure	228 psi (16 Bars)
Valve clearance	0.04 mm
Valve spring free length service limit	
Inner spring	30.1 mm
Outer spring	33.3 mm
Camshaft lobe height service limit	
Intake	26.038 mm
Exhaust	25.407 mm
Rocker arm inside diameter	10.000 to 10.015 mm
Service limit	10.1 mm

Transmission

Belt width	17.5 mm
Service limit	16.5 mm
Variator roller diameter service limit	15.4 mm
Clutch lining thickness service limit	1.5 mm
Clutch drum diameter service limit	107.5 mm
Spring free length service limit	154.6 mm
Gearbox oil type	SAE 90W gear oil
Gearbox oil capacity	100 ml

Fuel system

Fuel tank capacity	5 litres
Carburettor type	CVK 17 mm
Main jet	80
Pilot jet	35
Pilot screw setting	2 ± 1/2 turns out
Float height	17 mm
Automatic choke resistance	10 ohms
Throttle cable freeplay	2 to 6 mm

Ignition system

Spark plug type	NGK CR7HSA
Electrode gap	0.6 to 0.7 mm
Timing	
At idle (F mark)	13° BTDC @ 1700 rpm
At full advance	28° BTDC @ 4000 rpm
Pulse generator coil resistance	40 to 300 ohms
HT coil primary resistance	0.1 to 1.0 ohm
HT coil secondary resistance	
with plug cap	7 to 12 K-ohms
without plug cap	3 to 5 K-ohms

Brakes

Disc brake
    Fluid type . . . . DOT 4
    Disc thickness service limit . . . . 3 mm
Drum brake
    Drum diameter service limit . . . . 111 mm
    Shoe lining service limit . . . . 2 mm
    Drum brake lever freeplay . . . . 10 to 20 mm at lever ball end

Tyres

Sizes
    Front . . . . 120/70-12 (100/80-16 City model)
    Rear . . . . 130/70-12 (120/80-16 City model)
Pressures
    Front . . . . 22 psi (1.5 Bar)
    Rear . . . . 29 psi (2.0 Bar)

Electrical system

Battery 12V, 4Ah
    Voltage – fully charged 13.1V
    Voltage – undercharged 12.3V
Alternator
    Output (regulated). . . . . 14.5 ± 0.5V (DC)
    Charging coil resistance . . . . 0.2 to 1.2 ohm
    Lighting coil resistance . . . . 0.1 to 1.0 ohm
Fuse 7A
Starter motor brush length service limit . . . . 8.5 mm

Torque wrench settings

Spark plug . . . . 10 to 14 Nm
Cylinder head cover bolts . . . . 8 to 12 Nm
Cylinder head nuts . . . . 18 to 22 Nm
Crankcase bolts . . . . 8 to 12 Nm
Exhaust manifold nuts . . . . 10 to 14 Nm
Exhaust mounting bolts . . . . 30 to 36 Nm
Oil filter screen cap. . . . . 10 to 20 Nm
Oil drain bolt . . . . 11 to 15 Nm
Oil pump bolts . . . . 1 to 3 Nm
Alternator nut . . . . 35 to 45 Nm
Alternator stator bolts. . . . . 8 to 12 Nm
Variator centre nut . . . . 35 to 40 Nm
Clutch assembly nut. . . . . 50 to 60 Nm
Clutch centre nut . . . . 35 to 40 Nm
Rear shock absorber lower bolt . . . . 24 to 30 Nm
Rear shock absorber upper bolt . . . . 35 to 45 Nm
Steering head bearing locknut . . . . 60 to 80 Nm
Handlebar bolt and nut. . . . . 45 to 55 Nm
Front axle nut . . . . 50 to 70 Nm
Rear hub nut. . . . . 110 to 130 Nm

Kymco Agility 125

Engine

Type	124.6 cc single cylinder, air-cooled four-stroke
Bore x stroke	52.4 x 57.8 mm
Idle speed.	1700 ± 100 rpm
Oil type	SAE 15W/40 API SF four-stroke motorcycle oil
Oil capacity.	800 ml
Piston diameter service limit	52.3 mm
Cylinder bore diameter service limit	52.5 mm
Piston-to-bore clearance service limit	0.10 mm
Piston ring installed end gap service limit	0.5 mm
Cylinder compression pressure	184 psi (13 Bars)
Valve clearance	0.12 mm
Valve spring free length service limit	
Inner spring.	32.3 mm
Outer spring	35.0 mm
Camshaft lobe height service limit	
Intake	29.40 mm
Exhaust.	29.16 mm
Rocker arm inside diameter	10.000 to 10.015 mm
Service limit	10.1 mm

Transmission

Belt width	17.5 mm
Service limit	16.5 mm
Variator rollers	
Standard diameter	15.920 to 16.080 mm
Service limit	15.4 mm
Clutch lining thickness service limit	1.5 mm
Clutch drum diameter service limit.	125.5 mm
Spring free length service limit	147.6 mm
Gearbox oil type.	SAE 90W gear oil
Gearbox oil capacity	190 ml

Fuel system

Fuel tank capacity	5 litres
Carburettor type.	CVK 37 mm
Main jet	105
Pilot jet	35
Pilot screw setting	3 ± 1/2 turns out
Float height.	17.5 mm
Automatic choke resistance.	10 ohms
Throttle cable freeplay	2 to 6 mm

Ignition system

Spark plug type	NGK CR7HSA
Electrode gap.	0.6 to 0.7 mm
Timing	
At idle (F mark)	13° BTDC @ 1700 rpm
At full advance	27° BTDC @ 4000 rpm
Pulse generator coil resistance	40 to 300 ohms
HT coil primary resistance	0.1 to 1.0 ohm
HT coil secondary resistance	
with plug cap	7 to 12 K-ohms
without plug cap.	3 to 5 K-ohms

Brakes

Disc brake
  Fluid type . . . . DOT 4
  Disc thickness service limit . . . . 3 mm
Drum brake
  Drum diameter service limit . . . . 131 mm
  Shoe lining service limit . . . . 2 mm
  Brake lever freeplay . . . . 10 to 20 mm at lever ball end

Tyres

Sizes
  Front . . . . 120/70-12 (100/80-16 City model)
  Rear . . . . 130/70-12 (120/80-16 City model)
Pressures
  Front . . . . 25 psi (1.75 Bar)
  Rear . . . . 33 psi (2.25 Bar)

Electrical system

Battery 12V, 7Ah
  Voltage – fully charged 13.1V
  Voltage – undercharged 12.3V
Alternator
  Output (regulated) . . . . 14.5 ± 0.5V (DC)
  Charging coil resistance . . . . 0.2 to 1.2 ohm
  Lighting coil resistance . . . . 0.1 to 1.0 ohm
Fuse 7A
Starter motor brush length service limit . . . . 8.5 mm

Torque wrench settings

Spark plug . . . . 10 to 14 Nm
Cylinder head nuts . . . . 20 Nm
Crankcase bolts . . . . 8 to 12 Nm
Exhaust manifold nuts . . . . 10 to 14 Nm
Exhaust mounting bolts . . . . 30 to 36 Nm
Oil filter screen cap . . . . 10 to 20 Nm
Oil drain bolt . . . . 11 to 15 Nm
Oil pump bolts . . . . 1 to 3 Nm
Alternator nut . . . . 35 to 45 Nm
Alternator stator bolts . . . . 8 to 12 Nm
Variator centre nut . . . . 35 to 40 Nm
Clutch assembly nut . . . . 50 to 60 Nm
Clutch centre nut . . . . 35 to 40 Nm
Rear shock absorber lower bolt . . . . 24 to 30 Nm
Rear shock absorber upper bolt . . . . 35 to 45 Nm
Steering head bearing locknut . . . . 60 to 80 Nm
Handlebar bolt and nut . . . . 45 to 55 Nm
Front axle nut . . . . 50 to 70 Nm
Rear hub nut . . . . 110 to 130 Nm

Sym DD 50

Engine

Type . . . . 49.4 cc single cylinder air-cooled two-stroke
Bore x stroke . . . . 39.0 x 41.4 mm
Idle speed. . . . . 2000 rpm
Oil type. . . . . JASO FC, SAE 20 semi-synthetic
Oil tank capacity. . . . . 1.2 litres
Piston diameter service limit . . . . 38.935 mm
Cylinder diameter service limit. . . . . 39.050 mm
Piston-to-bore clearance:
  Standard. . . . . 0.04 to 0.05 mm
  Service limit . . . . 0.10 mm
Piston ring installed end gap
  Standard. . . . . 0.10 to 0.25 mm
  Service limit . . . . 0.40 mm

Transmission

Belt width
  Standard. . . . . 18.0 mm
  Service limit . . . . 16.5 mm
Variator rollers
  Standard diameter . . . . 15.92 to 16.08 mm
  Service limit . . . . 15.40 mm
Clutch lining thickness service limit . . . . 2.0 mm
Clutch spring free length service limit . . . . 92.7 mm
Gearbox oil. . . . . SAE 140 hypoid gear oil
Gearbox oil capacity . . . . 90 ml

Fuel system

Fuel tank capacity . . . . 6.1 litres
Throttle twistgrip freeplay. . . . . 2 to 6 mm
Carburettor. . . . . 14 mm PB2BE slide type
  Main jet. 82
  Pilot screw setting . . . . 1 3/8 turns out
  Float height. . . . . 8.6 mm
  Automatic choke resistance . . . . approx. 10.0 ohms @ 20°C

Ignition system

Spark plug type . . . . NGK BR8HSA
Electrode gap. . . . . 0.6 to 0.7 mm
Pulse generator coil resistance . . . . 50 to 200 ohms
HT coil primary resistance . . . . 0.19 to 0.23 ohms
HT coil secondary resistance. . . . . 2.8 to 3.4 K-ohms

Brakes

Disc brake
  Fluid type . . . . DOT 4
  Pad minimum thickness. . . . . 2.0 mm
  Disc thickness
    Standard. . . . . 3.5 mm
    Service limit . . . . 2.0 mm
Drum brake
  Brake shoe lining thickness
    Standard. . . . . 4.0 mm
    Service limit . . . . 2.0 mm
  Brake lever freeplay . . . . 10 to 20 mm at lever ball end

Tyres

Size.	3.00-10
Pressure	
Front.	22 psi (1.50 Bar)
Rear	32 psi (2.25 Bar)

Electrical system

Battery	
Capacity	12V, 3Ah
Voltage (fully charged)	13 to 13.2V
Alternator	
Output (regulated).	14 to 15V (DC)
Charging coil resistance	0.2 to 1.0 ohms
Lighting coil resistance.	0.2 to 0.8 ohms
Fuse (main)	7A
Bulbs	
Headlight (main/dipped).	35/35W
Sidelight	3.4W
Brake/tail light.	18/5W
Turn signal lights.	10W
Instrument and warning lights	1.7 and 3.4W

Torque wrench settings

Spark plug	14 Nm
Cylinder head bolts	10 Nm
Crankcase bolts	10 Nm
Engine mounting bolts	60 Nm
Exhaust manifold nuts	12 Nm
Exhaust system mounting bolts.	32 Nm
Alternator rotor nut.	38 Nm
Variator centre nut	38 Nm
Clutch centre nut	38 Nm
Clutch assembly nut.	55 Nm
Gearbox oil drain plug	13 Nm
Rear shock absorber lower bolt.	27 Nm
Rear shock absorber upper bolt	40 Nm
Steering head bearing locknut	70 Nm
Front fork leg clamp bolts	25 Nm
Front axle nut	60 Nm
Rear hub nut.	110 Nm
Rear wheel bolts.	25 Nm
Disc brake caliper mounting bolts	31 Nm
Disc mounting bolts	45 Nm
Brake hose banjo bolts.	35 Nm

Sym Mio 50 and 100

Engine

	50 cc	100 cc
Type	49.5/101 cc single cylinder air-cooled four-stroke	
Bore x stroke	37 x 46 mm	50 x 51.5 mm
Idle speed	2000 rpm	1700 rpm
Engine oil type	SAE 10W30 four-stroke engine oil	
Engine oil capacity	700 ml	650 ml
Cylinder compression service limit	130 ± 29 psi (9 ± 2 Bars)	174 ± 29 psi (12 ± 2 Bars)
Piston diameter service limit	36.900 mm	49.900 mm
Cylinder bore service limit	37.500 mm	50.500 mm
Piston-to-bore clearance service limit	0.10 mm	0.10 mm
Piston ring installed end gap (standard/service limit)		
Top and second rings	0.10 to 0.25 mm/0.50 mm	0.10 to 0.25 mm/0.50 mm
Valve clearance	0.05 mm intake, 0.1 mm exhaust	0.12 mm intake and exhaust
Valve spring free length service limit	31.5 mm	31.5 mm
Camshaft lobe height service limit		
Intake/service limit	24.100 mm/23.761 mm	25.969 mm/25.570 mm
Exhaust/service limit	23.850 mm/23.369 mm	25.891 mm/25.410 mm
Rocker arm inside diameter	10.000 to 10.015 mm	
Service limit	10.1 mm	

Transmission

Belt width	
Standard	17.800 to 18.200 mm
Service limit	17.2 mm
Variator rollers	
Standard diameter	15.920 to 16.080 mm
Service limit	15.40 mm
Clutch lining thickness service limit	1.5 mm
Clutch spring free length service limit	
50 cc	87.90 mm
100 cc	156.00 mm
Gear oil type	SAE 85W/140
Gear oil capacity	
50 cc	90 ml
100 cc	100 ml

Fuel system

	50 cc	100 cc
Fuel tank capacity	4.8 litres	
Throttle cable freeplay	2 to 6 mm at twistgrip flange	
Carburettor	CV type	
Main jet	88	95
Pilot jet	35	38
Pilot screw setting	2 ± ½ turn	2 5/8 ± ¾ turn
Float height	17.75 mm	16 mm
Automatic choke resistance	approx. 10.0 ohms @ 20°C	

Ignition system

Spark plug type	NGK C6HSA
Spark plug gap	0.6 to 0.7 mm
Pulse generator coil resistance	
50 cc	50 to 200 ohms
100 cc	92 to 138 ohms
HT coil primary resistance	
50 cc	0.19 to 0.23 ohms
100 cc	0.26 to 0.35 ohms
HT coil secondary resistance	
50 cc	3 to 5 K-ohms
100 cc	3.4 to 4.6 K-ohms

Brakes

Disc brake
Fluid type . . . . DOT 4
Disc thickness
Standard . . . . 3.5 mm
Service limit . . . . 2.0 mm
Drum brake
Brake shoe lining thickness service limit . . . . 2.0 mm
Brake lever freeplay . . . . 10 to 20 mm

Tyres

Size
50 cc . . . . 3.00-10 front, 90/90-10 rear
100 cc 90/90-10
Pressure
50 cc . . . . 22 psi (1.5 Bar) front, 33 psi (2.25 Bar) rear
100 cc . . . . 29 psi (2.0 Bar) front, 33 psi (2.25 Bar) rear

Electrical system

Battery 12V, 4Ah
Alternator
Output (regulated) . . . . 13 to 14V (DC)
Charging coil resistance – 50 cc . . . . 0.2 to 1.0 ohms
Charging coil resistance – 100 cc . . . . 0.6 to 0.9 ohms
Lighting coil resistance – 50 cc . . . . 0.1 to 0.8 ohms
Lighting coil resistance – 100 cc . . . . 0.4 to 0.6 ohms
Fuse (main) 7A
Bulbs
Headlight (main/dipped) 12V 30/30W
Brake/tail light 12V 18/5W
Turn signal lights 12V 10W

Torque wrench settings

Spark plug . . . . 10 to 14 Nm
Cylinder head nuts . . . . 18 to 22 Nm
Cylinder head bolts . . . . 10 to 14 Nm
Crankcase bolts . . . . 15 to 20 Nm
Engine oil drain plug . . . . 35 to 45 Nm
Engine oil filter cap . . . . 13 to 17 Nm
Engine mounting bolts . . . . 45 to 55 Nm
Exhaust manifold nuts . . . . 10 to 14 Nm
Exhaust system mounting bolts . . . . 30 to 36 Nm
Alternator rotor nut . . . . 50 to 60 Nm
Variator centre nut . . . . 50 to 60 Nm
Clutch centre nut . . . . 50 to 60 Nm
Clutch assembly nut . . . . 50 to 60 Nm
Gearbox oil drain plug . . . . 8 to 12 Nm
Gearbox oil filler plug . . . . 10 to 14 Nm
Rear shock absorber lower bolt . . . . 24 to 30 Nm
Rear shock absorber upper bolt . . . . 35 to 45 Nm
Steering head bearing locknut . . . . 10 to 20 Nm
Handlebar bolt nut . . . . 40 to 50 Nm
Front axle nut . . . . 50 to 70 Nm
Rear hub nut . . . . 110 to 130 Nm
Disc brake caliper mounting bolts . . . . 31 to 35 Nm
Disc mounting bolts . . . . 40 to 45 Nm
Brake hose banjo bolts . . . . 33 to 37 Nm

Sym Jet BasiX 50 and Jet Euro X 50/100

Engine

Type . . . . 49.4/101.3cc single cylinder air-cooled two-stroke
Bore x stroke . . . . 39.0 x 41.4 mm
Idle speed
    50 cc. . . . . 2000 rpm
    100 cc. . . . . 2100 rpm
Oil type. . . . . JASO FC, SAE 20 semi-synthetic
Oil tank capacity. . . . . 1.2 litres
Piston diameter service limit
    50 cc. . . . . 38.935 mm
    100 cc. . . . . 50.935 mm
Cylinder diameter service limit
    50 cc. . . . . 39.050 mm
    100 cc. . . . . 51.050 mm
Piston-to-bore clearance
    Standard. . . . . 0.04 to 0.05 mm
    Service limit . . . . 0.10 mm
Piston ring installed end gap
    Standard. . . . . 0.10 to 0.25 mm
    Service limit . . . . 0.40 mm
Cylinder compression pressure
    50 cc. . . . . 85 to 114 psi (6 to 8 Bars)
    100 cc. . . . . 114 to 171 psi (8 to 12 Bars)

Transmission

Belt width
    Standard. . . . . 18.0 mm
    Service limit . . . . 16.5 mm
Variator rollers
    Standard diameter . . . . 15.92 to 16.08 mm
    Service limit . . . . 15.40 mm
Clutch lining thickness (service limit) . . . . 2.0 mm
Clutch spring free length (service limit) . . . . 82.5 mm
Gearbox oil. . . . . SAE 140 hypoid gear oil
Gearbox oil capacity . . . . 110 ml

Fuel system

Fuel tank capacity . . . . 6.3 litres
Throttle twistgrip freeplay. . . . . 2 to 6 mm
Carburettor. . . . . Slide type 15 mm 50 cc, 16 mm 100 cc
    Float height. . . . . 8.8 ± 1 mm
    Automatic choke resistance . . . . approx. 10 ohms @ 20°C

Ignition system

Spark plug type
    50 cc. . . . . NGK BR8HSA
    100 cc. . . . . NGK BR6HSA
Electrode gap. . . . . 0.6 to 0.7 mm
Pulse generator coil resistance . . . . 50 to 200 ohms
HT coil primary resistance . . . . 0.19 to 0.23 ohms
HT coil secondary resistance. . . . . 2.8 to 3.4 K-ohms

Brakes

Disc brake
  Fluid type . . . . DOT 4
  Pad minimum thickness . . . . 2.0 mm
  Disc thickness
    Standard . . . . 3.5 mm
    Service limit . . . . 2.0 mm
Drum brake
  Brake shoe lining thickness
    Standard . . . . 4.0 mm
    Service limit . . . . 2.0 mm
  Brake lever freeplay . . . . 10 to 20 mm at lever ball end

Tyres

Sze . . . . 120/70-12 front, 130/70-12 rear
Pressure
  Front . . . . 25 psi (1.75 Bar)
  Rear . . . . 29 psi (2.0 Bar)

Electrical system

Battery 12V, 3Ah
Alternator output (regulated) . . . . 14 to 15V (DC)
Fuse (main) 7A

Torque wrench settings

Spark plug . . . . 14 Nm
Cylinder head bolts . . . . 10 Nm
Crankcase bolts . . . . 10 Nm
Engine mounting bolts . . . . 60 Nm
Exhaust manifold nuts . . . . 12 Nm
Exhaust system mounting bolts . . . . 32 Nm
Alternator rotor nut . . . . 38 Nm
Variator centre nut . . . . 38 Nm
Clutch centre nut . . . . 38 Nm
Clutch assembly nut . . . . 55 Nm
Gearbox oil drain plug . . . . 13 Nm
Rear shock absorber lower bolt . . . . 27 Nm
Rear shock absorber upper bolt . . . . 40 Nm
Steering head bearing locknut . . . . 15 Nm
Handlebar bolt . . . . 45 Nm
Front fork leg clamp bolts . . . . 27 Nm
Front axle nut . . . . 60 Nm
Rear hub nut . . . . 110 Nm
Rear wheel bolts . . . . 25 Nm
Disc brake caliper mounting bolts . . . . 31 Nm
Disc mounting bolts . . . . 45 Nm
Brake hose banjo bolts . . . . 35 Nm

Sym City Hopper 50

Engine

Engine type.	49 cc single cylinder air-cooled two-stroke
Bore x stroke	39.0 x 41.4 mm
Idle speed.	2000 rpm
Oil type.	JASO FC, SAE 20 semi-synthetic
Oil tank capacity.	1.2 litres
Piston diameter service limit	38.935 mm
Cylinder diameter service limit	39.050 mm
Piston-to-bore clearance:	
Standard.	0.04 to 0.05 mm
Service limit	0.10 mm
Piston ring installed end gap	
Standard.	0.10 to 0.25 mm
Service limit	0.40 mm

Transmission

Belt width	
Standard.	18.0 mm
Service limit	16.5 mm
Variator rollers	
Standard diameter	15.92 to 16.08 mm
Service limit	15.40 mm
Clutch lining thickness (service limit)	2.0 mm
Clutch spring free length (service limit)	82.5 mm
Gearbox oil	SAE 140 hypoid gear oil
Gearbox oil capacity	120 ml

Fuel system

Fuel tank capacity	6.5 litres
Throttle twistgrip freeplay.	2 to 6 mm
Carburettor.	14 mm PB2BE slide type
Pilot screw setting	1 3/8 turns out
Float height.	8.8 mm
Automatic choke resistance	approx. 10.0 ohms @ 20°C

Ignition system

Spark plug type	NGK BR8HSA
Electrode gap	0.6 to 0.7 mm
Pulse generator coil resistance	50 to 200 ohms
HT coil primary resistance	0.19 to 0.23 ohms
HT coil secondary resistance	3.6 to 3.9 K-ohms
Spark plug cap resistance	4.3 to 5.7 K-ohms

Brakes

Disc brake	
Fluid type	DOT 4
Pad minimum thickness	2.0 mm
Disc thickness	
Standard.	3.5 mm
Service limit	2.0 mm
Drum brake	
Brake shoe lining thickness	
Standard.	4.0 mm
Service limit	2.0 mm
Brake lever freeplay	10 to 20 mm at lever ball end

Tyres

Size	100/90-10
Pressure	
Front	22 psi (1.50 Bar)
Rear	25 psi (1.75 Bar)

Electrical system

Battery	
Capacity	12V, 4Ah
Voltage (fully charged)	13 to 13.2V
Alternator	
Output (regulated)	14 to 15V (DC)
Charging coil resistance	0.2 to 1.0 ohms
Lighting coil resistance	0.1 to 0.8 ohms
Fuse	7A
Bulbs	
Headlight (main/dipped)	35/35W
Sidelight	3W
Brake/tail light	18/5W
Turn signal lights	10W
Instrument and warning lights	3W and LEDs

Torque wrench settings

Cylinder head bolts	20 Nm
Crankcase bolts	15 Nm
Engine mounting bolt	55 Nm
Inlet manifold bolts	12 Nm
Exhaust manifold nuts	14 Nm
Exhaust system mounting bolts	32 Nm
Alternator rotor nut	45 Nm
Alternator stator bolts	10 Nm
Variator centre nut	60 Nm
Starter clutch centre nut	45 Nm
Clutch centre nut	45 Nm
Clutch assembly nut	60 Nm
Gearbox oil drain plug	13 Nm
Rear shock absorber lower bolt	30 Nm
Rear shock absorber upper bolt	45 Nm
Steering head bearing locknut	50 Nm
Handlebar stem bolt	50 Nm
Front suspension bolts	30 Nm
Front axle nut	70 Nm
Rear hub nut	130 Nm
Wheel rim nuts	25 Nm
Disc brake caliper mounting bolts	35 Nm
Disc mounting bolts	22 Nm
Brake hose banjo bolts	40 Nm

TGB 50 cc 202, 101R, Hawk, 302 & R50X models

Engine

Type	49.3 cc single cylinder air-cooled two-stroke
Bore x stroke	41.0 x 37.4 mm
Oil type	2T two-stroke engine oil to JASO FC
Oil tank capacity	800 ml

Piston diameter (15 mm above skirt)
Standard	40.945 to 40.955 mm
Service limit	40.900 mm

Cylinder bore diameter
Standard	41.005 to 41.020 mm
Service limit	41.070 mm

Piston-to-bore clearance
Standard	0.06 to 0.07 mm
Service limit	0.12 mm

Piston ring installed end gap
Standard	0.10 to 0.25 mm
Service limit	0.75 mm

Fuel tank capacity
202 and 101R models	5.1 litres
302, Hawk and R50X models	6.8 litres

Transmission

Belt width service limit	15 mm
Clutch lining thickness service limit	2 mm

Clutch drum inside diameter
Standard	110 to 110.15 mm
Service limit	110.40 mm

Clutch spring free length
Standard	98.1 mm
Service limit	96.9 mm

Gearbox oil	SAE 85W/90 gear oil
Gearbox oil capacity	90 ml

Ignition system

Spark plug type
202, 101R, Hawk and 302 model	NGK BPR6HS
R50X model	NGK BPR7HS
Electrode gap	0.6 to 0.7 mm
Ignition timing	15° BTDC @ 4000 rpm
Minimum spark gap	6 to 8 mm
HT coil secondary resistance	8 K-ohms ± 10%
Spark plug cap resistance	5 to 7.6 K-ohms

Brakes

Disc brake
Fluid type	DOT 4
Pad minimum thickness	2 mm

Drum brake

Brake drum diameter
Standard	110 mm
Service limit	110.7 mm

Brake shoe assembly diameter (across shoe mid-points)
Standard	109.2 mm
Service limit	106 mm

Brake lever freeplay
202, 101R, Hawk and 302 model	10 to 20 mm at lever ball end
R50X	15 to 35 mm at lever ball end

Tyres

Size
  202, 101R and Hawk models 120/70-12
  302 and R50X models 130/60-13
Pressure
  Front . . . .   25 psi (1.7 Bar)
  Rear . . . .   30 psi (2.1 Bar)

Electrical system

Battery capacity 12V, 4Ah
Alternator output (regulated) . . . .   13 to 15V
Starter motor brush minimum length . . . .   3 mm
Fuse 7A
Bulbs
  Headlight
    202, 101R, Hawk and 302 (main/dipped) 35/35W
    R50X . . . .   55W x 2 halogen
  Brake/tail light 21/5W
  Turn signal lights 10W
  Instrument lights 1.7W

Torque wrench settings

Spark plug . . . .   25 to 30 Nm
Cylinder head nuts . . . .   12 to 13 Nm
Crankcase bolts . . . .   5 to 8 Nm
Exhaust manifold nuts . . . .   8 to 12 Nm
Exhaust system mounting bolt . . . .   18 to 28 Nm
Alternator rotor nut . . . .   35 to 45 Nm
Variator centre nut . . . .   40 to 60 Nm
Clutch centre nut . . . .   40 to 60 Nm
Clutch assembly nut . . . .   40 to 60 Nm
Gearbox oil drain plug . . . .   4 to 7 Nm
Gearbox oil level/filler plug . . . .   9 to 15 Nm
Rear shock absorber bolts . . . .   20 to 30 Nm
Steering head bearing locknut . . . .   60 to 100 Nm
Handlebar stem bolt . . . .   55 to 60 Nm
Front axle nut . . . .   55 to 60 Nm
Rear hub nut . . . .   60 to 90 Nm
Brake caliper mounting bolts . . . .   21 to 25 Nm
Brake disc bolts . . . .   18 to 20 Nm
Brake master cylinder bolts . . . .   16.5 Nm

TGB 125 cc BK8, 204, 404, 304 and Hawk

Engine

Type	124 cc single cylinder air-cooled four-stroke
Bore x stroke	52.4 x 57.8 mm
Idle speed.	1800 ± 100 rpm
Oil type.	SAE 10W/40 motorcycle engine oil
Oil capacity.	900 ml
Valve clearances.	0.12 mm
Compression pressure	186 psi (12.8 Bar)
Piston diameter	
Standard.	52.002 to 52.390 mm
Service limit	52.300 mm
Cylinder bore diameter	
Standard.	52.400 to 52.410 mm
Service limit	52.500 mm
Piston-to-bore clearance service limit	0.10 mm
Piston ring installed end gap	
Standard.	0.10 to 0.25 mm
Service limit	0.50 mm
Valve spring free length	
Inner spring service limit.	31.2 mm
Outer spring service limit	34.1 mm
Fuel tank capacity	
404 model.	10.7 litres
BK8, 204, 304 and Hawk models.	6.8 litres
Throttle cable freeplay	2 to 6 mm of twistgrip rotation

Transmission

Belt width (service limit)	19 mm
Variator roller minimum diameter	17.4 mm
Clutch lining minimum thickness	1.5 mm
Clutch drum inside diameter service limit	125.5 mm
Clutch spring minimum free length	135 mm
Gearbox oil.	SAE 90 gear oil
Gearbox oil capacity	
BK8.	120 ml
204, 404, 304 and Hawk.	90 ml

Ignition system

Spark plug type	NGK CR7HSA
Electrode gap.	0.6 to 0.7 mm
Source coil resistance	300 to 1000 ohms
Pulse generator coil resistance	40 to 300 ohms
HT coil primary resistance	0.1 to 1.0 ohm
HT coil secondary resistance.	7 to 12 K-ohms

Brakes

Disc brake	
Fluid type	DOT 4
Pad minimum thickness.	to wear limit markers
Disc minimum thickness.	3 mm
Drum brake	
Shoe lining minimum thickness	2 mm
Brake drum minimum inside diameter	131 mm
Brake lever freeplay	
BK8 and 404 model	10 to 20 mm at lever ball end
304 and Hawk models	15 to 35 mm at lever ball end

Tyres

Size
BK8	80/80-14 (front), 110/80-14 (rear)
204	120/90-10 front and rear
404, 304 and Hawk	130/60-13 front and rear

Pressure
Front	25 psi (1.75 Bar)
Rear	30 psi (2.1 Bar)

Electrical system

Battery
Capacity	12V, 7Ah
Voltage (fully charged)	12.8V minimum
Alternator stator coil resistance	0.1 to 1.0 ohm
Starter motor brush minimum length	8.5 mm
Fuse	7.5A

Bulbs
Headlight (main/dipped)	35/35W
Brake/tail light	21/5W
Turn signal lights	10W

Torque wrench settings

Spark plug	10 to 12 Nm
Cylinder head nuts	8 to 10 Nm
Exhaust manifold nuts	10 to 12 Nm
Exhaust system mounting bolt	30 to 40 Nm
Engine oil drain bolt	15 Nm
Engine oil strainer cap bolt	15 to 20 Nm
Alternator rotor nut	55 Nm
Fan bolts	9 Nm
Clutch centre nut	40 to 60 Nm
Gearbox oil drain bolt and level/filler bolt	9 to 15 Nm
Rear shock absorber mounting bolts	20 to 30 Nm
Front axle nut	50 to 60 Nm
Rear hub nut	60 to 90 Nm
Brake caliper mounting bolts	21 to 25 Nm
Brake disc bolts	18 to 20 Nm

Standard torque settings

Specific torque settings aren't available for the majority of fasteners. Where the nut or bolt is of a standard fitment, and not of unusual pitch or material, these standard settings can be applied: Note that fasteners are identified by their thread diameter, e.g. an M6 bolt has a 6 mm thread diameter – this does not relate to the 'across flats' head size or spanner size.

M5 bolt or nut . . . . 5 Nm
M6 bolt or nut . . . . 10 Nm
M8 bolt or nut . . . . 21.5 Nm
M10 bolt or nut . . . . 35 Nm
M12 bolt or nut . . . . 55 Nm
M6 bolt or nut with flanged head . . . . 12 Nm
M8 bolt or nut with flanged head . . . . 27 Nm
M10 bolt or nut with flanged head . . . . 40 Nm

Reference

Tools and Workshop Tips

Buying tools

A toolkit is a fundamental requirement for servicing and repairing a scooter. Although there will be an initial expense in building up enough tools for servicing, this will soon be offset by the savings made by doing the job yourself. As experience and confidence grow, additional tools can be added to enable the repair and overhaul of the scooter. Many of the specialist tools are expensive and not often used so it may be preferable to hire them, or for a group of friends or scooter club to join in the purchase.

As a rule, it is better to buy more expensive, good quality tools. Cheaper tools are likely to wear out faster and need to be renewed more often, nullifying the original saving.

 Warning: To avoid the risk of a poor quality tool breaking in use, causing injury or damage to the component being worked on, always aim to purchase tools which meet the relevant national safety standards.

The following lists of tools do not represent the manufacturer's service tools, but serve as a guide to help the owner decide which tools are needed for this level of work. In addition, items such as an electric drill, hacksaw, files, soldering iron and a workbench equipped with a vice, may be needed. Although not classed as tools, a selection of bolts, screws, nuts, washers and pieces of tubing always come in useful.

For more information about tools, refer to the Haynes *Motorcycle Workshop Practice Techbook* (Bk. No. 3470).

Manufacturer's service tools

Inevitably certain tasks require the use of a service tool. Where possible an alter native tool or method of approach is recommended, but sometimes there is no option if personal injury or damage to the component is to be avoided. Where required, service tools are referred to in the relevant procedure.

Service tools can usually only be purchased from a scooter dealer and are identified by a part number. Some of the commonly-used tools, such as rotor pullers, are available in aftermarket form from mail-order motorcycle tool and accessory suppliers.

Maintenance and minor repair tools

☐ Set of flat-bladed screwdrivers-
☐ Set of Phillips head screwdrivers
☐ Combination open-end and ring spanners
☐ Socket set (3/8 inch or 1/2 inch drive)
☐ Set of Allen keys or bits
☐ Set of Torx keys or bits
☐ Pliers, cutters and self-locking grips (Mole grips)
☐ Adjustable spanners
☐ C-spanners
☐ Tread depth gauge and tyre pressure gauge
☐ Cable oiler clamp
☐ Feeler gauges
☐ Spark plug gap measuring tool
☐ Spark plug spanner or deep plug sockets
☐ Wire brush and emery paper
☐ Calibrated syringe, measuring vessel and funnel

☐ Oil filter adapters (4-stroke engines)
☐ Oil drainer can or tray
☐ Pump type oil can
☐ Grease gun
☐ Straight-edge and steel rule
☐ Continuity tester
☐ Battery charger
☐ Hydrometer (for battery specific gravity check)
☐ Anti-freeze tester (for liquid-cooled engines)

Repair and overhaul tools

☐ Torque wrench (small and mid-ranges)
☐ Conventional, plastic or soft-faced hammers
☐ Impact driver set
☐ Vernier gauge
☐ Circlip pliers (internal and external, or combination)
☐ Set of cold chisels and punches
☐ Selection of pullers
☐ Breaker bars
☐ One-man brake bleeder kit
☐ Wire stripper and crimper tool
☐ Multimeter (measures amps, volts and ohms)
☐ Stroboscope (for dynamic timing checks)
☐ Hose clamp
☐ Clutch holding tool

Specialist tools

☐ Micrometers (external type)
☐ Telescoping gauges
☐ Dial gauge
☐ Stud extractor
☐ Screw extractor set
☐ Bearing driver set
☐ Valve spring compressor (4-stroke engines)
☐ Piston pin drawbolt tool
☐ Piston ring clamp

1.1 Hydraulic motorcycle ramp

1.2 Use an approved can only for storing petrol (gasoline)

1.3 A fire extinguisher, goggles, mask and protective gloves should be at hand in the workshop

1 Workshop equipment and facilities

The workbench

● Work is made much easier by raising the scooter up on a ramp – components are much more accessible if raised to waist level. The hydraulic or pneumatic types seen in the dealer's workshop are a sound investment if you undertake a lot of repairs or overhauls **(see illustration 1.1)**.
● If raised off ground level, the scooter must be supported on the ramp to avoid it falling. Most ramps incorporate a front wheel locating clamp which can be adjusted to suit different diameter wheels. When tightening the clamp, take care not to mark the wheel rim or damage the tyre – use wood blocks on each side to prevent this.

Fumes and fire

● Refer to the Safety first! page at the beginning of the manual for full details. Make sure your workshop is equipped with a fire extinguisher suitable for fuel-related fires (Class B fire – flammable liquids) – it is not sufficient to have a water-filled extinguisher.
● Always ensure adequate ventilation is available. Unless an exhaust gas extraction system is available for use, ensure that the engine is run outside of the workshop.
● If working on the fuel system, make sure the

workshop is ventilated to avoid a build-up of fumes. This applies equally to fume build-up when charging a battery. Do not smoke or allow anyone else to smoke in the workshop.

Fluids

● If you need to drain fuel from the tank, store it in an approved container marked as suitable for the storage of petrol (gasoline) **(see illustration 1.2)**. Do not store fuel in glass jars or bottles.
● Use proprietary engine degreasers or solvents which have a high flash-point, such as paraffin (kerosene), for cleaning off oil, grease and dirt – never use petrol (gasoline) for cleaning. Wear rubber gloves when handling solvent and engine degreaser. The fumes from certain solvents can be dangerous – always work in a well-ventilated area.

Dust, eye and hand protection

● Protect your lungs from inhalation of dust particles by wearing a filtering mask over the nose and mouth. Many frictional materials still contain asbestos which is dangerous to your health. Protect your eyes from spouts of liquid and sprung components by wearing a pair of protective goggles **(see illustration 1.3)**.
● Protect your hands from contact with solvents, fuel and oils by wearing rubber gloves. Alternatively apply a barrier cream to your hands before starting work. If handling hot components or fluids, wear suitable gloves to protect your hands from scalding and burns.

What to do with old fluids

● Old cleaning solvent, fuel, coolant and oils should not be poured down domestic drains or onto the ground. Package the fluid up in old oil containers, label it accordingly, and take it to a garage or disposal facility. Contact your local authority for location of such sites.

2 Fasteners – screws, bolts and nuts

Fastener types and applications
Bolts and screws

● Fastener head types are either of hexagonal, Torx or splined design, with internal and external versions of each type **(see illustrations 2.1 and 2.2)**; splined head fasteners are not in common use on scooters. The conventional slotted or Phillips head design is used for certain screws. Bolt or screw length is always measured from the underside of the head to the end of the item **(see illustration 2.11)**.
● Certain fasteners on the scooter have a tensile marking on their heads, the higher the marking the stronger the fastener. High tensile fasteners generally carry a 10 or higher marking. Never replace a high tensile fastener with one of a lower tensile strength.

Washers **(see illustration 2.3)**

● Plain washers are used between a fastener

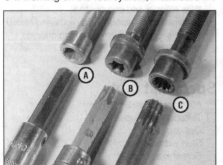

2.1 Internal hexagon/Allen (A), Torx (B) and splined (C) fasteners, with corresponding bits

2.2 External Torx (A), splined (B) and hexagon (C) fasteners, with corresponding sockets

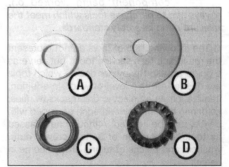

2.3 Plain washer (A), penny washer (B), spring washer (C) and serrated washer (D)

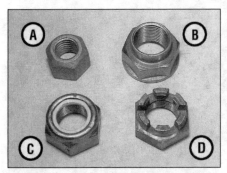

2.4 Plain nut (A), shouldered locknut (B), nylon insert nut (C) and castellated nut (D)

2.5 Bend split pin (cotter pin) arms as shown (arrows) to secure a castellated nut

2.6 Bend split pin (cotter pin) arms as shown to secure a plain nut

head and a component to prevent damage to the component or to spread the load when torque is applied. Plain washers can also be used as spacers or shims in certain assemblies. Copper or aluminium plain washers are often used as sealing washers on drain plugs.

● The split-ring spring washer works by applying axial tension between the fastener head and component. If flattened, it is fatigued and must be renewed. If a plain (flat) washer is used on the fastener, position the spring washer between the fastener and the plain washer.

● Serrated star type washers dig into the fastener and component faces, preventing loosening. They are often used on electrical earth (ground) connections to the frame.

● Cone type washers (sometimes called Belleville) are conical and when tightened apply axial tension between the fastener head and component. They must be installed with the dished side against the component and often carry an OUTSIDE marking on their outer face. If flattened, they are fatigued and must be renewed.

● Tab washers are used to lock plain nuts or bolts on a shaft. A portion of the tab washer is bent up hard against one flat of the nut or bolt to prevent it loosening. Due to the tab washer being deformed in use, a new tab washer should be used every time it is disturbed.

● Wave washers are used to take up endfloat on a shaft. They provide light springing and prevent excessive side-to-side play of a component. Can be found on rocker arm shafts.

Nuts and split pins

● Conventional plain nuts are usually six-sided **(see illustration 2.4)**. They are sized by thread diameter and pitch. High tensile nuts carry a number on one end to denote their tensile strength.

● Self-locking nuts either have a nylon insert, or two spring metal tabs, or a shoulder which is staked into a groove in the shaft – their advantage over conventional plain nuts is a resistance to loosening due to vibration. The nylon insert type can be used a number of times, but must be renewed when the friction of the nylon insert is reduced, ie when the nut spins freely on the shaft. The spring tab type

2.7 Correct fitting of R-pin. Arrow indicates forward direction

can be reused unless the tabs are damaged. The shouldered type must be renewed every time it is disturbed.

● Split pins (cotter pins) are used to lock a castellated nut to a shaft or to prevent slackening of a plain nut. Common applications are wheel axles and brake torque arms. Because the split pin arms are deformed to lock around the nut a new split pin must always be used on installation – always fit the correct size split pin which will fit snugly in the shaft hole. Make sure the split pin arms are correctly located around the nut **(see illustrations 2.5 and 2.6)**.

● R-pins (shaped like the letter R), or slip pins as they are sometimes called, are sprung and can be reused if they are otherwise in good condition. Always install R-pins with their closed end facing forwards **(see illustration 2.7)**.

Caution: If the castellated nut slots do not align with the shaft hole after tightening to the torque setting, tighten the nut until

the next slot aligns with the hole – never slacken the nut to align its slot.

Circlips **(see illustration 2.8)**

● Circlips (sometimes called snap-rings) are used to retain components on a shaft or in a housing and have corresponding external or internal ears to permit removal. Parallel-sided (machined) circlips can be installed either way round in their groove, whereas stamped circlips (which have a chamfered edge on one face) must be installed with the chamfer facing away from the direction of thrust load **(see illustration 2.9)**.

● Always use circlip pliers to remove and install circlips; expand or compress them just enough to remove them. After installation, rotate the circlip in its groove to ensure it is securely seated. If installing a circlip on a splined shaft, always align its opening with a shaft channel to ensure the circlip ends are well supported and unlikely to catch **(see illustration 2.10)**.

● Circlips can wear due to the thrust of components and become loose in their

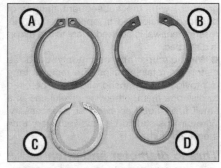

2.8 External stamped circlip (A), internal stamped circlip (B), machined circlip (C) and wire circlip (D)

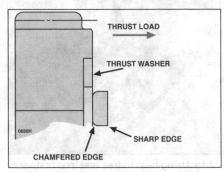

2.9 Correct fitting of a stamped circlip

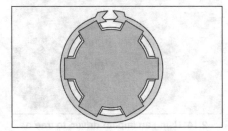

2.10 Align circlip opening with shaft channel

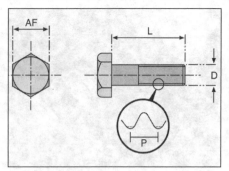

2.11 Fastener length (L), thread diameter (D), thread pitch (P) and head size (AF)

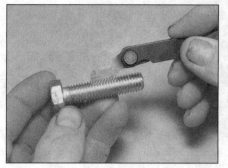

2.12 Using a thread gauge to measure pitch

2.13 A sharp tap on the head of a fastener will often break free a corroded thread

grooves, with the subsequent danger of becoming dislodged in operation. For this reason, renewal is advised every time a circlip is disturbed.

● Wire circlips are commonly used as piston pin retaining clips. If a removal tang is provided, long-nosed pliers can be used to dislodge them, otherwise careful use of a small flat-bladed screwdriver is necessary. Wire circlips should be renewed every time they are disturbed.

Thread diameter and pitch

● Diameter of a male thread (screw, bolt or stud) is the outside diameter of the threaded portion (see illustration 2.11). Most scooter manufacturers use the ISO (International Standards Organisation) metric system expressed in millimetres, eg M6 refers to a 6 mm diameter thread. Sizing is the same for nuts, except that the thread diameter is measured across the valleys of the nut.

● Pitch is the distance between the peaks of the thread (see illustration 2.11). It is expressed in millimetres, thus a common bolt size may be expressed as 6.0 x 1.0 mm (6 mm thread diameter and 1 mm pitch). Generally pitch increases in proportion to thread diameter, although there are always exceptions.

● Thread diameter and pitch are related for conventional fastener applications and the accompanying table can be used as a guide. Additionally, the AF (Across Flats), spanner or socket size dimension of the bolt or nut (see illustration 2.11) is linked to thread and pitch specification. Thread pitch can be measured with a thread gauge (see illustration 2.12).

● The threads of most fasteners are of the right-hand type, ie they are turned clockwise to tighten and anti-clockwise to loosen. The reverse situation applies to left-hand thread fasteners, which are turned anti-clockwise to tighten and clockwise to loosen. Left-hand threads are used where rotation of a component might loosen a conventional right-hand thread fastener.

AF size	Thread diameter x pitch (mm)
8 mm	M5 x 0.8
8 mm	M6 x 1.0
10 mm	M6 x 1.0
12 mm	M8 x 1.25
14 mm	M10 x 1.25
17 mm	M12 x 1.25

Seized fasteners

● Corrosion of external fasteners due to water or reaction between two dissimilar metals can occur over a period of time. It will build up sooner in wet conditions or in countries where salt is used on the roads during the winter. If a fastener is severely corroded it is likely that normal methods of removal will fail and result in its head being ruined. When you attempt removal, the fastener thread should be heard to crack free and unscrew easily – if it doesn't, stop there before damaging something.

● A smart tap on the head of the fastener will often succeed in breaking free corrosion which has occurred in the threads (see illustration 2.13).

● An aerosol penetrating fluid (such as WD-40) applied the night beforehand may work its way down into the thread and ease removal.

Depending on the location, you may be able to make up a Plasticine well around the fastener head and fill it with penetrating fluid.

● If you are working on an engine internal component, corrosion will most likely not be a problem due to the well lubricated environment. However, components can be very tight and an impact driver is a useful tool in freeing them (see illustration 2.14).

● Where corrosion has occurred between dissimilar metals (eg steel and aluminium alloy), the application of heat to the fastener head will create a disproportionate expansion rate between the two metals and break the seizure caused by the corrosion. Whether heat can be applied depends on the location of the fastener – any surrounding components likely to be damaged must first be removed (see illustration 2.15). Heat can be applied using a paint stripper heat gun or clothes iron, or by immersing the component in boiling water – wear protective gloves to prevent scalding or burns to the hands.

● As a last resort, it is possible to use a hammer and cold chisel to work the fastener head unscrewed (see illustration 2.16). This will damage the fastener, but more importantly extreme care must be taken not to damage the surrounding component.

Caution: Remember that the component being secured is generally of more value than the bolt, nut or screw – when the fastener is freed, do not unscrew it with force, instead work the fastener back and forth when resistance is felt to prevent thread damage.

2.14 Using an impact driver to free a fastener

2.15 Using heat to free a seized fastener

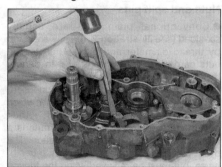

2.16 Using a hammer and chisel to free a seized fastener

2.17 Using a stud extractor tool to remove a broken crankcase stud

Broken fasteners and damaged heads

● If the shank of a broken bolt or screw is accessible you can grip it with self-locking grips. The knurled wheel type stud extractor tool or self-gripping stud puller tool is particularly useful for removing the long studs which screw into the cylinder mouth surface of the crankcase or bolts and screws from which the head has broken off **(see illustration 2.17)**. Studs can also be removed by locking two nuts together on the threaded end of the stud and using a spanner on the lower nut **(see illustration 2.18)**.

● A bolt or screw which has broken off below or level with the casing must be extracted using a screw extractor set. Centre punch the fastener to centralise the drill bit, then drill a hole in the fastener **(see illustration 2.19)**. Select a drill bit which is approximately half to three-quarters the diameter of the fastener and drill to a depth which will accommodate the extractor. Use the largest size extractor

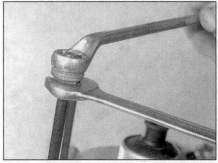

2.18 Two nuts can be locked together to unscrew a stud from a component

possible, but avoid leaving too small a wall thickness otherwise the extractor will merely force the fastener walls outwards wedging it in the casing thread.

● If a spiral type extractor is used, thread it anti-clockwise into the fastener. As it is screwed in, it will grip the fastener and unscrew it from the casing **(see illustration 2.20)**.

 Warning: Stud extractors are very hard and may break off in the fastener if care is not taken – ask an engineer about spark erosion if this happens.

● If a taper type extractor is used, tap it into the fastener so that it is firmly wedged in place. Unscrew the extractor (anti-clockwise) to draw the fastener out.

● Alternatively, the broken bolt/screw can be drilled out and the hole retapped for an oversize bolt/screw or a diamond-section thread insert. It is essential that the drilling is carried out squarely and to the correct depth, otherwise the casing may be ruined – if in

2.19 When using a screw extractor, first drill a hole in the fastener . . .

doubt, entrust the work to an engineer.

● Bolts and nuts with rounded corners cause the correct size spanner or socket to slip when force is applied. Of the types of spanner/socket available always use a six-point type rather than an eight or twelve-point type – better grip is obtained. Surface drive spanners grip the middle of the hex flats, rather than the corners, and are thus good in cases of damaged heads **(see illustration 2.21)**.

● Slotted-head or Phillips-head screws are often damaged by the use of the wrong size screwdriver. Allen-head and Torx-head screws are much less likely to sustain damage. If enough of the screw head is exposed you can use a hacksaw to cut a slot in its head and then use a conventional flat-bladed screwdriver to remove it. Alternatively use a hammer and cold chisel to tap the head of the fastener around to slacken it. Always replace damaged fasteners with new ones, preferably Torx or Allen-head type.

2.20 . . . then thread the extractor anti-clockwise into the fastener

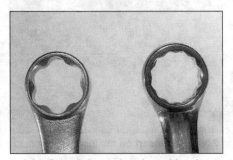

2.21 Comparison of surface drive ring spanner (left) with 12-point type (right)

A dab of valve grinding compound between the screw head and screw-driver tip will often give a good grip.

Thread repair

● Threads (particularly those in aluminium alloy components) can be damaged by overtightening, being assembled with dirt in the threads, or from a component working loose and vibrating. Eventually the thread will fail completely, and it will be impossible to tighten the fastener.

● If a thread is damaged or clogged with old locking compound it can be renovated with a thread repair tool (thread chaser) **(see illustrations 2.22 and 2.23)**; special thread

2.22 A thread repair tool being used to correct an internal thread

2.23 A thread repair tool being used to correct an external thread

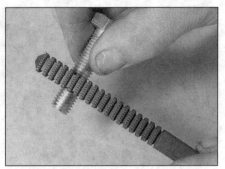

2.24 Using a thread restorer file

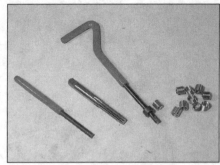

2.25 Obtain a thread insert kit to suit the thread diameter and pitch required

2.26 To install a thread insert, first drill out the original thread . . .

chasers are available for spark plug hole threads. The tool will not cut a new thread, but clean and true the original thread. Make sure that you use the correct diameter and pitch tool. Similarly, external threads can be cleaned up with a die or a thread restorer file **(see illustration 2.24)**.

● It is possible to drill out the old thread and retap the component to the next thread size. This will work where there is enough surrounding material and a new bolt or screw can be obtained. Sometimes, however, this is not possible – such as where the bolt/screw passes through another component which must also be suitably modified, also in cases where a spark plug or oil drain plug cannot be obtained in a larger diameter thread size.

● The diamond-section thread insert (often known by its popular trade name of Heli-Coil)

is a simple and effective method of renewing the thread and retaining the original size. A kit can be purchased which contains the tap, insert and installing tool **(see illustration 2.25)**. Drill out the damaged thread with the size drill specified **(see illustration 2.26)**. Carefully retap the thread **(see illustration 2.27)**. Install the insert on the installing tool and thread it slowly into place using a light downward pressure **(see illustrations 2.28 and 2.29)**. When positioned between a 1/4 and 1/2 turn below the surface withdraw the installing tool and use the break-off tool to press down on the tang, breaking it off **(see illustration 2.30)**.

● There are epoxy thread repair kits on the market which can rebuild stripped internal threads, although this repair should not be used on high load-bearing components.

Thread locking and sealing compounds

● Locking compounds are used in locations where the fastener is prone to loosening due to vibration or on important safety-related items which might cause loss of control of the scooter if they fail. It is also used where important fasteners cannot be secured by other means such as lockwashers or split pins.

● Before applying locking compound, make sure that the threads (internal and external) are clean and dry with all old compound removed. Select a compound to suit the component being secured – a non-permanent general locking and sealing type is suitable for most applications, but a high strength type is needed for permanent fixing of studs in castings. Apply a drop or two of the compound to the first few threads of the fastener, then thread it into place and tighten to the specified torque. Do not apply excessive thread locking compound otherwise the thread may be damaged on subsequent removal.

● Certain fasteners are impregnated with a dry film type coating of locking compound on their threads. Always renew this type of fastener if disturbed.

● Anti-seize compounds, such as copper-based greases, can be applied to protect threads from seizure due to extreme heat and corrosion. A common instance is spark plug threads and exhaust system fasteners.

2.27 . . . tap a new thread . . .

2.28 . . . fit insert on the installing tool . . .

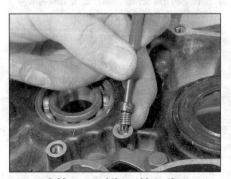

2.29 . . . and thread into the component . . .

2.30 . . . break off the tang when complete

3 Measuring tools and gauges

Feeler gauges

● Feeler gauges (or blades) are used for measuring small gaps and clearances **(see illustration 3.1)**. They can also be used to measure endfloat (sideplay) of a component on a shaft where access is not possible with a dial gauge.

● Feeler gauge sets should be treated with care and not bent or damaged. They are etched with their size on one face. Keep

3.1 Feeler gauges are used for measuring small gaps and clearances – thickness is marked on one face of gauge

3.2 Check micrometer calibration before use

them clean and very lightly oiled to prevent corrosion build-up.

● When measuring a clearance, select a gauge which is a light sliding fit between the two components. You may need to use two gauges together to measure the clearance accurately.

Micrometers

● A micrometer is a precision tool capable of measuring to 0.01 or 0.001 of a millimetre. It should always be stored in its case and not in the general toolbox. It must be kept clean and never dropped, otherwise its frame or measuring anvils could be distorted resulting in inaccurate readings.

● External micrometers are used for measuring outside diameters of components and have many more applications than internal micrometers. Micrometers are available in different size ranges, eg 0 to 25 mm, 25 to 50 mm, and upwards in 25 mm steps; some large micrometers have interchangeable anvils to allow a range of measurements to be taken. Generally the largest precision measurement you are likely to take on a scooter is the piston diameter.

● Internal micrometers (or bore micrometers) are used for measuring inside diameters, such as valve guides and cylinder bores. Telescoping gauges and small hole gauges are used in conjunction with an external micro-meter, whereas the more expensive internal micrometers have their own measuring device.

External micrometer

Note: *The conventional analogue type instrument is described. Although much easier to read, digital micrometers are considerably more expensive.*

● Always check the calibration of the micrometer before use. With the anvils closed (0 to 25 mm type) or set over a test gauge (for the larger types) the scale should read zero **(see illustration 3.2)**; make sure that the anvils (and test piece) are clean first. Any discrepancy can be adjusted by referring to the instructions supplied with the tool. Remember that the micrometer is a precision measuring tool – don't force the anvils closed, use the ratchet (4) on the end of the micrometer to close it. In this way, a measured force is always applied.

● To use, first make sure that the item being measured is clean. Place the anvil of the micrometer (1) against the item and use the thimble (2) to bring the spindle (3) lightly into contact with the other side of the item **(see illustration 3.3)**. Don't tighten the thimble down because this will damage the micrometer – instead use the ratchet (4) on the end of the micrometer. The ratchet mechanism applies a measured force preventing damage to the instrument.

● The micrometer is read by referring to the linear scale on the sleeve and the annular scale on the thimble. Read off the sleeve first to obtain the base measurement, then add the fine measurement from the thimble to obtain the overall reading. The linear scale on the sleeve represents the measuring range of the micrometer (eg 0 to 25 mm). The annular scale on the thimble will be in graduations of 0.01 mm (or as marked on the frame) – one full revolution of the thimble will move 0.5 mm on the linear scale. Take the reading where the datum line on the sleeve intersects the thimble's scale. Always position the eye directly above the scale otherwise an inaccurate reading will result.

In the example shown the item measures 2.95 mm **(see illustration 3.4)**:

Linear scale	2.00 mm
Linear scale	0.50 mm
Annular scale	0.45 mm
Total figure	**2.95 mm**

Most micrometers have a locking lever (6) on the frame to hold the setting in place, allowing the item to be removed from the micrometer.

● Some micrometers have a vernier scale on their sleeve, providing an even finer measurement to be taken, in 0.001 increments of a millimetre. Take the sleeve and thimble measurement as described above, then check which graduation on the vernier scale aligns with that of the annular scale on the thimble **Note:** *The eye must be perpendicular to the scale when taking the vernier reading – if necessary rotate the body of the micrometer to ensure this.* Multiply the vernier scale figure by 0.001 and add it to the base and fine measurement figures.

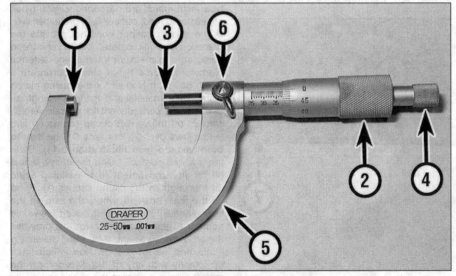

3.3 Micrometer component parts

1	Anvil	3	Spindle	5	Frame
2	Thimble	4	Ratchet	6	Locking lever

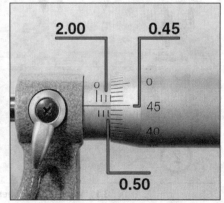

3.4 Micrometer reading of 2.95 mm

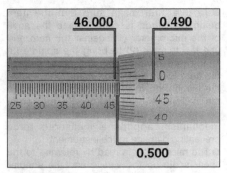

3.5 Micrometer reading of 46.99 mm on linear and annular scales . . .

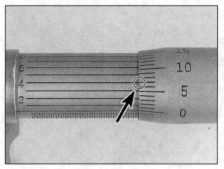

3.6 . . . and 0.004 mm on vernier scale

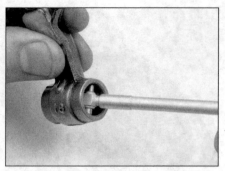

3.7 Expand the telescoping gauge in the bore, lock its position . . .

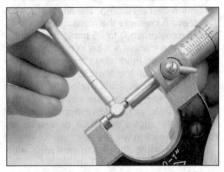

3.8 . . . then measure the gauge with a micrometer

3.9 Expand the small hole gauge in the bore, lock its position . . .

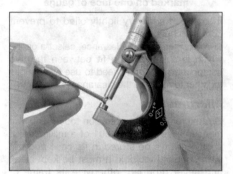

3.10 . . . then measure the gauge with a micrometer

In the example shown the item measures 46.994 mm **(see illustrations 3.5 and 3.6)**:

Linear scale (base)	46.000 mm
Linear scale (base)	00.500 mm
Annular scale (fine)	00.490 mm
Vernier scale	00.004 mm
Total figure	**46.994 mm**

Internal micrometer

● Internal micrometers are available for measuring bore diameters, but are expensive

and unlikely to be available for home use. It is suggested that a set of telescoping gauges and small hole gauges, both of which must be used with an external micrometer, will suffice for taking internal measurements on a scooter.
● Telescoping gauges can be used to measure internal diameters of components. Select a gauge with the correct size range, make sure its ends are clean and insert it into the bore. Expand the gauge, then lock its position and withdraw it from the bore (see

illustration 3.7). Measure across the gauge ends with a micrometer **(see illustration 3.8)**.
● Very small diameter bores (such as valve guides) are measured with a small hole gauge. Once adjusted to a slip-fit inside the component, its position is locked and the gauge withdrawn for measurement with a micrometer **(see illustrations 3.9 and 3.10)**.

Vernier caliper

Note: *The conventional linear and dial gauge type instruments are described. Digital types are easier to read, but are far more expensive.*
● The vernier caliper does not provide the precision of a micrometer, but is versatile in being able to measure internal and external diameters. Some types also incorporate a depth gauge. It is ideal for measuring clutch plate friction material and spring free lengths.
● To use the conventional linear scale vernier, slacken off the vernier clamp screws (1) and set its jaws over (2), or inside (3), the item to be measured **(see illustration 3.11)**. Slide the jaw into contact, using the thumb-wheel (4) for fine movement of the sliding scale (5) then tighten the clamp screws (1). Read off the main scale (6) where the zero on the sliding scale (5) intersects it, taking the whole number to the left of the zero; this provides the base measurement. View along the sliding scale and select the division which lines up exactly with any of the divisions on the main scale, noting that the divisions usually represents 0.02 of a millimetre. Add this fine measurement to the base measurement to obtain the total reading.

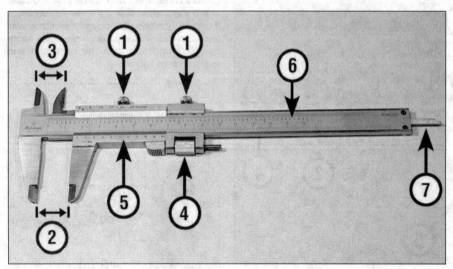

3.11 Vernier component parts (linear gauge)

1 Clamp screws	3 Internal jaws	5 Sliding scale	7 Depth gauge
2 External jaws	4 Thumbwheel	6 Main scale	

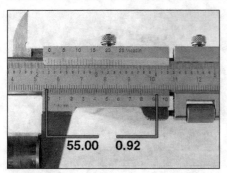

3.12 Vernier gauge reading of 55.92 mm

In the example shown the item measures 55.92 mm **(see illustration 3.12)**:

Base measurement	55.00 mm
Fine measurement	00.92 mm
Total figure	**55.92 mm**

● Some vernier calipers are equipped with a dial gauge for fine measurement. Before use, check that the jaws are clean, then close them fully and check that the dial gauge reads zero. If necessary adjust the gauge ring accordingly. Slacken the vernier clamp screw (1) and set its jaws over (2), or inside (3), the item to be measured **(see illustration 3.13)**. Slide the jaws into contact, using the thumbwheel (4) for fine movement. Read off the main scale (5) where the edge of the sliding scale (6) intersects it, taking the whole number to the left of the zero; this provides the base measurement. Read off the needle position on the dial gauge (7) scale to provide the fine measurement; each division represents 0.05 of a millimetre. Add this fine measurement to the base measurement to obtain the total reading.

In the example shown the item measures 55.95 mm **(see illustration 3.14)**:

Base measurement	55.00 mm
Fine measurement	00.95 mm
Total figure	**55.95 mm**

Dial gauge or DTI (Dial Test Indicator)

● A dial gauge can be used to accurately measure small amounts of movement. Typical uses are measuring shaft runout or shaft endfloat (sideplay) and setting piston position for ignition timing on two-strokes. A

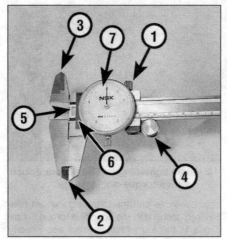

3.13 Vernier component parts (dial gauge)

1	Clamp screw	5	Main scale
2	External jaws	6	Sliding scale
3	Internal jaws	7	Dial gauge
4	Thumbwheel		

dial gauge set usually comes with a range of different probes and adapters and mounting equipment.

● The gauge needle must point to zero when at rest. Rotate the ring around its periphery to zero the gauge.

● Check that the gauge is capable of reading the extent of movement in the work. Most gauges have a small dial set in the face which records whole millimetres of movement as well as the fine scale around the face periphery which is calibrated in 0.01 mm divisions. Read off the small dial first to obtain the base measurement, then add the measurement from the fine scale to obtain the total reading.

In the example shown the gauge reads 1.48 mm **(see illustration 3.15)**:

Base measurement	1.00 mm
Fine measurement	0.48 mm
Total figure	**1.48 mm**

● If measuring shaft runout, the shaft must be supported in vee-blocks and the gauge mounted on a stand perpendicular to the shaft. Rest the tip of the gauge against the centre of the shaft and rotate the shaft slowly whilst watching the gauge reading **(see illustration 3.16)**. Take several measurements along the

length of the shaft and record the maximum gauge reading as the amount of runout in the shaft. **Note:** *The reading obtained will be total runout at that point – some manufacturers specify that the runout figure is halved to compare with their specified runout limit.*

● Endfloat (sideplay) measurement requires that the gauge is mounted securely to the surrounding component with its probe touching the end of the shaft. Using hand pressure, push and pull on the shaft noting the maximum endfloat recorded on the gauge **(see illustration 3.17)**.

● A dial gauge with suitable adapters can be used to determine piston position BTDC on two-stroke engines for the purposes of ignition timing. The gauge, adapter and suitable length probe are installed in the place of the spark plug and the gauge zeroed at TDC. If the piston position is specified as 1.14 mm BTDC, rotate the engine back to 2.00 mm BTDC, then slowly forwards to 1.14 mm BTDC.

4 Torque and leverage

What is torque?

● Torque describes the twisting force about a shaft. The amount of torque applied is determined by the distance from the centre of the shaft to the end of the lever and the amount of force being applied to the end of the lever; distance multiplied by force equals torque.

● The manufacturer applies a measured

3.14 Vernier gauge reading of 55.95 mm

3.15 Dial gauge reading of 1.48 mm

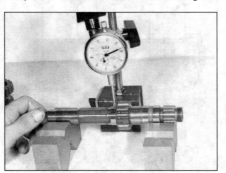

3.16 Using a dial gauge to measure shaft runout

3.17 Using a dial gauge to measure shaft endfloat

4.1 Set the torque wrench index mark to the setting required, in this case 12 Nm

4.2 Angle tightening can be accomplished with a torque-angle gauge . . .

4.3 . . . or by marking the angle on the surrounding component

torque to a bolt or nut to ensure that it will not slacken in use and to hold two components securely together without movement in the joint. The actual torque setting depends on the thread size, bolt or nut material and the composition of the components being held.

● Too little torque may cause the fastener to loosen due to vibration, whereas too much torque will distort the joint faces of the component or cause the fastener to shear off. Always stick to the specified torque setting.

Using a torque wrench

● Check the calibration of the torque wrench and make sure it has a suitable range for the job. Torque wrenches are available in Nm (Newton-metres), kgf m (kilograms-force metre), lbf ft (pounds-feet), lbf in (inch-pounds). Do not confuse lbf ft with lbf in.

● Adjust the tool to the desired torque on the scale **(see illustration 4.1)**. If your torque wrench is not calibrated in the units specified, carefully convert the figure (see *Conversion Factors*). A manufacturer sometimes gives a torque setting as a range (8 to 10 Nm) rather than a single figure – in this case set the tool midway between the two settings. The same torque may be expressed as 9 Nm ± 1 Nm. Some torque wrenches have a method of locking the setting so that it isn't inadvertently altered during use.

● Install the bolts/nuts in their correct location and secure them lightly. Their threads must be clean and free of any old locking compound. Unless specified the threads and flange should be dry – oiled threads are necessary in certain

circumstances and the manufacturer will take this into account in the specified torque figure. Similarly, the manufacturer may also specify the application of thread-locking compound.

● Tighten the fasteners in the specified sequence until the torque wrench clicks, indicating that the torque setting has been reached. Apply the torque again to double-check the setting. Where different thread diameter fasteners secure the component, as a rule tighten the larger diameter ones first.

● When the torque wrench has been finished with, release the lock (where applicable) and fully back off its setting to zero – do not leave the torque wrench tensioned. Also, do not use a torque wrench for slackening a fastener.

Angle-tightening

● Manufacturers often specify a figure in degrees for final tightening of a fastener. This usually follows tightening to a specific torque setting.

● A degree disc can be set and attached to the socket **(see illustration 4.2)** or a protractor can be used to mark the angle of movement on the bolt/nut head and the surrounding casting **(see illustration 4.3)**.

Loosening sequences

● Where more than one bolt/nut secures a component, loosen each fastener evenly a little at a time. In this way, not all the stress of the joint is held by one fastener and the components are not likely to distort.

● If a tightening sequence is provided, work

in the REVERSE of this, but if not, work from the outside in, in a criss-cross sequence **(see illustration 4.4)**.

Tightening sequences

● If a component is held by more than one fastener it is important that the retaining bolts/nuts are tightened evenly to prevent uneven stress build-up and distortion of sealing faces. This is especially important on high-compression joints such as the cylinder head.

● A sequence is usually provided by the manufacturer, either in a diagram or actually marked in the casting. If not, always start in the centre and work outwards in a criss-cross pattern **(see illustration 4.5)**. Start off by securing all bolts/nuts finger-tight, then set the torque wrench and tighten each fastener by a small amount in sequence until the final torque is reached. By following this practice, the joint will be held evenly and will not be distorted. Important joints, such as the cylinder head and big-end fasteners often have two- or three-stage torque settings.

Applying leverage

● Use tools at the correct angle. Position a socket wrench or spanner on the bolt/nut so that you pull it towards you when loosening. If this can't be done, push the spanner without curling your fingers around it **(see illustration 4.6)** – the spanner may slip or the fastener loosen suddenly, resulting in your fingers being crushed against a component.

● Additional leverage is gained by extending the length of the lever. The best way to do this is to use a breaker bar instead of the regular length tool, or to slip a length of tubing over the end of the spanner or socket wrench.

● If additional leverage will not work, the fastener head is either damaged or firmly corroded in place (see *Fasteners*).

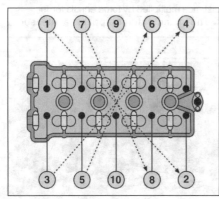

4.4 When slackening, work from the outside inwards

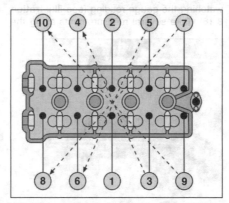

4.5 When tightening, work from the inside outwards

4.6 If you can't pull on the spanner to loosen a fastener, push with your hand open

5.1 Using a bearing driver against the bearing's outer race

5.2 Using a large socket against the bearing's outer race

5.3 This bearing puller clamps behind the bearing and pressure is applied to the shaft end to draw the bearing off

5 Bearings

Bearing removal and installation

Drivers and sockets

● Before removing a bearing, always inspect the casing to see which way it must be driven out – some casings will have retaining plates or a cast step. Also check for any identifying markings on the bearing and if installed to a certain depth, measure this at this stage. Some roller bearings are sealed on one side – take note of the original fitted position.

● Bearings can be driven out of a casing using a bearing driver tool (with the correct size head) or a socket of the correct diameter. Select the driver head or socket so that it contacts the outer race of the bearing, not the balls/rollers or inner race. Always support the casing around the bearing housing with wood blocks, otherwise there is a risk of fracture. The bearing is driven out with a few blows on the driver or socket from a heavy mallet. Unless access is severely restricted (as with wheel bearings), a pin-punch is not recommended unless it is moved around the bearing to keep it square in its housing.

● The same equipment can be used to install bearings. Make sure the bearing housing is supported on wood blocks and line up the bearing in its housing. Fit the bearing as noted on removal – generally they are installed with their marked side facing outwards. Tap the bearing squarely into its housing using a driver or socket which bears only on the bearing's outer race – contact with the bearing balls/rollers or inner race will destroy it **(see illustrations 5.1 and 5.2)**.

● Check that the bearing inner race and balls/rollers rotate freely.

Pullers and slide-hammers

● Where a bearing is pressed on a shaft a puller will be required to extract it **(see illustration 5.3)**. Make sure that the puller clamp or legs fit securely behind the bearing and are unlikely to slip out. If pulling a bearing off a gear shaft for example, you may have

to locate the puller behind a gear pinion if there is no access to the race and draw the gear pinion off the shaft as well **(see illustration 5.4)**.

Caution: Ensure that the puller's centre bolt locates securely against the end of the shaft and will not slip when pressure is applied. Also ensure that puller does not damage the shaft end.

● Operate the puller so that its centre bolt exerts pressure on the shaft end and draws the bearing off the shaft.

● When installing the bearing on the shaft, tap only on the bearing's inner race – contact with the balls/rollers or outer race with destroy the bearing. Use a socket or length of tubing as a drift which fits over the shaft end **(see illustration 5.5)**.

5.4 Where no access is available to the rear of the bearing, it is sometimes possible to draw off the adjacent component

5.6 Expand the bearing puller so that it locks behind the bearing . . .

● Where a bearing locates in a blind hole in a casing, it cannot be driven or pulled out as described above. A slide-hammer with knife-edged bearing puller attachment will be required. The puller attachment passes through the bearing and when tightened expands to fit firmly behind the bearing **(see illustration 5.6)**. By operating the slide-hammer part of the tool the bearing is jarred out of its housing **(see illustration 5.7)**.

● It is possible, if the bearing is of reasonable weight, for it to drop out of its housing if the casing is heated as described opposite. If this method is attempted, first prepare a work surface which will enable the casing to be tapped face down to help dislodge the bearing – a wood surface is ideal since it will not damage the casing's gasket surface.

5.5 When installing a bearing on a shaft use a piece of tubing which bears only on the bearing's inner race

5.7 . . . attach the slide hammer to the bearing puller

5.8 Tapping a casing face down on wood blocks can often dislodge a bearing

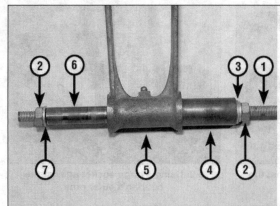

1 Bolt or length of threaded bar
2 Nuts
3 Washer (external diameter greater than tubing internal diameter)
4 Tubing (internal diameter sufficient to accommodate bearing)
5 Suspension arm with bearing
6 Tubing (external diameter slightly smaller than bearing)
7 Washer (external diameter slightly smaller than bearing)

5.10 Drawing the bearing out

5.9 Drawbolt component parts assembled on a suspension arm

Wearing protective gloves, tap the heated casing several times against the work surface to dislodge the bearing under its own weight (see illustration 5.8).

● Bearings can be installed in blind holes using the driver or socket method described above.

Drawbolts

● Where a bearing or bush is set in the eye of a component, such as a suspension linkage arm or connecting rod small-end, removal by drift may damage the component. Furthermore, a rubber bushing in a shock absorber eye cannot successfully be driven out of position. If access is available to a engineering press, the task is straightforward. If not, a drawbolt can be fabricated to extract the bearing or bush.

● To extract the bearing/bush you will need a long bolt with nut (or piece of threaded bar with two nuts), a piece of tubing which has

an internal diameter larger than the bearing/bush, another piece of tubing which has an external diameter slightly smaller than the bearing/bush, and a selection of washers (see illustrations 5.9 and 5.10). Note that the pieces of tubing must be of the same length, or longer, than the bearing/bush.

● The same kit (without the pieces of tubing) can be used to draw the new bearing/bush back into place (see illustration 5.11).

Temperature change

● If the bearing's outer race is a tight fit in the casing, the aluminium casing can be heated to release its grip on the bearing. Aluminium will expand at a greater rate than the steel bearing outer race. There are several ways to do this, but avoid any localised extreme heat

(such as a blow torch) – aluminium alloy has a low melting point.

● Approved methods of heating a casing are using a domestic oven (heated to 100°C) or immersing the casing in boiling water (see illustration 5.12). Low temperature range localised heat sources such as a paint stripper heat gun or clothes iron can also be used (see illustration 5.13). Alternatively, soak a rag in boiling water, wring it out and wrap it around the bearing housing.

> ⚠ **Warning: All of these methods require care in use to prevent scalding and burns to the hands. Wear protective gloves when handling hot components.**

● If heating the whole casing note that plastic components, such as the oil pressure switch, may suffer – remove them beforehand.

● After heating, remove the bearing as described above. You may find that the expansion is sufficient for the bearing to fall out of the casing under its own weight or with a light tap on the driver or socket.

● If necessary, the casing can be heated to aid bearing installation, and this is sometimes the recommended procedure if the scooter manufacturer has designed the housing and bearing fit with this intention.

● Installation of bearings can be eased by placing them in a freezer the night before installation. The steel bearing will contract slightly, allowing easy insertion in its housing. This is often useful when installing steering head outer races in the frame.

Bearing types and markings

● Plain bearings, ball bearings, needle roller bearings and tapered roller bearings will all be found on scooters (see illustrations 5.14 and 5.15). The ball and roller types are usually caged between an inner and outer race, but uncaged variations may be found.

● Plain bearings are sometimes found at the crankshaft main and connecting rod big-end where they are good at coping with high loads. They are made of a phosphor-bronze material and are impregnated with self-lubricating properties.

of the suspension arm

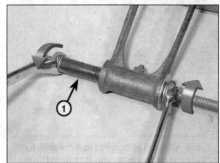

5.11 Installing a new bearing (1) in the suspension arm

5.12 A casing can be immersed in a sink of boiling water to aid bearing removal

5.13 Using a localised heat source to aid bearing removal

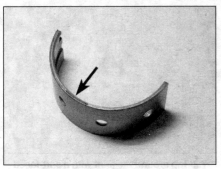

5.14 Bearings are either plain or grooved. They are usually identified by colour code (arrow)

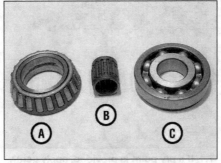

5.15 Tapered roller bearing (A), needle roller bearing (B) and ball journal bearing (C)

5.16 Typical bearing marking

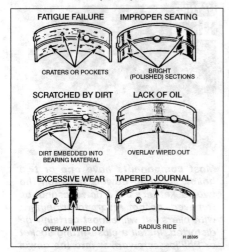

5.17 Typical bearing failures

5.18 Example of ball journal bearing with damaged balls and cages

5.19 Hold outer race and listen to inner race when spun

● Ball bearings and needle roller bearings consist of a steel inner and outer race with the balls or rollers between the races. They require constant lubrication by oil or grease and are good at coping with axial loads. Tapered roller bearings consist of rollers set in a tapered cage set on the inner race; the outer race is separate. They are good at coping with axial loads and prevent movement along the shaft – a typical application is in the steering head.

● Bearing manufacturers produce bearings to ISO size standards and stamp one face of the bearing to indicate its internal and external diameter, load capacity and type (see illustration 5.16).

● Metal bushes are usually of phosphor-bronze material. Rubber bushes are used in suspension mounting eyes. Fibre bushes have also been used in suspension pivots.

Bearing fault finding

● If a bearing outer race has spun in its housing, the housing material will be damaged. You can use a bearing locking compound to bond the outer race in place if damage is not too severe.

● Plain bearings will fail due to damage of their working surface, as a result of lack of lubrication, corrosion or abrasive particles in the oil (see illustration 5.17). Small particles

of dirt in the oil may embed in the bearing material whereas larger particles will score the bearing and shaft journal. If a number of short journeys are made, insufficient heat will be generated to drive off condensation which has built up on the bearings.

● Ball and roller bearings will fail due to lack of lubrication or damage to the balls or rollers. Tapered roller bearings can be damaged by overloading them. Unless the bearing is sealed on both sides, wash it in paraffin (kerosene) to remove all old grease then allow it to dry. Make a visual inspection looking to dented balls or rollers, damaged cages and worn or pitted races (see illustration 5.18).

● A ball bearing can be checked for wear by listening to it when spun. Apply a film of light oil to the bearing and hold it close to the ear – hold the outer race with one hand and spin the inner race with the other hand (see illustration 5.19). The bearing should be almost silent when spun; if it grates or rattles it is worn.

6 Oil seals

Oil seal removal and installation

● Oil seals should be renewed every time a component is dismantled. This is because the seal lips will become set to the sealing surface and will not necessarily reseal.

● Oil seals can be prised out of position using a large flat-bladed screwdriver (see

illustration 6.1). In the case of crankcase seals, check first that the seal is not lipped on the inside, preventing its removal with the crankcases joined.

● New seals are usually installed with their marked face (containing the seal reference code) outwards and the spring side towards the fluid being retained. In certain cases, such as a two-stroke engine crankshaft seal, a double lipped seal may be used due to there being fluid or gas on each side of the joint.

● Use a bearing driver or socket which bears only on the outer hard edge of the seal to install it in the casing – tapping on the inner edge will damage the sealing lip.

Oil seal types and markings

● Oil seals are usually of the single-lipped type. Double-lipped seals are found where a liquid or gas is on both sides of the joint.

6.1 Prise out oil seals with a large flat-bladed screwdriver

6.2 These oil seal markings indicate inside diameter, outside diameter and seal thickness

● Oil seals can harden and lose their sealing ability if the scooter has been in storage for a long period – renewal is the only solution.
● Oil seal manufacturers also conform to the ISO markings for seal size – these are moulded into the outer face of the seal **(see illustration 6.2)**.

7 Gaskets and sealants

Types of gasket and sealant

● Gaskets are used to seal the mating surfaces between components and keep lubricants, fluids, vacuum or pressure contained within the assembly. Aluminium gaskets are sometimes found at the cylinder joints, but most gaskets are paper-based. If the mating surfaces of the components being joined are undamaged the gasket can be installed dry, although a dab of sealant or grease will be useful to hold it in place during assembly.
● RTV (Room Temperature Vulcanising) silicone rubber sealants cure when exposed to moisture in the atmosphere. These sealants are good at filling pits or irregular gasket faces, but will tend to be forced out of the joint under very high torque. They can be used to replace a paper gasket, but first make sure that the width of the paper gasket is not essential to the shimming of internal components. RTV sealants should not be used on components containing petrol (gasoline).
● Non-hardening, semi-hardening and hard

7.1 If a pry point is provided, apply gently pressure with a flat-bladed screwdriver

setting liquid gasket compounds can be used with a gasket or between a metal-to-metal joint. Select the sealant to suit the application: universal non-hardening sealant can be used on virtually all joints; semi-hardening on joint faces which are rough or damaged; hard setting sealant on joints which require a permanent bond and are subjected to high temperature and pressure. **Note:** *Check first if the paper gasket has a bead of sealant impregnated in its surface before applying additional sealant.*
● When choosing a sealant, make sure it is suitable for the application, particularly if being applied in a high-temperature area or in the vicinity of fuel. Certain manufacturers produce sealants in either clear, silver or black colours to match the finish of the engine.
● Do not over-apply sealant. That which is squeezed out on the outside of the joint can be wiped off, whereas an excess of sealant on the inside can break off and clog oilways.

Breaking a sealed joint

● Age, heat, pressure and the use of hard setting sealant can cause two components to stick together so tightly that they are difficult to separate using finger pressure alone. Do not resort to using levers unless there is a pry point provided for this purpose **(see illustration 7.1)** or else the gasket surfaces will be damaged.
● Use a soft-faced hammer **(see illustration 7.2)** or a wood block and conventional hammer to strike the component near the mating surface. Avoid hammering against cast extremities since they may break off. If this method fails, try using a wood wedge between the two components.

7.2 Tap around the joint with a soft-faced mallet if necessary – don't strike cooling fins

Most components have one or two hollow locating dowels between the two gasket faces. If a dowel cannot be removed, do not resort to gripping it with pliers – it will almost certainly be distorted. Install a close-fitting socket or Phillips screwdriver into the dowel and then grip the outer edge of the dowel to free it.

Caution: If the joint will not separate, double-check that you have removed all the fasteners.

Removal of old gasket and sealant

● Paper gaskets will most likely come away complete, leaving only a few traces stuck on the sealing faces of the components. It is imperative that all traces are removed to ensure correct sealing of the new gasket.
● Very carefully scrape all traces of gasket away making sure that the sealing surfaces are not gouged or scored by the scraper **(see illustrations 7.3, 7.4 and 7.5)**. Stubborn

7.3 Paper gaskets can be scraped off with a gasket scraper tool . . .

7.4 . . . a knife blade . . .

7.5 . . . or a household scraper

7.6 Fine abrasive paper is wrapped around a flat file to clean up the gasket face

7.7 A kitchen scourer can be used on stubborn deposits

deposits can be removed by spraying with an aerosol gasket remover. Final preparation of the gasket surface can be made with very fine abrasive paper or a plastic kitchen scourer **(see illustrations 7.6 and 7.7)**.

● Old sealant can be scraped or peeled off components, depending on the type originally used. Note that gasket removal compounds are available to avoid scraping the components clean; make sure the gasket remover suits the type of sealant used.

8 Hoses

Clamping to prevent flow

● Small-bore flexible hoses can be clamped to prevent fluid flow whilst a component is worked on. Whichever method is used, ensure that the hose material is not permanently distorted or damaged by the clamp.

a) A brake hose clamp available from auto accessory shops **(see illustration 8.1)**.

b) A wingnut type hose clamp **(see illustration 8.2)**.

c) Two sockets placed each side of the hose and held with straight-jawed self-locking grips **(see illustration 8.3)**.

d) Thick card each side of the hose held between straight-jawed self-locking grips **(see illustration 8.4)**.

Freeing and fitting hoses

● Always make sure the hose clamp is moved well clear of the hose end. Grip the hose with your hand and rotate it whilst pulling it off the union. If the hose has hardened due to age and will not move, slit it with a sharp knife and peel its ends off the union **(see illustration 8.5)**.

● Resist the temptation to use grease or soap on the unions to aid installation; although it helps the hose slip over the union it will equally aid the escape of fluid from the joint. It is preferable to soften the hose ends in hot water and wet the inside surface of the hose with water or a fluid which will evaporate.

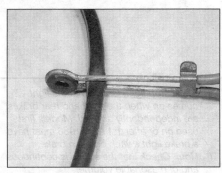

8.1 Hoses can be clamped with an automotive brake hose clamp . . .

8.2 . . . a wingnut type hose clamp . . .

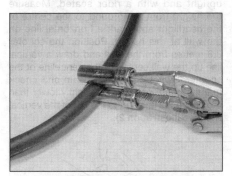

8.3 . . . two sockets and a pair of self-locking grips . . .

8.4 . . . or thick card and self-locking grips

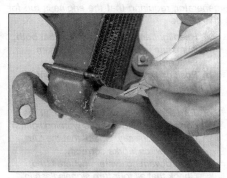

8.5 Cutting a coolant hose free with a sharp knife

About the MOT Test

In the UK, all vehicles more than three years old are subject to an annual test to ensure that they meet minimum safety requirements. A current test certificate must be issued before a machine can be used on public roads, and is required before a road fund licence can be issued. Riding without a current test certificate will also invalidate your insurance.

For most owners, the MOT test is an annual cause for anxiety, and this is largely due to owners not being sure what needs to be checked prior to submitting the scooter for testing. The simple answer is that a fully roadworthy scooter will have no difficulty in passing the test.

This is a guide to getting your scooter through the MOT test. Obviously it will not be possible to examine the scooter to the same standard as the professional MOT tester, particularly in view of the equipment required for some of the checks. However, working through the following procedures will enable you to identify any problem areas before submitting the scooter for the test.

It has only been possible to summarise the test requirements here, based on the regulations in force at the time of printing. Test standards are becoming increasingly stringent, although there are some exemptions for older vehicles. More information about the MOT test can be obtained from the TSO publications, *How Safe is your Motorcycle* and *The MOT Inspection Manual for Motorcycle Testing.*

Many of the checks require that one of the wheels is raised off the ground. Additionally, the help of an assistant may prove useful.

Check that the frame number is clearly visible.

Electrical System

Lights, turn signals, horn and reflector

● With the ignition on, check the operation of the following electrical components. **Note:** *The electrical components on certain small-capacity machines are powered by the generator, requiring that the engine is run for this check.*

a) *Headlight and tail light. Check that both illuminate in the low and high beam switch positions.*

b) *Position lights. Check that the front position (or sidelight) and tail light illuminate in this switch position.*

c) *Turn signals. Check that all flash at the correct rate, and that the warning light(s) function correctly. Check that the turn signal switch works correctly.*

d) *Hazard warning system (where fitted). Check that all four turn signals flash in this switch position.*

e) *Brake stop light. Check that the light comes on when the front and rear brakes are independently applied. Models first used on or after 1st April 1986 must have a brake light switch on each brake.*

f) *Horn. Check that the sound is continuous and of reasonable volume.*

● Check that there is a red reflector on the rear of the machine, either mounted separately or as part of the tail light lens.
● Check the condition of the headlight, tail light and turn signal lenses.

Headlight beam height

● The MOT tester will perform a headlight beam height check using specialised beam setting equipment **(see illustration 1)**. This equipment will not be available to the home mechanic, but if you suspect that the headlight is incorrectly set or may have been maladjusted in the past, you can perform a rough test as follows.

● Position the scooter in a straight line facing a brick wall. The scooter must be off its stand, upright and with a rider seated. Measure the height from the ground to the centre of the headlight and mark a horizontal line on the wall at this height. Position the scooter 3.8 metres from the wall and draw a vertical line up the wall central to the centreline of the scooter. Switch to dipped beam and check that the beam pattern falls slightly lower than the horizontal line and to the left of the vertical line **(see illustration 2)**.

Headlight beam height checking equipment

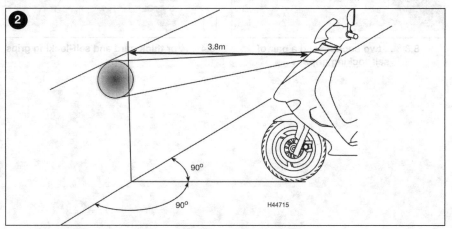

3.8m

90°

90°

H44715

Home workshop beam alignment check

Exhaust System

Exhaust

● Check that the exhaust mountings are secure and that the system does not foul any

of the rear suspension components.
● Start the scooter. When the revs are increased, check that the exhaust is neither holed nor leaking from any of its joints. On a linked system, check that the collector box is not leaking due to corrosion.
● Note that the exhaust decibel level ("loudness" of the exhaust) is assessed at

the discretion of the tester. If the scooter was first used on or after 1st January 1985 the silencer must carry the BSAU 193 stamp, or a marking relating to its make and model, or be of OE (original equipment) manufacture. If the silencer is marked NOT FOR ROAD USE, RACING USE ONLY or similar, it will fail the MOT.

Steering and Suspension

Steering

● With the front wheel raised off the ground, rotate the steering from lock to lock. The handlebar or switches must not contact anything. Problems can be caused by damaged lock stops on the lower yoke and frame, or by the fitting of non-standard handlebars.

● When performing the lock to lock check, also ensure that the steering moves freely without drag or notchiness. Steering movement can be impaired by poorly routed cables, or by overtight head bearings or worn bearings. The tester will perform a check of the steering head bearing lower race by mounting the front wheel on a surface plate, then performing a lock to lock check with the weight of the machine on the lower bearing **(see illustration 3)**.
● Grasp the fork sliders (lower legs) and attempt to push and pull on the forks **(see**

illustration 4). Any play in the steering head bearings will be felt. Note that in extreme cases, wear of the front fork bushes can be misinterpreted for head bearing play.
● Check that the handlebars are securely mounted.
● Check that the handlebar grip rubbers are secure. They should by bonded to the bar left end and to the throttle twistgrip on the right end.

Front suspension

● With the scooter off the stand, hold the front brake on and pump the front suspension up and down **(see illustration 5)**. Check that the movement is adequately damped.
● Inspect the area above and around the front fork oil seals **(see illustration 6)**. There should be no sign of oil on the fork tube (stanchion) nor leaking down the slider (lower leg).
● On models with leading or trailing link front suspension, check that there is no freeplay in the linkage when moved from side to side.

Front wheel mounted on a surface plate for steering head bearing lower race check

Checking the steering head bearings for freeplay

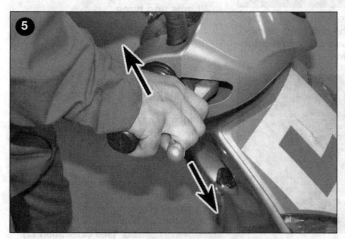

Hold the front brake on and pump the front suspension up and down to check operation

Inspect the area around the fork dust seal for oil leakage

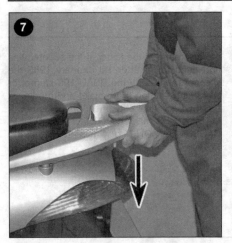

Bounce the rear of the scooter to check rear suspension operation

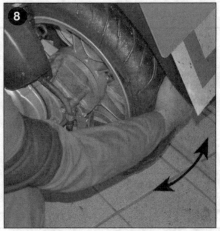

Grasp the rear wheel to check for play in the engine-to-frame mountings

Rear suspension

● With the scooter off the stand and an assistant supporting the scooter by its handlebars, bounce the rear suspension **(see illustration 7)**. Check that the suspension components do not foul the bodywork and check that the shock absorber(s) provide adequate damping.

● Visually inspect the shock absorber(s) and check that there is no sign of oil leakage from its damper.

● With the rear wheel raised off the ground, grasp the wheel as shown and attempt to move it from side to side **(see illustration 8)**. Any play in the engine-to-frame mountings will be felt as movement.

Brakes, Wheels and Tyres

Brakes

● With the wheel raised off the ground, apply the brake then free it off, and check that the wheel is about to revolve freely without brake drag.

Brake pad wear can usually be viewed without removing the caliper. Some pads have wear indicator grooves (arrow)

● On disc brakes, examine the disc itself. Check that it is securely mounted and not cracked.

● On disc brakes, view the pad material through the caliper mouth and check that the pads are not worn down beyond the limit **(see illustration 9)**.

● On drum brakes, check that when the brake is applied the angle between the operating

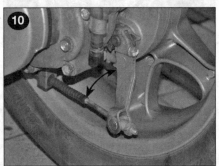

On drum brakes, check the angle of the operating lever with the brake fully applied. Most drum brakes have a wear indicator pointer and scale

lever and cable or rod is not too great **(see illustration 10)**. Check also that the operating lever doesn't foul any other components.

● On disc brakes, examine the flexible hoses from top to bottom. Have an assistant hold the brake on so that the fluid in the hose is under pressure, and check that there is no sign of fluid leakage, bulges or cracking. If there are any metal brake pipes or unions, check that these are free from corrosion and damage.

● The MOT tester will perform a test of the scooter's braking efficiency based on a calculation of rider and scooter weight. Although this cannot be carried out at home, you can at least ensure that the braking systems are properly maintained. For hydraulic disc brakes, check the fluid level, lever/pedal feel (bleed of air if its spongy) and pad material. For drum brakes, check adjustment, cable or rod operation and shoe lining thickness.

Wheels and tyres

● Check the wheel condition. Cast wheels should be free from cracks and if of the built-up design, all fasteners should be secure.

● With the wheel raised off the ground, spin the wheel and visually check that the tyre and wheel run true. Check that the tyre does not foul the suspension or mudguards.

● With the wheel raised off the ground, grasp the wheel and attempt to move it about the axle **(see illustration 11)**. Any play felt here indicates wheel bearing failure.

● Check the tyre tread depth, tread condition and sidewall condition **(see illustration 12)**.

● Check the tyre type. Front and rear tyre types must be compatible and be suitable for

Check for wheel bearing play by trying to move the wheel about the axle (spindle)

Checking the tyre tread depth

Tyre direction of rotation arrow can be found on tyre sidewall

Two straight-edges are used to check wheel alignment

road use. Tyres marked NOT FOR ROAD USE, COMPETITION USE ONLY or similar, will fail the MOT.

● If the tyre sidewall carries a direction of rotation arrow, this must be pointing in the direction of normal wheel rotation **(see illustration 13)**.

● Check that the wheel axle nuts (where applicable) are properly secured. A self-locking nut or castellated nut with a split-pin or R-pin can be used.

● Wheel alignment is checked with the scooter off the stand and a rider seated. With the front wheel pointing straight ahead, two

perfectly straight lengths of metal or wood and placed against the sidewalls of both tyres **(see illustration 14)**. The gap each side of the front tyre must be equidistant on both sides. Incorrect wheel alignment may be due to a cocked rear wheel or in extreme cases, a bent frame.

General checks and condition

● Check the security of all major fasteners, bodypanels, seat and mudguards.

● Check that the pillion footrests, handlebar levers and stand are securely mounted.

● Check for corrosion on the frame or any load-bearing components. If severe, this may affect the structure, particularly under stress.

Conversion Factors

Length (distance)

Inches (in)	x 25.4	= Millimetres (mm)	x 0.0394	=	Inches (in)
Feet (ft)	x 0.305	= Metres (m)	x 3.281	=	Feet (ft)
Miles	x 1.609	= Kilometres (km)	x 0.621	=	Miles

Volume (capacity)

Cubic inches (cu in; in^3)	x 16.387	= Cubic centimetres (cc; cm^3)	x 0.061	=	Cubic inches (cu in; in^3)
Imperial pints (Imp pt)	x 0.568	= Litres (l)	x 1.76	=	Imperial pints (Imp pt)
Imperial quarts (Imp qt)	x 1.137	= Litres (l)	x 0.88	=	Imperial quarts (Imp qt)
Imperial quarts (Imp qt)	x 1.201	= US quarts (US qt)	x 0.833	=	Imperial quarts (Imp qt)
US quarts (US qt)	x 0.946	= Litres (l)	x 1.057	=	US quarts (US qt)
Imperial gallons (Imp gal)	x 4.546	= Litres (l)	x 0.22	=	Imperial gallons (Imp gal)
Imperial gallons (Imp gal)	x 1.201	= US gallons (US gal)	x 0.833	=	Imperial gallons (Imp gal)
US gallons (US gal)	x 3.785	= Litres (l)	x 0.264	=	US gallons (US gal)

Mass (weight)

Ounces (oz)	x 28.35	= Grams (g)	x 0.035	=	Ounces (oz)
Pounds (lb)	x 0.454	= Kilograms (kg)	x 2.205	=	Pounds (lb)

Force

Ounces-force (ozf; oz)	x 0.278	= Newtons (N)	x 3.6	=	Ounces-force (ozf; oz)
Pounds-force (lbf; lb)	x 4.448	= Newtons (N)	x 0.225	=	Pounds-force (lbf; lb)
Newtons (N)	x 0.1	= Kilograms-force (kgf; kg)	x 9.81	=	Newtons (N)

Pressure

Pounds-force per square inch (psi; lbf/in^2; lb/in^2)	x 0.070	= Kilograms-force per square centimetre (kgf/cm^2; kg/cm^2)	x 14.223	=	Pounds-force per square inch (psi; lbf/in^2; lb/in^2)
Pounds-force per square inch (psi; lbf/in^2; lb/in^2)	x 0.068	= Atmospheres (atm)	x 14.696	=	Pounds-force per square inch (psi; lbf/in^2; lb/in^2)
Pounds-force per square inch (psi; lbf/in^2; lb/in^2)	x 0.069	= Bars	x 14.5	=	Pounds-force per square inch (psi; lbf/in^2; lb/in^2)
Pounds-force per square inch (psi; lbf/in^2; lb/in^2)	x 6.895	= Kilopascals (kPa)	x 0.145	=	Pounds-force per square inch (psi; lbf/in^2; lb/in^2)
Kilopascals (kPa)	x 0.01	= Kilograms-force per square centimetre (kgf/cm^2; kg/cm^2)	x 98.1	=	Kilopascals (kPa)
Millibar (mbar)	x 100	= Pascals (Pa)	x 0.01	=	Millibar (mbar)
Millibar (mbar)	x 0.0145	= Pounds-force per square inch (psi; lbf/in^2; lb/in^2)	x 68.947	=	Millibar (mbar)
Millibar (mbar)	x 0.75	= Millimetres of mercury (mmHg)	x 1.333	=	Millibar (mbar)
Millibar (mbar)	x 0.401	= Inches of water (inH$_2$O)	x 2.491	=	Millibar (mbar)
Millimetres of mercury (mmHg)	x 0.535	= Inches of water (inH$_2$O)	x 1.868	=	Millimetres of mercury (mmHg)
Inches of water (inH$_2$O)	x 0.036	= Pounds-force per square inch (psi; lbf/in^2; lb/in^2)	x 27.68	=	Inches of water (inH$_2$O)

Torque (moment of force)

Pounds-force inches (lbf in; lb in)	x 1.152	= Kilograms-force centimetre (kgf cm; kg cm)	x 0.868	=	Pounds-force inches (lbf in; lb in)
Pounds-force inches (lbf in; lb in)	x 0.113	= Newton metres (Nm)	x 8.85	=	Pounds-force inches (lbf in; lb in)
Pounds-force inches (lbf in; lb in)	x 0.083	= Pounds-force feet (lbf ft; lb ft)	x 12	=	Pounds-force inches (lbf in; lb in)
Pounds-force feet (lbf ft; lb ft)	x 0.138	= Kilograms-force metres (kgf m; kg m)	x 7.233	=	Pounds-force feet (lbf ft; lb ft)
Pounds-force feet (lbf ft; lb ft)	x 1.356	= Newton metres (Nm)	x 0.738	=	Pounds-force feet (lbf ft; lb ft)
Newton metres (Nm)	x 0.102	= Kilograms-force metres (kgf m; kg m)	x 9.804	=	Newton metres (Nm)

Power

Horsepower (hp)	x 745.7	= Watts (W)	x 0.0013	=	Horsepower (hp)

Velocity (speed)

Miles per hour (miles/hr; mph)	x 1.609	= Kilometres per hour (km/hr; kph)	x 0.621	=	Miles per hour (miles/hr; mph)

Fuel consumption*

Miles per gallon, Imperial (mpg)	x 0.354	= Kilometres per litre (km/l)	x 2.825	=	Miles per gallon, Imperial (mpg)
Miles per gallon, US (mpg)	x 0.425	= Kilometres per litre (km/l)	x 2.352	=	Miles per gallon, US (mpg)

Temperature

Degrees Fahrenheit = (°C x 1.8) + 32   Degrees Celsius (Degrees Centigrade; °C) = (°F - 32) x 0.56

It is common practice to convert from miles per gallon (mpg) to litres/100 kilometres (l/100km), where mpg x l/100 km = 282

This Section provides an easy reference-guide to the more common faults that are likely to afflict your machine. Obviously, the opportunities are almost limitless for faults to occur as a result of obscure failures, and to try and cover all eventualities would require a book. Indeed, a number have been written on the subject.

Successful troubleshooting is not a mysterious 'black art' but the application of a bit of knowledge combined with a systematic and logical approach to the problem. Approach any troubleshooting by first accurately identifying the symptom and then checking through the list of possible causes, starting with the simplest or most obvious and progressing in stages to the most complex.

Take nothing for granted, but above all apply liberal quantities of common sense.

The main symptom of a fault is given in the text as a major heading below which are listed the various systems or areas which may contain the fault. Details of each possible cause for a fault and the remedial action to be taken are given, in brief, in the paragraphs below each heading. Further information should be sought in the relevant Chapter.

1 Engine doesn't start or is difficult to start
- [ ] Starter motor doesn't rotate
- [ ] Starter motor rotates but engine does not turn over
- [ ] Starter works but engine won't turn over (seized)
- [ ] No fuel flow
- [ ] Engine flooded
- [ ] No spark or weak spark
- [ ] Compression low
- [ ] Stalls after starting
- [ ] Rough idle

2 Poor running at low speed
- [ ] Spark weak
- [ ] Fuel/air mixture incorrect
- [ ] Compression low
- [ ] Poor acceleration

3 Poor running or no power at high speed
- [ ] Firing incorrect
- [ ] Fuel/air mixture incorrect
- [ ] Compression low
- [ ] Knocking or pinking
- [ ] Miscellaneous causes

4 Overheating
- [ ] Engine overheats
- [ ] Firing incorrect
- [ ] Fuel/air mixture incorrect
- [ ] Compression too high
- [ ] Engine load excessive
- [ ] Lubrication inadequate
- [ ] Miscellaneous causes

5 Transmission problems
- [ ] No drive to rear wheel
- [ ] Vibration
- [ ] Poor performance
- [ ] Clutch not disengaging completely

6 Abnormal engine noise
- [ ] Knocking or pinking
- [ ] Piston slap or rattling
- [ ] Valve noise (four-stroke engines)
- [ ] Other noise

7 Abnormal frame and suspension noise
- [ ] Front end noise
- [ ] Shock absorber noise
- [ ] Brake noise

8 Excessive exhaust smoke
- [ ] White smoke (four-stroke engines)
- [ ] White/blue smoke (two-stroke engines)
- [ ] Black smoke
- [ ] Brown smoke

9 Poor handling or stability
- [ ] Handlebar hard to turn
- [ ] Handlebar shakes or vibrates excessively
- [ ] Handlebar pulls to one side
- [ ] Poor shock absorbing qualities

10 Braking problems – disc brakes
- [ ] Brakes are ineffective
- [ ] Brake lever pulsates
- [ ] Brakes drag

11 Braking problems – drum brakes
- [ ] Brakes are ineffective
- [ ] Brake lever pulsates
- [ ] Brakes drag

12 Electrical problems
- [ ] Battery dead or weak
- [ ] Battery overcharged

1 Engine doesn't start or is difficult to start

Starter motor doesn't rotate

☐ Fuse blown. Check fuse and starter circuit (Chapter 9).
☐ Battery voltage low. Check and recharge battery (Chapter 9).
☐ Starter motor defective. Make sure the wiring to the starter is secure. Make sure the starter relay clicks when the start button is pushed. If the relay clicks, then the fault is in the wiring or motor.
☐ Starter relay faulty. Check it (Chapter 9).
☐ Starter switch on handlebar not contacting. The contacts could be wet, corroded or dirty. Disassemble and clean the switch (Chapter 9).
☐ Wiring open or shorted. Check all wiring connections and harnesses to make sure that they are dry, tight and not corroded. Also check for broken or frayed wires that can cause a short to earth.
☐ Ignition switch defective. Check the switch according to the procedure in Chapter 9. Renew the switch if it is defective.

Starter motor rotates but engine does not turn over

☐ Starter pinion assembly or starter clutch defective. Inspect and repair or renew (Chapter 2).
☐ Damaged pinion assembly or starter gears. Inspect and renew the damaged parts (Chapter 2).

Starter works but engine won't turn over (seized)

☐ Seized engine caused by one or more internally damaged components. Failure due to wear, abuse or lack of lubrication. On all engines damage can include piston, cylinder, connecting rod, crankshaft, bearings and additionally on four-strokes, valves, camshaft, camchain. Refer to Chapter 2 for engine disassembly.

No fuel flow

☐ No fuel in tank.
☐ Fuel hose or tank vent hose trapped. Check the hoses.
☐ Fuel filter clogged. Remove the tap and clean the filter, or check the in-line fuel filter.
☐ Fuel tap vacuum hose split or detached. Check the hose.
☐ Fuel tap diaphragm split. Renew the tap (Chapter 3).
☐ Fuel hose clogged. Remove the fuel hose and carefully blow through it.
☐ Float needle valve or carburettor jets clogged. The carburettor should be removed and overhauled if draining the float chamber doesn't solve the problem.

Engine flooded

☐ Float height or fuel level too high. Check as described in Chapter 3.
☐ Float needle valve worn or stuck open. A piece of dirt, rust or other debris can cause the valve to seat improperly, causing excess fuel to be admitted to the float chamber. In this case, the float chamber should be cleaned and the needle valve and seat inspected. If the needle and seat are worn, then the leaking will persist and the parts should be renewed (Chapter 3).

No spark or weak spark

☐ Ignition switch OFF.
☐ Battery voltage low. Check and recharge the battery as necessary (Chapter 9).
☐ Spark plug dirty, defective or worn out. Locate reason for fouled plug using spark plug condition chart at the end of this manual and follow the plug maintenance procedures (Chapter 1). Condition is especially applicable to two-stroke engines due to the oily nature of their lubrication system.
☐ Spark plug cap or secondary (HT) wiring faulty. Check condition. Replace either or both components if cracks or deterioration are evident (Chapter 4).
☐ Spark plug cap not making good contact. Make sure that the plug cap fits snugly over the plug end.

☐ Ignition control unit (ICU) defective. Check the unit, referring to Chapter 4 for details.
☐ Pulse generator coil or source coil defective. Check the unit, referring to Chapter 4 for details.
☐ Ignition HT coil defective. Check the coil, referring to Chapter 4.
☐ Ignition switch shorted. This is usually caused by water, corrosion, damage or excessive wear. The switch can be disassembled and cleaned with electrical contact cleaner. If cleaning does not help, renew the switch (Chapter 9).
☐ Wiring shorted or broken. Make sure that all wiring connections are clean, dry and tight. Look for chafed and broken wires (Chapters 4 and 9).

Compression low

☐ Spark plug loose. Remove the plug and inspect its threads (Chapter 1).
☐ Cylinder head not sufficiently tightened down. If the cylinder head is suspected of being loose, then there's a chance that the gasket or head is damaged if the problem has persisted for any length of time. The head nuts should be tightened to the proper torque in the correct sequence (Chapter 2).
☐ Low crankcase compression on two-stroke engines due to worn crankshaft oil seals. Condition will upset the fuel/air mixture. Renew the seals (Chapter 2C).
☐ Improper valve clearance (four-strokes). This means that the valve is not closing completely and compression pressure is leaking past the valve. Check and adjust the valve clearances (Chapter 1).
☐ Cylinder and/or piston worn. Excessive wear will cause compression pressure to leak past the rings. This is usually accompanied by worn rings as well. A top-end overhaul is necessary (Chapter 2).
☐ Piston rings worn, weak, broken, or sticking. Broken or sticking piston rings usually indicate a lubrication or carburation problem that causes excess carbon deposits or seizures to form on the pistons and rings. Top-end overhaul is necessary (Chapter 2).
☐ Cylinder head gasket damaged. If a head is allowed to become loose, or if excessive carbon build-up on the piston crown and combustion chamber causes extremely high compression, the head gasket may leak. Retorquing the head is not always sufficient to restore the seal, so gasket renewal is necessary (Chapter 2).
☐ Cylinder head warped. This is caused by overheating or improperly tightened head nuts. Machine shop resurfacing or head renewal is necessary (Chapter 2).
☐ Valve spring broken or weak (four-stroke engines). Caused by component failure or wear; the springs must be renewed (Chapter 2A or 2B).
☐ Valve not seating properly (four-stroke engines). This is caused by a bent valve (from over-revving or improper valve adjustment), burned valve or seat (improper carburation) or an accumulation of carbon deposits on the seat (from carburation or lubrication problems). The valves must be cleaned and/or renewed and the seats serviced if possible (Chapter 2A or 2B).

Stalls after starting

☐ Faulty automatic choke. Check connections and movement (Chapter 3).
☐ Ignition malfunction (Chapter 4).
☐ Carburettor malfunction (Chapter 3).
☐ Fuel contaminated. The fuel can be contaminated with either dirt or water, or can change chemically if the machine is allowed to sit for several months or more. Drain the tank and carburettor (Chapter 3).
☐ Inlet air leak. Check for loose carburettor-to-inlet manifold connection, loose carburettor top (Chapter 3).
☐ Engine idle speed incorrect. Turn idle adjusting screw until the engine idles at the specified rpm (Chapter 1).

1 Engine doesn't start or is difficult to start (continued)

Rough idle

☐ Ignition malfunction (Chapter 4).
☐ Idle speed incorrect (Chapter 1).
☐ Carburettor malfunction (Chapter 3).
☐ Fuel contaminated. The fuel can be contaminated with either dirt or water, or can change chemically if the machine is allowed to

sit for several months or more. Drain the tank and carburettor (Chapter 3).
☐ Inlet air leak. Check for loose carburettor-to-inlet manifold connection, loose carburettor top (Chapter 3).
☐ Air filter clogged. Clean or renew the air filter element (Chapter 1).

2 Poor running at low speeds

Spark weak

☐ Battery voltage low. Check and recharge battery (Chapter 9).
☐ Spark plug fouled, defective or worn out. Refer to Chapter 1 for spark plug maintenance.
☐ Spark plug cap or HT wiring defective. Refer to Chapter 4 for details on the ignition system.
☐ Spark plug cap not making contact.
☐ Incorrect spark plug. Wrong type, heat range or cap configuration. Check and install correct plug listed in the Data section.
☐ Ignition control unit (ICU) defective. See Chapter 4.
☐ Pulse generator coil defective. See Chapter 4.
☐ Ignition HT coil defective. See Chapter 4.

Fuel/air mixture incorrect

☐ Pilot screw out of adjustment (Chapter 3).
☐ Pilot jet or air passage clogged. Remove and clean the carburettor (Chapter 3).
☐ Air bleed hole clogged. Remove carburettor and blow out all passages (Chapter 3).
☐ Air filter clogged, poorly sealed or missing (Chapter 1).
☐ Air filter housing poorly sealed. Look for cracks, holes or loose screws and renew or repair defective parts.
☐ Fuel level too high or too low. Check the float height and fuel level (Chapter 3).
☐ Carburettor inlet manifold loose. Check for cracks, breaks, tears or loose fixings.

Compression low

☐ Spark plug loose. Remove the plug and inspect its threads (Chapter 1).
☐ Cylinder head not sufficiently tightened down. If the cylinder head is suspected of being loose, then there's a chance that the gasket or head is damaged if the problem has persisted for any length of time. The head nuts should be tightened to the proper torque in the correct sequence (Chapter 2).
☐ Improper valve clearance (four-stroke engines). This means that the valve is not closing completely and compression pressure is leaking past the valve. Check and adjust the valve clearances (Chapter 1).
☐ Low crankcase compression on two-stroke engines due to worn

crankshaft oil seals. Condition will upset the fuel/air mixture. Renew the seals (Chapter 2C).
☐ Cylinder and/or piston worn. Excessive wear will cause compression pressure to leak past the rings. This is usually accompanied by worn rings as well. A top-end overhaul is necessary (Chapter 2).
☐ Piston rings worn, weak, broken, or sticking. Broken or sticking piston rings usually indicate a lubrication or carburation problem that causes excess carbon deposits or seizures to form on the pistons and rings. Top-end overhaul is necessary (Chapter 2).
☐ Cylinder head gasket damaged. If a head is allowed to become loose, or if excessive carbon build-up on the piston crown and combustion chamber causes extremely high compression, the head gasket may leak. Retorquing the head is not always sufficient to restore the seal, so gasket renewal is necessary (Chapter 2).
☐ Cylinder head warped. This is caused by overheating or improperly tightened head nuts. Machine shop resurfacing or head replacement is necessary (Chapter 2).
☐ Valve spring broken or weak (four-stroke engines). Caused by component failure or wear; the springs must be replaced (Chapter 2A or 2B).
☐ Valve not seating properly (four-stroke engines). This is caused by a bent valve (from over-revving or improper valve adjustment), burned valve or seat (improper carburation) or an accumulation of carbon deposits on the seat (from carburation or lubrication problems). The valves must be cleaned and/or renewed and the seats serviced if possible (Chapter 2A or 2B).

Poor acceleration

☐ Carburettor leaking or dirty. Overhaul the carburettor (Chapter 3).
☐ Faulty automatic choke (Chapter3).
☐ Timing not advancing. The pulse generator coil or the ignition control unit (ICU) may be defective (Chapter 4). If so, they must be renewed, as they can't be repaired.
☐ Engine oil viscosity too high (four-stroke engines). Using too heavy an oil can damage the oil pump or lubrication system and cause drag on the engine.
☐ Brakes dragging. On disc brakes, usually caused by debris which has entered the brake piston seals, or from a warped disc or bent axle. On drum brakes, cable out of adjustment, shoe return spring broken. Repair as necessary (Chapter 7).
☐ Clutch slipping or drive belt worn (Chapter 5).

3 Poor running or no power at high speed

Firing incorrect

- [ ] Air filter clogged. Clean or renew filter (Chapter 1).
- [ ] Spark plug fouled, defective or worn out. See Chapter 1 for spark plug maintenance.
- [ ] Spark plug cap or HT wiring defective. See Chapter 4 for details of the ignition system.
- [ ] Spark plug cap not in good contact (Chapter 4).
- [ ] Incorrect spark plug. Wrong type, heat range or cap configuration. Check and install correct plug.
- [ ] Ignition control unit or HT coil defective (Chapter 4).

Fuel/air mixture incorrect

- [ ] Main jet clogged. Dirt, water or other contaminants can clog the main jet. Clean the fuel tap filter, the in-line filter, the float chamber and the jets and carburettor orifices (Chapter 3).
- [ ] Main jet wrong size. The standard jetting is for sea level atmospheric pressure and oxygen content.
- [ ] Air bleed holes clogged. Remove and overhaul carburettor (Chapter 3).
- [ ] Air filter clogged, poorly sealed, or missing (Chapter 1).
- [ ] Air filter housing or duct poorly sealed. Look for cracks, holes or loose clamps or screws, and renew or repair defective parts.
- [ ] Fuel level too high or too low. Check the float height or fuel level (Chapter 3).
- [ ] Carburettor inlet manifold loose. Check for cracks, breaks, tears or loose fixings.

Compression low

- [ ] Spark plug loose. Remove the plug and inspect its threads. Reinstall and tighten to the specified torque (Chapter 1).
- [ ] Cylinder head not sufficiently tightened down. If the cylinder head is suspected of being loose, then there's a chance that the gasket or head is damaged if the problem has persisted for any length of time. The head nuts should be tightened to the proper torque in the correct sequence (Chapter 2).
- [ ] Improper valve clearance (four-stroke engines). This means that the valve is not closing completely and compression pressure is leaking past the valve. Check and adjust the valve clearances (Chapter 1).
- [ ] Low crankcase compression on two-stroke engines due to worn crankshaft oil seals. Condition will upset the fuel/air mixture. Renew the seals (Chapter 2C).
- [ ] Cylinder and/or piston worn. Excessive wear will cause compression pressure to leak past the rings. This is usually accompanied by worn rings as well. A top-end overhaul is necessary (Chapter 2).
- [ ] Piston rings worn, weak, broken, or sticking. Broken or sticking piston rings usually indicate a lubrication or carburation problem that causes excess carbon deposits or seizures to form on the pistons and rings. Top-end overhaul is necessary (Chapter 2).

- [ ] Cylinder head gasket damaged. If a head is allowed to become loose, or if excessive carbon build-up on the piston crown and combustion chamber causes extremely high compression, the head gasket may leak. Retorquing the head is not always sufficient to restore the seal, so gasket replacement is necessary (Chapter 2).
- [ ] Cylinder head warped. This is caused by overheating or improperly tightened head nuts. Cylinder head skimming or head replacement is necessary (Chapter 2).
- [ ] Valve spring broken or weak (four-stroke engines). Caused by component failure or wear; the springs must be renewed (Chapter 2A or 2B).
- [ ] Valve not seating properly (four-stroke engines). This is caused by a bent valve (from over-revving or improper valve adjustment), burned valve or seat (improper carburation) or an accumulation of carbon deposits on the seat (from carburation or lubrication problems). The valves must be cleaned and/or renewed and the seats serviced if possible (Chapter 2A or 2B).

Knocking or pinking

- [ ] Carbon build-up in combustion chamber. Use of a fuel additive that will dissolve the adhesive bonding the carbon particles to the crown and chamber is the easiest way to remove the build-up. Otherwise, the cylinder head will have to be removed and decarbonised (Chapter 2). On two-stroke engines, the regular service interval for cylinder head decarbonisation should be adhered to.
- [ ] Incorrect or poor quality fuel. Old or improper grades of fuel can cause detonation. This causes the piston to rattle, thus the knocking or pinking sound. Drain old fuel and always use the recommended fuel grade.
- [ ] Spark plug heat range incorrect. Uncontrolled detonation indicates the plug heat range is too hot. The plug in effect becomes a glow plug, raising cylinder temperatures. Install the proper heat range plug (Chapter 1).
- [ ] Improper air/fuel mixture. This will cause the cylinders to run hot, which leads to detonation. Clogged jets or an air leak can cause this imbalance. See Chapter 3.

Miscellaneous causes

- [ ] Throttle valve doesn't open fully. Adjust the throttle twistgrip freeplay (Chapter 1).
- [ ] Clutch slipping or drive belt worn (Chapter 5).
- [ ] Timing not advancing (Chapter 4).
- [ ] Engine oil viscosity too high (four-stroke engines). Using too heavy an oil can damage the oil pump or lubrication system and cause drag on the engine.
- [ ] Brakes dragging. On disc brakes, usually caused by debris which has entered the brake piston seals, or from a warped disc or bent axle. On drum brakes, cable out of adjustment, shoe return spring broken. Repair as necessary (Chapter 7).

4 Overheating

Engine overheats

☐ Air cooling ducts or engine cowling blocked or incorrectly fitted.
☐ Problem with cooling fan.

Firing incorrect

☐ Spark plug fouled, defective or worn out. See Chapter 1 for spark plug maintenance.
☐ Incorrect spark plug.
☐ Ignition control unit defective (Chapter 4).
☐ Faulty ignition HT coil (Chapter 4).

Fuel/air mixture incorrect

☐ Main jet clogged. Dirt, water or other contaminants can clog the main jet. Clean the fuel tap filter, the in-line filter, the float chamber and the jets and carburettor orifices (Chapter 3).
☐ Main jet wrong size. The standard jetting is for sea level atmospheric pressure and oxygen content.
☐ Air bleed holes clogged. Remove and overhaul carburettor (Chapter 3).
☐ Air filter clogged, poorly sealed, or missing (Chapter 1).
☐ Air filter housing or duct poorly sealed. Look for cracks, holes or loose clamps or screws, and renew or repair defective parts.
☐ Fuel level too high or too low. Check the float height or fuel level (Chapter 3).
☐ Carburettor inlet manifold loose. Check for cracks, breaks, tears or loose fixings.

Compression too high

☐ Carbon build-up in combustion chamber. Use of a fuel additive that will dissolve the adhesive bonding the carbon particles to the piston crown and chamber is the easiest way to remove the build-up. Otherwise, the cylinder head will have to be removed and decarbonised (Chapter 2). On two-stroke engines, the regular service interval for cylinder head decarbonisation should be adhered to.
☐ Improperly machined head surface or installation of incorrect size cylinder base gasket during engine assembly.

Engine load excessive

☐ Clutch slipping or drive belt worn (Chapter 4).
☐ Engine oil level too high (four-stroke engines). The addition of too much oil will cause pressurisation of the crankcase and inefficient engine operation. Check the specifications in your handbook and drain to proper level (Chapter 1 and *Pre-ride checks*).
☐ Engine oil viscosity too high (four-stroke engines). Using too heavy an oil can damage the oil pump or lubrication system as well as cause drag on the engine.
☐ Brakes dragging. On disc brakes, usually caused by debris which has entered the brake piston seals, or from a warped disc or bent axle. On drum brakes, cable out of adjustment, shoe return spring broken. Repair as necessary (Chapter 7).

Lubrication inadequate

☐ Engine oil level too low (four-stroke engines). Friction caused by intermittent lack of lubrication or from oil that is overworked can cause overheating. The oil provides a definite cooling function in the engine. Check the oil level (Chapter 1 and *Pre-ride checks*).
☐ Oil pump out of adjustment (two-stroke engines) . Adjust pump cable (Chapter 1).
☐ Poor quality oil or incorrect viscosity or type. Oil is rated not only according to viscosity but also according to type. Some oils are not rated high enough for use in this engine. Check the specifications in your handbook or the *Data* section and change to the correct oil (Chapter 1). On two-stroke engines, make sure that you use a two-stroke oil which is suitable for oil injection engines.

Miscellaneous causes

☐ Modification to exhaust system. Most aftermarket exhaust systems cause the engine to run leaner, which makes them run hotter. When installing an accessory exhaust system, always obtain advice on rejetting the carburettor.

5 Transmission problems

No drive to rear wheel

☐ Drive belt broken (Chapter 5).
☐ Clutch not engaging (Chapter 5).
☐ Clutch or drum excessively worn (Chapter 5).

Transmission noise or vibration

☐ Bearings worn. Also includes the possibility that the shafts are worn. Overhaul the transmission (Chapter 5).
☐ Gears worn or chipped (Chapter 5).
☐ Clutch drum worn unevenly (Chapter 5).
☐ Worn bearings or bent shaft (Chapter 5).
☐ Loose clutch nut or drum nut (Chapter 5).

Poor performance

☐ Variator worn or insufficiently greased (Chapter 5).
☐ Weak or broken driven pulley spring (Chapter 5).
☐ Clutch or drum excessively worn (Chapter 5).
☐ Grease on clutch friction material (Chapter 5).
☐ Drive belt excessively worn (Chapter 5).

Clutch not disengaging completely

☐ Weak or broken clutch springs (Chapter 5).
☐ Engine idle speed too high (Chapter 1).

6 Abnormal engine noise

Knocking or pinking

☐ Carbon build-up in combustion chamber. Use of a fuel additive that will dissolve the adhesive bonding the carbon particles to the piston crown and chamber is the easiest way to remove the build-up. Otherwise, the cylinder head will have to be removed and decarbonised (Chapter 2). On two-stroke engines, always decarbonise the cylinder head and piston crown at the recommended service interval (Chapter 1).

☐ Incorrect or poor quality fuel. Old or improper fuel can cause detonation. This causes the piston to rattle, thus the knocking or pinking sound. Drain the old fuel and always use the recommended grade fuel (Chapter 3).

☐ Spark plug heat range incorrect. Uncontrolled detonation indicates that the plug heat range is too hot. The plug in effect becomes a glow plug, raising cylinder temperatures. Install the proper heat range plug (Chapter 1).

☐ Improper air/fuel mixture. This will cause the cylinder to run hot and lead to detonation. Clogged jets or an air leak can cause this imbalance. See Chapter 3.

Piston slap or rattling

☐ Cylinder-to-piston clearance excessive. Caused by improper assembly. Inspect and overhaul top-end parts (Chapter 2).

☐ Connecting rod bent. Caused by over-revving, trying to start a badly flooded engine or from ingesting a foreign object into the combustion chamber. Renew the damaged parts (Chapter 2).

☐ Piston pin or piston pin bore worn or seized from wear or lack of lubrication. Renew damaged parts (Chapter 2).

☐ Piston ring(s) worn, broken or sticking. Overhaul the top-end (Chapter 2).

☐ Piston seizure damage. Usually from lack of lubrication or overheating. Renew the piston and cylinder, as necessary (Chapter 2). On two-stroke engines, check that the oil pump is correctly adjusted.

☐ Connecting rod small or big-end bearing clearance excessive. Caused by excessive wear or lack of lubrication. Renew worn parts.

Valve noise – four-stroke engines

☐ Incorrect valve clearances. Adjust the clearances by referring to Chapter 1.

☐ Valve spring broken or weak. Check and renew weak valve springs (Chapter 2A or 2B).

☐ Camshaft bearings worn or damaged. Lack of lubrication at high rpm is usually the cause of damage. Insufficient oil or failure to change the oil at the recommended intervals are the chief causes (Chapter 2A or 2B).

Other noise

☐ Exhaust pipe leaking at cylinder head connection. Caused by improper fit of pipe or loose exhaust flange. All exhaust fasteners should be tightened evenly and carefully. Failure to do this will lead to a leak.

☐ Crankshaft runout excessive. Caused by a bent crankshaft (from over-revving) or damage from an upper cylinder component failure.

☐ Engine mounting bolts loose. Tighten all engine mount bolts (Chapter 2).

☐ Crankshaft bearings worn (Chapter 2).

☐ Camshaft drive gear assembly defective (four-stroke engines). Replace according to the procedure in Chapter 2A or 2B.

7 Abnormal frame and suspension noise

Front end noise

☐ Steering head bearings loose or damaged. Clicks when braking. Check and adjust or replace as necessary (Chapters 1 and 6).

☐ Bolts loose. Make sure all bolts are tightened to the specified torque (Chapter 6).

☐ Fork tube bent. Good possibility if machine has been dropped. Renew the tube or the fork assembly (Chapter 6).

☐ Front axle nut loose. Tighten to the specified torque (Chapter 7).

☐ Loose or worn wheel or hub bearings. Check and renew as needed (Chapter 7).

Shock absorber noise

☐ Fluid level incorrect. Indicates a leak caused by defective seal. Shock will be covered with oil. Renew the shock (Chapter 6).

☐ Defective shock absorber with internal damage. This is in the body of the shock and can't be remedied. The shock must be renewed (Chapter 6).

☐ Bent or damaged shock body. Renew the shock (Chapter 6).

☐ Loose or worn suspension linkage components. Check and renew as necessary (Chapter 6).

Brake noise

☐ Squeal caused by dust on brake pads or shoes. Usually found in combination with glazed pads or shoes. Clean using brake cleaning solvent (Chapter 7).

☐ Contamination of brake pads or shoes. Oil, brake fluid or dirt causing brake to chatter or squeal. Clean or renew pads or shoes (Chapter 7).

☐ Pads or shoes glazed. Caused by excessive heat from prolonged use or from contamination. Do not use sandpaper, emery cloth, carborundum cloth or any other abrasive to roughen the pad surfaces as abrasives will stay in the pad material and damage the disc or drum. A very fine flat file can be used, but pad or shoe renewal is advised (Chapter 7).

☐ Disc or drum warped. Can cause a chattering, clicking or intermittent squeal. Usually accompanied by a pulsating lever and uneven braking. Check the disc runout and the drum ovality (Chapter 7).

☐ Loose or worn wheel (front) or transmission (rear) bearings. Check and renew as needed (Chapters 7 or 5).

8 Excessive exhaust smoke

White smoke – four-stroke engines (oil burning)

☐ Piston oil control ring worn. The ring may be broken or damaged, causing oil from the crankcase to be pulled past the piston into the combustion chamber. Renew the rings (Chapter 2A or 2B).

☐ Cylinder worn, or scored. Caused by overheating or oil starvation. A new cylinder and piston will have to be installed (Chapter 2A or 2B).

☐ Valve stem oil seal damaged or worn. Renew oil seals (Chapter 2A or 2B).

☐ Valve guide worn. Inspect the valve guides and if worn seek the advice of a scooter specialist (Chapter 2A or 2B).

☐ Engine oil level too high, which causes the oil to be forced past the rings. Check the specifications in your handbook and drain to proper level (*Pre-ride checks*).

☐ Head gasket broken between oil return and cylinder. Causes oil to be pulled into the combustion chamber. Renew the head gasket and check the head for warpage (Chapter 2A or 2B).

☐ Abnormal crankcase pressurisation, which forces oil past the rings.

White/blue smoke – two-stroke engines (oil burning)

☐ Oil pump cable adjustment incorrect. Check throttle cable/oil pump cable adjustment (Chapter 1).

☐ Accumulated oil deposits in the exhaust system. If the scooter is used for short journeys only, the oil residue from the exhaust gases will condense in the cool silencer. Take the scooter for a long run in hot weather to burn off the accumulated oil residue.

Black smoke (over-rich mixture)

☐ Air filter clogged. Clean or renew the element (Chapter 1).

☐ Main jet too large or loose. Compare the jet size to the Specifications (Chapter 3).

☐ Automatic choke faulty (Chapter 3).

☐ Fuel level too high. Check and adjust the float height or fuel level as necessary (Chapter 3).

☐ Float needle valve held off needle seat. Clean the float chamber and fuel line and renew the needle and seat if necessary (Chapter 3).

Brown smoke (lean mixture)

☐ Main jet too small or clogged. Lean condition caused by wrong size main jet or by a restricted orifice. Clean float chamber and jets and compare jet size to specifications (Chapter 3).

☐ Fuel flow Insufficient. Float needle valve stuck closed due to chemical reaction with old fuel. Float height or fuel level Incorrect. Restricted fuel hose. Clean hose and float chamber and adjust float if necessary.

☐ Carburettor inlet manifold clamp loose (Chapter 3).

☐ Air filter poorly sealed or not installed (Chapter 1).

☐ Ignition timing incorrect (Chapter 4).

9 Poor handling or stability

Handlebar hard to turn

☐ Steering head bearing adjuster nut too tight. Check adjustment as described in Chapters 1 and 6.

☐ Bearings damaged. Roughness can be felt as the bars are turned from side-to-side. Replace bearings and races (Chapter 6).

☐ Races dented or worn. Denting results from wear in only one position (e.g. straight ahead), from a collision or hitting a pothole or from dropping the machine. Renew races and bearings (Chapter 6).

☐ Steering stem lubrication inadequate. Causes are grease getting hard from age or being washed out by high pressure car washes. Disassemble steering head and repack bearings (Chapter 6).

☐ Steering stem bent. Caused by a collision, hitting a pothole or by dropping the machine. Renew damaged part. Don't try to straighten the steering stem (Chapter 6).

☐ Front tyre air pressure too low (*Pre-ride checks*).

Handlebar shakes or vibrates excessively

☐ Tyres worn (*Pre-ride checks*).

☐ Swingarm pivots worn. Renew worn components (Chapter 6).

☐ Wheel rim(s) warped or damaged. Inspect wheels for runout (Chapter 7).

☐ Wheel bearings worn. Worn wheel bearings (front) or transmission bearings (rear) can cause poor tracking. Worn front bearings will cause wobble (Chapter 7).

☐ Handlebar mountings loose (Chapter 6).

☐ Front suspension bolts loose. Tighten them to the specified torque (Chapter 6).

☐ Engine mounting bolts loose. Will cause excessive vibration with increased engine rpm (Chapter 2).

Handlebar pulls to one side

☐ Frame bent. Definitely suspect this if the machine has been dropped. May or may not be accompanied by cracking near the bend. Renew the frame (Chapter 6).

☐ Wheels out of alignment. Caused by improper location of axle spacers or from bent steering stem or frame (Chapter 6 or 7).

☐ Steering stem bent. Caused by impact damage or by dropping the machine. Renew the steering stem (Chapter 6).

☐ Fork tube bent (telescopic fork models). Disassemble the forks and renew the damaged parts (Chapter 6).

Poor shock absorbing qualities

Too hard:
a) Fork oil quantity excessive (Chapter 6).
b) Fork oil viscosity too high. Refer to your scooter handbook or check with a scooter specialist.
c) Fork or front shock internal damage (Chapter 6).
d) Suspension bent. Causes a harsh, sticking feeling (Chapter 6).
e) Rear shock internal damage (Chapter 6).
f) Tyre pressure too high (*Pre-ride checks*).

Too soft:
a) Fork oil viscosity too light. Refer to your scooter handbook or check with a scooter specialist.
b) Fork or shock spring(s) weak or broken (Chapter 6).
c) Shock internal damage or leakage (Chapter 6).

10 Braking problems – disc brakes

Brakes are ineffective

- ☐ Air in brake hose. Caused by inattention to master cylinder fluid level or by leakage (*Pre-ride checks*). Locate problem and bleed brake (Chapter 7).
- ☐ Pads or disc worn (Chapter 7).
- ☐ Brake fluid leak. Locate problem and rectify (Chapter 7).
- ☐ Contaminated pads. Caused by contamination with oil, grease, brake fluid, etc. Renew pads. Clean disc thoroughly with brake cleaner (Chapter 7).
- ☐ Brake fluid deteriorated. Fluid is old or contaminated. Drain system, replenish with new fluid and bleed the system (Chapter 7).
- ☐ Master cylinder internal parts worn or damaged causing fluid to bypass (Chapter 7).
- ☐ Master cylinder bore scratched by foreign material or broken spring. Repair or renew master cylinder (Chapter 7).
- ☐ Disc warped. Renew disc (Chapter 7).

Brake lever pulsates

- ☐ Disc warped. Renew disc (Chapter 7).
- ☐ Axle bent. Renew axle (Chapter 7).
- ☐ Brake caliper bolts loose (Chapter 7).
- ☐ Wheel warped or otherwise damaged (Chapter 7).
- ☐ Wheel bearings damaged or worn (Chapter 7).

Brakes drag

- ☐ Master cylinder piston seized. Caused by wear or damage to piston or cylinder bore (Chapter 7).
- ☐ Lever balky or stuck. Check pivot and lubricate (Chapter 7).
- ☐ Brake caliper piston seized in bore. Caused by wear or ingestion of dirt past deteriorated seal (Chapter 7).
- ☐ Brake pads damaged. Pad material separated from backing plate. Usually caused by faulty manufacturing process or from contact with chemicals. Renew pads (Chapter 7).
- ☐ Pads improperly installed (Chapter 7).

11 Braking problems – drum brakes

Brakes are ineffective

- ☐ Cable incorrectly adjusted. Check cable (Chapter 1).
- ☐ Shoes or drum worn (Chapter 7).
- ☐ Contaminated shoes. Caused by contamination with oil, grease, etc. Renew shoes. Clean drum thoroughly with brake cleaner (Chapter 7).
- ☐ Brake lever arm incorrectly positioned, or cam excessively worn (Chapter 7).

Brake lever pulsates

- ☐ Drum warped. Renew drum (Chapter 7).
- ☐ Axle bent. Renew axle (Chapter 7).
- ☐ Wheel warped or otherwise damaged (Chapter 7).
- ☐ Transmission bearings damaged or worn (Chapter 5).

Brakes drag

- ☐ Cable incorrectly adjusted or requires lubrication. Check cable (Chapter 1).
- ☐ Shoe return springs broken (Chapter 7).
- ☐ Lever balky or stuck. Check pivot and lubricate (Chapter 7).
- ☐ Lever arm or cam binds. Caused by inadequate lubrication or damage (Chapter 7).
- ☐ Brake shoe damaged. Friction material separated from shoe. Usually caused by faulty manufacturing process or from contact with chemicals. Renew shoes (Chapter 7).
- ☐ Shoes improperly installed (Chapter 7).

12 Electrical problems

Battery dead or weak

- ☐ Battery faulty. Caused by sulphated plates which are shorted through sedimentation. Also, broken battery terminal making only occasional contact (Chapter 9).
- ☐ Battery cables making poor electrical contact (Chapter 9).
- ☐ Load excessive. Caused by addition of high wattage lights or other electrical accessories.
- ☐ Ignition switch defective. Switch either earths internally or fails to shut off system. Renew the switch (Chapter 9).
- ☐ Regulator/rectifier defective (Chapter 9).
- ☐ Alternator stator coil open or shorted (Chapter 9).
- ☐ Wiring faulty. Wiring either shorted to earth or connections loose in ignition, charging or lighting circuits (Chapter 9).

Battery overcharged

- ☐ Regulator/rectifier defective. Overcharging is noticed when battery gets excessively warm (Chapter 9).
- ☐ Battery defective. Renew battery (Chapter 9).
- ☐ Battery amperage too low, wrong type or size. Install manufacturer's specified amp-hour battery to handle charging load (Chapter 9).

Note: *References throughout this index are in the form* **"Chapter number"** • **"Page number".** *So, for example, 2A•10 refers to page 10 of Chapter 2A.*

Note: *References throughout this index are in the form* "**Chapter number**" • "**Page number**". *So, for example, 2A•10 refers to page 10 of Chapter 2A.*

Note: *References throughout this index are in the form* **"Chapter number"** • **"Page number"**. *So, for example, 2A•10 refers to page 10 of Chapter 2A.*

Preserving Our Motoring Heritage

<
The Model J Duesenberg Derham Tourster. Only eight of these magnificent cars were ever built – this is the only example to be found outside the United States of America

Almost every car you've ever loved, loathed or desired is gathered under one roof at the Haynes Motor Museum. Over 300 immaculately presented cars and motorbikes represent every aspect of our motoring heritage, from elegant reminders of bygone days, such as the superb Model J Duesenberg to curiosities like the bug-eyed BMW Isetta. There are also many old friends and flames. Perhaps you remember the 1959 Ford Popular that you did your courting in? The magnificent 'Red Collection' is a spectacle of classic sports cars including AC, Alfa Romeo, Austin Healey, Ferrari, Lamborghini, Maserati, MG, Riley, Porsche and Triumph.

A Perfect Day Out

Each and every vehicle at the Haynes Motor Museum has played its part in the history and culture of Motoring. Today, they make a wonderful spectacle and a great day out for all the family. Bring the kids, bring Mum and Dad, but above all bring your camera to capture those golden memories for ever. You will also find an impressive array of motoring memorabilia, a comfortable 70 seat video cinema and one of the most extensive transport book shops in Britain. The Pit Stop Cafe serves everything from a cup of tea to wholesome, home-made meals or, if you prefer, you can enjoy the large picnic area nestled in the beautiful rural surroundings of Somerset.

>
John Haynes O.B.E., Founder and Chairman of the museum at the wheel of a Haynes Light 12.

<
The 1936 490cc sohc-engined International Norton – well known for its racing success

The Museum is situated on the A359 Yeovil to Frome road at Sparkford, just off the A303 in Somerset. It is about 40 miles south of Bristol, and 25 minutes drive from the M5 intersection at Taunton.
Open 9.30am - 5.30pm (10.00am - 4.00pm Winter) 7 days a week, *except Christmas Day, Boxing Day and New Years Day*
Special rates available for schools, coach parties and outings Charitable Trust No. 292048